# TRAVELLER'S LITERARY COMPANION
## TO
## ITALY

## Martin Garrett

TRAVELLER'S
LITERARY COMPANION

Read your
way around
the world

## In Print

*Titles in the Traveller's Literary Companion series:*
South and Central America
Africa
Eastern and Central Europe
The Indian Sub-continent
Japan
South-east Asia
The Caribbean
France
Italy

British Library Cataloguing in Publication Data: A catalogue record for this
book is available from the British Library.

Paperback ISBN 1 873047 91 6

Paperback cover design by Russell Townsend
Maps drawn by Russell Townsend
Additional artwork by Zana Juppenlatz
Typeset by J&L Composition Ltd, Filey, North Yorkshire
Printed by Bookcraft, Midsomer Norton, Somerset

First published in 1998 by
In Print Publishing Ltd, Montpelier House, Montpelier Road, Brighton, BN1 3BE
Tel: (01273) 720891 Fax: (01273) 778244

# SERIES FOREWORD

This series of *Traveller's Literary Companions* is the series I have been looking for all my travelling life. Discovering new writers and new countries is one of the greatest pleasures we know, and these books will greatly increase the enjoyment of all who consult them. Each volume is packed with scholarly and entertaining historical, geographical, political and above all literary information. A country lives through its literature, and we have here an illustrated survey not only of a country's own writers, but also of the views of foreigners, explorers, tourists and exiles. The only problem I foresee is that each volume will bring about a compulsive desire to book a ticket on the next flight out.

The writers take us back in the past to each country's cultural origins, and bring us right up to the present with extracts from novels, poems and travel writings published in the 1980s and 1990s. The biographical information about the writers is invaluable, and will give any traveller an easy and immediate access to the past and present state of each nation. Conversation with hosts, colleagues or strangers on trains will be greatly assisted. An enormous amount of work has gone into the compiling and annotating of each volume, and the balance of fact and comment seems to me to be expertly judged.

Margaret Drabble

FOR ROY AND DELWEN

## Acknowledgements

I should like to thank John Edmondson for his untiring help and encouragement, Sarie Forster for her hard work on the manuscript, and Helen, Philip, and Edmund for their interest and understanding at all stages. Earlier, John and Anne Rao's annual visits helped to keep Italy alive for me during a period when I was unable to go there. Thanks are also due to the staff of the information centre, the Conservatorio di Musica Girolamo Frescobaldi, and the Biblioteca Ariostea, in Ferrara, of Casa Guidi in Florence, and of the Italian National Tourist Office in London.

This is also perhaps the place to salute some of the notable authors for whom I didn't, in the end, find a suitable space: Ugo Betti, Oriana Fallaci, Anna Maria Ortese, Gesualdo Buffalino, the baroque poet Giambattista Marino.

# CONTENTS

Series Foreword (by Margaret Drabble) .......................... iii
Using the companion ............................................... vi
About the author ................................................. vii
Introduction ..................................................... viii
Italian map ........................................................ x

**Venice** ........................................................... 1
**The Veneto and the North-East** ............................... 29
**Lombardy** ........................................................ 46
**Piedmont** ........................................................ 67
**Liguria** .......................................................... 79
**Emilia-Romagna** ................................................. 89
**Florence** ........................................................ 110
**Tuscany** ......................................................... 141
**Umbria and the Marche** ......................................... 159
**Rome** ............................................................ 173
**Lazio** ........................................................... 209
**Naples and Campania** ............................................ 217
**Abruzzo, Calabria and the South-East** ......................... 245
**Sicily** .......................................................... 259
**Sardinia** ........................................................ 292

Map of Northern Italy ............................................. 30
Map of Central Italy .............................................. 90
Map of Southern Italy ............................................. 174
Map of Sicily and Sardinia ........................................ 260

Acknowledgements .................................................. 302
Index of places ................................................... 305
Index of people ................................................... 308

# USING THE COMPANION

Each chapter is divided into four sections: (1) a general introduction to the country and its literature, with supporting historical and cultural background; (2) a Booklist which gives details of works mentioned in the introduction or extracted; (3) Extracts from prose and poetry focusing on particular places or the country in general; (4) biographical and literary notes on the authors extracted.

The extracts are arranged by place, alphabetically, and each has a number to make it easy to locate from elsewhere in the chapter. A quick list of published sources can be found in the Booklist, where the extract numbers are highlighted in bold type. Fuller references are included under 'Acknowledgements and Citations' at the end of the book.

The symbol ◊ after an author's name indicates that there is a biographical entry. Where this entry is in another chapter, this is indicated after the symbol, which is then printed in parentheses.

There is an index of authors and other significant personal names at the end of the book, as well as an index of places.

## About the author

Martin Garrett read English at St Edmund Hall, Oxford, where he went on to write a D.Phil. thesis on Jacobean drama. Since 1983 he has worked as a writer, examiner, and tutor (teaching for colleges of the universities of Oxford and Cambridge and on American study abroad programmes). He is keenly interested in southern European culture and literature and travels frequently in Italy, France and Greece. He is the author of *Greece: a Literary Companion* (John Murray, 1994) and has written or edited three books on Renaissance literature.

# INTRODUCTION

'There are two Italies; one composed of the green earth and the mighty ruins of ancient times, and aerial mountains, and the warm and radiant atmosphere which is interfused through all things. The other consists of the Italians of the present day, their works and ways. The one is the most sublime and lively contemplation that can be conceived of by the imagination of man; the other the most degraded disgusting and odious. – What do you think? Young women of rank actually eat – you will never guess what – *garlic*. Our poor friend Lord Byron is quite corrupted by living among these people.'

So wrote Shelley to his friend Leigh Hunt in December 1818. Writers and others have often constructed ideal Italies: Aeneas and his Trojan refugees must strive, on divine instructions, to reach the mighty and fertile western land where, Virgil is confidently able to state, their descendants will build the greatest of all cities; some *Risorgimento* ideologues and activists projected a united Italy in which all corruption, all inequalities of class and region, would be removed; northern Europe dreamt of the 'warm and radiant atmosphere' of the southern land – or, earlier, of its murderous machiavels, its lust for stabbing and fine clothes (as combined when a character banished from Rome in John Webster's play *The White Devil* threatens to 'make Italian cut-works' – open-work embroidery – in his enemies' 'guts').

Myth meets or contrasts with reality – or different constructions of reality encounter each other – in many different ways; there are more than 'two Italies', and localities are often more important than 'Italy'. Byron explored poetry, politics, social life and garlic-eaters (both 'of rank' and not) in the distinct environments of Venice, Ravenna, and Pisa. The Trojans cried simply 'Italia!' when they first sighted the low coastline in Book Three of *The Aeneid*, but when they return in Book Six find that they can establish themselves only (even with the help of Virgilian hindsight) by making the right local sacrifices and alliances. Only thus, and by hard-fought victory in war, can they carve out for themselves the territory in the Alban Hills which will eventually grow into an empire. Dante wants more Italian unity, under the Holy

Roman Emperor, than many of his contemporaries, but it is difficult to imagine *The Divine Comedy* without its Florence and Florentines, idealised, vilified, unforgotten by the exiled poet. There have been attempts to limit Italian diversity – laws, customs and language which the more powerful and more prosperous north of the country sought to impose on the poor south from the 1860s onwards; national broadcasting and communications have done much to erode the more extreme differences. But since the late 19th century, partly in reaction to such threats, books about 'the Italians of the present day, their works and ways' have frequently concerned themselves with roots and regions, with the practical and the metaphysical connections between particular human beings and particular landscapes, industries, hardships, speech-patterns, family structures, traditions: the Sicily of Pirandello or Sciascia, Grazia Deledda's Sardinia, Carlo Levi's isolated, bare Basilicata, the poor quarters of Pratolini's Florence, to give only a few examples.

Fortunately readers and travellers are not obliged to choose between myths. (Even so-called realistic settings are arrived at by a process of selection, function within individual narrative and thematic structures, and may spawn new myths.) It is possible to move swiftly, imaginatively as well as physically, from Pratolini's Via del Corno to Dante's Baptistry, to walk simultaneously in Veronica Franco's Venice, Thomas Mann's, and your own, and perhaps in so doing to experience something of the same eclectic process, garnering, glimpsing, apparently forgetting, as the authors themselves.

Martin Garrett,
Cambridge

N

TRENTINO-
ALTO ADIGE

FRIULI-
VENEZIA
GIULIA

VALLE
D'AOSTA

LOMBARDY

VENETO

PIEDMONT

Venice

EMILIA-ROMAGNA

LIGURIA

SAN
MARINO

Florence

TUSCANY

MARCHE

UMBRIA

ABRUZZO

Rome

LAZIO

MOLISE

CAMPANIA

APULIA

Naples

BASILICATA

SARDINIA

CALABRIA

SICILY

## THE REGIONS OF
## ITALY

—·—·— International boundary
— — — Regional boundary

0    Kilometres    160

# VENICE

'I sat in front of Florian's *café*, eating ices, listening to music, talking with acquaintances: the traveller will remember how the immense cluster of tables and little chairs stretches like a promontory into the smooth lake of the Piazza.'
Henry James,
*The Aspern Papers*

Everyone, said Théophile Gautier (◊Naples and Campania), chooses one or two towns, 'ideal countries' whose palaces, streets, houses he builds in imagination on the basis of an 'inner architecture'. The foundations of this *ville intuitive* are stories, engravings, maps, 'sometimes the euphony or singularity of the name' (*Voyage en Italie (Italian Journey)*, 1851). For Gautier as for many Venice (in French the more euphonious *Venise*) was such a place, long only an image in 'the dark chamber of the brain'. For Byron◊ it was 'one of those places which I know before I see them', made by his reading a fairy-city 'Rising like water-columns from the sea,/Of joy the sojourn and of wealth the mart' (*Childe Harold's Pilgrimage*, Canto Four, 1818). Even the actual decline and decay of the once proud city tended less to contradict than to enrich such imaginings; the 'water-columns' which once reflected the Serenissima in her full magnificence now remember it in a more subtly poetic way, so that Venice becomes 'Perchance even dearer in her day of woe,/Than when she was a boast, a marvel, and a show'. The way was open to such melancholy Venices as that of Thomas Mann◊ in *Der Tod in Venedig (Death in Venice)*, 1912, both beautiful and seedy, site of love and death. (Extract 4). It remained as much a place of the mind as of stone and water, a place appropriately to be written about and painted in terms of wavering magical light, of objects dissolved in vapour or sheen. Turner became the interpreter – as *his* interpreter John Ruskin◊ puts it in *Modern Painters*, Part Two, 1846 – of palaces which are 'pale ranks of motionless flame', of 'those azure, fathomless depths of crystal mystery, on which the swiftness of the poised gondola floats double . . . its scarlet draperies flashed from the

1

kindling surface, and its bent oar breaking the radiant water into a dust of gold'.

Before the melancholy set in, visitors were attracted by Venice's power as the centre of a sea-borne empire with the great **Arsenal** at its heart, and by the splendour which expressed this power: the sort of scenes witnessed by John Evelyn (◊Lazio) in 1645 when the cannon of the Arsenal roared in loud echoing acclamation as the Doge per-formed the annual ceremony of wedding the sea by casting a gold ring and a gold cup from the prow of his 'gloriously painted, carved and gilded' boat the *Bucintoro*, which was 'environed and followed' by galleys and gondolas filled with 'spectators . . . trumpets, music and more cannons'. Many foreigners were also interested in the Venetian constitution – in the ideas intended, in theory at least, to be made manifest in the spectacle. Only in Venice could Renaissance visitors encounter 'a republican ideology' which was not merely theoretical but 'bedfellow with a real, observable commonwealth' (Edward Muir), only here could the civilized amenities of Italy be enjoyed by Protes-tants in a city which prided itself on its vigorous tradition of indepen-dence from the Papacy and the Inquisition. (Many Protestants confined their Italian itineraries to the Veneto; the reputation for tolerance also encouraged the proliferation of printing-presses, although the presence of Greek scholars was the main inducement to Aldus Manutius – Aldo Manuzio (1449–1515) – to establish here his Aldine Press, which produced among other clearly, crisply printed works more than thirty major editions of ancient Greek authors).

For centuries the patricians of the republic worked to promote the image of Venice as exemplar of freedom within discipline, oligarchy in the public interest. Visitors were usually persuaded; the Venetians' 'principal profession [i.e. what they profess] is liberty', declared William Thomas in his *History of Italy*, 1549. In *Othello* Brabantio, woken by Iago and Roderigo with the news that he has been robbed of his daughter, protests that 'This is Venice; my house is not a grange' – an isolated farmhouse – because Venice is surely too civilized and well regulated for such skulduggery to be possible. The play goes on to show that violence and deceit are not far beneath the surface, but they erupt only in distant Cyprus; such doings 'would not be believed in Venice'.

Probably the most popular Venetian author in England in the early 17th century was Fra Paolo Sarpi, who had close links with Protes-tants including the English ambassadors Sir Henry Wotton and Sir Dudley Carleton, and who undertook the legal and theological defence of the republic when it came under papal interdict in 1606. The conflict concerned Venice's extension of restrictions on ecclesias-tical landholding and assertion of the state's right to try clergy for major crimes. Sarpi argues the Venetian case vigorously in *Trattato dell'Interdetto* (*Treatise on the Interdict*), 1606, maintaining that in secular matters the authority of sovereign states derives directly from God and is not subject to papal decrees. On occasion the case for the defence is enlivened by passages of rhetorical indignation: Paul V's sentence of excommunication has been 'thundered out against the Duke and Senate, and all their dominions interdicted, because they will not suffer the liberty of the commonwealth to be defrauded; . . . because they do not deprive her of the power granted by God . . . to maintain the tranquillity and peace of her dominions; because they defend the lives, honour, and goods of those people committed to their government'. Protestants rejoiced to hear Sarpi's defiance, and the Catholic powers were too well aware of the importance of their own secular aims to act against Venice on the Pope's behalf. In April 1607 the pontiff reluctantly lifted his interdict. A blow had been struck for the autonomy of the modern secular state. Sarpi, who had wounded the Pope's pride as well as his authority, survived three assassination attempts. The first, which happened on the steps of the **Santa Fosca** bridge in the Cannaregio district in October 1607, left him with a badly scarred face. Sarpi is commemorated by a late 19th century bronze statue in **Campo Santa Fosca**.

There was a reputation also for sexual liberality. The fame of bold, beautiful and even learned courtesans perhaps attracted more male visitors than did study of the Venetian constitution. Thomas Coryat, who gives one of the fullest accounts of these women in *Coryat's Crudities*, 1611, claims that the safest policy for the traveller is to keep your eyes shut or 'turn them aside from these venereous Venetian objects'. He keeps his own eyes open, arguing a little disingenuously that 'the knowledge of evil is not evil' so it is no dishonour 'to see a courtesan in her house, and note her manners and conversation'. The superior sort of 'amorous Calypso' will allure her clients with glorious and glittering tapestried rooms, pictures of herself decked out like Venus, cosmetics ('sordid trumperies', the discerning man will realise), elaborately dressed hair, damask gowns, gold and jewels, carnation stockings, perfume; moreover, 'she will endeavour to enchant thee partly with her melodious notes that she warbles out upon her lute . . . and partly with that heart-tempting harmony of her voice', and is a persuasive rhetorician.

For all this apparent power, however, even the most (financially and socially) valued courtesans were in a precarious position. Those who were accomplished musicians or rhetoricians were not only employing marketable skills – advertising for 'dalliances' – but entering into dangerous competition with the traditionally male practitioners of these arts, themselves part of the highly patriarchal system which regulated severely the conduct and dress of other Venetian women. The late 16th century courtesan and poet Veronica Franco, competing with men in poems and familiar letters, could easily be stereotyped by them as a whore or simply as a woman. She was one of the easier targets for the satirical barbs of Pietro Aretino◊. The strategies by which Franco coped with this problem, studied by Margaret F. Rosenthal, include the poetic creation of an 'elegant self-portrait' of one 'unconcerned with sexual pleasure and financial profit' – one who, for example, when Henri III of France visited her, could defy negative male views of courtesans, offering him not sexual favours but an enamelled portrait of herself and a sonnet introducing it. (This royal encounter, however, contributed not only to her prestige but to the number of her envious enemies.)

Most women lacked the articulacy of Franco or, a generation before, Gaspara Stampa◊, or the opportunity to express it. The usual literary image of Venetian women was Iago's – 'super-subtle Venetians' who spend their time with their 'curled darlings' and 'do let God see the pranks /They dare not show their husbands' – or at the other extreme, the one embodied in the pure Desdemona, or Celia in Ben Jonson's *Volpone*, 1607. As the power and glory of Venice decreased – as it lost its reputation as a city of eastern wealth where acquistive Volpones could wake with cries of 'Good morning to the day and next my gold!' and there was always important financial 'news on the Rialto' (*The Merchant of Venice*) – the image of corruption spread more widely. Many, outsiders and Venetians, blamed the decline on general decadence. The carnival attracted particular censure, as did the exploits of Giacomo Casanova◊, shamelessly retold in his Memoirs. The music of the 18th century composer Baldassare Galuppi suggests to the speaker of Robert Browning's (◊Florence) *A Toccata of Galuppi's* (1855) a frivolous Venice of balls 'begun at midnight, burning ever to midday', chatter and black velvet masks; 'What of soul was left, I wonder, when the kissing had to stop?' But the poem regrets and delicately, attempting to verbalise the soft toccata, makes present and fixes the ephemeral world described. The speaker lacks 'the heart to scold' and ends the poem equally aware of the present dissolution in death and the past splendour of the 'Dear dead women, with such hair, too – what's become of all the gold?' (The golden hair – usually dyed in real life – had long featured in Venetian paintings, whether of goddesses or of Carpaccio's two languid ladies on a balcony in the **Museo Correr**.)

## PIAZZA SAN MARCO

The power, commodiousness, and splendour of Venice were impressed on visitors to the Piazza at the height of the Republic. Thomas Coryat, in *Coryat's Crudities*, 1611, dedicates many pages to the square and its buildings, since 'the variety of the curious objects which it exhibiteth to the spectator is such, that a man shall wrong it to speak [only] a little of it'. 'Truly such is the stupendious (to use a strange Epitheton for so strange and rare a place as this) glory of it, that at my first entrance thereof it did even amaze or rather ravish my senses'. Not only is the architecture more magnificent than that yielded by any place under the sun, but everyone under the sun is gathered here: 'you may both see all manner of fashions of attire, and hear all the languages of Christendom, besides those that are spoken by the barbarous ethnics' (peoples later listed by Coryat are 'Polonians, Slavonians, Persians, Grecians, Turks, Jews, Christians of all the famousest regions of Christendom'); in the morning and the early evening there is such 'frequency of people' that 'a man may very properly call it rather Orbis than Urbis forum, that is, a market place of the world, not of the city'.

In 1910 the Futurist poet Filippo Tommaso Marinetti◊ was less impressed by the 'Venice of foreigners, market for counterfeit anti-quarians, magnet for snobbery and universal imbecility' (Extract 5). Into the midst of this objectionable place, from the **Orologio** or clock-tower in Piazza San Marco, his supporters dropped copies of his pamphlet *Contro Venezia passatista (Against Past-Loving Venice)*. The collapse of the *Campanile* into the Piazza in 1902 might seem already to have confirmed Marinetti's view that this was a 'putrefying city', but it was rebuilt and around it the lovers of the past continued to drift, although then as now often in present pursuit of refreshment, music from the bands outside the cafés, or the general relaxed atmosphere of the paved and vehicle-free expanse – the atmosphere of the 'open air saloon dedicated to cooling drinks and . . . finer degustation' described by Henry James's narrator in *The Aspern Papers*, 1888 (Extract 3). (**Florian's**, where he takes his ice, had 22 years earlier lost its more urgent significance as the café for Venetians intent on peacefully displaying their patriotism by boycotting Quadri's, haunt of the occupying Austrians; it was *de rigueur* for locals and their sym-pathisers not to applaud the Austrian military band).

Even St Mark's, observes James in the 1882 essay revised for *Italian Hours*, 1909, can be used for relaxation once you are familiar with it and can 'pass in under the pictured porticoes with a feeling of habit and friendliness and a desire for something cool and dark'. On the grounds that 'the reader has been served too well already' where 'the best-described building in the world' is concerned, he gives not a detailed description but a more impressionistic account of 'the molten colour that drops from the hollow vaults and thickens the air with its richness', the burnished gold catching the light on its little uneven cubes, the tabernacles 'whose open doors disclose a dark Byzantine image spotted with dull, crooked gems'. In substance this is not very different to the more expansive passages of the authors he cites as among those responsible for serving readers 'too well', Ruskin◊ and Théophile Gautier (◊Naples and Campania). Ruskin (Extract 6) is rather more precise even in his rapture, and Gautier characteristically phantasmagoric in his vision of mosaics coming to life in *Voyage en*

*Italie* (*Italian Journey*), 1851: golden lightning flashes suddenly, the saints stir:

> 'the stiff folds of their dalmatics seem to soften and float, fixed eyes move . . . sealed feet begin to walk; the cherubim revolve their eight wings like wheels; angels unfurl their long purple and azure feathers, nailed to the wall by the implacable mosaicist . . . The martyrs get up from their grills or detach themselves from their crosses. The prophets talk with the evangelists. Doctors make observations to young saints, who smile with their porphyry lips; the figures . . . become processions of phantoms which . . . pass before you shaking their haloes of long golden hair. It is dazzling, dizzying, hallucinatory!'

Writers on San Marco generally register a jewelled gloom and a sense of the Other or the strangely, distinctively mingled – Gautier claims to see not only Byzantine or later medieval figures in the mosaic but, at least potentially, Egyptian and Hindu, blending mysteriously in 'a Christianity before Christ, a church made before religion'. Yet the impact is at the same time intensely personal, the effect, as James points out, not of 'beauty of proportion or perspective; there is nothing grandly balanced or far-arching; there are no long lines nor triumphs of the perpendicular', but of 'beauty of surface, of tone, of detail, of things near enough to touch and kneel upon and lean against'.

The **Baptistry** of San Marco has a peculiarly personal significance in Marcel Proust's *A la recherche du temps perdu* (*Remembrance of Things Past*), 1913–27. When Marcel, having long tried in vain to recapture moments of past happiness, steps on the uneven paving stones in the courtyard of the Hôtel de Guermantes, he is suddenly filled with at first inexplicable joy. All worry about the future, all doubt about his literary ability, are immediately removed. There are images of deep blue, of coolness and dazzling light. And at last Marcel realises: 'it was Venice'. In the baptistry with his mother he had stood on two uneven tiles. Now, as he experiences at once present and past, his impressions are 'in some way . . . extra-temporal'. The idea of returning to the temporal city can now be rejected; as Tony Tanner puts it, 'the only Venice he will revisit will be the Venice within, that old Venice of anticipation and desire'.

## THE DOGES' PALACE

The many chambers of the ducal palace aim to impress visitors, through grandeur, scale, celebratory painting and huge maps, with Venetian power. It is difficult to imagine the Doge and senators in *Othello* (more at home, of course, in a Jacobean playhouse) hurriedly meeting in these great halls. The one which impressed visitors most was usually the **Sala del Maggior Consilio**, the great hall in which, under the oligarchic system established in 1297, the council of the nobility met to elect government officials. (They also selected the committee which would in turn produce smaller committees to elect the Doge.) It is an immense room; it is claimed that three thousand people feasted with Henri III of France here in 1574. (During his visit Venice also treated Henri to the sort of spectacular entertainments remembered thirty-odd years later by Jonson's *Volpone*, unsuccessfully wooing the chaste Celia with his claims to be now just as 'fresh,/ As hot, as high' as when:

> 'For entertainment of the great Valois,
> I acted young Antinous, and attracted
> The eyes and ears of all the ladies present,
> T'admire each graceful gesture, note, and footing.')

The power of the Doge was much more limited than that of the great Valois; the fate of Marin Falier, who was executed having plotted to overthrow his fellow patricians in 1355, stood as a warning to his successors. His place among the Doges portrayed in the frieze of the Sala is taken by a black curtain and a stern Latin inscription noting that he was decapitated for his crimes. Byron, struck by the black veil and by the sight of 'the Giants' staircase, where he was crowned, and discrowned, and decapitated' (in fact the **Scala dei Giganti** was a later addition to the palace), gives a romantic account of the ruler's 'fiery character and strange story' in his verse drama *Marino Faliero, Doge of Venice*, 1821.

It was in this chamber, too, that the republic finally dissolved itself, as Napoleonic troops advanced on Venice, in 1797. The last Doge, Ludovico Manin, had just stutteringly advised the Great Council in effect to surrender its power when the sound of musket-shots from outside forced a hasty vote in favour of the motion and the patricians' precipitate flight from the building in fear of mobs and guillotines. (In fact the shots were a parting salute by Dalmatian soldiers who had been in Venetian service.) To many citizens, as to the narrator of Ippolito Nievo's historical novel *Le confessioni d'un italiano* (*The Castle of Fratta*), 1867, the Doge's action was 'a baseness without example'. 'For the half of such a crime, Marin Faliero had perished on the scaffold'. But annalists have also remembered the quiet, melancholy words of Manin after his colleagues' flight from the palace. Removing his ducal hat or *corno*, he handed the cap beneath it to his servant and told him 'take this; I shall not be needing it again.' The capitulation of the once mighty oligarchs, unglamorous though it may have been, prevented much bloodshed.

Another, unrelated and more happily remembered Manin, Daniele, proclaimed a new republic in the crowded Sala in 1848; it survived for 17 months before the Austrians regained control. But except during this interlude, the Doges' palace features in writing about Venice more often as an aesthetic centre than a political. Henry James, for instance, enjoys the way 'the reflected sunshine plays up through the great windows from the glittering lagoon and shimmers and twinkles over gilded walls and ceilings'; the stately past 'glows around you in a strong sea-light'. He joys in particular in the works of Veronese – 'a kind of breezy festival' where 'the white colonnades sustain the richest cano-pies, under which the first gentlemen and ladies in the world both render homage and receive it. Their glorious garments rustle in the air of the sea and their sun-lighted faces are the very complexion of Venice'. Veronese 'revels in the gold-framed ovals of the ceilings, multiplies himself there with the fluttering movement of an embroi-dered banner that tosses itself into the blue'.

## THE PRISONS

'I stood in Venice, on the Bridge of Sighs;/A palace and a prison on each hand'. The opening lines of Byron's *Childe Harold's Pilgrimage*, Canto Four, 1818, did much to associate the city with prisons. That the serene but ominously nick-named Bridge of Sighs should lead from the splendours of the ducal palace to the horror of the dungeons increased the poignancy of the prisoners' fate. Historians of Venice including John Julius Norwich have pointed out that conditions in Venetian prisons were no worse than those elsewhere in Europe, and that they were not, as Napoleon for one imagined, full of political prisoners. Apparently Casanova is (characteristically) exaggerating somewhat when he says that the underground cells in the palace – the *pozzi* or wells – were so named because they were always flooded with two feet of sea-water, forcing the inmates to sleep, eat, and live on small platforms above the water (*Histoire de ma vie* (*History of My Life*), 1821). But to be confined to the *pozzi* was clearly a grim enough fate.

Casanova himself was confined in the *piombi* – the 'leads', named for their position beneath the roof of the palace – in 1755-6. He was a prisoner of the State Inquisition, denounced by the spy Giovanni Battista Manuzzi for libertinism, unbelief, cheating gullible noblemen of money through claims about his power over spirits or knowledge of alchemy, and a long list of other offences, real or imagined. Casanova's escape, if one believes even some of the account of it in his memoirs, was daring, difficult, and lucky. He forced his way out onto the sloping roof of the palace, dragged himself up it, and, after a long wait for the full moon to go down and a near plummet to his death, succeeded in entering part of the palace through a window. At every stage he was hindered by the company of a panic-stricken and unreliable monk, Marin Balbi. Eventually, with Casanova covered in cuts and scratches and Balbi unscathed, they reached a room adjoining the **Sala delle Quattro Porte**. Casanova put on his spare set of clothes, including a magnificent plumed hat, and gave the monk his cloak. Thus attired (the usually elegant libertine looking like someone 'roughed up' at 'some house of ill-fame' or, because of the strange appearance of the hatless cloaked monk, 'a charlatan or an astronomer'), they were let into the hall by an official who fortunately supposed that they must have been accidentally locked in. Forthwith the escapees, 'neither dawdling nor running', marched down the Scala dei Giganti, out of the Porta della Carta, off to the quay and into a gondola which took them to Mestre on the mainland. By coach they went on to Treviso, and on foot (Casanova eventually forcing his irritating companion to separate from him) until they were safely out of Venetian territory.

Silvio Pellico, a liberal imprisoned by the Austrians between 1820 and 1830, spent an early period of his captivity in the *piombi*. He was afflicted by company even worse than that of Father Balbi: multitudes of mosquitoes infested the bed, table, chair, floor, walls and ceiling of his cell, 'while the air was filled with an infinity of them coming and going unendingly' with 'a diabolical whirr'. The view from the window of 'a forest of cupolas and campanili' might have been consoling, but in the intense heat the leaden roof of San Marco 'hammered back at me with stunning force'. Such conditions nearly drove Pellico to suicide, but, as he explains in *Le mie prigioni* (My Prisons), 1832, he forced himself to think through his life, sustaining himself with long meditations on religion and 'the duties of men and myself in particular'. These, to eke out his supply of paper, he scraped onto the rough table in his cell with a piece of glass, writing in code. Each day he wrote laboriously until the surface of the table was covered, pondered at length what he had written, and then 'forced myself (often regretfully) to scrape everything away . . . so that the surface should be ready to receive new thoughts'. The process was methodically repeated through the days until the death sentence on Pellico and other political prisoners was solemnly pronounced in Piazza San Marco. Commutations – Pellico endured eight years' hard labour at Spielberg in Moravia – were then read out. (A copy of the whole document, which takes what must have been a terrifying time to progress from condemnation to commutation, can be seen in the Risorgimento section of the **Museo Correr** in the Piazza.)

## THE GRAND CANAL

The canals have always been the most distinctive feature of Venice, together with their gondolas, whose qualities successive writers have striven to define, from the functional but lustrous 'water coach' of John Evelyn's diary (◊Lazio) to Mann's deathly boat 'black as nothing else on earth save a coffin'. (For Byron too, in the comic verse tale *Beppo*, the gondola glides 'Just like a coffin clapt in a canoe', but also, usefully, 'Where none can make out what you say or do'.)

The smaller canals have had their chroniclers. Gautier, with a catholic taste for the unexpected and different as opposed to the merely beautiful, delighted in the quiet alleys and waterways around the **Cannaregio Canal**, the crumbling houses and the green, creeping water full of vegetable leftovers and straw from old mattresses. Thomas Coryat in 1608 had seen canals and rubbish more practically: the 'channels' (which also function as swifter versions of streets) helpfully carry away 'all the garbage and filthiness that falleth into them from the city'. But particular attention has been paid to the Grand Canal, the curve and sweep of Henry James's 'noble waterway that begins in its glory at [Santa Maria della] Salute and ends in its abasement at the railway station', crossed by the **Rialto bridge** with its shops (and beneath the bridge, claims Coryat, 'vicious and licentious varlets' working as ferrymen), and lined by Coryat's 'goodly' and 'sumptuous' palazzi.

Probably the most talked-of inhabitant of a palace on the Grand Canal (up the length of which he once swam from the Lido) was Byron, living in **Palazzo Mocenigo** as leaseholder in 1818 and 1819. In this sprawling house he lived with 14 servants, a menagerie of monkeys, a fox, and mastiffs on the ground floor, and various of the 'more women than I can count or recount' with whom he was involved in Venice. Byron's letters of the period dwell on the most dominant of these women, his fiery housekeeper, Margharita Cogni, 'La Fornarina' ('the baker's wife'). She knocked down her rivals amid 'great confusion – and demolition of head dresses and handkerchiefs'; 'she was the terror of men, women and children, for she had the strength of an Amazon with the temper of Medea. She was a fine animal – but quite untameable', Byron recalled after Margharita had – following failed attempts to knife him and to drown herself in the canal – finally accepted that their liaison was over.

At Palazzo Mocenigo Byron also began work on his longest, wittiest and most insightful poem, *Don Juan*, 1819–24. He had first experimented with a similar tone of voice in *Beppo*, 1818, the deliberately digressive story of a Venetian woman who lives with her lover (or 'vice-husband') during the prolonged absence of her spouse; all three come to an easy accommodation when the husband unexpectedly reappears. Topic and manner are appropriate to the role reversals, licensed anarchy and sexual freedom of the carnival, into which Byron entered with enthusiasm during his years in Venice. Laura (named ironically after Petrarch's unobtainable beloved) meets her lover at carnival, the time when:

> 'The people take their fill of recreation,
> And buy repentance, ere they grow devout,
> However high their rank, or low their station,
> With fiddling, feasting, dancing, drinking, masking,
> And other things which may be had for asking.'

Other popular Venetian rendez-vous include the many theatres, where 'the deep damnation' of Laura's lover's 'bah' is so feared that 'Soprano, basso, even the contra-alto,/Wished him five fathom under the Rialto', and where Byron enjoyed the 18th-century comedies of Carlo Goldoni, whose birthplace (the small **Goldoni museum** and centre for theatre studies in the Palazzo Centani, Calle dei Nomboli), is not far from the other bank of the canal, roughly opposite Palazzo Mocenigo. Goldoni began as a deviser of scenarios for *commedia dell'arte* actors and went on to write plays which added a degree of social and psychological realism to the traditional *commedia* types to create aristocrats, lovers distressed or accident-prone, irascible old men descended from the *pantalone* figure, fishermen, innkeepers, obtuse or canny country people, loyal or cunning servants recognisable to theatre-goers as new versions of themselves and their favourite types. Some audiences, however, preferred the *fiabe* of Carlo Gozzi, romantic fables with more fantastic elements including *L'amore delle tre melarance* (*The Love of Three Oranges*), 1761.

Moving along the Grand Canal in the direction of the Accademia bridge one comes to the magnificent **Palazzo Rezzonico**, where Robert Browning, staying with his son Pen, died in an upper room on 12 December 1889. The palace is now a museum which opulently celebrates 18th century Venice. On the other side of the canal, just after the Accademia bridge, is one of several buildings associated with Henry James, the **Palazzo Barbaro**. James's impressions here, garnered on visits to his compatriots the Curtises in the 1880s and 1890s, helped him to create Palazzo Leporelli in *The Wings of the Dove*, the 'high florid rooms' where 'hard cool pavements took reflexions in their lifelong polish' and the sun on the stirred sea-water flickered over ceilings with 'medallions of purple and brown, of brave old melancholy colour, medals as of old reddened gold, embossed and beribboned, all toned with time and flourished and scolloped and gilded about, set in their great moulded and figured concavity'. For Milly Theale, the rich young American who rents this splendour, 'the romance . . . would be to sit there for ever, through all her time, as in a fortress', but time and human nature will destroy the prospect of this idyll – she is fatally ill and Kate Croy and Merton Densher seek her money not, as she is deceived into thinking, her love.

James was also a guest at Ca' Alvisi (now Hotel Regina) and the adjoining **Palazzo Giustiniani-Recanati**, owned by the expatriate American Katharine de Kay Bronson. Thanks partly to its location on the Canal opposite 'the high, broad-based, florid church of **Santa Maria della Salute**' and especially thanks to its benevolent and tactful hostess, Ca' Alvisi acted as 'a friendly private-box at the constant operatic show' with 'withdrawing rooms behind for more detached conversation'. The talk was enriched by the circulation of 'delicate tobacco and little gilded glasses', while, below, the gondolas of the many guests waited at 'her well-plashed water-steps' (*Italian Hours*, 1910). Passing on along the Molo and across the Ponte della Paglia to Riva degli Schiavoni, one comes to a third place important to James. On the top floor of no. 4161, now Pensione Wildner, he worked on *The Portrait of a Lady* in 1880 and reflected, in the preface added 25 years later, on the effect of 'romantic and historic sites' on art of which they are not themselves to be the subject:

> 'the waterside life, the wondrous lagoon spread before me, and the ceaseless human chatter of Venice came in at my windows, to which I seem to myself to have been constantly driven, in the fruitless fidget of composition, as if to see whether, out in the blue channel, the ship of some right suggestion, of some better phrase, of the next happy twist of my subject, the next true touch for my canvas, mightn't come into sight.'

Concentration was not, James recalls as he chews it over, much helped. Such places express 'only too much'. But doubtless in some way 'one's book, and one's "literary effort" at large' benefited, and some pages now make him 'see again the bristling curve of the wide Riva, the large colour-spots of the balconied houses and the repeated undulation of the little hunch-backed bridges, marked by the rise and drop again, with the wave, of foreshortened clicking pedestrians'.

## The Lagoon

Byron, ever eager for original experience, varied his carnal, carnival and writing experiences in Venice by regular visits to the Armenian monastery on the island of **San Lazzaro**, just off the Lido, where he studied Armenian with Father Pasqual Aucher: 'I found,' he wrote to his friend the poet Thomas Moore, 'that my mind wanted something craggy to break upon; and this – as the most difficult thing I could discover here for an amusement – I have chosen, to torture me into attention'. On the **Lido** itself, then still a lonely place, Byron sought stimulus in vigorous riding. When Shelley came to Venice in September 1818 the two rode together; Shelley describes the 'bare strand/Of hillocks, heaped from ever-shifting sand' (Extract 1) and draws on their long conversations here and at Palazzo Mocenigo in his poem *Julian and Maddalo* (published 1824), an account both of their fascination for each other and of their fundamentally different philosophies. Julian's atheism and optimism about the possibility of human betterment are opposed to Maddalo's vestigial religion and Byronic scepticism. But the tension and readability of the poem result from the insistence on exploring both points of view, from the poet's awareness that Maddalo's or Byron's 'more serious conversation is a sort of intoxication; men are held by it as a spell', the acknowledgement by the idealist that just possibly, as Maddalo pithily observes, 'You talk Utopia'.

Boats proceeding north across the Lagoon to the islands of Murano, Burano, and Torcello, first pass the cemetery island of **San Michele**, the 'gloomy cypressed isle of the dead' of Bernard Malamud's Venetian novel *Pictures of Fidelman*, 1969. Here are buried Frederick Rolfe, 'Baron Corvo'◊ and Ezra Pound (◊Tuscany).

**Torcello**, colonised (traditionally, at least) by refugees from the Roman city of Altinum and for a time more populous and important than the islands which◊ became Venice, is used by John Ruskin◊ as a symbol of the purity which Venice lost. The first settlers came 'seeking, like Israel of old, a refuge from the sword in the paths of the sea'. They built a cathedral – really the process took several centuries, but Ruskin imagines it, persuasively, as an immediate, hasty piece of work – whose outside with its massy stone shutters suitably resembles 'a refuge from Alpine storm' and whose interior freely admitted sunshine. This unusual 'luminousness' is 'especially touching in a church built by men of sorrow'. 'There was fear and depression upon them enough, without a material gloom', and so – to the comfort also of Ruskin, nervous often of Catholic glooms in Venice – they cast no artificial shadows on their mosaics and used no dark colours in them. 'They sought for comfort in their religion, for tangible hopes and promises, not for threatenings and mysteries'. Physically and metaphorically the cathedral can be compared with the traditional Ship of the Church, the ark of refuge in the midst of destruction. To learn in what (quasi-Protestant) spirit the dominion of Venice was begun, the stranger should not consider wealth, arsenals, 'the pageantry of her palaces' or 'the secrets of her councils' but should:

> 'ascend the highest tier of the stern ledges that sweep round the altar of Torcello, and then, looking as the pilot did of old along the marble ribs of the goodly temple-ship, let him repeople its veined deck with the shadows of its dead mariners, and strive to feel in himself the strength of heart that was kindled within them, when first, after the pillars of it had settled in the sand, and the roof of it had been closed against the angry sky that was still reddened by the fires of their homesteads, – first, within the shelter of its knitted walls, amidst the murmur of the waste of waves and the beating of the wings of the sea-birds round the rock that was strange to them, – rose that ancient hymn, in the power of their gathered voices:
> THE SEA IS HIS, AND HE MADE IT
> AND HIS HANDS PREPARED THE DRY LAND.'

Torcello was long ago superseded by Venice, but even its quiet, depopulated state contributes to the vision of primal purity, for the only incense 'that fills the temple of their ancient worship' is the scent of soft grass, cut at dawn by the mower's scythe, in the 'little meadow which was once the Piazza of the city', 'hardly larger than an ordinary

English farmyard, and roughly enclosed on each side by broken pal-
ings and hedges of honeysuckle'.

## OTHER LITERARY LANDMARKS

**Ca' Foscari**: the palace where Doge Iacopo Foscari, subject of Byron's
verse play *The Two Foscari*, 1821, died in 1457.

**Campo San Bartolomeo**: 1883 bronze statue of Goldoni as genial
18th century gentleman with cane and three-cornered hat.

**Hotel Danieli**: among the guests have been John and Effie Ruskin
and the novelist Georges Sand (1804–76) and her lover the poet and
dramatist Alfred de Musset (1810–57).

**Palazzo Dario**: palace on the Grand Canal where the French Symbolist poet Henri de Régnier (1864–1936) lived.

**Palazzo Vendramin-Callergi**: here Richard Wagner (1813–83) died.

**Santa Maria Gloriosa dei Frari**: here are the tombs of Titian
(c.1485–1576), erected in the mid-19th century, and of Antonio
Canova (1757–1822). Canova's, which he designed himself, is, in the
opinion of Ruskin, 'consummate in science, intolerable in affectation, ridiculous in conception'.

**Scuola Grande di San Rocco**: Ruskin was 'crushed to the earth' by
the power of Tintoretto's huge canvases, including the resurrection
where 'the rocks of the sepulchre [are] crashed all to pieces and
roaring down upon you, while the Christ soars forth into a torrent
of angels'.

**Teatro Fenice** ('Phoenix'): opera-house, scene of the first night of
Verdi's *Rigoletto*, 1851, and *La Traviata*, 1853, founded in 1791, burnt
down in 1836 and 1996.

**Teatro Goldoni**: theatre, built in the 17th century, for which Goldoni
worked in 1753–62, when it was called the San Luca.

**Teatro Malibran**: formerly the San Giovanni Grisostomo opera-
house, where Goldoni was director in 1737.

## BOOKLIST

Adler, Sara Maria, 'Veronica
Franco's Petrarchan *Terze
Rime*: Subverting the Master's
Plan', *Italica* vol. 65, 1988, pp.
213–33.

Bassanese, Fiora, *Gaspara Stampa*,
Twayne, Boston, 1982.

Browning, Robert, *The Poems*,
*Volume I*, John Pettigrew and
Thomas J. Collins, ed, Penguin,
London, 1993.

Byron, George Gordon, Lord,
'*The Flesh is Frail*': *Byron's Letters
and Journals, Volume 6, 1818–19*,
Leslie A. Marchand, ed, John
Murray, London, 1976.

*Booklist continued*

Casanova, Giacomo, *History of My Life* [1821], Willard R. Trask, trans, Longmans, London, 1967.

Clegg, Jeanne, *Ruskin and Venice*, Junction Books, London, 1981.

Collier, Peter, *Proust and Venice*, Cambridge University Press, Cambridge, 1989.

Coryat, Thomas, *Coryat's Crudities* [1611], James MacLehose, Glasgow, 1905.

Evelyn, John, *The Diary of John Evelyn*, Guy de la Bédoyère, ed, Boydell, Woodbridge, 1995.

Goldoni, Carlo, *Four Comedies*, Frederick Davies, trans, Penguin, Harmondsworth, 1968. **Extract 2.**

Gozzi, Carlo, *Useless Memories* [1797–8], J.A. Symonds, trans, Oxford University Press, 1962.

Hayman, Ronald, *Thomas Mann: a Biography*, Scribner, New York, 1995; Bloomsbury, London, 1996.

Holmes, Richard, *Shelley: the Pursuit*, Penguin, London, 1987.

James, Henry, *The Aspern Papers* [1888], Daniel Aaron and Julian Taylor, ed, Dent, London, 1994. **Extract 3.**

James, Henry, *Italian Hours* [1909], John Auchard, ed, Penguin, New York and London, 1995.

James, Henry, *The Portrait of a Lady* [1881], Geoffrey Moore and Patricia Crick, ed, Penguin, Harmondsworth, 1984.

James, Henry, *The Wings of the Dove* [1902], Peter Brooks, ed, Oxford University Press, Oxford, 1984.

Littlewood, Ian, *Venice: a Literary Companion*, John Murray, London, 1991.

Mann, Thomas, *Death in Venice* [1912]. *Tristan. Tonio Kroger*, H.T. Lowe-Porter, trans, Penguin Harmondsworth, 1975. **Extract 4.**

Marchand, Leslie A., *Byron: a Portrait*, John Murray, London, 1970.

Marinetti, Filippo Tomasso, *Selected Writings*, R.W. Flint and Arthur Coppotelli, trans, Secker and Warburg, London, 1972. **Extract 5.**

Marinetti, Filippo Tomasso, *The Futurist Cookbook* [1932], Suzanne Brill, trans, introduction by Lesley Chamberlain, Trefoil Publications, London, 1989.

Muir, Edward, *Civic Ritual in Renaissance Venice*, Princeton University Press, Princeton, 1981.

Nievo, Ippolito, *The Castle of Fratta* [1867], Lovett F. Edwards, trans, Oxford University Press, London, 1957.

Norwich, John Julius, *A History of Venice*, Penguin, London, 1983.

Pellico, Silvio, *My Prisons* [1832], I.G. Capaldi, trans, Oxford University Press, London, 1963

Proust, Marcel, *Remembrance of Things Past* [1913–27], C.K.S. Moncrieff and T. Kilmartin, trans, Penguin, Harmondsworth, 1984.

Rosenthal, Margaret F., *The Honest Courtesan: Veronica Franco, Citizen and Writer in Sixteenth-Century Venice*, University of Chicago Press, Chicago and London, 1992.

Ruskin, John, *The Stones of Venice* [1851–3], Jan Morris, ed, Bellew Publishing, London, 1989. **Extract 6.**

Shelley, Percy Bysshe, *Selected Poetry and Prose*, Alasdair D.F. Macrae, ed, Routledge, London, 1991. **Extract 1.**

Tanner, Tony, *Venice Desired*, Blackwell, Oxford and Cambridge, Mass., 1992.

Thomas, William, *The History of Italy* [1549]. George B. Parkes, ed, Cornell University Press, Ithaca, 1963.

Booklist continued

Tusiani, Joseph, trans, *Italian Poets of the Renaissance*, Baroque Press, Long Island City, New York, 1971. [Includes poems by Gaspara Stampa].

Wootton, David, *Paolo Sarpi: Between Renaissance and Enlightenment*, Cambridge University Press, Cambridge, 1983.

# Extracts

## (1) THE LIDO

### Percy Bysshe Shelley, *Julian and Maddalo*, 1818

*The poem draws on the long conversations of Shelley and Byron in 1818. Maddalo, a spell-binding Byronic talker, has great capacity for noble action but 'derives, from a comparison of his own extraordinary mind with the dwarfish intellects that surround him, an intense apprehension of the nothingness of human life'. The Shelley-like Julian is 'passionately attached to those philosophical notions which assert the power of man over his own mind'.*

I rode one evening with Count Maddalo
Upon the bank of land which breaks the flow
Of Adria towards Venice: a bare strand
Of hillocks, heaped from ever-shifting sand,
Matted with thistles and amphibious weeds,
Such as from earth's embrace the salt ooze breeds,
Is this; an uninhabited sea-side,
Which the lone fisher, when his nets are dried,
Abandons; and no other object breaks
The waste, but one dwarf tree and some few stakes
Broken and unrepaired, and the tide makes
A narrow space of level sand thereon,
Where 'twas our wont to ride while day went down.
This ride was my delight. I love all waste
And solitary places; where we taste
The pleasure of believing what we see
Is boundless, as we wish our souls to be:
And such was this wide ocean, and this shore
More barren than its billows; and yet more
Than all, with a remembered friend I love

To ride as then I rode; – for the winds drove
The living spray along the sunny air
Into our faces; the blue heavens were bare,
Stripped to their depths by the awakening north;
And, from the waves, sound like delight broke forth
Harmonizing with solitude, and sent
Into our hearts aerial merriment.
So, as we rode, we talked; and the swift thought,
Winging itself with laughter, lingered not,
But flew from brain to brain, – such glee was ours,
Charged with light memories of remembered hours,
None slow enough for sadness: till we came
Homeward, which always makes the spirit tame.
This day had been cheerful but cold, and now
The sun was sinking, and the wind also.
Our talk grew somewhat serious, as may be
Talk interrupted with such raillery
As mocks itself, because it scorn
The thoughts it would extinguish: – 'twas forlorn,
Yet pleasing, such as once, so poets tell,
The devils held within the shades of Hell
Concerning God, freewill and destiny:
Of all the earth has yet been or yet may be,
All that vain men imagine or believe,
Or hope can paint or suffering may achieve,
We descanted, and I (for ever still
Is it not wiser to make the best of ill?)
Argued against despondency, but pride
Made my companion take the darker side.

## (2) VENICE

### Carlo Goldoni, *The Venetian Twins*, 1748

*The twins of the title, Tonino of Venice and Zanetto of Bergamo,
separated since birth, are habitually mistaken for each other,
leaving themselves and others in a state of often farcical confusion. (To make matters worse, Tonino is using the name
Zanetto.) Lelio, Tonino's rival for Beatrice, takes the twins for
one strangely unpredictable person, by turns fierce and cowardly.
Here he decides to see 'what a little flattery can do'. Such scenes
of mutual incomprehension are rooted in the playing traditions
of commedia dell'arte, which Goldoni both drew on and
sought to reform into scripted drama.*

LELIO I bow before the exalted, before the noblest of all the most celebrated heroes of Venice.

TONINO Your servant, you loud-mouthed proclaimer of your own importance.

LELIO I beg your pardon if, with the tedious articulation of my pronunciation, I dare to offend the tympanum of your ear.

TONINO Regurgitate the trumpet of your eloquence, lest I touch not only its tympanum but also its drum.

LELIO I must make known to you that I am overcome with the most delirious madness.

TONINO I suspected it from the first.

LELIO Love's poisoned arrows have pierced my impenetrable heart.

TONINO And your brain as well, I'd say.

LELIO Ah, Signor Zanetto, you who are of the family Bisognosi, deny not your aid to one who has need of you.

TONINO *You* have need of *me*? For what?

LELIO I am burning with love.

TONINO Well, if it's sympathy you want . . .

LELIO You alone can heal me of my wounds.

TONINO Where was it you said you came from?

LELIO I come from a city where misfortune reigns. I was born under an unlucky star and raised among desperadoes and reckless men.

TONINO You mean you've escaped from a lunatic asylum?

LELIO I will cut the thread of my labyrinthine discourse and come to the point. I love Beatrice. I desire her. I pant for her. My fate depends on you. I appeal to your immeasurable, to your more than illimitable kindness, to give her to me.

TONINO I will cut the knot of my reply with my knife of frankness. Beatrice is mine. I will surrender all the wealth of India before I surrender the beauteous beauty of my beautiful one. [*To himself*] Damn him, he's started me doing it as well.

LELIO You sentence me to death!

TONINO That'll be one lunatic the less.

LELIO Oh, horror!

TONINO Oh – go away.

## (3) Venice

### Henry James, *The Aspern Papers*, 1888

*James's unnamed narrator, plotting to obtain, by fair means or foul, papers connected with the poet he idolizes, describes the Piazza. In so doing he shows at the same time his arrogance and shallowness and a degree of Jamesian perception, almost as if James is parodying the manner of his own travel-writing.*

I was seldom at home in the evening, for when I attempted to occupy myself in my apartments the lamplight brought in a swarm of noxious insects, and it was too hot for closed windows. Accordingly I spent the late hours either on the water (the moonlight of Venice is famous), or in the splendid square which serves as a vast forecourt to the strange old basilica of Saint Mark. I sat in front of Florian's *café*, eating ices, listening to music, talking with acquaintances: the traveller will remember how the immense cluster of tables and little chairs stretches like a promontory into the smooth lake of the Piazza. The whole place, of a summer's evening, under the stars and with all the lamps, all the voices and light footsteps on marble (the only sounds of the arcades that enclose it), is like an open-air saloon dedicated to cooling drinks and to a still finer degustation – that of the exquisite impressions received during the day. When I did not prefer to keep mine to myself there was always a stray tourist, disencumbered of his Baedeker, to discuss them with, or some domesticated painter rejoicing in the return of the season of strong effects. The wonderful church, with its low domes and bristling embroideries, the mystery of its mosaic and sculpture, looked ghostly in the tempered gloom, and the sea-breeze passed between the twin columns of the Piazzetta, the lintels of a door no longer guarded, as gently as if a rich curtain were swaying there.

## (4) Venice

### Thomas Mann, Death in Venice, 1912

*Mann's Aschenbach, after a life of discipline, experiences the painful pleasures of a return of the repressed when, holidaying in Venice, he falls obsessively in love with an unattainable boy.*

Tadzio and his sisters at length took a gondola. Aschenbach hid behind a portico or fountain while they embarked and directly they pushed off did the same. In a furtive whisper he told the boatman he would tip him well to follow at a little distance the other gondola, just rounding a corner, and fairly sickened at the man's quick, sly grasp and ready acceptance of the go-between's role.

Leaning back among soft, black cushions he swayed gently in the wake of the other black-snouted bark, to which the strength of his passion chained him. Sometimes it passed from his view, and then he was assailed by an anguish of unrest. But his guide appeared to have long practice in affairs like these; always, by dint of short cuts or deft manoeuvres, he contrived to overtake the coveted sight. The air was heavy and foul, the sun burnt down through a slate-coloured haze. Water slapped gurgling against wood and stone. The gondolier's cry, half warning, half salute, was answered with singular accord from far within the silence of the labyrinth. They passed little gardens high up the crumbling wall, hung with clustering white and purple flowers that sent down an odour of almonds. Moorish lattices showed shadowy in the gloom. The marble steps of a church descended into the canal, and on them a beggar squatted, displaying his misery to view, showing the whites of his eyes, holding out his hat for alms. Farther on a dealer in antiquities cringed before his lair, inviting the passer-by to enter and be duped. Yes, this was Venice, this the fair frailty that fawned and that betrayed, half fairy-tale, half snare; the city in whose stagnating air the art of painting once put forth so lusty a growth, and where musicians were moved to accords so weirdly lulling and lascivious. Our adventurer felt his senses wooed by this voluptuousness of sight and sound, tasted his secret knowledge that the city sickened and hid its sickness for love of gain, and bent an ever more unbridled leer on the gondola that glided on before him.

# (5) VENICE

## Filippo Tommaso Marinetti,
## *Against Past-Loving Venice*, 1910

*Copies of Marinetti's provocative manifesto were dropped into
St Mark's Square by his fellow Futurists.*

We renounce the old Venice, enfeebled and undone by worldly luxury, although we once loved and possessed it in a great nostalgic dream.

We renounce the Venice of foreigners, market for counterfeiting antiquarians, magnet for snobbery and universal imbecility, bed unsprung by caravans of lovers, jewelled bathtub for cosmopolitan courtesans, *cloaca maxima* of passéism.

We want to cure and heal this putrefying city, magnificent sore from the past. We want to cheer and ennoble the Venetian people, fallen from their ancient grandeur, drugged by a contemptible mean cowardice in the practice of their little one-eyed businesses.

We want to prepare the birth of an industrial and military Venice that can dominate the Adriatic sea, that great Italian lake.

Let us hasten to fill in its little reeking canals with the shards of its leprous, crumbling palaces.

Let us burn the gondolas, rocking chairs for cretins, and raise to the heavens the imposing geometry of metal bridges and howitzers plumed with smoke, to abolish the falling curves of the old architecture.

Let the reign of the holy Electric Light finally come, to liberate Venice from its venal moonshine of furnished rooms.

# (6) VENICE

## John Ruskin, *The Stones of Venice*, 1851–3

*Like many observers, Ruskin is entranced by the glittering interior of San Marco. He is also anxious, however, to see through the lustre to truths amenable to the religious, and specifically Protestant, beliefs which he held at this time.*

There opens before us a vast cave, hewn out into the form of a Cross, and divided into shadowy aisles by many pillars. Round the domes of its roof the light enters only through narrow apertures like large stars; and here and there a ray or two from some far-away casement wanders into the darkness, and casts a narrow phosphoric stream upon the waves of marble that heave and fall in a thousand colours along the floor. What else there is of light is from torches, or silver lamps, burning ceaselessly in the recesses of the chapels; the roof sheeted with gold, and the polished walls covered with alabaster, give back at every curve and angle some feeble gleaming to the flames; and the glories round the heads of the sculptured saints flash out upon us as we pass them, and sink again into the gloom. Under foot and over head, a continual succession of crowded imagery, one picture passing into another, as in a dream; forms beautiful and terrible mixed together; dragons and serpents, and ravening birds of prey, and graceful birds that in the midst of them drink from running fountains and feed from vases of crystal; the passions and the pleasures of human life symbolized together, and the mystery of its redemption; for the mazes of interwoven lines and changeful pictures lead always at last to the Cross, lifted and carved in every place and upon every stone; sometimes with the serpent of eternity wrapped round it, sometimes with doves beneath its arms, and sweet herbage growing forth from its feet; but conspicuous most of all on the great rood that crosses the church before the altar, raised in bright blazonry against the shadows of the apse. And although in the recesses of the aisles and chapels, when the mist of the incense hangs heavily, we may see continually a figure traced in faint lines upon their marble, a woman standing with her eyes raised to heaven, and the inscription above her, 'Mother of God', she is not here the presiding deity. It is the Cross that is first seen, and always burning at the centre of the temple; and every dome and hollow of its roof has a figure of Christ in the utmost height of it, raised in power, or returning in judgment.

# Biographies and important works

ARETINO, Pietro (1492–1556), took his name from the town of his birth, Arezzo. He studied literature and painting in Perugia. He lived in Rome during much of 1517–25, where the Medici Popes Leo X and Clement VII were among his protectors. But he made too many enemies with his libellous attacks, particularly his *pasquinate* – lampoons affixed to the statue Pasquino – and left Rome following an attempt on his life. From 1527 he was based, on the whole more safely, in Venice. Here his skill in ridiculing the mighty made him some friends in high places: both François I of France and the Emperor Charles V were prepared to pay for his printed good word.

Among Aretino's extant works are *I raggionamenti* (*The Dialogues*), 1534–6, which ironically apply the familiar form of the philosophical dialogue to arguments in favour of prostitution, prose comedies including *La cortegiana* (*The Courtesan*), 1534 (written in 1525), and the more academic verse tragedy *L'Orazia* (*The Horatii*), 1546. Aretino had a widespread reputation for obscenity, but also for robust satire and language free of literary elaboration. His *Lettere*, 1537–57, contain examples of his breadth of interests, his friendships (especially with the painter Titian) and his dislikes.

BYRON, George Gordon Noel, Lord (1788–1824), was the most famous living English poet when, in 1816, he came to Switzerland and then Italy in the wake of the scandal surrounding the collapse of his marriage to Annabella Milbanke.

In 1816–19 he lived (engaging in much sex, riding, swimming, and writing) chiefly in Venice, which became for him, in Leslie Marchand's words, 'a magic world, a theatrical setting for life, with a melancholy history that touched a chord of sympathy in him'. In April 1819 a quieter period of his personal life (the writing continued unabated) began when he fell in love with Countess Teresa Guiccioli. He lived with her, mainly in Ravenna and Pisa, until his departure to join the struggle for Greek independence in 1823. He died of fever at Missolonghi in April 1824.

Byron wrote much of his best work in Italy. In *Childe Harold's Pilgrimage*, Canto Four, 1818, eagerly read by the public who had bought the earlier cantos and his eastern tales, he fixed images of Italian towns and natural features for generations of European travellers. Rome and Venice in particular are also part of a larger meditation on time and its casualties. Byron's deceptively easy colloquial later style in *Beppo*, 1818, and *Don Juan*, 1819–24, owed some of its inspiration to Italian burlesque and particularly Luigi Pulci's late 15th century mock-heroic romance *Morgante*, part of which Byron translated. Another inspiration, seen also in Byron's irresistibly readable, witty and multifaceted letters to his friends, was his experience of Italy's often comparatively relaxed sexual mores. Italy contrasted in this respect with England, and was also a useful vantage point from which to observe and satirise the social and political hypocrisies of the country from which he had exiled himself.

CASANOVA, Giacomo (1725–98), of Venice, studied at the university of Padua and was expected to enter the church. Instead he entered on a career of travel, gambling, seductions and longer love-affairs. He bestowed on himself the title Chevalier de Seingalt. Arrested by the State Inquisition in 1755, he escaped in 1756. In 1774 he returned to Venice to work as an Inquisition spy, but was banished in 1782 and withdrew to Austria. There he wrote, in French, an extensive account of his adventures up to1774, *Histoire de ma vie* (*History of My Life*), 1821. In the fourth book of the *History* Casanova outlines the philosophy of his life as a 'reasoning voluptuary': while animal nature, in order to perpetuate itself, satisfies itself habitually with 'hunger, appetite for coitus, [and] hate which tends to destroy the enemy', 'Man alone is capable of true pleasure, for, endowed with the faculty of reason, he foresees it, seeks it, creates it, and reasons about it after enjoying it'.

CORYAT or CORYATE, Thomas (c.1577–1617), travelled in Europe, mostly on foot, in 1608. He recorded his expedition in *Coryat's Crudities*, 1611. In 1612 he embarked on a more ambitious journey as far as India, where he died. He was renowned both for amusing anecdote and comprehensive enquiry into places and people, rendered in sometimes extravagant prose interspersed with verses. The writing is suffused with the presence of the author in his guise as the honest, popular 'character' Tom Coryat. Some measure of the spirit – and spiritedness – of his work is evident on the title-page, announcing 'Crudities' (undigested matter) 'hastily gobbled up in five months' travels . . . Newly digested in the hungry air of Odcombe in the County of Somerset, and now

dispersed to the nourishment of the travelling members of this Kingdom'.

FRANCO, Veronica (1546–91), was a Venetian *cortigiana onesta* or high-class courtesan. She was part of the circle or salon of the well-connected Domenico Venier. (Her influence with Domenico and his nephew Marco, however, gained her the enmity of the younger nephew, Maffio, who played on her name in a sonnet as *Veronica, ver unica puttana* – 'Veronica, veritably unique whore'.) In 1580 she was investigated by the Inquisition on charges of witchcraft, but the case was soon dropped.

Franco's chief publications are *Terze rime* (*Poems in Terza Rima*), 1575, and *Lettere familiari* (*Familiar Letters*), 1580. The letters contain eloquently expressed practical counsels including advice to a woman not – given the physical dangers, hardships and male persecution involved – to let her daughter become a courtesan. The first part of the *Rime* includes poems by male authors as well as Franco's verse responses to them. The contrast between the directness and honesty of most of her poems and the more conventionally Petrarchan male pieces contributes to the sequence's assault on Petrarchism and its passive or silent females. She speaks honestly and directly, counselling what Sara Maria Adler calls 'a sane hedonism'; in contrast with the Petrarchan tradition, hers is a 'poetics of release, not repression and sublimation; her art is generated not by the suffering of love denied but rather by aspirations toward love fulfilled, by the energy of her exuberant sensuality'.

GOLDONI, Carlo (1707–93), born in Venice, provided scenarios for *commedia dell'arte* actors while practising (with little success) as a lawyer in the 1730s. He was briefly director of the San Giovanni Grisostomo opera house (later Teatro Malibran). In 1743 he set up as a lawyer in Pisa, but in 1748 was persuaded by Cesare d'Arbes (a well known *commedia* Pantalone) to return to Venice as house dramatist at Teatro Sant'Angelo. In this small theatre (subsequently demolished) and then from 1753 at the San Luca (later Teatro Goldoni) were performed most of Goldoni's many comedies: fully scripted works, breaking with the improvisatory mode of *commedia dell'arte* while often, especially in the earlier plays, retaining some of its stylized figures, dialects, and typical plots. (Some of his ideas for theatrical reform are discussed on-stage in *Il teatro comico*, 1750.) Goldoni's chief rival in the theatre was Pietro Chiari (1712–85), while Carlo Gozzi) opposed both of them, upholding the value of improvisation and fantasy. Tradition has it that the success of Gozzi's plays drove Goldoni to move, in 1762, to Paris, where he wrote for the *Comédie italienne*, taught Italian at Versailles, and composed in French his *Mémoires*, 1787.

*I due gemelli veneziani* (*The Venetian Twins*), 1748, gave Cesare d'Arbes opportunities for virtuoso comic acting as each of the brothers. In structure the play resembles Plautus' *Menaechmi* and Shakespeare's *The Comedy of Errors*, other tales of twins' mistaken identity, but the ending includes deaths and revelations of corruption and venality which, although clearly meant to be played in stylised fashion, may introduce a somewhat more sober note. *La casa nova* (*The Superior Residence*), 1760, is representative of a number of Goldoni's later plays with more detailed social settings. The new house is in confusion because the owner has been living above his means and fallen out with his rich uncle, his new wife demands a lifestyle to match her 'airs and graces', his sister feels displaced, the servants haven't been paid for months, and the workmen refuse to do more to the house until they too are paid. The scene is set for farce or broad social satire, but resolution is achieved more subtly through a combination of love, swallowing of pride, and human generosity (and, of course, a clever plot).

GOZZI, Carlo (1720–1806), a Venetian aristocrat who supported *commedia dell'arte* and its masked, stylised performance traditions, had considerable theatrical success with his series of fantastic *fiabe* (fables) in the early 1760s. These include *L'amore delle tre melarance* (*The Love of Three Oranges*), 1761, the subject of Sergei Prokofiev's opera, and *Turandot*, 1762, a source of the operas by Mascagni and Puccini. Gozzi also wrote *Memorie inutile* (*Useless Memories*), 1797–8.

JAMES, Henry (1843–1916), came to Italy, especially Venice, Florence, and Rome, many times between 1869 and 1907. In *Italian Hours*, 1909, he revised and made some additions to essays mostly of the 1870s. (Much of the Venetian material dates from the 1890s, however.) Here 'the fond appeal of the observer concerned', says James in his preface, 'is all to aspects and appearances'. The essays look lovingly at surfaces (especially marble floors, paintings, light-filled spaces, examples of 'old Italian sketchability'), atmospheres and their effect on the writer.

In James' novels and tales Americans in Italy, as in Europe more widely, encounter superficial ease and delight; real and metaphorical surfaces are again described. In

*Daisy Miller*, 1879, Daisy's ignorance of old-fashioned European proprieties breeds scandal and misunderstanding. In *Roderick Hudson*, 1875, the luxuriant artistic environment is one factor in the young sculptor's downfall. In *The Portrait of a Lady*, 1881, Gilbert Osmond is an American who has slyly adapted himself to European ways and is able to use the patina and obfuscations of expatriate life in his deception of the apparently clear-sighted Isabel Archer. *The Wings of the Dove*, 1902, written in James' subtle, complex, glancing late style, puts Venice to more delicate psychological and atmospheric use. The appearance of Palazzo Leporelli, where hope or at least a temporary stasis seems possible for the dying Milly Theale, is as often suggested as described.

The genesis of *The Aspern Papers*, 1888, was an anecdote about an American Shelley enthusiast's attempt to obtain papers from Claire Clairmont, Mary Shelley's step-sister and mother of a child by Byron, who died in Florence, aged 81, in 1879. James transfers the setting to Venice, makes the poet an American, Jeffrey Aspern, and has his 'publishing scoundrel' narrator tell his story 'with such candour and ingenuousness that he discloses his own duplicity, his easy rationalizations and his failure to grasp the fact that, in his zeal for literary history, he is an invader of private lives' (Leon Edel).

MANN, Thomas (1875–1955), holidayed in Venice in the early summer of 1911. Observation of the Polish boy Wladyslaw Moes was the main immediate source of *Der Tod in Venedig* (*Death in Venice*), 1912, and the external features of Gustav von Aschenbach are based on those of the composer Gustav Mahler, whom Mann had met and who died in May 1911. But the conflicts inherent in the life of the successful artist had long interested Mann. Ronald Hayman argues that *Death in Venice* is 'an expression of regret that the author had made too many sacrifices to Apollo [art] and too few to Dionysus [pleasure, self-fulfilment]'; at the same time it works as a safety-valve since 'anarchic impressions are projected onto a character . . . as part of a carefully structured and highly polished narrative'. Aschenbach's submission to Dionysus entails both bliss and, in the beautiful, cholera-infested Venice, death.

MARINETTI, Filippo Tommaso (1876–1944), born at Alexandria in Egypt, was educated partly in France and wrote most of his early poems in French. He became, from 1909, the theorist and chief proponent of Futurism. Discarding accepted syntax and punctuation, using infinitives in preference to other verb forms, the Futurist should, according to Marinetti's manifestoes (various of which are collected in *Manifesti del futurismo*, 1914) write about machines, cars, aeroplanes, speed, war. He attempted to enact such beliefs in poems, novels, short stories, and theatre pieces, and to proclaim their applicability to film, fashion, even, in *La cucina futurista* (*The Futurist Cookbook*), 1932, cooking. (Light 'aerofood' and edible sculpture will help to harmonise people's palates and their life of today and tomorrow; Neapolitan 'sentimental scepticism' comes of eating too much heavy pasta.) The long poem *Zang Tum Tum*, 1914, concerning the Balkans war of 1912–13, realises the sounds of battle with the aid of much onomatopoeia. The title of *Uccidiamo la chiara di luna* (*Let's Kill the Moonlight*), 1911 (in French 1909) sums up the Futurist attitude to much earlier poetry.

Marinetti, a convinced nationalist (in apparent contradiction of his more anarchistic views on most subjects), fought and was wounded in the First World War and served also in the Second, including a period on the eastern front in 1942–3. (On a somewhat lighter note, his cookbook suggested native terms with which to replace those of foreign provenance: *quisibeve* – 'here one drinks' – for 'bar'; *pranzoalsole* – 'lunch in the sun' – for 'picnic'; *guidapalato* – 'palate guide' – for 'maître d'hôtel'.) For a period after the First World War he was associated with Mussolini, who later honoured him by appointing him to the Italian Academy in 1929.

Marinetti provided an explosive stimulus to other artists inside and outside Italy, among them Ezra Pound and the English Vorticists. Part of his appeal is the apparent seriousness with which he announces his views even when – as often surely in *La cucina futurista* – his tongue is in his cheek; in photographs he always contrives to strike an attitude of unsmiling defiance which is unmistakably, thought-provokingly, meant to be read as an attitude.

NIEVO, Ippolito (1831–61), from Padua, lived in various parts of Italy during his short life, but felt a special loyalty to the Friuli region, home of his mother's family; he was strongly influenced by his maternal grandfather, Carlo Marin, once a patrician of the Venetian republic and present at its dissolution in 1797. Marin partly inspired the octogenarian narrator of Nievo's most notable work, *Le confessioni d'un italiano* (*The Castle of Fratta*), 1867 (written 1857–8). This is concerned with the political history of Italy from the 1790s to the 1850s as well as with the narrator's personal history including his relationship with the elusive Pisana. The patriotic senti-

ments of the novel soon found a practical outlet: Nievo served under Garibaldi from 1859 and was one of his Thousand in Sicily in 1860. Nievo's death when his ship went down in the Tyrrhenian Sea was mourned in a letter to his family by Garibaldi, who remembered him as one of his most valiant followers. He entered the pantheon of Risorgimento heroes.

PELLICO, Silvio (1789–1854), was born at Saluzzo in Piedmont. From 1809 he lived in Milan, where his tragedy *Francesca da Rimini* was widely acclaimed in 1815. He was a co-founder and editor of the liberal newspaper *Il Conciliatore* of 1818–19, and subsequently involved with the anti-government *Carbonari*. As a result he was arrested by order of the Austrian authorities in 1820 and held first in Milan and then in Venice. A sentence of death was commuted to hard labour (1822–30) at the Spielberg fortress in Moravia, where conditions were notoriously harsh.

*Le mie prigioni* (*My Prisons*), 1832, was intended to 'help console some unhappy creature by the account of the evils that I suffered' and to 'bear witness that . . . I did not find humanity so wicked, so unworthy of forgiveness, as it is usually made out to be'. The book dwells on the prisoner's early desolation and subsequent religious comfort, records the histories of his warders and fellow-captives, and deliberately excludes discussion of politics and many of the details of what he endured, especially at Spielberg. Pellico's account initially offended both conservatives and many of their opponents, who found it hard to accept his religious emphasis, complete forgiveness of enemies, and dislike of the use of force even in a good cause. It was later popular, nevertheless, with Risorgimento activists and sympathisers.

PROUST, Marcel (1871–1922), visited Venice in May and October 1900, mainly inspired by reading Ruskin on the city. In *A la Recherche du temps perdu* (*Remembrance of Things Past*), 1913–27, Venice and its art occur as 'a topos of cultural and sexual fulfilment' and later 'a latent figure of Marcel's memory and creativity' (Peter Collier). The sudden evocation of Venice by the uneven paving is an important instance, like the more generally known memory-releasing *madeleine*, of Proust's notion of 'involuntary memory'.

ROLFE, Frederick, (1860–1913), who called himself Baron Corvo, worked as a teacher until his conversion to Roman Catholicism in 1886. He attended seminaries in England and Rome but was rejected for the priesthood in 1890. His novel *Hadrian the Seventh*, 1904, involves the wish fulfilling elevation of an unlikely candidate to the papacy.

Rolfe lived, in England and then, from 1908, in Venice, mainly by 'borrowing' the money and enjoying the hospitality of various friends and patrons whom he usually went on to alienate and abuse. *The Desire and Pursuit of the Whole: a Romance of Modern Venice*, 1934 (written 1909) contains thinly veiled attacks on some of these friends but also impressions of Venice, sometimes querulous, sometimes poetic, and his life there as homosexual lover or would-be lover.

RUSKIN, John (1819–1900), English writer, artist, and social visionary/campaigner, first visited Italy with his parents in the early 1830s. His first Italian expedition without them came in 1845 and is chronicled in detailed, vigorously opinonated letters home. In 1849–50 he brought his wife Effie to Venice, where she conducted an enthusiastic social life while he drew, wrote, and clambered about buildings in preparation for *The Stones of Venice*, 1851–3. (The difference in interests, as well as non-consummation, helped to end the marriage in 1854.) There were later visits, culminating in 1888, after the onset of the mental illness which increasingly afflicted him in later years.

His reactions to Italy – positive and negative – are expressed most clearly in *The Stones of Venice*, 1851–3, which set out to show how the rise and fall of the Venetian builders' art depended on 'the moral or immoral temper of the State'. Gothic, and sometimes earlier 'Byzantine' work, true to the free patterns of nature and centred on craftsmen and their skills, is championed (with the aid both of sweeping generalisations and of minutely detailed study of decoration). Renaissance palaces in Venice draw their picturesqueness only from their contrast with 'the rude confusion of the sea-life' and green waves beneath them, or with Gothic palaces. The adversaries of art and morality include also the modernizing of Venice with railway and gas-lamps, the whole Industrial Revolution, and both callous Italian neglect of old buildings and misguided attempts to restore them. Ruskin also shared his parents' wariness of Catholicism, but this was increasingly dissipated by his enthusiasm for the Venetian painters, especially Tintoretto.

*The Stones* was a highly influential work. It contributed to the Gothic revival (much though Ruskin disliked the movement's actual works), indulging the self-image of the British, as Jan Morris puts it, with the argument that Venetian Gothic 'represented the combination of mercantile success, social justice, and godly thanksgiving'. The new middle-class British tourists took their Ruskin to Italy; and in Venice, says Ruskin with some bitterness, helped themselves 'through the tedium of the business by due quantity of ices at Florian's, music by moonlight on the Grand Canal, paper lanterns' and English newspapers. Why they bothered, nevertheless, to read Ruskin is summed up by Morris: 'he worked always, right or wrong, in the fire of conviction, just as the medieval master-masons of his imagination stood on the dizzy scaffold of their towers, or paced their echoing vaults, in the certainty that they were doing the work of God'.

SARPI, Fra Paolo (1552–1623), a Servite monk born in Venice, rose rapidly in his order. In 1606 he was appointed as legal adviser to the Venetian senate, entrusted with the defence of the city against the papal interdict of 1606–7 in such works as *Trattato dell'Interdetto* (*Treatise on the Interdict*), 1606. Sarpi's massive *Istoria del Concilio Tridentino* (*History of the Council of Trent*) was published in England in 1619 since Venice had accepted Trent's Counter-Reformation reforms while the *History* seeks to expose the council's proceedings as riddled with corruption and intrigue – with what the work's 1620 translator Nathanael Brent calls 'an infinity of intolerable abuses'. John Milton called Sarpi 'the Great Unmasker'.

David Wootton's book on Sarpi presents evidence for the controversial view that he was in fact an atheist. He draws on the manuscript *pensieri* ('thoughts'), largely unpublished during Sarpi's lifetime, to suggest how radical was the monk's secularism, his desire to overthrow all religious authority, and his 'conception of man as answerable only to himself'.

STAMPA, Gaspara (c.1523–54), came to Venice from Padua in 1531 after the death of her father, a successful jeweller. Her mother's house became known as a *ridotto* (a centre for artistic activity, especially the performance of music and poetry). Gaspara and her sister Cassandra enjoyed esteem as musicians; whether they were also courtesans, as has often been suggested, is unclear. In 1548 she fell in love with Count Collaltino di Collalto, who was often away from Venice and seems only partially to have reciprocated her love; her emotions in these circumstances provide the main matter of *Rime di Madonna Gaspara Stampa* (*Poems of the Lady Gaspara Stampa*), published soon after her death in 1554.

# THE VENETO AND THE NORTH-EAST

The Villa Rotonda 'is on a small hill, of very easy access, and it is watered on one side by the Bacchiglione, a navigable river, and on the other it is encompassed with most pleasant risings, which look like a very great theatre, and all are cultivated, and abound with most excellent fruits and most exquisite vines.'
*Andrea Palladio,*
*The Four Books of*
*Architecture*

Many writers have emanated from or described the cities of the Veneto – Verona, Padua, Vicenza – but, in retreat from these and the powerful and splendid Venice, have also colonized smaller towns, villages, and hills. Petrarch spent the last few years of his life at Arquà – now **Arquà Petrarca** – in the Euganean Hills (then much more wooded than now) south of Padua. The Casa Petrarca displays the poet's desk, his chair, and the embalmed body of his cherished cat, proclaimed in Latin inscription 'a second Laura'. Here, acting on the precedent of Roman poets and men of affairs, he withdrew from the complications of city-life (although besieged at times by devotees and people who wanted to say that they had seen him). He planted a garden and vineyard, read Virgil, wrote letters on his peace of mind ('long since freed from youthful passions'), his continued thirst for knowledge, and the passing of friends, and made last alterations to the great sequence inspired by the first Laura, the *Canzoniere* (*Lyric Poems*), 1342–74 (Extract 1). His tomb, a raised sarcophagus of Veronese red marble, stands further down the hill by the church of Santa Maria.

From 1489 'the fair and pleasant castle of **Asolo**, built in the foothills of our mountains overlooking the marches of Treviso' was attractive to courtiers like Pietro Bembo, who set here the discourses on love of *Gli Asolani* (*The Asolani*), 1505. In 1489 Venice had conferred the surrounding area (and a sizeable annual income) on Bembo's kinswoman Caterina Cornaro, widow of the King of Cyprus. In

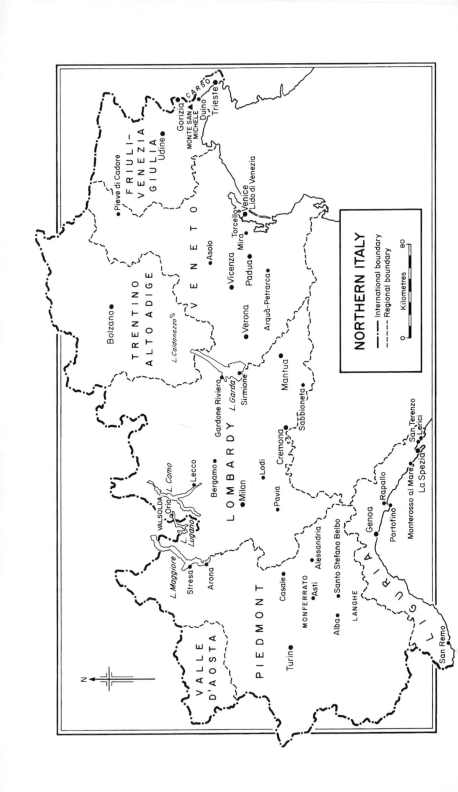

NORTHERN ITALY

International boundary
Regional boundary

0     Kilometres     80

N

FRIULI-VENEZIA GIULIA
Pieve di Cadore
Udine
Gorizia
MONTE SAN MICHELE
CARSO
Duino
Trieste

VENETO
Asolo
Torcello
Mira
Venice
Lido di Venezia
Vicenza
Padua
Verona
Arquà-Petrarca

TRENTINO ALTO ADIGE
Bolzano
L. Caldonazzo

Mantua
Gardone Riviera
L. Garda
Sirmione
Sabbioneta

LOMBARDY
Cremona
Lodi
Lecco
L. Como
Oria
VALSOLDA
L. Lugano
Bergamo
Milan
Pavia

San Terenzo
Lerici
Monterosso al Mare
La Spezia
Rapallo
Genoa
Portofino

LIGURIA

L. Maggiore
Stresa
Arona

PIEDMONT
Alessandria
Casale
MONFERRATO
Asti
Santo Stefano Belbo
Alba
LANGHE
Turin

VALLE D'AOSTA

San Remo

exchange she ceded the island to the republic, whose puppet and at times virtual prisoner she had been for some years. Having lost her political importance, the Queen was free for 20 years to preside over debates and dances. The wedding celebrations for a maid of honour are prolonged, at least in Bembo's fictionalized account, 'day after day with music, singing, dancing, and most solemn feasts'. In *Gli Asolani* these delights are followed by the civilized discourses of noble young men to noble young women, beginning in the royal garden. Here the natural and the artificial combine pleasingly in a fair pergola of vines, a walk 'bestrewed with shining flint', and a fountain, carved from the living rock, which descends into 'a miniature canal of marble'. Only the main tower of the Castello survived after 1820. What remained of 'delicious Asolo', however, had a strong attraction for Robert Browning (◊Florence) on his first visit in 1838 as on his last 51 years later, when he was entertained at La Mura, a villa which was once part of the ramparts, by his close friend Katharine de Kay Bronson. Asolo and Bembo provided Browning with a title for his last volume of poems, *Asolando*, 1889, where, as he says in his dedication to Katharine Bronson, 'I unite . . . the disconnected poems by a title-name popularly ascribed to the inventiveness' of Bembo: '*Asolare* – "to disport in the open air, amuse oneself at random".'

The fertile Veneto is, by modern transport at least, close to very different Italian lands: the Dolomites, for instance, or the partly German speaking and German dominated area around **Bolzano** or **Bozen**, which became part of Italy only in 1919. Its heritage is remembered in the main square, Piazza Walther, by a statue of the great Middle High German lyric poet Walther von der Vogelweide (c.1170–c.1230). Nevertheless even here the Grand Tourist William Beckford (◊Lombardy) detected, in 1780, 'indications of approaching Italy' – 'the rocks cut into terraces, thick set with melons, and Indian corn; gardens of fig-trees and pomegranates hanging over walls, clustered with fruit'. Impatient 'to reach the promised land' he travelled on through the night, along the Adige 'rolling its full tide between precipices' to near Trento and, after a few hours' sleep, to the shaded creeks and 'purest and most transparent water' of **Lago di Caldonazzo**, whose 'shores present one continual shrubbery, interspersed with knots of larches and slender almonds starting from the underwood'. (*Dreams, Waking Thoughts, and Incidents*, 1783).

## PADUA

Théophile Gautier (◊Naples and Campania), arriving in Padua from Venice, was at first disappointed. Too close to a centre which draws life to itself, Padua is 'a dead town', almost deserted apparently. There is nothing of Venetian elegance and graciousness in the sad streets. The buildings are lumpish, serious, a little sullen, and the dark porches are like mouths yawning with boredom (*Voyage en Italie* (*Italian Journey*), 1851). Gautier's view was somewhat coloured – or drained of colour – by the fact that his amorous sojourn in Venice with Maria Mattei had just come to an end, but there has been a tendency for outsiders to slight the city as poor sister of La Serenissima, its ruler from 1405. Natives, however, have remained culturally proud and independent. The University (centred on the mainly 16th century **Palazzo del Bo**) was founded in 1222. Later it was noted particularly for medical education; the 16th century anatomical theatre survives at the Bo. The Paduan playwright Angelo Beolco, 'Il Ruzzante'◊, takes frequent opportunity to declare his city, in *L'Anconitana* (*The Woman from Ancona*), c. 1529–32, magnificent, full of scholars, keen on the arts and kind to strangers like the woman of the title. Local identity is more solidly asserted in his use of Pavano, the dialect of the area to the north of Padua, in many of his plays and particularly for his own regular character, whose name he took, the clever and comical servant Ruzzante. In *L'Anconitana* noble lovers exchange compliments in formal Tuscan, while in quick Pavano the servant abuses, runs verbal rings around, and occasionally helps his master, the octogenarian Venetian-speaking Sier Tomao. (The master, absurdly or touchingly, is in love with a courtesan.) Ruzzante 'wouldn't swap my tongue for any other when it comes to storytelling'; his wit, inventiveness, rude jests and gestures, rapid monologues and frequent songs dominate the play which he besides – Tuscan, Pavano and Venetian alike – composed.

Pilgrims come to worship and leave ex votos at the shrine of St Antony, Portuguese missionary, friend of St Francis, and patron of childbirth, the poor, and lost property, in the 13th and 14th century **Basilica di Sant'Antonio**, known as Il Santo. Hester Piozzi (◊Piedmont) recalled that 'the shrine of St. Antonio is . . . sufficiently venerated; and the riches of his church really amazed me: such silver lamps! Such votive offerings! Such glorious sculpture'. She felt, however, that the numerous cupolas 'distract attention and create confusion of ideas' and contrasted them with the less magnificent but more pleasing **Santa Giustina** (*Observations and Reflections Made in the Course of a Journey Though France, Italy, and Germany*, 1789). Gautier disliked the interior of the Santo as 'excessively rich', crowded out with tombs and chapels of every period. (The Renaissance contributes a monument to Pietro Bembo◊.) His particular scorn was reserved for 18th century 'bewigged angels' playing 'on small fiddles like dancing-masters' and performing an *avant-deux* on the clouds'. But tastes had changed since Piozzi's time: to Gautier, even the 'mad exuberance' of the Rococo (which he has, after all, had fun describing) was preferable to the boring and bare sobriety of Santa Giustina.

Gautier, like most 19th and 20th century visitors, expressed a more unalloyed enthusiasm for the **Cappella degli Scrovegni**, built by Enrico Scrovegni in expiation for the sin of usury for which Dante (◊Florence) consigned his father to the seventh circle of Hell. Inside the chapel are Giotto's frescoes (c. 1305–10), an 'uninterrupted tapestry' of ultramarine, 'calm, azured, starred like a fine clear sky'. This is the general impression; others have been struck more by the sense – almost unique in early 14th century painting – of perspective space, of human emotion (Jesus and Judas looking into each other's eyes), and of physical volume. (Gautier does note that while the angels and virtues are slender, the devils and vices are obese, for in one group the spirit is preponderant, and in the other, matter.)

The chapel was built in the remains of the Roman amphitheatre (whence its alternative name *Arena*) – in 1850 Gautier's garden of 'thick, luxuriant growth' where one certainly wouldn't have expected to find the chapel without prior warning. A more well-kempt garden can be seen between the Santo and Santa Giustina: the **Orto Botanico**, the oldest botanic garden in Europe (1545). This, says Thomas Coryat (◊Venice) in *Coryat's Crudities*, 1611, was 'famoused over most places in Christendom for the sovereign virtue of medicinable herbs'. Here he was pleased by the sight of 'a very pretty fruit which is esteemed far more excellent than apricocks, or any other dainty fruit whatsoever growing in Italy. They call it pistachi, a fruit much used in their dainty banquets'. And here Goethe ruminated on higher things than pistachio, pressing forward, with the help of a small palm still shown in a greenhouse, in 'my hypothesis that it might be possible to derive all plant forms from one original plant' (*Italian Journey*, 1816–17).

## VERONA

'There is no world without Verona walls', cries Romeo, confronting the prospect of exclusion for killing Tybalt:

> 'But purgatory, torture, hell itself;
> Hence banished is banish'd from the world,
> And world's exile is death!'

Within the walls the bare indications of place in Shakespeare's play – the house with walled grounds and balcony, the monument of the Capels or Capulets – have been given 'a local habitation and a name'. It is possible to visit **Casa di Giulietta** and its fine balcony (23 Via Cappello) and **Casa di Romeo** (2–4 Via delle Arche Scaligere), beautiful medieval houses with or without later literary associations, and the **Tomba di Giulietta**, a marble sarcophagus at the former church of San Francesco al Corso. Driven by performance, school curricula, quotation, parody, and the tourist industry, *Romeo and Juliet* or some version of it continues to live in 'Verona streets', with which it first became connected in 1530 when Luigi da Porto in *Historia . . . di due* *nobili amanti* (*History of Two Noble Lovers*) – Shakespeare's source at several removes – transferred the setting of the story from the Siena of *his* source.

Long before the star-crossed lovers came to Verona, it was a Roman city, much of which survives, most notably the Porta dei Borsari and Porta dei Leoni gates, the (restored) Ponte Pietra crossing the rushing river Adige near the theatre and, above all, the **Arena** which once accommodated up to 25,000 spectators. For Grand Tourists who had yet to reach Rome itself, this was a particularly important destination and one which rarely disappointed. At twilight one evening in September 1780 William Beckford (◊Lombardy), having bought the absence of a garrulous local antiquary who was 'very profound in the doctrine of conduits', 'traversed a gloomy arcade, and emerged alone into the arena'. Nothing stirred, 'save the weeds and grasses which skirt the walls, and tremble with the faintest breeze'. 'Abandoned to a stillness and solitude I was so peculiarly disposed to taste', as he watched the light fade behind the highest arches, Beckford was able to induce the shiver of sublimity which he habitually sought: 'red and fatal were the tints of the western sky; the wind blew chill and hollow, and something more than common seemed to issue from the withering herbage on the walls. I started up; and arrived, panting, in the great square before the ruins'.

Generations later than Beckford's, led by John Ruskin (◊Venice), sought their frissons in such medieval remains as the churches of **San Zeno** and **Sant' Anastasia**. In Verona Ruskin located Gothic style 'in the simplicity of its youthful power, and the tenderness of its accomplished beauty' (*The Political Economy of Art*, 1857). Unusually for one so often disappointed in his quest for the pristine or pure, Ruskin liked almost everything about Verona and remembered enthusiastically for an audience in Manchester the 'serenity of effortless grace' of the Renaissance buildings and the foaming Alpine river 'from whose shore the rocks rise in a great crescent, dark with cypress, and misty with olive'. Another attraction was the **tombs of the della Scala** or Scaliger family, lords of Verona in the 13th and 14th centuries, outside the church of Santa Maria Antica. Among them stands out the ebullient equestrian statue of Cangrande ('great dog') della Scala (co-ruler from 1308, ruled 1311–29), fearless warrior and generous protector of the exiled Dante (◊Florence). (The present statue at Santa Maria is a copy. The original is displayed dramatically in the **Castelvecchio museum**.)

Ironically it was in the city of chivalrous protectors and noble lovers that a particularly unsavoury murder took place in January 1900. The dismembered body of Isolina Canuti, aged 19, was found in the River Adige. She was several months pregnant by Lieutenant Carlo Trivulzio, stationed in Verona with the respected and glamorous Alpini regiment at a time when the city was, as Dacia Maraini says, 'a garrison city . . .

bristling with towers, turrets, forts, gunpowder magazines, barracks' and soldiers who 'considered themselves the true sons of the city, the ones who gave it class and style'. Maraini's reconstruction and investigation *Isolina, o la donna tagliata a pezzi* (*Isolina*), 1985 (Extract 4), reviews the evidence and the social setting of the crime and reaches the conclusion that Trivulzio – the acquitted main suspect – was almost undoubtedly guilty of the crime (probably with the collaboration of several other officers). The military and national establishment and their press supporters connived to suppress or ignore the incriminating evidence and to brand their opponents as socialists hostile to the army; inconvenient witnesses were labelled by Trivulzio's lawyers as 'ill or alcoholic or mad'. And Isolina, because she had two lovers and was poor and expendable, was deemed to be a prostitute. 'What, finally, did the life of a girl from a poor, obscure family count for, when opposed to the honour of the army?' A dead woman, she was vilified even more successfully than the Jewish Alfred Dreyfus in France, still a prisoner at this time.

## VICENZA

In 1562 a lavish production of *Sofonisba* (*Sophonisba*), 1515, by the Vicentine nobleman and epic poet Giangiorgio Trissino (1478–1550), was given in the **Basilica** (or Palazzo Pubblico) of Vicenza. The play commended itself to the city's Olympic Academy, founded in 1556, not only as a local product but as the first modern, blank-verse tragedy closely to follow Greek models. In order further to demonstrate their classicism and the prestige of their city (whose Roman past they liked to vaunt at the expense of their ruler, Venice) the noble and learned Olympians later commissioned the architect who had converted the Basilica for *Sofonisba*, the architect Andrea Palladio (1508–80), to design a permanent performance place in stone. (He himself was elected to the Academy. Only later in the century were those actually tainted by practice of the 'mechanic arts' barred from membership.)

Palladio's **Teatro Olimpico** is an interpretation of what was known of Roman theatres, largely on the basis of the writings of his first-century B.C. '*maestro e guida*' Vitruvius. Since Palladio died in August 1580 when only the outer walls were complete, the plan was carried out by Vincenzo Scamozzi, who conspicuously modified Palladio's design for the stage by introducing the perspective streets. These featured first in the 1585 production of a version of Sophocles' *Oedipus Rex*, a noted theatrical occasion announced by drums, trumpets, song and 'sudden fragrance'. But the Olympic theatre itself is perhaps more the incarnation of an architectural theory than a practical aid to production, especially since only some viewers can see the perspectives from the necessary angle; changeable scenery was already being used to good effect in other contemporary theatres. Goethe (◊Naples and Campania) found it 'indescribably beautiful' but felt that 'compared to our modern theatres, it looks like an aristocratic, rich and well-educated child as against a clever man of the world who, though not as rich, distinguished or educated, knows better what it is in his means to do' (*Italian Journey*, 1816–17).

Villa Almerico, known as **Villa Rotonda**, near Vicenza, has been a more influential building: one of those works by Palladio which became 'the three-dimensional blue-prints for the architecture of 18th-century England and America' (Charles FitzRoy) and in this case particularly for Lord Burlington's Chiswick House. In *I quattro libri dell' architettura* (*The Four Books of Architecture*), 1570, Palladio describes the Rotonda (built in the late 1560s for Monsignor Paolo Almerico) and the fine views to be surveyed from the four loggias around the central domed saloon. The site is one of the most agreeable that can be:

> 'because it is on a small hill, of very easy access, and is watered on one side by the Bacchiglione, a navigable river; and on the other it is encompassed with most pleasant risings, which look like a very great theatre, and all are cultivated, and abound with most excellent fruits, and most exquisite vines.'

The well preserved interior of the villa was used by Joseph Losey for his 1979 film of Mozart's *Don Giovanni*.

## TRIESTE

Trieste, a cosmopolitan port on the frontier between the Italian, German and Slav-speaking lands, first emerged as an important commercial centre in the 18th century, when it provided the Austrian empire with its only important access to the sea. During the 19th century the population rose from about 33,000 to 220,000. The Italian-speaking inhabitants were the most numerous, and made Trieste a centre of Irredentism (from *irredento* – 'unredeemed' or unliberated as applied to culturally or geographically Italian regions still not part of a united Italy after 1861), but a mixture of Austrian repression and concessions helped to delay 'redemption' until the end of the First World War.

In cosmopolitan Trieste, between 1905 and 1915, lived James Joyce◊, writing, surviving on loans and his (or his brother Stanislaus') earnings as English language teacher, and renting a succession of small flats with his wife and children. (The generally long-suffering Stan eventually took separate lodgings in despair at his brother's drinking habits, improvidence, and irregular hours.) Here Joyce learned, as his biographer Richard Ellmann puts it, 'what he had unlearned in Dublin, to be a Dubliner'; here he finished *Portrait of the Artist as a Young Man* and embarked on *Ulysses*. But he also responded more directly to the city and its people and language, as Ellmann explains:

> 'Like Dublin, Trieste had a large population but remained a small town. Everyone looked familiar; the same people went to the same cafés, to the opera and to the theatre. Joyce was particularly taken with the dialect; if Dublin speech is distinctive, Triestine speech is much more so, having its own spellings and verb forms and an infusion of Slovene and other words. Not only was *Triestino* a special dialect, but the residents of Trieste, who had congregated there from Greece, Austria, Hungary, and Italy, all spoke the dialect with special pronunciations. The puns and international jokes that resulted delighted Joyce.'

Among Joyce's language pupils was Ettore Schmitz, now better known as the novelist Italo Svevo٥ but then a successful businessman and, as Joyce told him on reading *Una Vita* (*A Life*), 1893 and *Senilità* (*As a Man Grows Older*), 1898, 'a neglected writer'. Some of the contradictions and complexities of the life and work of Schmitz/Svevo are characteristic both of his own background – he was a German-educated Italophone and an Italophile non-practising Jew, nominally Catholic – and of his mixed and divided city. His complex, ironic novels of neurosis and self-deception mix dialect forms with the pedantically correct, the 19th-century novel of ideas with the 20th-century psychological novel. (*La coscienza di Zeno* (*Confessions of Zeno*), 1923, the belated third novel (Extract 3) which resulted partly from Joyce's encouragement, draws to some extent on the new notions of Freudian psychoanalysis.) Svevo, suspect for his inelegant language and at first for using a surname indicative of German origins, was read less in Italy than elsewhere until recent decades. Now he is probably Trieste's most famous native. A plaque marks his birthplace at 16 Viale XX Settembre (formerly Via dell' Acquedotto). (Svevo is buried, inconspicuously, in the tomb of his wife's family, the Veneziani, in the cemetery of Sant' Anna.)

Alfonso Nitti, in *Una Vita*, climbs up, above Trieste, to the edge of the **Carso**, 'the vast silent deserted plateau with its innumerable stone hillocks of all shapes, pointed, round, squat, heaps of stones fallen from above and arranged . . . haphazardly'. The grey limestone contrasts strangely with the colours of sea and green land beside Trieste: a primitive world removed, for a moment, from commerce, self-advancement, the social conventions and delusions to which Nitti, like other Svevo protagonists, is prey. Further into the stony hills – first around **Monte San Michele**, south of Gorizia, later to the east of Trieste in what is now Slovene territory – the Italian and Austrian armies engaged in one of the most fierce conflicts of the First World War. It was sometimes while resting behind the lines, but frequently in the lulls of battle, that Giuseppe Ungaretti٥ wrote poems – in pencil, in notebooks when possible, otherwise on cardboard cartridge-containers or anything else that came to hand. The heightened senses of one confronting death, his love of life, and his belief in spare, unpunctuated, unrhetorical expression, combine to produce the short, urgent lyrics of *Il porto sepolto* (*The Buried Harbour*), 1916 (Extract 1).

Only four years before Ungaretti went to the front line, and only about twenty miles away, Rainer Maria Rilke (1875–1926) spent a quiet winter (1911–12) at **Duino**, north-west along the coast from Trieste. Here, at the castle of Princess Marie von Thurn und Taxis, Rilke could look out across a large expanse of sea, either from his corner-room or from the 200 foot cliffs. Living an almost solitary life after his hostess' departure, and recuperating from an unsettled and unproductive period, he determined, he explains in a letter, to see 'what the inner self offers as a counterweight' to the 'prodigious elemental forces' of sea, rock, storm. The inner self obliged with poems, among them, most importantly, the first elements of the *Duineser Elegie* (*Duino Elegies*), 1911–22.

## OTHER LITERARY LANDMARKS

**Asolo**: the Museo Civico, Piazza Maggiore, contains exhibits connected with the colourful life of the actress Eleonora Duse (1858–1924). She is buried in the cemetery at the church of Sant' Anna.

**Colloredo di Montalbano**, near **Udine**: Ippolito Nievo (◊Venice) spent some of his youth at the castle here; it is one of the sources for the castle in *Le confessioni d'un italiano* (*The Castle of Fratta*), 1867.

**Gorizia**: as part of the Austro-Hungarian Empire, one of the multicultural settings of *Un altro mare* (*A Different Sea*), 1991, by the novelist Claudio Magris (b. 1939).

**Mira**: in 1817 Byron lived in Palazzo Foscarini, now a post-office, and worked on *Childe Harold's Pilgrimage*, Canto Four.

**Pieve di Cadore**: museum on the site of the birthplace of the painter Titian (Tiziano Vecellio, c.1485–1576).

**Romano d'Ezzelino** (near Bassano del Grappa): remains of the stronghold of Ezzelino III, 'the firebrand', ferocious lord of the March of Treviso 1225–59, placed among the tyrants in the seventh circle of Hell in Dante's *Inferno*.

## BOOKLIST

Bembo, Pietro, *Gli Asolani* [1505], Rudolf B. Gottfried, trans, Indiana University Press, Bloomington, 1954.

Ellmann, Richard, *James Joyce. New and Revised Edition*, Oxford University Press, New York, 1982.

*Booklist continued*

Gatt-Rutter, John, *Italo Svevo: a Double Life*, Clarendon Press, Oxford, 1988.

Goethe, Johann Wolfgang von, *Italian Journey* [1816–17], W.H. Auden and Elizabeth Mayer, trans, Penguin, London, 1970.

Mann, Nicholas, *Petrarch*, Oxford University Press, Oxford and New York, 1984.

Maraini, Dacia, *Isolina* [1985], Siân Williams, trans, Peter Owen, London and Chester Springs, PA, 1993. **Extract 4.**

Palladio, Andrea, *The Four Books of Architecture* [1570], Dover, New York, 1965.

Petrarca, Francesco, *For Love of Laura: Poetry of Petrarch*, Marion Shore, trans, University of Arkansas Press, Fayetteville, 1987. **Extract 1.**

Piozzi, Hester Lynch, *Observations and Reflections Made in the Course of a Journey Through France, Italy, and Germany* [1789], Herbert Barrows, ed, University of Michigan Press, Ann Arbor, 1967.

Prater, Donald, *A Ringing Glass: the Life of Rainer Maria Rilke*, Clarendon Press, Oxford, 1986.

Ruzzante (Angelo Beolco), *L'Anconitana/The Woman from Ancona* [c.1529–32], Nancy Dersofi, trans, University of California Press, Berkeley, Los Angeles, London, 1994.

Svevo, Italo, *Confessions of Zeno* [1923], Beryl de Zoete, trans, Secker and Warburg, London, 1962. **Extract 3.**

Svevo, Italo, *A Life* [1893], Archibald Colquhoun, trans, Penguin, Harmondsworth, 1982.

Ungaretti, Giuseppe, *Selected Poems*, Patrick Creagh, trans, Penguin, Harmondsworth, 1971. **Extract 2.**

# *Extracts*

## (1) Arquà Petrarca

### Francesco Petrarca, *Lyric Poems*, 1342–74

*Petrarch's introductory sonnet announces the theme of painful, unrequited, repented but (it will emerge) potentially transcendent love which he will pursue in many different ways through 366 poems.*

> You who hear within my scattered verse
> the troubled sighs on which I fed my heart
> in youthful error, now that I in part
> am someone other than I was at first;
> for all the varied ways I cry and curse

amid the empty hope and wasted art,
I ask that those who suffer by Love's dart
may pardon me, and pity me my worst.
But now when I reflect how I became
a common tale to all, it brings me grief,
so that I grow ashamed that now it seems
the fruit of all my wandering is shame,
and true repentance, and the clear belief
that what the world adores are fleeting dreams.

## (2) MONTE SAN MICHELE

### Giuseppe Ungaretti, 'Watch', 23 December 1915

*One of the intense, condensed poems from the front line in Ungaretti's The Buried Harbour, 1916.*

A whole night through
thrown down beside
a butchered comrade
with his clenched teeth
turned to the full moon
and the clutching
of his hands
thrust
into my silence
I have written
letters full of love

Never have I
clung
so fast to life

## (3) TRIESTE

### Italo Svevo, *Confessions of Zeno*, 1923

*Walking, after dark, up the streets towards the heights of Trieste, the narrator's brother-in-law broods on his financial and marital woes. The approach of the narrator is, as usual in this psychological, partly Freudian novel, more analytic and self-examining.*

He ended by exclaiming mournfully:
  'Life is hard and unjust.'

I felt it was impossible for me to say a single word that implied any criticism of him or Ada. But I felt I must say something. He had ended by discussing life and had found two epithets for it which certainly did not err on the side of originality. If I succeeded in finding something better it was because I was able to start by criticising what he had said. One is often led to say things because of some chance association in the sound of the words; and directly one has spoken one begins to wonder if what one has said was worth the breath spent on it, and occasionally discovers that one has started a new idea. I said:

'Life is neither good nor bad; it is original.'

When I thought it over I felt as if I had said something rather important. Looking at it like that I felt as if I were seeing life for the first time, with all its gaseous, liquid, and solid bodies. If I had talked about it to someone who was strange to it, and therefore deprived of an ordinary common sense, he would have remained gasping at the thought of the huge, purposeless structure. He would have asked: 'But how could you endure it?' And if he had inquired about everything in detail, from the heavenly bodies hung up in the sky which can be seen but not touched, to the mystery that surrounds death, he would certainly have exclaimed: 'Very original!' . . . The more I thought of it the more original life seemed to me. And one did not need to get outside it in order to realise how fantastically it was put together. One need only remind oneself of all that we men expect from life to see how very strange it is, and to arrive at the conclusion that man has found his way into it by mistake and does not really belong there.

## (4) VERONA

### Dacia Maraini, *Isolina*, 1985

*Verona in 1900 was a garrison city. A lieutenant of the Alpini regiment was almost undoubtedly responsible for the murder and dismemberment of Isolina Canuti, who was pregnant by him, but the military and conservative establishment and their press ensured that he was not found guilty. Maraini investigates the known facts and draws conclusions on attitudes to women in Italian society of the time.*

The officers led a frantically gay life, dragging along with them for entertainment girls they considered of little importance who, if they became pregnant, would not demand marriage. The young women from good families were kept well locked-up in their palaces, and when they did emerge for some ball at the Villa Canossa or the Officers' Club, would always be accompanied by aunts, mothers, grandmothers and cousins who never let them out of sight.

For girls who had more freedom because they were poorer, the temptations were such that they were almost irresistible. How could you say no to the poised, extravagant courting of so many officers who hid their brutality beneath impeccable manners and glittering uniforms?

To race down dusty roads on a bicycle, sowing terror amongst the hens and geese; to attend a horse race wearing a new jacket and see so many beautiful young ladies with their hair covered in flowers and fruit; to glide over the ice whirling around in the middle of a colourful crowd of young officers; to have dinner by candlelight in a well-known restaurant like the Chiodo or the Torcolo; to kiss in a dark hallway as carriages rolled by outside . . . what could be more seductive for a restless girl greedy for life?

Everywhere you went you were met by dozens of dashing officers with blond moustaches, sparkling eyes, bodies sheathed in fantastic uniforms the colour of green meadows, gold, forget-me-nots, blood. How could you resist the urge to throw yourself headlong into the parties, to play, to fall in love, to let yourself go?

# Biographies and important works

BEMBO, Pietro (1470–1547), a Venetian nobleman, travelled widely in Italy as scholar, courtier, and churchman (he eventually became a Cardinal in 1539). His many literary activities include editing Petrarch and Dante and writing poems, courtly 'love letters' to Lucrezia Borgia, the Latin dialogue *De Aetna* (*On Etna*), 1496, *Prose della volgar lingua* (*Writings in the Vernacular Language*), 1525, where the use of purified Tuscan is promoted, and *Gli Asolani* (*The Asolani*), 1505.

The seed of *Gli Asolani* was probably a wedding which Bembo attended in Asolo in 1495. The three discourses on love culminate in praise of Platonic love. Bembo is himself cast as exponent of divine love in *The Courtier* of Castiglione (◊Umbria and the Marche), whom he knew at the court of Urbino in 1506–12.

JOYCE, James (1882–1941), first

came to Italy in 1904, worked as a bank clerk in Rome in 1906–7, and left Trieste (then under Austrian rule) only after Italy's entry into the First World War in 1915 made the city a dangerous place for foreigners. (His outspokenly pro-Italian brother Stanislaus was interned.) During these years Joyce worked on much of *A Portrait of the Artist as a Young Man*, 1914–15, and parts of *Dubliners*, 1914, and *Ulysses*, 1922. Italo Svevo◊, a Jew who shared Leopold Bloom's 'amiably ironic view of life' (Richard Ellmann), is one of the many people known to Joyce who provided elements of the character in *Ulysses*. Later he used the name of Svevo's wife Livia, and her long tresses, for Anna Livia Plurabelle in *Finnegan's Wake*, 1939.

MARAINI, Dacia (born in Florence 1936), a prolific writer in many forms, has addressed feminist issues in works including *L'età di malessere* (*The Age of Discontent*), 1963, *Lettere a Marina* (*Letters to Marina*), 1981, and *La lunga vita di Marianna Ucrìa* (*The Silent Duchess*), 1990, the story of a Sicilian aristocrat of the 18th century who as a child is raped by the uncle who later marries her. The shock of this abuse renders her deaf and dumb, but she gradually achieves wholeness through extensive reading and the rediscovery of her own body. Women in Maraini's work are silenced by men, forced into marriages or abortions, even murdered and cut up as in *Isolina: la donna tagliata a pezzi* (*Isolina*), 1985. But in reconstructing the context of Isolina's killing or enabling the Duchess' non-oral self-realisation, Maraini contributes actively to the freeing of women's space.

PETRARCA, Francesco (1304–74), known in English as Petrarch, was born in Arezzo, the son of a Florentine banished, like Dante (◊Florence), as a member of the White Guelf faction. In 1311 the family moved to Carpentras, near Avignon, seat of the papacy from 1309 to 1377. Petrarch's house at Vaucluse, near Avignon, remained one of his main homes until 1353. He studied law (but says that he spent more time studying literature) at Montpellier and Bologna. He claims first to have seen Laura, the subject of his *Canzoniere* (*Lyric Poems*), 1342–74, in church in Avignon on 6 April 1327. (The date fits too neatly with other dates patterning the poems to be accurate. Laura probably existed, but the effect of her presence in Petrarch's work is more metaphorical than biographical.) From 1330 he was in church minor orders, and developed protectors in the Roman Colonna family. Petrarch was deeply involved in classical scholarship

– he was interested in Cicero, Virgil and St Augustine in particular – and Latin composition, notably *Africa*, a verse epic on the Roman general and moral exemplar Scipio Africanus, begun in 1333 and laid aside only in the early 1350s.

In 1341 Petrarch was crowned as Poet Laureate in Rome. (The words *lauro*, *Laura*, *l'aura*, *l'aureo* – laurel, Laura, the breeze, the golden – intertwine in the *Canzoniere*.) His enthusiasm for Rome fired his support, from a distance, for Cola di Rienzo's republican-inspired Roman regime of 1347. Later he served more conservative political masters, spending much of 1353–61 under the protection of the Visconti in Milan and much of 1362–8 in Venice. These and other states entrusted him with diplomatic missions. His last years were spent mainly in Padua and Arquà.

In addition to *Africa*, the Latin works include *De vita solitaria* (*On the Solitary Life*), 1346, the Virgil-influenced *Bucolicum Carmen* (*Bucolic Song*), 1346–66, and the series of letters known as *Familiares* and *Seniles* (*Letters on Familiar Matters and Letters of Old Age*), <1366 and 1366–74. In the letters Petrarch carefully crafted images of himself and his poetry for posterity; indeed, as Nicholas Mann says, all Petrarch's writing 'constitutes a vast, diffuse, and constantly evolving portrait of the self . . . seen through so many prisms as to become almost kaleidoscopic'.

The results of the process of constant evolution are conspicuous in the long vernacular poem *I trionfi* (*The Triumphs*), c. 1356–74. This began as a simple Triumph of Love where Cupid's captives include Laura, Petrarch, Dante, and many others. But the poem gradually expanded so that Love is now conquered by Chastity – physically, Cupid becomes Laura's prisoner – and Chastity in turn by Death, Death by Fame, Fame by Time, and Time by Eternity. The status of each of these powers (except Eternity, whose closure of the poem Petrarch could apparently bring himself to effect only at the end of his own life) becomes provisional, and the reader concentrates as much on the *vari stati* – the 'changing states' – of the poet's ('Petrarch's') mind as on the nature of Love or Fame. (Since the conquests are realised as processions, *I trionfi* was a popular topic for illustration. Either directly or though the illustrations the poem influenced the Renaissance tendency to regard or re-enact the Roman victory parade as a primarily allegorical spectacle.)

The *Canzoniere* also evolved gradually, through careful revision and re-alignment, from separate, often unconnected pieces (mostly sonnets) into a larger structure. But since this is not a narrative work – in fact, as Mann points out, it is the first non-narrative long poem – the structure remains loose enough, partly because of the method of composition, for individual poems to counterpoint, even contradict each other, within the more general movement towards the divine love of the ending. It is possible to experience both aspects of the oxymoronic 'icy fire' of loving Laura, unobtainable in the first half of the *Canzoniere*, dead in the second. Equally, the partly fragmented structure, apparent to a degree whenever a shorter piece begins or ends, gives the poet an opportunity to dwell not on love or a love-story but on the paradoxical process of the writing itself: the poet's dilemma is that 'he is unable to write, yet forced to write; he finds writing therapeutic, and yet it is writing that creates the suffering – love – for which only writing can provide the cure' (Mann). But whether or not words can win

Laura or provide consolation for her death, Petrarch is clearly aware that they can win posterity. They did so most of all during the Renaissance, when there were 'Petrarchist' love-poets almost everywhere in Europe. Petrarchan or Petrarch-derived sonnets were translated, imitated, or parodied by Lorenzo de' Medici (◊Florence), the French Pléiade group, the English poets Sir Thomas Wyatt, the Earl of Surrey, Sir Philip Sidney, Shakespeare. The lover in Sidney's *Astrophil and Stella* laments, but cannot easily avoid, the continual reprocessing of Petrarch's 'long deceasèd woes'.

RUZZANTE (from *ruzzare*, to frolic, play about) was the name adopted by the Paduan actor and playwright Angelo Beolco (c. 1502–42). His plays, mostly in Pavano dialect but often designed to appeal to aristocratic audiences in Padua and Venice, draw on sources from Roman comedy and academic Italian comedy to folk entertainments like the Venetian *momarie* ('mummings'). The plays centre on the Ruzzante character, a wily, talkative peasant with a good singing voice.They include *La moscheta* (*The Well-Spoken Lady*), c.1528, *Il parlamento di Ruzzante* (*Ruzzante Returns from the Wars*), c.1528, and the more classical and linguistically diverse *L'Anconitana* (*The Woman from Ancona*), c.1529–32.

SVEVO, Italo, is the pseudonym of Ettore Schmitz (1861–1928) of Trieste. (The pseudonym is intended to indicate mixed Italian/ German – *svevo*, Swabian – ancestry, and loyalty to Italy in spite of this background.) He was educated in Germany and Trieste before becoming a bank clerk and later, as a result of his marriage to Livia Veneziani, manager of a large and successful specialist paint business. Circumstances rather than inclination drove him into a business career; he had hoped to become a writer, and pursued his preference in articles for newspapers and reviews and in the novels *Una vita* (*A Life*), 1893 and *Senilità* (*As a Man Grows Older*), 1898. Both novels were poorly received; a third, *La coscienza di Zeno* (*Confessions of Zeno*, followed only in 1923.

The main characters of Svevo's three novels 'embody the equivocation, delusions, frustrations and flabby adaptations of everyday living, the reality which never gets to grips with itself, which does not determine but is determined, and which is the reality of many or most of us' (John Gatt-Rutter). This is already true of Alfonso Nitti in *Una vita*, a bank clerk with unfulfillable aspirations, whose story is told in largely realist manner. It is in *Senilità* that the point is made more challengingly, more experientially, through surprising shifts in narrative point of view, and this technique is developed further in *La coscienza*, where the narrator Zeno is introduced as unreliable from the opening inclusion of a note by his psychoanalyst, Dr S. (Doubt is also thrown not so much on the validity but on the efficacy of psychoanalysis). To complicate matters, Zeno is a skilful and humorous story-teller and by no means always unaware of his evasions in love, business, and smoking (his continually deferred 'last cigarettes' were also Svevo's). Thus the implications of the narrative remain finally indeterminable; it demands repeated reading. In Zeno's consciousness (*coscienza* means both 'conscience' and 'consciousness') the past is less faced or falsified than re-shaped.

UNGARETTI, Giuseppe (1888–1970), was born at Alexandria in Egypt to parents originally from Lucca. The bright, crumbling near-eastern city, where he lived until 1912, is a recurrent presence in his poems. During 1912–15 he studied in France and met artists including the painters Picasso and Modigliani and the poet Apollinaire. French influences (especially Baudelaire and Mallarmé) combined with Ungaretti's experience of heavy fighting on the Carso front to produce a poetry of brevity, of language stripped bare. In the war-poems of *Il porto sepolto* (*The Buried Harbour*), 1916 (later included in *L'allegria* (*Joy*), 1931) the 'buried harbour' is the place from which the poet comes back to the light, bearing songs which he then scatters abroad.

After the First World War Ungaretti worked as journalist and poet in Rome before becoming Professor of Italian at Sao Paulo in Brazil (1936–42). Here his nine-year-old son Antonietto died in 1939. Against the background of this loss, and the troubled state of the Italy to which Ungaretti returned in 1942, he wrote the poems of *Il dolore* (*Grief*), 1947. These are mostly more traditional in character than his earlier work. Later volumes include *Il tacuino del vecchio* (*The Old Man's Notebook*), 1960.

# LOMBARDY

The Germanic Lombards or Lan-
gobards who descended into Italy
in the sixth century gave their
name at one time to the whole
north of the country. The plains
which retain their name continued to be much invaded and
fought over. Starting in 1494 the
French came frequently. (In 1525,
however, they were crushingly
defeated, and François I himself
captured, when an army of the
emperor Charles V relieved
**Pavia**.) In 1796 Napoleon Bonaparte swept to victory against the
Austrians at **Lodi**, opening the
road to the greatest prize to be
won by successful invaders, **Milan**. Here there has been a mighty
city since late Roman and early Byzantine times, when its bishop, Saint
Ambrose, had the courage, influence and power to cajole and for a
time excommunicate the emperor Theodosius. Its power now is as a
rich European centre of commerce and fashion.

Among the southern Lombard cities are **Mantua**, a Renaissance city
artistically and imaginatively linked with Ferrara and Urbino, and
**Cremona**, celebrated for centuries for violin-making – Antonio
Stradivari (c.1644–1737) worked here. **Bergamo**, further north
towards the mountains, has enjoyed and suffered from more rural
associations: after the tragical mirth of the death of Pyramus and
Thisbe, Bottom in *A Midsummer Night's Dream* offers his duke the
chance either 'to see the epilogue, or to hear a Bergomask dance
between two of our company'. The 'Bergomask', some kind of appropriately rustic performance, duly goes ahead. Bergamo is the home of
clowns in the *commedia dell' arte*.

The Lakes of northern and eastern Lombardy, only in parts still
countrified enough to please a Bergamasco rustic, have for centuries
provided a respite from the heat of the plain and the cities, with,

beyond the hills at hand, the Alps whose 'stern authority recalls to one so much of the sorrows of life as is necessary to enhance one's immediate pleasure' (Stendhal, Extract 1).

## MILAN

Milan is 'just a great modern city, but well worth a visit', feels the 'civilized' civil servant Martin Whitby in E.M. Forster's unfinished story *Arctic Summer* (written mostly in 1911); 'two or three days are plenty'. First and foremost, one should see the **cathedral** and the **Galleria Vittorio Emanuele II**, the great glass-roofed 1870s shopping arcade. 'One does them together,' says Whitby; indeed the Galleria, 'in the heart of modern Italy', with its transepts and naves, strollers, vermouth-drinkers and shops selling 'artistic furniture, and silk pyjamas, and Dante as a paperweight, and dubious literature and corsets and pianos' is the real cathedral of Milan. The building more conventionally regarded as such, begun in the 14th century and eventually completed in the early 19th, has been much described. To Heinrich Heine it looked like 'white note-paper', 'lace-like scissoring' which startles the observer by proving, at closer view, to be of 'unde-niable white marble'. Sculpted saints rise everywhere to form a bewild-ering 'petrified multitude' and the whole cathedral is 'a playground for giant children' ('Journey from Munich to Genoa', 1829).

'Then,' says the more prosaic Whitby, 'there is Leonardo's Last Supper. A tram takes you there from the Cathedral'. Leonardo da Vinci painted his masterpiece for the Refectory of **Santa Maria delle Grazie** between 1495 and 1497. (Giorgio Vasari's account (Extract 5) of the painter's attitude later furthered his reputation as divinely inspired founder of modern style.) Leonardo had come to Milan probably in 1482, attracted by the cultured court of Lodovico 'Il Moro' (effectively Duke from 1476 although he officially replaced his nephew Gian Galeazzo Sforza only at his death in 1494). For the court he painted, designed scenes and machines for spectacles like the 'Festa del Paradiso' presented to Gian Galeazzo and his new wife Isabella in 1490 at the **Castello Sforzesco** (where Leonardo's decorated **Sala delle Asse** survives, if in damaged form). He also engaged in debate or *duello* on topics like the rival excellences of painting, poetry, music and sculpture. Leonardo's notes for such a debate were arranged by 16th and 17th century editors into a prelude to the *Trattato* (*Treatise*) on painting, with the convenient name, from 1817, *Paragone* (*Comparison*). Painting is finally superior to poetry because

'the eye embraces the beauty of the whole world. It is the lord of astronomy and the maker of cosmography; it counsels and cor-rects all the arts of mankind; it leads men to different parts of the world; it is the prince of mathematics, and the sciences founded on it are absolutely certain. It has measured the distances and sizes of the stars; it has found the elements and their locations; it divines the future from the course of the stars; it has given birth to architecture, and to perspective, and to the divine art of painting. . . . Owing to the eye the soul is content to stay in its bodily prison, for without it such bodily prison is torture.'

Ludovico, deposed by the French in 1499 and again in 1500 (he died a prisoner in the Château of Loches in 1508), was a casualty of the wave of invasions which he had helped to bring about by offering his support for the Italian expedition of Charles VIII of France in 1494–5. Italy was plunged into decades of disorder followed by centuries of foreign domination. Lombardy came under Spanish sway in 1535; the novelist Alessandro Manzoni, unable directly to attack later Austrian rule, set *I promessi sposi* (*The Betrothed*), 1840–2, in the fraught Spanish years 1628–30, when German *landsknechte* despoiled the countryside and in Milan there was riot (Extract 4), famine, and plague. Manzoni's hero and heroine suffer mainly because of the longer term problem of the abuse of power by local noblemen like Manzoni's Don Rodrigo and his hired *bravi*. But their personal vicissitudes are virtually submerged, in mid-novel, by the spectacle of a major city brought near to anarchy. In the famine everyone pours into the city: out of work servants, *bravi* now cowed and bewildered, peasants ruined by war or taxes or the poor harvest. The new arrivals are 'amazed and indignant' at finding themselves in a crowd of equally afflicted people 'in the very place where they had hoped to be unusual objects of compassion'.

But firm against despair stand Cardinal Federigo Borromeo and his priests, struggling valiantly to feed, heal, or spiritually uplift as many sufferers as they can reach. Readers who shared Manzoni's political liberalism but not his loyal Catholicism distrusted this vein in *I promessi sposi*; but if some priests – like Manzoni's comically cowardly Don Abbondio – were compliant tools of oppression and unlikely bastions against famine and disease, Federigo Borromeo (1564–1631) was, in history as in fiction, a strong-minded leader prepared to enforce his legal rights as archbishop against Spanish jurisdiction and to combat however possible the disasters of 1628–30. In organizing spiritual and practical counter-attacks on disease he was following consciously in the footsteps of his cousin, Saint Carlo Borromeo (1538–84), who had played a similar role in the pestilence year 1576. San Carlo's body is preserved in the crypt of the cathedral, an object of devotion to many Catholics but to Charles Dickens (◊Liguria), 'a shrunken heap of poor earth' amidst great glitter; 'there is not a ray of imprisoned light in all the flash and fire of jewels, but seems to mock the dusty holes where eyes were once'. Protestants would have less difficulty in appreciating Federigo Borromeo's principal memorial,

product of Counter-Reformation zeal though it once was: his extensive collections of books and paintings were the foundation of the
**Biblioteca Ambrosiana** and the **Pinacoteca Ambrosiano** in the
(much altered and war-damaged) **Palazzo dell' Ambrosiana**.

Manzoni, one of the most famous Milanese of the 19th century (he
lived almost all his adult life in or near Milan, owning from 1813 the
house at 1 Via Morone, now the **Museo Manzoniano**, where he died
in 1873) set his most important work in the 17th century. In the 18th
century, as Stendhal͗ sees it in the opening chapter of *La Chartreuse de
Parme* (*The Charterhouse of Parma*), 1839, foreign domination dried up
that 'thirst for pleasure natural in southern countries' and once pre-
valent at the court of the Visconti and Sforza dukes. In its place came
the 'grande affaire' of 'printing of sonnets upon handkerchiefs of rose-
coloured taffeta' to salute the marriages of rich or noble young ladies.
Meanwhile the monks, as the work of Voltaire and the *Encyclopédie*
came out in France, had long been 'dinning into the ears of the good
people of Milan that to learn to read . . . was a great waste of labour'.
But the rationalism of a few Milanese Enlightenment authors like
Giuseppe Parini͗ did, Stendhal allows, help to prepare the way for
Napoleon, who in 1796 'came with the crash of cannon at Lodi to
awaken Italy from her age-old slumbers' (*Rome, Naples et Florence*,
1817). For three years, until the withdrawal of the French in 1799,
the thirst for pleasure returned to such a degree that instances were
reported of old millionaire merchants and money-lenders 'who, during this interval, quite forgot to pull long faces and to amass money'.
(Amassing money was made more difficult, an author less friendly to
Napoleon might have pointed out, by the taxes the French needed to
impose to pay for the war. But to many those days did come to seem
like a golden age from the perspective of the newly repressive rule of
the Austrians from 1814 onwards.)

The 17-year-old Henri Beyle (it was in *Rome, Naples et Florence* that
he first used the name Stendhal) had arrived in Milan in June 1800 in
the wake of Napoleon's triumphant reconquest ('imagine a whole
populace madly in love'). From then on nothing damped his enthusiasm for the city. After a decade of enforced absence he visited in
1811, much extending the 'few days" leave he had been granted from
his administrative post. And then in 1814, when no preferment was
offered by the restored French monarchy, Stendhal left Paris once
again for the beloved city and its *cotolette alla milanese*, its people's
unusual combination of 'shrewdness and generosity', its fine streets
and its porticoes of granite columns (quarried from Baveno on Lake
Maggiore). He remained until 1821, pursuing his liaison with Angela
Pietragrua and hoping to begin one with Metilde Dembowski, and
enjoying above all the **Teatro alla Scala**. Here, apart from the music of
Rossini, Mozart, and others less known today, was to be experienced a
stage 'afire with wealth and magnificence', with 'all that is most baroque

and most bizarre, all that is most sumptuous in architectural devising, all that can be made to live and breathe through the soft brilliance of draperies'. La Scala was also the social hub of the city, where 'from 200 miniature *salons* which go by the name of boxes, each with its curtain-draped window giving a view across the vastness of the auditorium there rises a lively buzz of conversation'.

After 1821, suspect for Bonapartism and liberal connections, Stendhal was allowed only the briefest of visits to Milan by the increasingly cautious Austrian authorities. He was, dangerously, acquainted with contributors to the newspaper *Il Conciliatore*, suppressed in 1819, including Silvio Pellico (◊Venice), who was arrested in 1820. He also knew of Carlo Porta◊, the Milanese dialect poet, author of inventive satires on conservative society.

Some of the most cutting and comic satire in modern Milan has come from the actor and playwright Dario Fo◊, much of whose work was first performed here, whether in conventional theatres or in factories and their car-parks, clubs, or, as in *Morte accidentale di un anarchico* (*Accidental Death of an Anarchist*), 1970, in a converted warehouse. In December 1969 a bomb had exploded at the bank in Piazza Fontana, killing 16 people. The police arrested and interrogated Giuseppe Pinelli, who 'flew' from the fourth-floor window of police headquarters to his death. Ten years later, three right-wingers, one a police agent, were convicted of the bombing. Fo's play had already exposed through outrageous farce the ineptitude of a police cover-up. Fo himself originally played the 'Maniac', diagnosed as suffering from 'histrionomania', who impersonates a senior judge and makes the policemen re-enact the moments leading up to the death of the anarchist. Their attempts to improve on the truth result in absurd contradictions which rapidly reveal their complicity and corruption. As the first audiences realised, according to Fo, the horrible reality of what they were watching, their 'grins froze on their faces and in most cases turned into a kind of *Grand Guignol* scream which had nothing liberating about it, nothing to make things palatable – on the contrary, it made them impossible to swallow'.

## THE LAKES

**Lake Maggiore** provided imaginative relief for Edward Gibbon in 1764: while Milan Cathedral 'is an unfinished monument of Gothic superstition and wealth', 'the fancy is amused by a visit to the **Borromean islands**, an enchanted palace, a work of the fairies in the midst of a lake encompassed with mountains, and far removed from the haunts of men'. **Isola Bella** in particular was already known for the luxurious palace and 'rare' gardens of the Counts Borromeo (members of the same family as the Milanese cardinals). Such carefully cultivated delights are not to the taste of some people and some generations;

Byron, who 'navigated Lake Maggiore' in 1816, wrote to Augusta Leigh that the islands were 'fine but too artificial'.

By the time Dario Fo was born at Sangiano, near the eastern shore of the lake, in 1926, the region was somewhat less 'removed from the haunts of men'. But he found his own fairies in the old tales related by local fishermen, smugglers, and story-tellers. His sister, Bianca Fo Rambois, remembers in her memoir *Io, da grande mi sposo un partigiano* (*When I Grow Up I'll Marry a Partisan*), 1976, how he would sit on the jetty steps listening to the 'legends of the Lake' told by the fishermen as they mended their nets. At night he would adapt what he had heard for his brother and sister as they lay in bed, and even pass it off as true. The stories, food for Fo's abiding love of the incongruous, were about 'green, mossy, enchanted towns buried under the waters of the lake, inhabited by giant silver fish with human heads'.

Between Lakes Maggiore and Como is Lake Lugano. Much of the shoreline is Swiss territory, but on the northern shore just east of the border is the **Valsolda**, associated with Antonio Fogazzaro's novel *Piccolo mondo antico* (*The Little World of the Past*), 1895 (Extract 2). This is set in the 1850s and mostly in **Oria** and other nearby villages, or on the steep mountain paths above, or, often, on the lake itself. Small boats cross the water carrying people paying courtesy calls, officials of the Austrian regime searching for suspected liberals, liberals coming at evening publicly to sing and play the bassoon and privately to talk patriotic politics into the night. The moon moves on the lake, it is shrouded in mist or rain, mountains move in and out of view, a child is drowned. Along the shore priests, doctors, village elders and others fish in silence, looking like spiritual contemplatives but in fact, in their daydreams, hoping to hook bishoprics, government advancement or, in a cook's case, simply a fine mountain tench. Increasingly the inhabitants of the 'piccolo mondo' are becoming involved in the larger world. But as yet, for much of the novel, peace reigns on the steep shores and the vineyards, the jasmine, verbena, and festooned blue passion-flowers, on the cypresses which stand for the faith of Franco Maironi and the one glistening carob-tree which suggests his romantic southern sensibility.

Alessandro Manzoni's *I promessi sposi* (*The Betrothed*), begins with a description – traditionally learnt in Italian schools – of the lower eastern branch of **Lake Como**, sometimes called Lake Lecco, as it narrows towards the town of Lecco and broadens again into Lake Garlate. The peaceful woods, fields, vineyards and small villages of the 'vast surrounding countryside' contrast both with the scenes of riot and plague in Milan later in the novel and with the menacing presence, more locally, of rapacious Spanish soldiers and hired thugs. For Stendhal's Contessa Gina Pietranera Lake Lecco is 'grimly severe' where the Como branch is 'voluptuous'. The lake in general, however, is 'noble and tender, everything speaks of love, not recalling the ugliness of civilisation' (*La Chartreuse de Parme* (*The Charterhouse of Parma*), 1839; Extract 1). Even Dr Thomas Arnold (1795–1842), the energetic reforming headmaster of Rugby school, glimpsed what the Countess means as he mused, for a moment, on what it would be like to bring one's family to live on Lake Como. The 'voluptuous enjoyment', he concluded, would not repay the abandonment of 'the line of usefulness and activity which I have in England'. But to see it for recreation, 'to strengthen us for work to come, and to gild with beautiful recollections our daily life of home duties . . . is delightful, and is a pleasure which I think we may enjoy without restraint'. England has 'other destinies' – her citizens must work to 'do good to themselves and to the world. Therefore, these lovely valleys, and this surpassing beauty of lake and mountain, and garden, and wood, are least, of all men, for us to covet; and our country, so entirely subdued as it is to man's uses, with its gentle hills and valleys, its innumerable canals and coaches, is best suited as an instrument of usefulness'.

**Lake Garda**, the Roman Lake Benacus on whose shores the rich then as later built fine villas, was familiar to the poet Catullus◊, who, at least in verse, usually has none of Dr Arnold's suspicion of 'voluptuous enjoyment'. Arnold, however, no doubt had no objection to the poem in which Catullus, returning from foreign service, hails the peninsula of **Sirmione** (Roman Sirmio) as the jewel of 'almost islands' and the place of contented homecomimg. Although he probably lived mainly in Rome the poet, of a rich family based in Verona, presumably retained or had access to a villa on the lake. This fact is commemorated in Grotte di Catullo.

On the western side of Lake Garda, at **Gardone Riviera**, lived a later, equally sensuous poet, Gabriele D'Annunzio◊. From 1921 he crammed the buildings and grounds at **Il Vittoriale degli Italiani** with objects expressive of his own powerful conception of himself: the prow of the battleship *Puglia* involved in his seizure of the disputed city of Fiume in 1919; the bi-plane in which he flew over Vienna during the First World War; the mirror with the inscription, aimed particularly at the visiting Mussolini, 'Remember that you are made of glass and I of steel' (the attitude of the older man of action to the Duce, who had benefited from association with him, was distinctly ambiguous); and D'Annunzio's mausoleum. In December 1923 he had proclaimed that Vittoriale was to be given to the state; for, he says with characteristic confidence in the self he spent a lifetime creating, and equally characteristic rhetorical emphasis 'not only every house furnished by me, not only every room carefully arranged by me, but every object chosen or collected by me . . . was always a mode of self-expression, . . . a mode of spiritual revelation, like any of my poems, like any of my dramas, like any of my political and military deeds'.

# MANTUA

In 1844 Dickens (◊Liguria) walked through a Mantua of tumbledown disused churches, a 'marshy town . . . so intensely dull and flat, that the dirt seemed not to have come there in the ordinary course, but to have settled and mantled on its surface as on standing water'. William Beckford◊ had already found damp and decay in the 1780s, but for him enough remained, even in the overgrown courtyard of the **Palazzo Ducale**, to suggest the 'refined enjoyments' available during 'the elegant reign of the Gonzagas' (*Dreams, Waking Tours, and Incidents*, 1783; Extract 3).

Before the woes of Mantua – Duke Vincenzo II's sale of most of the portable art treasures to Charles I of England in 1628, the sack of the city by imperial troops in 1630, Austrian rule in the 18th century (source of the 'German whiskers' abhorred by Beckford) – the court of the Gonzaga had been elegant indeed. Marquis Ludovico Gonzaga (ruled 1444–78) commissioned some of the finest works which do remain *in situ* in the Ducal Palace: Andrea Mantegna's wall-paintings of Ludovico and his relaxedly self-confident court in the **Camera degli Sposi**, and the more fragmentary and romantic scenes in Antonio Pisanello's frescoes, rediscovered only in the 1960s, of battling Arthurian knights and their ladies in the **Sala del Pisanello**. For generations the Gonzaga went on enriching and extending their palace (it would eventually, under the Austrians, have five hundred rooms). Culturally, the court reached its apogee under Isabella d'Este (1474–1539), wife of Marquis Francesco II (ruled 1484–1519) and mother of Marquis (later Duke) Federico II (1519–40). Isabella continued to employ Mantegna, was painted by Leonardo da Vinci and Titian, and presided over a circle which included Baldassare Castiglione (◊Umbria and Marche) during his periods in Mantuan service.

It was Federico who invited to Mantua, in 1524, the painter and architect Giulio Romano (1499–1546). His **Palazzo del Tè** (from an area of meadowland called Teietto) was designed as a summer residence for the Duke. Its most talked of room has always been the **Sala dei Giganti**, which seeks however possible – through echoing acoustics, minimal lighting, softening of the angles, painting from floor to ceiling and even over the doors – to create the illusion that the spectator is present amid the chaos and destruction caused by Jupiter hurling his thunderbolts at the Giants. To art historians this is a defining Mannerist moment; where 'Mantegna's illusionism in the Camera degli Sposi is charming, carefree, and plausible . . . Giulio's has as its sole end the striking of terror into the spectator and the exhibition of the artist's virtuosity' (Peter Murray). In Dickens's terms, Giulio achieves 'unaccountable nightmares' of interior decoration, an 'apoplectic performance' in which the ugly and grotesque giants:

'are depicted as staggering under the weight of falling buildings, and being overwhelmed in the ruins; upheaving masses of rock, and burying themselves beneath; vainly striving to sustain the pillars of heavy roofs that topple down upon their heads; and in a word, undergoing and doing every kind of mad and demoniacal destruction. The figures are immensely large, and exaggerated to the utmost pitch of uncouthness; the colouring is harsh and dis-agreeable; and the whole effect more like (I should imagine) a violent rush of blood to the head of the spectator, than any real picture set before him by the hand of an artist'.

But in a novel, Dickens would have to agree, such a picture might do much: he relishes the thought that the sickly-looking caretaker might be 'too much haunted by the Giants, and they were frightening her to death, all alone in that exhausted cistern of a Palace, among the reeds and rushes, with the mists hovering about outside, and stalking round and round it continually'.

## OTHER LITERARY LANDMARKS

**Arona**: near here, on the western shore of Lake Maggiore, is the San Carlone, a colossal statue (1697) of San Carlo Borromeo.

   **Bergamo**: Museo (Gaetano) Donizetti, in the 1stituto Musiale Doni-zetti, 9 Via Arena, presents the life and work of the opera composer (1797–1848) born in Bergamo.

   **Cremona**: the cathedral, 'of a mixed Grecian and Gothic architec-ture,' 'has a respectable appearance; while two enormous lions, of red marble, frown at its door' (Hester Piozzi◊ Piedmont).

   **Lecco**: Manzoni spent much of his youth at Villa Manzoni in Via Amendola.

   **Mantua**: 13th century statue of Virgil (◊Naples and Campania) in Piazza delle Erbe.

   **Milan**: models from the drawings of Leonardo◊ at the Museo Nazionale della Scienza e della Tecnica 'Leonardo da Vinci'.

   **Milan**: Museo Teatrale attached to La Scala opera-house.

   **Milan**: Manzoni◊ is buried in the Cimitero Monumentale.

   **Sabbioneta**: Scamozzi's Teatro Olimpico (1590) is a Palladian thea-tre in many ways similar to its namesake in Vicenza. (See Veneto and North-East.)

   **Santa Maria delle Grazie**, west of Mantua: tomb of Baldassare Castiglione (◊Umbria and Marche).

   **Stresa**: the Hôtel des Iles Borromées features in Book IV of Ernest Hemingway's *A Farewell to Arms*, 1929.

# BOOKLIST

Beckford, William, *The Grand Tour of William Beckford: Selections from Dreams, Waking Thoughts and Incidents* [1783], Elizabeth Mavor, ed, Penguin, Harmondsworth, 1986. **Extract 3.**

Fo, Dario, *Accidental Death of an Anarchist* [1970], adapted by Gavin Richards from Gillian Hanna, trans, Methuen, London, 1987.

Fo, Dario, *Accidental Death of an Anarchist* [1970] and *Mistero buffo* [1969], Ed Emery, trans, in *Plays One*, introduced by Stuart Hood, Methuen, London, 1992.

Fogazzaro, Antonio, *The Little World of the Past* [1895], W.J. Strachan, trans, Oxford University Press, London, 1962. **Extract 2.**

Forster, E.M., *Arctic Summer and Other Fiction*, Edward Arnold, London, 1980.

Ginzburg, Natalia, *The Manzoni Family* [1983], Marie Evans, trans, Paladin Books, London, 1989.

Hirst, David, *Dario Fo and Franca Rame*, Macmillan, Basingstoke and London, 1989.

Jones, Pamela M., *Federigo Borromeo and the Ambrosiana: Art Patronage and Reform in 17th Century Milan*, Cambridge University Press, Cambridge, 1993.

Keates, Jonathan, *Stendhal*, Sinclair-Stevenson, London, 1994.

Leonardo da Vinci, *The Literary Works*, Jean Paul Richter, ed and trans, 2 vols, Phaidon, London, 1970.

Manzoni, Alessandro, *The Betrothed* [1840–2], Archibald Colqohoun, trans, Dent, London, and Dutton, New York, 1968. **Extract 4.**

Hugh and Pauline Massingham, *The Englishman Abroad*, Phoenix House, London, 1962

Mitchell, Tony, *Dario Fo: People's Court Jester*, Methuen, London, 1984.

Murray, Peter, *The Architecture of the Italian Renaissance*, Thames and Hudson, London, 1969.

Rame, Franca and Dario Fo, *A Woman Alone and Other Plays*, Methuen, London, 1991.

Stendhal, *The Charterhouse of Parma* [1839], C. K. Scott Moncrieff, trans, David Campbell, London, 1992. **Extract 1.**

Stendhal, *Rome, Naples and Florence* [1817], Richard N. Coe, trans, John Calder, London, 1959.

Vasari, Giorgio, *Lives of the Artists* [1568], George Bull, trans, 2 vols, Penguin, Harmondsworth, 1987. **Extract 5.**

# *Extracts*

## (1) LAKE COMO

### Stendhal, *The Charterhouse of Parma*, 1839

*Gina, Contessa Pietranera, later Duchessa Sanseverina, once at
the centre of a lively social circle in Napoleonic Milan, helps to
banish boredom from the 'feudal castle' of her mean-spirited
legitimist brother-in-law. Her delight in 'immediate pleasure',
highly significant to her own and her nephew Fabrizio's fortunes
in the rest of the novel, is for Stendhal a defining feature of the
true Italian character.*

The Contessa set out to visit, with Fabrizio, all those enchanting spots
in the neighbourhood of Grianta, which travellers have made so
famous: the Villa Melzi on the other shore of the lake, opposite the
castle, and commanding a fine view of it; higher up, the sacred wood of
the Sfrondata, and the bold promontory which divides the two arms
of the lake, that of Como, so voluptuous, and the other which runs
towards Lecco, grimly severe: sublime and charming views which the
most famous sight in the world, the Bay of Naples, may equal, but
does not surpass. It was with ecstasy that the Contessa recaptured the
memories of her earliest childhood and compared them with her
present sensations. 'The Lake of Como,' she said to herself, 'is not
surrounded, like the Lake of Geneva, by wide tracts of land enclosed
and cultivated according to the most approved methods, which suggest money and speculation. Here, on every side, I see hills of irregular
height covered with clumps of trees that have grown here at random,
which the hand of man has never yet spoiled and forced to *yield a
return*. Standing among these admirably shaped hills which run down
to the lake at such curious angles, I can preserve all the illusions of
Tasso's and Ariosto's descriptions. All is noble and tender, everything
speaks of love, nothing recalls the ugliness of civilisation. The villages
halfway up their sides are hidden in tall trees, and above the tree-tops
rises the charming architecture of picturesque belfries. If some little
field 50 yards across comes here and there to interrupt the clumps of
chestnuts and wild cherries, the satisfied eye sees growing on it plants
more vigorous and happier than elsewhere. Beyond these hills, the
crests of which offer one hermitages in all of which one would like to
dwell, the astonished eye perceives the peaks of the Alps, always
covered in snow, and their stern austerity recalls to one so much of
the sorrows of life as is necessary to enhance one's immediate pleasure. The imagination is touched by the distant sound of the bell of
some little village hidden among the trees: these sounds borne across

the waters which soften their tone, assume a tinge of gentle melancholy and resignation, and seem to be saying to man: 'Life is fleeting:
do not therefore show yourself so obdurate towards the happiness
that is offered you, make haste to enjoy it.' The language of these
enchanted spots, which have not their like in the world, restored to the
Contessa the heart of a girl of 16.

## (2) Lake Lugano

### Antonio Fogazzaro,
### *The Little World of the Past*, 1895

*The novel is set in the 1850s, between the revolutionary attempts
of the late 1840s and the successful unification of much of Italy
after 1859. In this extract naive but sympathetic enthusiasm has
been generated by a (several years premature) rumour that Piedmont under Count Cavour is about to enter a war which will
bring about the liberation of northern Italy from the Austrians.
With hindsight Fogazzaro can see that even this liberation will
not bring perfect political solutions, any more than there will be
easy solutions in the troubled relationship of his protagonists
Luisa and Franco.*

Franco shook his fist in the air, trembling with excitement.

'*Viva* Cavour!' murmured Luisa.

'Ah, Demosthenes himself could hardly have praised the Count
more eloquently,' said the lawyer.

Franco's eyes filled with tears. 'I'm a fool,' he said. 'What do you
expect anyone to say?'

Pedraglio asked Luisa where the deuce she had hidden the bottle.
Luisa smiled, left them, and immediately returned with the wine and
some glasses.

'To Count Cavour!' said Pedraglio in a low voice. They raised their
glasses, repeating 'To Count Cavour!' and drained them; even Luisa,
who never drank in the ordinary way.

Pedraglio refilled the glasses and rose to his feet.

'To the war!' he said.

The other three leaped to their feet, seizing their glasses in silence,
too moved to speak.

'We must all join in!' said Pedraglio.

'Yes, all!' repeated Franco. Luisa kissed him impulsively on the
neck. Her husband cupped her head between his hands and planted
a kiss on her hair.

One of the windows facing on the lake was open. In the silence that
followed this kiss the rhythmic beat of oars could be heard.

'The customs people,' whispered Franco. As the customs launch slid by beneath the window, Pedraglio exclaimed 'Swine!' so loudly that the other two hushed him. The boat went by. Franco leaned his head out of the window.

It was becoming cool, the moon was setting behind the Carona hills, throwing a long, golden bar across the water. How strange it seemed to be contemplating this quiet corner when one's mind was filled with thoughts of a major war that was brewing. The mountains, sombre and melancholy, seemed to be brooding over the portentous future. Franco closed the window and they resumed their conversation in undertones, sitting round the table. They were all preoccupied with their speculations about the future and they all spoke of it as of a drama of which the script was ready to the last line, with all the i's dotted and t's crossed, in Count Cavour's desk.

## (3) MANTUA

### William Beckford,
### *Dreams, Waking Thoughts and Incidents*, 1783

*Beckford searches for 'refined enjoyments', whether in Mantua's association with Virgil, its painting and architecture, or its romantic desolation after the age of the Gonzaga. The drums and 'German whiskers' belong to the Austrian garrison.*

Mantua . . . rises out of a morass formed by the Mincio; whose course, in most places, is so choked up with reeds as to be scarcely discernible. It requires a creative imagination to discover any charms at such a prospect; and a strong prepossession not to be disgusted with the scene where Virgil was born. For my own part, I approached this neighbourhood with proper deference, and began to feel the God; but finding no tufted tree on which I could suspend my lyre, or verdant bank which invited to repose, I abandoned poetry, and entered the city in despair. The beating of drums, and the sight of German whiskers, finished what croaking frogs and stagnant ditches had begun. Every classic idea being scared by such sounds and such objects, I dined in dudgeon; and refused stirring out, till late in the evening. A few paces from the town stand the remains of the palace where the Gonzagas formerly resided. This, I could not resist looking at; and was amply rewarded. Several of the apartments, adorned by the bold pencil of Julio Romano, merit the most exact attention. . . . When it was too late to examine the paintings any longer, I walked into a sort of court, or rather garden, which had been decorated with fountains and antique statues. Their fragments still remain, amongst beds of weeds and flowers; for every corner of the place is smothered in vegetation. Here, nettles grow thick and rampant; there, tuberoses and jessamine climb around mounds of ruins; which, during the elegant reign of the Gonzagas, led to grottos and subterraneous apartments, concealed from vulgar eyes and sacred to the most refined enjoyments. I gathered a tuberose, that sprung from a shell of white marble, once trickling with water, now half filled with mould; and carrying it home, shut myself up for the rest of the night, inhaled its perfume, and fell a dreaming.

## (4) MILAN

### Alessandro Manzoni, *The Betrothed,* 1840–2

*Renzo, a 17th-century countryman who has just arrived in the city, finds himself in the middle of a riot directed against the officer responsible for food prices.*

Among the spectators was one – a debauched looking old man – who was a spectacle in himself. With his deep-set, bloodshot eyes stretched as wide open as they would go, with the wrinkles of his face distorted into a smirk of fiendish pleasure, with hands held high above his unreverend white locks, he was brandishing a hammer, a rope and four large nails. When the commissioner had been killed, he said, these things would be used to hang his body up on the front door of his own house.

'For shame!' cried Renzo. . . . 'For shame! Do we want to do the hangman out of a job? Do we want to kill a fellow-Christian? How can we expect God to send us bread, if we do terrible things like that? It's thunderbolts, not bread, that he'd be sending us!'

'You swine! You traitor to your country!' cried a bystander who had managed to hear this praiseworthy speech among the general din, turning a face contorted with devilish passion towards Renzo. 'Look at him! He's one of the commissioner's servants, disguised as a peasant!' – 'It's the commissioner himself, trying to escape disguised as a servant!' 'Where?' 'Kill him!' – 'Kill him!'

Renzo kept quiet and tried to look as small as possible. He would gladly have vanished altogether. One or two of his neighbours gathered round him protectively, and shouted other slogans as loudly as they could to confuse and drown the voices of those who were crying for blood. But what really saved him was a great cry of 'Make way! make way!' which suddenly rang out close at hand. 'Make way! Here it comes! This is what we want! Make way!'

What could it be? – It was a long ladder, which some men were bringing up, with the intention of leaning it against the wall and getting in at an upper window. Once in position, it would have made the task easy enough: but getting it there fortunately proved very difficult. It was carried by a man at each end and others on either side; they were pushed, jostled, and separated from each other by the crowd, so that their advance was slow and irregular. One man had his head between two rungs, and the supports on his shoulders; he was weighed down and shaken from side to side as if beneath a yoke, and was roaring with pain. . . . The fateful object staggered and wound its way forward. It arrived just in time to distract and disorganize Renzo's enemies. He took advantage of the local confusion which was now superimposed on the general one, and made off. He covered the first few yards bent almost double, as unobtrusively as possible, and then made free use of his elbows to get away from a spot which was clearly unhealthy for him.

## (5) Milan

### Giorgio Vasari, *Lives of the Artists, 1568*

*Leonardo da Vinci lived in Milan between 1482 and 1499 and worked on his Last Supper in about 1495–7. Although Leonardo 'accomplished far more in words than in deeds', he was important to Vasari as originator of 'the third style or period, which we like to call the modern age'. Endowed by heaven beyond all others of his time, 'all his actions seem inspired, and indeed everything he does clearly comes from God rather than human art'. Such pronouncements were highly influential in the later history of the idea of the man of genius.*

Leonardo also executed in Milan, for the Dominicans of Santa Maria delle Grazie, a marvellous and beautiful painting of the Last Supper. Having depicted the heads of the apostles full of splendour and majesty, he deliberately left the head of Christ unfinished, convinced he would fail to give it the divine spirituality it demands. This all but finished work has ever since been held in greatest veneration by the Milanese and others. In it Leonardo brilliantly succeeded in envisaging and reproducing the tormented anxiety of the apostles to know who had betrayed their master; so in their faces one can read the emotions of love, dismay, and anger, or rather sorrow, at their failure to grasp the meaning of Christ. And this excites no less admiration than the contrasted spectacle of the obstinacy, hatred, and treachery in the face of Judas or, indeed, than the incredible diligence with which every detail of the work was executed. The texture of the very cloth on the table is counterfeited so cunningly that the linen itself could not look more realistic.

It is said that the prior used to keep pressing Leonardo, in the most importunate way, to hurry up and finish the work, because he was puzzled by Leonardo's habit of sometimes spending half a day at at a time contemplating what he had done so far; if the prior had had his way, Leonardo would have toiled like one of the labourers hoeing in the garden and never put his brush down for a moment. Not satisfied with this, the prior then complained to the duke, making such a fuss that the duke was constrained to send for Leonardo and, very tactfully, question him about the painting, although he showed perfectly well that he was only doing so because of the prior's insistence. Leonardo, knowing he was dealing with a prince of acute and discerning intelligence, was willing (as he never had been with the prior) to explain his mind at length; and so he talked to the duke for a long time about the art of painting. He explained that men of genius often accomplish most when they work the least; for, he added, they are thinking out inventions and forming in their minds the perfect ideas which they subsequently express and reproduce with their hands. . . . Then, he said, he had yet to do the head of Judas, and this troubled him since he did not think he could imagine the features that would form the countenance of a man who, despite all the blessings he had been given, could so cruelly steel his will to betray his own master and the creator of the world. However, added Leonardo, he would try to find a model for Judas, and if he did not succeed in doing so, why then he was not without the head of that tactless and importunate prior. The duke roared with laughter at this and said that Leonardo had every reason in the world for saying so. The unfortunate prior retired in confusion to worry the labourers working in his garden, and he left off worrying Leonardo, who skilfully finished the head of Judas and made it seem the very embodiment of treachery and inhumanity.

# Biographies and important works

BECKFORD, William (1759–1844), immensely wealthy English traveller, connoisseur, creator of the Gothic fantasy Fonthill Abbey and author of the Gothic novel *Vathek, an Arabian Tale*, 1786, was in Italy in 1780–1 and 1782. *Dreams, Waking Thoughts, and Incidents*, 1783 (revised 1834) gives, as its title suggests, as much weight to subjective moods and intuitions as to more factual accounts of places and works of art. For Beckford reason and fancy 'are my sun and moon. The first dispels vapours and clears up the face of things, the other throws over all Nature a dim haze and may be styled the Queen of Delusions'.

CATULLUS, Gaius Valerius (c. 84–c.54 B.C.) came from a wealthy Veronese family. In 57–56 B.C. he served under the Roman governor of Bithynia; otherwise, he seems to have spent most of his life in Rome, but also had a villa at Sirmione (the Roman Sirmio). He was a political or personal enemy of Julius Caesar, who is mocked outrageously in several poems. (It is just possible that these attacks are a private joke to be enjoyed by their victim.)

Catullus' work was almost entirely lost from ancient times until the appearance of the crucial codex in Verona in the early 14th century. (This was itself lost, but three surviving later 14th century manuscripts derive from it directly or at one remove.) For most of the time since then Catullus has been known particularly as a writer of short epigrammatic and lyric poems like 'Vivamus, mea Lesbia, atque amemus . . . ' ('Let us live, my Lesbia, and let us love . . . '). Lesbia features in a number of poems. She is in some sense equivalent, almost certainly, to Clodia, infamous in Rome for promiscuity and as sister of the recklessly unconventional and violent Publius Clodius Pulcher. The sexual explicitness of many of the shorter poems made Catullus himself notorious to generations more prudish than his own; it seems to be a given of the Greek and Roman epigrammatic tradition. Perhaps the most read poem by Catullus not about sexual relationships is his brief lament for his dead brother, whose funeral rites he celebrates, ending atque in perpetuum, frater, ave atque vale ('and for ever, brother, greeting and farewell'). Catullus' undeservedly less renowned poems include a joyously devout hymn to Diana (an uncharacteristic choice, probably connected with a festival of the goddess), and an epyllion ('small epic') with an extended digression on the grief of Ariadne abandoned by Theseus and sought by the loving, rescuing Bacchus with his troops of satyrs, Sileni, and other frenzied followers.

D'ANNUNZIO, Gabriele (1863–1938), was born in Pescara as Gaetano Rapagnetta; he adopted names intended to suggest a bringer of revelations – the Annunciation and its bringer the Angel Gabriel. He settled in Rome in 1881 and there published several volumes of verse, including Canto novo (New Song), 1882 (revised 1896), which follows Carducci (◊Emilia-Romagna) in the adventurous use of classical metres. D'Annunzio's poems, and the novels which followed – among them Il piacere (The Child of Pleasure), 1889, and Il trionfo della morte (The Triumph of Death), 1894 – were, however, more sensuous and erotic than anything in Carducci or most literature of the time. Il piacere, the story of two love affairs of Count Andrea Sperelli, who tries (even if in the end he fails) to make his life a work of art, has been seen as a seminal work of fin-de-siècle Decadence.

Elected as a right-wing parliamentary deputy in 1897, D'Annunzio switched to socialism in 1898. (His involvement in parliamentary politics ended in 1900.) Already he was well known for extreme views, extravagance, and love affairs; no-one seems to have written about him without calling him 'flamboyant'. From 1898 he lived in a sumptuous Tuscan villa, La Capponcina, with the actress Eleonora Duse (1858–1924), with whom his tempestuous affair lasted for some years. In the novel Il fuoco (The Flame of Life), 1900, he draws freely on this relationship and outlines his ideas for a new, non-naturalistic, non-bourgeois theatre. Something of this aim was achieved in his verse plays for Duse, Francesca da Rimini, 1901, and La figlia di Iorio (The Daughter of Iorio), 1904, a stylised tale of peasant life in D'Annunzio's native Abruzzo. (Abruzzo is also the setting of the earlier more naturalistic stories collected in *Novelle di Pescara*, 1902.) The verse sequence *Alcyone* (*Halcyon*), 1903, has enjoyed more lasting popularity.

In the First World War D'Annunzio took on a new image as fearless military hero, fighting the Austrians at sea, on the land and in the air (he took part in a daring flight over Vienna), and sustaining wounds. In September 1919, disgusted at Italy's failure to obtain Fiume (now Rijeka) he formed a volunteer force and seized the town, holding it as dictator until December 1920. This episode was a useful precedent for the Fascist March on Rome of 1922. Association with the hero of Fiume remained politically advantageous to Mussolini, but the relationship between them was never entirely easy. In his last years, ill from war wounds and a fall from a window at Il Vittoriale in 1922, tired, politically superseded, honoured to the mirth of some as Prince of Montenevoso, D'Annunzio at last lost much of the energy which had informed his earlier work. His influence on poetry, declamatory prose, fashion, and political expression in Italy was, between the 1890s and the 1930s, immense: he was much copied and reviled and reacted against, and difficult to avoid.

FO, Dario (born 1926 at Sangiano near Lake Maggiore), actor and prolific playwright who communicates his radically 'subversive' ideas through farce, mime, song, improvisation; laughter, he says, is 'the people's way of cutting through the rotting body of bourgeois culture'. Fo studied art at the Accademia di Brera in Milan and architecture at the Polytechnic while already devising farces and performing practical jokes (staging a reception for a 'Picasso' played by a caretaker from the Brera, for instance). He then wrote and performed for radio and in revue, as a song-writer and for television, most famously in a variety show, *Canzonissima* (1962) which came to a rapid end as a result of censorship problems. Between 1959 and 1967 he and his wife and equally notable fellow actor Franca Rame performed at 'bourgeois' theatres including the Teatro Odeon in Milan, but in 1968, in order to unfetter their satire, to be more effective 'minstrels' to the exploited, as Franca Rame puts it, they made a decision to use only Communist party venues, mainly workers' clubs. In 1970 they broke with the party, not least because some of its officials disliked their inclusion among the objects of satire, and set up a theatre collective, La Comune.

Fo's sources of inspiration are diverse: the tall stories of his childhood (see Lake Maggiore), medieval legends, current affairs, discussions with the audience following productions, Brecht's 'epic theatre', the *giullare* – the medieval, anti-establishment, popular entertainer, or at least Fo's conception of this figure – whose influence is most evident in the one-man show *Mistero buffo* (*Comical Mystery Play*), 1969. The church is a major target of the satire in *Mistero*; in *Morte accidentale di un anarchico* (*Accidental Death of an Anarchist*), 1970, probably Fo's best known play outside Italy, the police are the target in what the author sees as a 'tragic farce'.

The exploitation of women has become one of the main concerns of Fo's and particularly Rame's theatre in their more recent work; a useful selection from this body of work is Franca Rame and Dario Fo, *A Woman Alone and Other Plays*, 1991.

FOGAZZARO, Antonio (1842–1911), spent much of his life in the city of his birth, Vicenza.

From childhood onwards, however, summers were often spent in the Valsolda on Lake Lugano. This is the principal setting of his most popular and approachable novel *Piccolo mondo antico* (*The Little World of the Past*), 1895. The troubled relationship of Franco and Luisa revolves around his romantic sensibilities and unshakeable Catholic belief and (for much of the novel) her colder rationality and desire to see action and justice in this world rather than the next. Although Fogazzaro's own Catholic sympathies are very evident by the end, he approaches the relationship with some psychological subtlety. (Subsequent novels, which bring the story of the Maironi family forward to times closer to his own, are more polemical; the Catholic reformism of *Il santo*, 1905, and *Leila*, 1910, resulted in their being placed on the Vatican's Index of prohibited books.) Luisa, Franco, and the author do largely agree in their support for the Risorgimento cause. Writing 40 years after the events, however, Fogazzaro is able simultaneously to celebrate the idealism of the past and to acknowledge that many ideals have remained unfulfilled. He writes with avowed nostalgia for the 'piccolo mondo' which fostered not only the small-mindedness and hypocrisy of Franco's grandmother the pro-Austrian Marchesa Maironi Scremin and those who placate her, but the old-world integrity and wisdom of Luisa's uncle, Piero Ribera. The 'smallness' of the world of the lake, where everyone knows everyone else's business and foibles, is often exploited to comic effect. The attitude to the characters is one primarily of tolerant affection, increased by the frequent use of various local dialects (not so far very convincingly rendered in translation).

MANZONI, Alessandro (1785–1873), was born in Milan and, except for the years 1805–10 which were spent mainly in Paris, remained in or near it for most of his life. After a period of scepticism Manzoni was reconverted to Catholicism in 1810. His early work consisted mostly of poetry, including the *Inni sacri* (*Sacred Hymns*) of 1812–22. In *Lettera sul romanticismo* (*Letter on Romanticism*), 1823, he argued against the application of neo-classical rules in literature. The first edition of his novel *I promessi sposi* (*The Betrothed*) appeared in 1825–7. (He had worked on an earlier, simpler version of the central story, *Fermo e Lucia*, in 1821–3.) In 1827 he visited Florence to 'rinse my clothes in the Arno' and began the process of revision of the novel from Lombard to Tuscan linguistic usages, thus striking one more blow for the acceptance of the modern descendant of the language of Dante as official 'Italian'. The definitive version of *The Betrothed* appeared in 1840–2. Manzoni's troubled family life – he outlived two wives and eight of his ten children – is described by Natalia Ginzburg (◊Piedmont) in *La famiglia Manzoni* (*The Manzoni Family*), 1983. Verdi's *Requiem*, originally begun in memory of Rossini, was dedicated to Manzoni and first performed at the church of San Marco in Milan on 22 May 1874, one year after his death.

*I Promessi sposi* is set, in the years 1628–30, in the area of Lecco, Milan, and Bergamo. The main plot concerns the proud and lustful Don Rodrigo's attempts to prevent the honest, sometimes naive, sometimes hot-headed Renzo (Lorenzo) from marrying the mostly perfect Lucia. Among the other most memorable characters are Lucia's loyal mother, the lovers' easily pressurized, comically cowardly parish priest Don Abbondio, the holy and courageous Capuchin Fra Cristoforo, and the 'Unnamed' (*l'innominato*), an agent of evil far more powerful than Don Rodrigo who kidnaps Lucia for him but recognises the error of his ways mainly because of her. There is a strong didactic element in the novel; Renzo, for instance, long dreams of revenge but is, in the end, deemed worthy of Lucia only when he forgives the plague-smitten Don Rodrigo.

Manzoni also acts on a historical imperative – the declared object of giving a detailed account of the Milanese plague is 'not only to set the stage for our characters, but also to give an adequate picture ... of a period in our country's history which, although famous enough in a general way, is little known in detail'. More immediately, the picture of the ill effects of foreign rule could be read by nationalists as support for Italian unification. (Manzoni himself, however, had some reservations about the Risorgimento.)

*The Betrothed*, generally esteemed as Italy's only major 19th-century novel, became a national institution. Fortunately it is less turgid than this might lead one to fear. Manzoni can even laugh at himself: at one point he pulls back from what sounds like the beginning of another long account to reassure the reader 'But there is no cause for alarm; I am not going to tell you the story of the pestilence of Bergamo too'.

PARINI, Giuseppe (1729–99), was born into a middle-class family at Bosisio – now Bosisio Parini – south of Lake Como. In Milan he was ordained priest and worked as tutor in a noble household and later, from 1769, professor at the Palatine Schools. His most important work is the long satirical poem *Il giorno* (*The Day*; first two books

1763–5, second two published posthumously 1801–4), an account of a young nobleman's trifling way of passing the day, from toilette through various divertissements to bed.

PORTA, Carlo (1775–1821), Milanese dialect poet, actor, and government official, is best known for such narrative satires as *Desgrazzi di Giovannin Bongee* (*The Misadventures of Giovannino Bongeri*), 1812, and *La nomina del cappellan* (*The Choosing of the Chaplain*), 1819. As not in Porta's non-dialect models, who included Giuseppe Parini, all levels of society are objects of laughter and criticism. He avoided direct attacks on Austrian rule after its restoration in 1814, but was prepared to risk identification with liberal beliefs by publishing *Il Romanticismo* (*Romanticism*), 1818, where a poetry of the passions is opposed to outmoded neo-classical rules.

STENDHAL is the pseudonym of Henri Beyle (1783–1842), born in Grenoble, who first came to Italy as a soldier in 1800–1 and frequently returned after 1811. He lived chiefly in Milan from 1814 to 1821, and was French consul at Civitavecchia from 1830. He gathered political and musical opinions, travel notes, and anecdotes as *Rome, Naples et Florence en 1817*, 1817 (expanded 1826). *Promenades dans Rome* (*Walks in Rome*), containing elements of a tourist-guide both serious and parodic, followed in 1829. *De l'Amour* (*On Love*), 1822, had its beginnings in Stendhal's passion for Metilde Dembowski in Milan. (He also, famously, followed her to press his suit in Volterra.) Many other of his works have Italian sources or themes. *La Chartreuse de Parme* (*The Charterhouse of Parma*), 1839, is set in the 19th century but founded in part on a 17th century manuscript account of the love-relationship between Vandozza Farnese and her nephew Alessandro, eventually Pope Paul III. The novel is a late, often playful example of what Jonathan Keates calls Stendhal's 'consistent vision of Italy as a place animated and empowered by violent physical response, expressed through sex or murder, a land which after three centuries continued to rehearse the cloak-and-dagger melodrama of the Renaissance as a kind of vitalizing rhetoric'. He wished to be remembered as 'Arrigo Beyle, Milanese'.

VASARI, Giorgio (1511–74), born in Arezzo, was a pupil of Michelangelo (◊Rome), Mannerist painter in Rome and at the court of Cosimo I de' Medici in Florence, architect of the Ufizzi, and perhaps the most influential of all art historians. The first edition of *Le vite de' più eccellenti architettori, pittori, e scultori italiani* (*The Lives of the Artists*), 1550, charts a progress from the first stirrings of a *rinascimento* – what later became known as the Renaissance – in Giotto and Cimabue, through the developing excellence of Donatello and others, to artistic perfection in Michelangelo. The second edition, 1568, extends the scope of the work to include more Venetians and more living artists, but retains the idea of a clear progression towards the achievements of the age of Leonardo, Raphael, and Michelangelo. Individual lives often exhibit the same structural clarity, skilfully shaping anecdotes into biographical and artistic patterns and sequences.

# PIEDMONT

'Along the rough country road which follows the Belbo I came to the parapet of the little bridge and to the reed-bed. I saw on the bank the wall of the cottage with its huge blackened stones, the twisted fig-tree and the gaping window and I thought of the terrible winters there.'
Cesare Pavese,
*The Moon and The Bonfires*

Hester Lynch Piozzi◊ was enthusiastic about the 'model of elegance, exact **Turin**' she came to in 1784. 'This town is the *salon* of Italy' – the room where guests, having crossed the Alps, are received – and it is 'a finely-proportioned and well-ornamented salon'. She particularly admired the regular grid of streets, which the rulers of the House of Savoy had developed from what remained of the original symmetrical plan of the Roman Augusta Taurinorum. What had been a little-known fortified northern town had become, since the 17th century, a dignified capital for an expanding kingdom. (The Dukes of Savoy acquired the Kingdom of Sardinia in 1720.) It was a well-ordered place, except, Piozzi feels obliged to note, for the townsfolk's habit of using their tasteful arches 'for the very grossest purposes'. Exhibiting more usually the same sense of ordered progress as its street-plan, Turin went on to become the engine of the Risorgimento and then, from the 1870s, the new industrial centre of Italy.

The Risorgimento was steered to its final destination, with the House of Savoy installed as kings of a united Italy, by the Piedmontese prime minister, Count Camillo di Cavour. He worked to this end cautiously, gradually, and always with a politic regard to the views and position of other powers, especially France. (Piedmont had traditional links with France, and the participation of Napoleon III was crucial to the achievement of Cavour's aims). Cavour's image, especially when seen in the light of the republican idealism of Mazzini (◊Liguria) or the inspirational heroics of Garibaldi (◊Sardinia) is one of cool, almost nordic rationality. Such qualities have often been associated with Piedmont in general. Novelists rather than poets flourish here. Italo Calvino (◊Liguria) when he arrived in Turin in 1948, found it 'more serious, more austere' than Milan. Because it had been 'the city of the anti-fascist intellectual', he told his translator William Weaver, it appealed to 'that part of me that is fascinated by a kind of Protestant severity. Turin is the most Protestant city of Italy, a kind of Italian Boston'.

Einaudi, the great publishing house for whom Calvino had come to work, had itself been a centre of anti-Fascist activity from its foundation by Giulio Einaudi in 1933. Early associates included Leone Ginzburg, married from 1938 to Natalia Ginzburg◊. Leone died after being tortured in prison in Rome in 1944, and most of the early Einaudi group were jailed or sent into internal exile at one time or another during the Fascist period; later one of their most notable authors was a survivor of Auschwitz, Primo Levi.◊

After the war Einaudi entered a more settled period, moving into new premises in Corso Re Umberto, where Natalia Ginzburg remembered the editorial director, Cesare Pavese,◊ smoking his pipe and rapidly correcting proofs. When there was nothing else to do he would either recite from *The Iliad* or work on his own novels, 'crossing things out with furious speed' (*Lessico famigliare* (*Family Sayings*), 1963). But the Turin in which the publishers re-established themselves was an altered place, much busier, for instance, than that of Primo Levi's childhood at 75 Corso Re Umberto (the house where he lived most of his life until his death in 1987), when there was pasture-land nearby and the family were woken in the morning by the sound of carts from the country jolting across cobblestones on their way into town. Allied bombing had destroyed half the roads and nearly a third of the city's housing. The rebuilding programme, together with the growth of the car industry (already indelibly associated with Turin; FIAT had been founded in 1899) brought thousands of immigrant workers from southern Italy into the new suburbs. The population doubled between 1951 and 1967.

Already in 1949 the large, often damp and misty city and its new commercial showcases seems an uninviting place to Clelia in Pavese's *Tra donne sole* (*Among Women Only*), although it is she, returning to work in her native city after establishing a career in Rome, who has changed as much as Turin. She is alienated from her childhood poverty and the streets and people who survive from that time. Equally, the social elite to which she now has access seems empty and superficial. The same faces are to be seen in the hotels, the salons, the fashion-shows, the gallery event where there is no need to look at the paintings. In the glossy post-war centre:

'everything seemed to be busy. The streets weren't for living in, but only to escape by. To think that when I used to pass the central avenues with my big box on my arm they seemed to me a kingdom of carefree people on holiday, in a way in which I then pictured seaside resorts. When one wants a thing one sees it everywhere!'
(*Il sistema periodico*, 1975.)

With two rich friends who can find no purpose in life Clelia drives, towards the end of the novel, up to the prominent Baroque basilica of **Superga** which, above the city, might be expected to function as a symbol of hope or transcendence; Clelia has until now seen it only from the Po, 'its rising black bulk sparkling with lights at the top, like a necklace carelessly thrown on the shoulders of a beautiful woman'. The three women look down at Turin, which to Rosetta is a place frighteningly full of people; but at least with money, says Momina, 'You damn well don't have to have them in the house.' Later Rosetta kills herself in a rented room looking up at Superga.

Smaller towns have their own brand of tedium, as Natalia Ginzburg suggests in *Le voci della sera* (*Voices in the Evening*), 1961 (Extract 2). For some, an alternative reality is to be found, not far from Turin, in the Alps – the white and brown peaks, fissured granite prisms, grassy ledges covered in fern and wild stawberry which were 'an island, an elsewhere' for Primo Levi even as catastrophe approached in 'Iron', *Il sistema periodico* (*The Periodic Table*, Extract 3). But city-dwellers have also been aware of the harsh realities of country living in Piedmont until very recent times. Rosetta Loy's *Le strade di polvere* (*The Dust Roads of Monferrato*), 1987, which delicately traces the emotional history of several generations of a family living in close proximity in their farmhouse in the **Monferrato** region (north of Alessandria), counterpoints the interior movements with the crises outside: as well as adultery, longing, death in childbirth, there is the flooding of the river Tanaro, the spread of cholera, troop movements.

Cesare Pavese's land – its vineyards, grimy huts, watercourses, bare threshing-floors – is more emphatically present in *La luna e i falò* (*The Moon and the Bonfires*), 1950, set in a village which is clearly **Santo Stefano Belbo** in the **Langhe** area of southern Piedmont. The steep valleys here, where agricultural cultivation is just – with patience – possible and winters hard, allow only a meagre living to poor inhabitants like the family who adopt the novel's narrator Anguillla and the one which he finds, 20 years later, living in deep misery in the same croft. Somewhat paradoxically Anguilla longs for the deep roots which he lacks in 'his' village but can offer Cinto, the boy who is (unhappily) rooted there, only the opportunity to leave.

The house where Pavese was born in Santo Stefano, now 20 Via Cesare Pavese, has become a place of pilgrimage. (It is the starting-point and information centre for visits to the local 'Luoghi di Pavese'.)

This fate is less likely to be suffered by the city of **Alessandria**, praised wittily and persuasively by its son Umberto Eco⟩ (Extract 1) as the place that never had any enthusiasm for 'a heroic cause, not even one preaching the necessity of exterminating those who are different'. It has 'given us no linguistic models for radio announcers, it has created no miracles of art that could inspire subscriptions to save them'. Alessandria has never been proud of itself. 'But how proud people can feel, discovering themselves to be children of a city without bombast and without myths, without missions and without truths' (*Il secondo diario minimo* (*How to Travel With a Salmon and Other Essays*), 1992). Places in Eco's novels are usually not so much locations you can readily visit as centres of actual and metaphysical labyrinths (like the multivalent, teasingly laid out library of *Il nome della rosa* (*The Name of the Rose*), 1980) or keys or apparent keys to codes. **Casale**, north of Alessandria, can be visited, and partly recognized from the descriptions of its siege of 1643 in *L'isola del giorno prima* (*The Island of the Day Before*), 1994, but entered only imaginatively as the place which the main figure Roberto, in love, constructs as 'a Casale of his own passion' whose alleys, fountains, and squares become 'the River of Inclination, the Lake of Indifference, or the Sea of Hostility', the island of his solitude; the narrator who affects to piece together (what may be) Roberto's papers concludes that here 'while he lost both his father and himself in a war of too many meanings and of no meaning at all, Roberto learned to see the universal world as a fragile tissue of enigmas, beyond which there was no longer an Author; or if there was, He seemed lost in the remaking of Himself from too many perspectives'.

## OTHER LITERARY LANDMARKS

**Alba**: setting of *I ventitre giorni della città di Alba* (*The 23 Days of the City of Alba*), 1952, autobiographical stories of the Resistance by Beppe Fenoglio (1922–63).

**Asti**: the dramatist Vittorio Alfieri (1749–1803) was born at Palazzo Alfieri, Piazza Cairoli.

**Turin**: the philosopher Friedrich Nietzsche lived and worked at 6 Via Carlo Alberto in 1888–9. He found the city dignified, serious, full of 'aristrocratic tranquillity'. See Lesley Chamberlain, *Nietzsche in Turin: the End of the Future*, Quartet, London, 1996.

## BOOKLIST

Camon, Ferdinando, *Conversations With Primo Levi* [1987], John Shepley, trans, Marlboro Press, Marlboro, Vermont, 1989.

*Booklist continued*

Cannon, JoAnn, *Postmodern Italian Fiction: the Crisis of Reason in Calvino, Eco, Sciascia, Malerba*, Fairleigh Dickinson University Press, Rutherford, 1989.

Cicioni, Mirna, *Primo Levi: Bridges of Knowledge*, Berg, Oxford and Washington, D.C., 1995.

Eco, Umberto, *How to Travel with a Salmon and Other Essays* [1992], William Weaver, trans, Secker and Warburg, London, 1994. **Extract 1**.

Eco, Umberto, *The Island of the Day Before* [1994], William Weaver, trans, Secker and Warburg, London, 1995.

Eco, Umberto, *The Name of the Rose*, [1980], William Weaver, trans, Secker and Warburg, London, 1992.

Ginzburg, Natalia, *Family Sayings* [1963], D.M. Low, trans (revised), Carcanet, Manchester, 1984.

Ginzburg, Natalia, *Voices in the Evening* [1961], D.M. Low, trans, Carcanet, Manchester, 1990. **Extract 2**.

Inge, M. Thomas, ed, *Naming the Rose: Essays on Eco's 'The Name of the Rose'*, University Press of Mississippi and London, 1988.

Levi, Primo, *If This Is a Man; the Truce* [1947, 1963], Stuart Woolf, trans, Vintage, London, 1996.

Levi, Primo, *Other People's Trades* [1985], Raymond Rosenthal, trans, Summit Books, New York, 1989 and Abacus, London, 1991.

Levi, Primo, *The Periodic Table* [1975], Raymond Rosenthal, trans, Sphere Books, London, 1986 **Extract 3**.

Loy, Rosetta, *The Dust Roads of Monferrato* [1987], William Weaver, trans, William Collins Sons, London, 1990.

Weaver, William, *Calvino: an Interview and its Story*, in *Calvino Revisited*, Franco Ricci, ed, Dovehouse Editions, Ottawa, 1989.

Pavese, Cesare, *Among Women Only* [1949], D.D. Paige, trans, Quartet, London, 1980.

Pavese, Cesare, *The Moon and the Bonfire* [1950], Louise Sinclair, trans, Quartet, London, 1978. **Extract 4**.

Pavese, Cesare, *This Business of Living: Diaries 1935–50* [1952], A.E. Murch and Jeanne Molli, trans, Quartet, London, 1980.

# *Extracts*

## (1) ALESSANDRIA

### Umberto Eco,
### The Miracle of San Baudolino, 1965–90

*Eco deftly transforms what might only be a wryly witty account of his native city as a colourless, unemphatic, negative place into a tribute to the virtues of the 'children of a city without bombast and without myths, without missions and without truths'.*

Alessandria is made up of great spaces. It is empty. And sleepy. But all of a sudden, on certain evenings in autumn or winter, when the city is submerged in fog, the voids vanish, and from the milky grayness, in the beams of headlights, corners, edges, unexpected facades, dark perspectives emerge from nothingness, in a new play of nuanced forms, and Alessandria becomes 'beautiful'. A city made to be seen in half-light, as you grope along, sticking to the walls. You must look for its identity not in sunshine but in haze. In the fog you walk slowly, you have to know the way if you don't want to get lost; but you always, somehow, arrive somewhere.

Fog is good and loyally rewards those who know it and love it. Walking in fog is better than walking in snow, trampling it down in hobnailed boots, because the fog comforts you not only from below but also from above, you don't soil it, you don't destroy it, it enfolds you affectionately and resumes its form after you have passed. It fills your lungs like a good tobacco; it has a strong and healthy aroma; it strokes your cheeks and slips between your lapels and your chin, tickling your neck, it allows you to glimpse from the distance ghosts that dissolve as you move closer, or it lets you suddenly discern in front of you forms, perhaps real, that dodge you and disappear into the emptiness. (Unfortunately, what you really need is a permanent war, with a blackout; it is only in such times that the fog is at its best, but you can't always have everything.) In the fog you are sheltered against the outside world, face to face with your inner self. *Nebulat ergo cogito.*

Luckily, when there is no fog on the Alessandrian plain, and especially in the early morning, *scarnebbia*, as we say; it 'unfogs'. A kind of nebulous dew, instead of illuminating the fields, rises to confuse sky and earth, lightly moistening your face. Now – in contrast to the foggy days – visibility is excessive, but the landscape remains sufficiently monochrome; everything is washed in delicate hues of grey and nothing offends the eye. You have to go outside the city, along the secondary roads or, better, along the paths flanking a straight canal, on a bicycle, without a scarf, a newspaper stuffed under your jacket to protect your chest. On the fields of Marengo, open to the moon and where, dark between the Bormida and the Tanaro, a forest stirs and lows, two battles were won long ago (1174 and 1800), the climate is invigorating.

## (2) PIEDMONT

### Natalia Ginzburg, *Voices in the Evening*, 1961

*Elsa and Tommasino are from the same village and know the same people. The people before them have, Tommasino says, 'already lived enough'; they have 'consumed all the reserves, all the vitality that there was for us.'*

He sat down. I had my hands in my jacket pockets, and looked at him. I looked at him, I looked at his head, his ruffled hair, his long big pullover, his thin hands which could not keep still and made continuous gestures.

'I have come to return the ring to you,' I said.

I drew it out of my pocket; it was small with a small pearl; this ring which he had given to me had belonged to his mother, Signora Cecilia.

He took it and laid it on the table.

'You don't want to marry me,' he said.

'No,' I said. 'How can you think that I want to marry you still after the things that you said to me yesterday?'

'Yesterday,' he said, 'I was depressed, taking a gloomy view of things. I probably felt that I was going to have a temperature.'

'However, of course,' he said, 'you are right; it is better so.'

I gazed around, and said,

'I have pictured everything, only too clearly. I have pictured you and me, here, in this house. I have pictured everything with great exactness down to the smallest details. And when one sees the things of the future so clearly as though they were already happening, it is a sign that they should never happen. They have already happened in a sense in our minds, and it is really not possible to experience them further.'

. . .

'How a place can get one down!' he said. 'It has a weight of lead, with all its dead. This village of ours, it just gets me down; it is so small, a handful of houses. I can never free myself from it, I cannot forget it. Even if I end up in Canada, I shall take it with me!'

## (3) PIEDMONT

### Primo Levi, *The Periodic Table*, 1975

> *Each story in Levi's collection is concerned with one of the elements of Mendeleev's Periodic Table and its actual or metaphorical role in individuals' lives. In the days just before the Second World War, the autobiographical narrator shares with his fellow-student Sandro his youthful belief in science as the noble human conquest of matter, an antidote to the lies and vagueness of Fascist propaganda, and in return the iron-like Sandro educates him into a more fundamentally physical contact with matter which, together with skill as a chemist and considerable luck, will enable him to survive Auschwitz.*

If necessary he carried a 30-kilo pack, but usually he travelled without it; his pockets were sufficient, and in them he put some vegetables . . . a chunk of bread, a pocketknife, sometimes the dog-eared Alpine Club guide, and a skein of wire for emergency repairs. In fact he did not carry the guide because he believed in it, but for the opposite reason. He rejected it because he felt that it shackled him; not only that, he also saw it as a bastard creature, a detestable hybrid of snow and rock mixed up with paper. He took it into the mountains to vilify. Happy if he could catch it in an error, even if it was at his and his climbing companion's expense. He could walk for two days without eating, or eat three meals all together and then leave. . . . He dragged me along on exhausting treks through the fresh snow, far from any sign of human life, following routes that he seemed to intuit like a savage. In the summer, from shelter to shelter, inebriating ourselves with the sun, the effort, and the wind, and scraping the skin of our fingertips on rocks never before touched by human hands: but not on the famous peaks, nor in quest of memorable feats; such things did not matter to him at all. What mattered was to know his limitations, to test and improve himself; more obscurely, he felt the need to prepare himself (and to prepare me) for an iron future, drawing closer month by month.

To see Sandro in the mountains reconciled you to the world and made you forget the nightmare weighing on Europe. This was his place, what he had been made for, like the marmots whose whistle and snout he imitated: in the mountains he became happy, with a silent, infectious happiness, like a light that is switched on. He aroused a new communion with the earth and sky, into which flowed my need for freedom, the plenitude of my strength, and a hunger to understand the things he had pushed me toward. We would come out at dawn, rubbing our eyes, through the small door of the Martinotti bivouac, and there, all around us, barely touched by the sun, stood the white and brown mountains, new as if created during the night that had just ended and at the same time innumerably ancient. They were an island, an elsewhere.

## (4) SANTO STEFANO BELBO

### Cesare Pavese,
### *The Moon and the Bonfires,* 1950

*The narrator, known to the reader only by his nick-name Angu-illa ('Eel'), returns after 20 years to the farm where, as an illegitimate child paid for at first by the orphanage, he grew up in a poor foster family.*

Last year, the first time I came back to the village, I went almost stealthily to look at the hazels again. The hill at Gaminella was a long slope covered as far as the eye could see with vineyards and terraces, a slant so gradual that if you looked up you could not see the top – and on the top, somewhere, there are other vineyards and other woods and paths – this hill, then, looked as if it had been flayed by the winter and showed up the bareness of the earth and of the tree trunks. In the wintry light I saw its great mass falling gradually away towards Canelli, where our valley finishes. Along the rough country road which follows the Belbo I came to the parapet of the little bridge and to the reed-bed. I saw on the bank the wall of the cottage with its huge blackened stones, the twisted fig-tree and the gaping window and I thought of the terrible winters there. But round about it the face of the land and the trees were changed; the clump of hazels had disappeared and our closely cut patch of millet grass grown smaller. From the byre an ox lowed and in the cold evening air I smelt the manure heap. So the man who had the crop now was not so badly off as we had been. I had always expected something like this or perhaps even that the cottage would have collapsed; I had imagined myself so often on the parapet of the bridge wondering how I could possibly have spent so many years in this hole, walking these few paths, taking the goat to pasture and looking for apples which had rolled down the bank, sure that the world ended where the road overhung the Belbo. But I had not expected not to find the hazels any more. That was the end of everything. These changes made me so cast down that I didn't call out or go on to the threshing floor. There and then I understood what it meant not to be born in a place, not to have it in my blood and be already half-buried there along with my forebears so that any change of crops didn't matter much.

# Biographies and important works

ECO, Umberto was born in Alessandria in 1936. He is Professor of Semiotics at the University of Bologna. In addition to influential writing on semiotics (the 'science of signs') and the nature of reading, Eco has published three novels which explore some of the themes of these academic works but have also succeeded in appealing to a much wider audience. The immensely popular *Il nome della rosa* (*The Name of the Rose*), 1980, sold 500,000 copies in hardback translation in the USA alone in 1983, and more than a million in paperback.

In *The Name of the Rose* William of Baskerville, a Franciscan whose name suggests his Holmesian methods of detection, investigates a series of deaths at a monastery in northern Italy. The answer to the mystery lies in the labyrinth-library and the location of the lost second part of Aristotle's *Poetics*, on comedy. Laughter, defended by William against the strictures of Brother Jorge of Burgos, who regards it as an agent of misbelief, functions in a way analogous to the postmodern idea of the 'open' story: while the closed novel tells a tale much as the reader expects, the open relies on acts of reader participation and involvement. Events in *The Name of the Rose* must, for instance, effectively be decoded from the account of the conventionally medievally educated novice Adso, who plays Watson to William's Holmes. And William, working like a good semiotician, must read the signs and codes which can reveal the cause of the deaths and the working of the killer or killers' mind. In fact, exceptional though his deductive skills are, he arrives at the right culprit but on the wrong conjectures, thus further emphasizing the indeterminacy of signs, meaning, reading. Any interpretation of this open novel – as of life – is partial, a fact recognised when the 1986 film by Jean-Jacques Annaud introduces itself not as the film of the book but as 'a palimpsest of Umberto Eco's novel'.

*Il pendolo di Foucault* (*Foucault's Pendulum*), 1987, and *L'isola del giorno prima* (*The Island of the Day Before*), 1994, are, similarly, at once challenging and entertaining, intercutting and playing with a vast range of ideas, structures, genres. Like Eco's first novel they are, as Jo Ann Cannon says in her study of Postmodern Italian fiction, 'an eloquent tribute to the acrobatics that allow us to orient ourselves in the entangled network of signs that constitutes our existence'.

GINZBURG, Natalia (1916–91), was born in Palermo, as Natalia Levi, of a Jewish father and Catholic mother (both non-practising). From 1919 she lived in Turin, where her father was Professor of Anatomy. The family was prominent in left-wing anti-Fascist circles in the 1930s. In 1938 she married Leone Ginzburg, a leading anti-Fascist Jew. She and their children joined him in internal exile at the village of Pizzoli, in Abruzzo. Leone was later arrested in Nazi-ruled Rome and died or was killed in prison there in 1944. From 1945 to 1950 Natalia Ginzburg worked for the publishers Einaudi in Turin, before moving to Rome. In 1983 she was elected to the Chamber of Deputies as an independent Communist. Her best known novels, written in a plain and sometimes deliberately repetitive style, are usually concerned with isolating or claustrophobic situations, often within marriage. The main characters are marginal to the larger currents of history, often living, as in *Le voci della sera* (*Voices in the Evening*), 1961, in small towns. Ginzburg's belief in the family is subordinated to the detailed reality of her characters' relationships; on the whole the situation of women is seen simply as part of the general difficulty of relationships in the uncertain, ill-defined post-war world, rather than as a spur to feminism. *Lessico famigliare* (*Family Sayings*), 1963, is an autobiographical work centred on the life, attitudes, and above all the language – idiosyncratic expressions, catchphrases, nonce-words and nonsense – of her family in Turin.

LEVI, Primo (1919–87), was born in Turin and lived there for almost all his life apart from the period of his deportation to and arduous return from Auschwitz. He graduated in chemistry at the university of Turin in 1941. Having joined the Partito d'Azione group of anti-Fascists he went as a resistance fighter to the Val d'Aosta, where he was captured in December 1943. In February 1944 he was sent to Auschwitz with 500 other people, nearly four out of five of whom were immediately consigned to the gas chambers. Levi's survival is the subject of his first and most popular book, *Se questo è un uomo* (*If This Is a Man*), 1947. He escaped death partly because his skill as a chemist was useable in the rubber factory at Monowitz (Auschwitz III). For the rest of his life he was dedicated to the task of educating and reminding others about the camps and the Holocaust. On the whole calm, lucid statement and description characterize *Se questo* (the preface rejects accusation in favour of 'dispassionate study' of the human mind) and Levi's numerous related writings; the novelist Ferdinando Camon, who recorded a series of conversations with Levi between 1982 and 1986, explains his personal gentleness of manner, his refusal to shout and accuse, as a way of achieving something much greater: making other people shout.

From 1946 to 1975 Levi worked as an industrial chemist. One of his main interests was in bridging the 'crevasse which has always seemed to me absurd' between scientific and literary cultures. Therefore *Il sistema periodico* (*The Periodic Table*), 1975, not only uses the elements, in literary fashion, as metaphors for human characteristics, but – often simultaneously – tells the story of their role in his scientific career. (The stories are highly autobiographical.) The physical atmosphere of the laboratory – the 'dense, hoary mist of ammonium chloride . . . depositing minute scintillating crystals on the windowpanes' in 'Iron', for instance – is frequently observed. And writing itself, Levi says in 'Chromium', recalling his work on *Se questo*, became 'the work of a chemist who weighs and divides, measures and judges on the basis of assured proofs, and strives to answer questions'.

Levi died in 1987, after some months of exhaustion and depression, in a probably deliberate fall from the third-floor landing of his home in Turin.

LOY, Rosetta (born 1931), has lived in Rome for much of her life. *Le strade di polvere* (*The Dust Roads of Monferrato*), 1987, is the only novel by Loy which has so far been translated into English. Her other books include *La bicicletta* (*The Bicycle*), 1974, and *La porta dell' acqua* (*The Gate in the Water*), 1974, a searching account of childhood and the repression of the female.

PAVESE, Cesare (1908–50), was born at Santo Stefano Belbo, where his family spent summers in his early years. After school and university in Turin, he worked briefly as a teacher and was an early associate of the publishers Einaudi. At this time Pavese developed a special interest in American literature, its archetypes and language (especially slang), partly as a reaction or protest against the 'pure' Italian emphasis encouraged by Fascist censors. From 1931 onwards he translated many American and English books, including work by Melville, Stein, and Dos Passos. His first collection of poems, *Lavorare stanca* (*Work Wearies*) was published in 1936. In May 1935 Pavese had been arrested as a result of associating with anti-Fascists and, specifically, receiving letters on behalf of his more politically committed and suspect lover, Tina Pizzardi, and refusing to betray her. He remained on the whole unaligned, becoming a Communist in 1945 to some extent out of guilt at his relative inaction during the war years, but maintaining an uneasy relationship with the party, whose non-individual focus he distrusted. The story which came out of his confinement in 1935–6 at Brancaleone in Calabria, *Il carcere* (*Prison*), 1948 (written in 1938–9) develops from the physical situation of an exile in the burning south not into an indictment of Fascist Italy but to a realisation of the irreducible solitariness of the central figure Stefano, prison or no prison.

After the Second World War Pavese worked at Einaudi as editorial director and produced most of his novels, including *Tra donne sole* (*Among Women Only*), 1949, and culminating in *La luna e i falò* (*The Moon and the Bonfires*), 1950. Throughout these works he is concerned with alienation or rootlessness. Realistic situations increasingly take on a mythic dimension; as he says in an August 1949 entry in his diary *Il mestiere di vivere* (*This Business of Living*), 1952, the writer should not at once amaze the reader with 'the symbolic fable of Ulysses' but should take 'a simple, ordinary man' and gradually 'give him the significance of a Ulysses'. *La luna* accordingly tells a simple story of a man's return, after 20 years, to the village where he grew up as an illegitimate child of unknown origin, and makes it a steadily more resonant or 'mythic' tale of loss (both of the past and of various futures which had been assumed or expected). On his return 'Anguilla' ('Eel': his sense of rootlessness is suggested by the fact that we know only his nickname) finds that there is still grinding poverty at Gaminella, the croft where he first lived, but that those natural features and people who gave him, temporarily, a sense of belonging – the hazel trees, the young ladies of La Mora with their pretensions, parasols, and apparent prospects – have disappeared. The fires of the title are lit first as a superstitious fertility rite (for which, as with moon superstitions, Anguilla's old friend the more rooted Nuto has a sympathy which he cannot feel), next in the climactic explosion of violence at Gaminella, and finally to remove all trace of the last La Mora girl, killed by the partisans when she changed sides too many times in the fighting of 1943–5. Except for Anguilla's understanding and material aid for the lame boy at Gaminella, Cinto, this is mostly a melancholy novel, a search for time past which discovers only partial and temporary consolations.

Pavese's suicide in August 1950 was carefully planned. One immediate cause was the failure of a love relationship, but this only contributed to the recurrent sense of alienation and depression recorded in the diaries and, less directly, the novels.


PIOZZI, Hester Lynch (1740–1821), is well known, under her first married name Mrs Thrale, as a friend of Dr Samuel Johnson. Her *Anecdotes* of Johnson appeared in 1786. In 1784, to Johnson's alarm, she married an Italian musician, Gabriele Piozzi. In *Observations and Reflections Made in the Course of a Journey Through France, Italy, and Germany*, 1789, she is, without being uncritical, generally well-disposed to her husband's country. Her friendly tone is conceived in opposition to the censoriousness and unwillingness to be pleased of many 18th century travellers, most obviously Tobias Smollett (◊Tuscany).

# LIGURIA

Leisured and literary English and Americans could, in the earlier 20th century, venture into the sunny, relatively temperate and 'civilized' Ligurian Riviera while remaining conveniently placed for the Côte d'Azur and Paris. With the exception of Genoa, the area was for most of its history less populous and cosmopolitan, more the land of turbulent seas and remote fishing villages in which Percy Bysshe Shelley (◊Rome) spent his last months in 1822.

Shelley lived at **Casa Magni**, by the beach at **San Terenzo** on the bay of Lerici, then a very small village. He had troubled dreams and visions (in one of which he saw 'the figure of himself which met him as he walked on the terrace and said to him "How long do you mean to be content?"'); he was haunted by the sea, as was Mary Shelley, who remembered that:

> 'an intense presentiment of coming evil brooded over my mind, and covered this beautiful place and genial summer with the shadow of coming misery . . . The beauty of the place seemed unearthly in its excess: the distance we were at from all signs of civilisation, the sea at our feet, its murmur or its roaring forever in our ears, – all these things led the mind to brood over strange thoughts, and, lifting it from everyday life, caused it to be familiar with the unreal.'

On 1 July 1822 Shelley left San Terenzo for the last time, sailing for Livorno.

Sea and sky were also essential to the poems of Eugenio Montale, who was born in Genoa in 1896 and spent many summers as a child and young adult at **Monterosso al Mare**, one of the **Cinque Terre** further up the coast from Lerici and La Spezia. Montale's work, especially the early *Ossi di seppia* (*Cuttlefish Bones*), 1925, dwells on marine scenes and images, the rough shore, rolled pebbles gnawed by salt, or the two jays which, 'whiteblue arrow-shots', flash towards the roaring waters; inland are cracked earth, cicadas, red ants amid the vetch. To some extent this is just nostalgia. But there is also a larger contrast between natural forces and human limitations; in *Mediterraneo* (Extract 3) the poet is futile, possessed only of tired 'dictionary letters' while the sea is endlessly powerful and mutable. (In recognizing and expressing the contrast, however, the poet does achieve some power).

Quieter seas inspired the sparer, more 'hermetic' poet Giuseppe Ungaretti) Veneto and North-East in the still morning of *Silenzio in Liguria* (*Silence in Liguria*), 1922 (Extract 2).

## SAN REMO

Edward Lear lived his last years at San Remo, dying at his Villa Tennyson in January 1888; he is buried in the **English Cemetery** next to Giorgis Kokalis, his Greek servant and companion on painting expeditions to the more exotic eastern climes which the warm and fertile Riviera could at least echo.

In 1902 San Remo was, to the ten-year-old Osbert Sitwell, as exciting as Greece or India had been to Lear. He first decided that Italy was 'my second country, the complement and perfect contrast to my own' when he was sent for a period of convalescence in the 'serene and aromatic air' of what was 'then a comfortable international settlement of square villas and oblong hotels, in cream and white and pink, set among tufted palms, with gardens of exhibition tangerine-trees' (*The Scarlet Tree*, 1949). Until the Second World War the lower town remained both comfortable and international, with its casinos, Russian Orthodox church (in Via Nuvolini) and Corso degli Inglesi. In the cinemas, where the young Italo Calvino) spent as much time as possible in the 1930s, there were of course American films. But beyond all this was *la pigna* ('the fir-cone'), the old upper town of steep cobbled alleyways. And much further up was the landscape of Calvino's *La strada di San Giovanni* (*The Road to San Giovanni*), 1962. Together he and his father would climb up the mule-tracks, past a vast range of plants which fascinated the botanist father and not, at the time, the future writer, to the ancestral Calvino home at **San Giovanni Battista** (Extract 4). Here the sea, distantly visible 'in a triangular cleft in the valley, V-shaped', seemed 'alien'. Up among the pines and chestnut-trees of the 'winding valleys of the Ligurian pre-Alps' was already 'his' (Calvino's) landscape. But it was only his time fighting here in a partisan group in 1944–5 which enabled him to use and describe it in his first novel *Il sentiero dei nidi di ragno* (*The Path to the Nest of Spiders*), 1947. It was then that 'the daily setting of my whole life' was rendered 'extraordinary and romantic'. A viewpoint had, as often in the more adventurous and fantastical stories which followed, been revealingly shifted.

## GENOA

In the middle ages Genoa was the rival of Venice and Pisa for maritime dominance in much of the Mediterranean. The magnificent facade of the **Cathedral of San Lorenzo** and the massy **Palazzo Ducale** proudly asserted its status. In the 14th century Genoese fleets, under the first Doge, Simon Boccanegra, defeated the Turks, the Tartars, and the Moors in close succession. But domestic politics were more compli-cated, as classes and clans, old and new nobility struggled for power or at the least revenge. Boccanegra, advanced by the popular party, was much conspired against by fellow aristocrats, although his position was not quite as impossibly difficult as it becomes in Verdi's opera *Simon Boccanegra*, 1857. Here, not content with supplanting the patri-cian party, he has seduced the daughter of its leader, Iacopo Fiesco; 25 years later he is happily reunited with the child of this liaison, and reconciled with Fiesco, but dies poisoned by a former suitor of his daughter. Not surprisingly, as he expires amid the splendours of the Palazzo Ducale – lovingly recreated or imagined by many a production – he wishes he had simply died at sea in his days of ecstatic marine glory.

Genoese politics may not have been quite as entwined as Verdi's librettist made them, but the internal feuding did help to subject the city to foreign domination. Eventually, however, some of the city's prestige was restored by another sea victor, the veteran admiral and administrator Andrea Doria (1466–1560), who established a new republic in 1528–9. (Doria was effectively an absolute prince, and the whole scheme was dependent on Spanish and imperial support, having been made possible by Doria's shift of allegiance, after many years, from François I of France to the Emperor Charles V.) The arts, and especially those involved in building and decorating palaces, flourished under the new order. Cramped edifices of sandstone and slate gave way to the more spacious and costly palaces inaugurated by Doria's own residence just outside the city walls, now the **Palazzo Doria-Pamphili** (not open to the public). The many fine palaces of what are now Via Balbi, Via Lomellini, and Via Garibaldi (formerly the Strada Nova) followed. The republican thinker Giuseppe Mazzi-ni, not on the whole a friend of palaces, was born in 1805 at 13 Via Lomellini, now the important **Museo del Risorgimento**.

Charles Dickens used Genoa as a base for his travels in Italy in 1844. He lived at first, before moving down into the city, in a 'Pink Jail' in Albaro, **Villa Bagnerello**, which survives in Via San Nazzaro. It was a 'sequestered spot' with a view of the bay, the hills, and 'monstrous old desolate houses and palaces . . . dotted all about', and trellised vines stretching down towards the seashore (*Pictures of Italy*, 1846). Dickens' first Italian city provided – or he sought out – subjects in plenty to be described with Dickensian gusto: palaces, gardens, splendour and squalor side by side (Extract 1); high views of the harbours; ravioli and 'small pieces of some unknown part of a calf, twisted into small shreds, fried, and served up in a great dish like whitebait'; wines of all sorts promiscuously classified, in the suburban trattorie, as either Champagne or Madeira, and ranging 'from cool Gruel up to old Marsala, and down again to apple Tea'.

## RAPALLO

Rapallo, beyond Genoa on the Riviera di Levante, was popular with writers as diverse as Thomas Mann (◊Venice), Ezra Pound (◊Tuscany) and the cartoonist and satirist Max Beerbohm (1872–1956). Beerbohm lived most of his life after 1910 (World Wars excepted) in seclusion at the **Villino Chiaro** on the once fairly peaceful coast road south of the town.

Pound lived at first in an apartment at 12 Via Marsala. W.B. Yeats, escaping the Dublin winter, came to see Pound and discussed with him, by the sea, the *Cantos*, examples of an art 'the opposite of mine'. Yeats describes Rapallo in *A Packet for Ezra Pound*, 1929:

> 'Houses mirrored in an almost motionless sea, mountains that shelter the bay from all but the south wind, bare brown branches of low vines and of tall trees blurring their outline as though with a soft mist; a verandahed gable a couple of miles away bringing to mind some Chinese painting, and Rapallo's thin line of broken mother of pearl along the water's edge.'

Such accessible delights made the town and bay increasingly crowded with foreigners. Yeats in a seaside café heard an English voice talking about singing *God save the King* and *For He's a Jolly Good Fellow* at choir-practice in 'the hotel at the end of the esplanade where they have the best beer.' Pound from 1929 often escaped, up the steep paths from Rapallo, to the flat he had found for the violinist Olga Rudge, mother of his daughter Maria, on the upper floor of a traditional peasant house in **Sant'Ambrogio.**

## OTHER LITERARY LANDMARKS

**Genoa**: Mazzini◊ is buried in the **Camposanto di Staglieno**.

**Portofino**: the Castello is the main setting of Elizabeth von Arnim's novel *The Enchanted April*, 1922.

## BOOKLIST

Calvino, Italo, *The Road to San Giovanni* [1962/1990], Tim Parks, trans, Jonathan Cape, London, 1993. **Extract 4.**

Calvino, Italo, *The Path to the Nest of Spiders* [1947], Archibald Colqohoun, trans, Ecco Press, New York, 1976.

Calvino, Italo, *Marcovaldo or the Seasons in the City* [1963], William Weaver, trans, Secker and Warburg, London, 1983.

Carpenter, Humphrey, *A Serious Character: the Life of Ezra Pound*, Faber, London, 1988.

Dickens, Charles, *Pictures from Italy* [1846], David Paroissien, ed, Robinson, London, 1989; Ecco Press, New York, 1988. **Extract 1.**

Hume, Kathryn, *Calvino's Fictions: Cogito and Cosmos*, Clarendon Press, Oxford, 1992.

Montale, Eugenio, *Poesie/Poems*, George Kay, trans, Edinburgh University Press, Edinburgh, 1964. **Extract 3.**

Sitwell, Sir Osbert, *The Scarlet Tree, Being the Second Volume of Left Hand, Right Hand! an Autobiography*, Macmillan, London, 1949.

Ungaretti, Giuseppe, *Selected Poems*, Patrick Creagh, trans, Penguin, Harmondsworth, 1971. **Extract 2.**

Weaver, William, *Calvino: an Interview and its Story*, in *Calvino Revisited*, Franco Ricci, ed, Dovehouse Editions, Ottawa, 1989.

Yeats, William Butler, *A Packet for Ezra Pound* [1929], Irish University Press, Shannon, 1970.

# *Extracts*

## (1) GENOA

### Charles Dickens, *Pictures from Italy,* 1846

*Dickens thrives on the extreme contrasts – 'stately edifices' and 'vilest squalor' side-by-side – of the city from which he toured Italy in 1844–5.*

The endless details of these rich Palaces; the walls of some of them, within, alive with masterpieces by Vandyke! The great, heavy, stone balconies, one above another, and tier over tier: with here and there, one larger than the rest, towering high up – a huge marble platform; the doorless vestibules, massively barred lower windows, immense public staircases, thick marble pillars, strong dungeon-like arches, and dreary, dreaming, echoing vaulted chambers: among which the eye wanders again, and again, and again, as every palace is succeeded by another – the terrace gardens between house and house, with green arches of the vine, and groves of orange-trees, and blushing oleander in full bloom, 20, 30, 40 feet above the street – the painted halls, mouldering, and blotting, and rotting in the damp corners, and still shining out in beautiful colours and voluptuous designs, where the walls are dry – the faded figures on the outside of the houses, holding wreaths, and crowns, and flying upward, and downward, and standing in niches, and here and there looking fainter and more feeble than elsewhere, by contrast with some fresh little Cupids, who on a more recently decorated portion of the front, are stretching out what seems to be the semblance of a blanket, but is, indeed, a sun-dial – the steep, steep, up-hill streets of small palaces (but very large palaces for all that) with marble terraces looking down into close by-ways – the magnificent and innumerable Churches; and the rapid passage from a street of stately edifices, into a maze of the vilest squalor, steaming with unwholesome stenches, and swarming with half-naked children and whole worlds of dirty people – make up, altogether, such a scene of wonder: so lively, and yet so dead: so noisy, and yet so quiet: so obtrusive, and yet so shy and lowering: so wide awake, and yet so fast asleep: that it is a sort of intoxication to a stranger to walk on, and on, and on, and look about him. A bewildering phantasmagoria, with all the inconsistency of a dream, and all the pain and all the pleasure of an extravagant reality!

## (2) LIGURIA

### Giuseppe Ungaretti, *Silence in Liguria*, 1922

*Ungaretti's limpid scene is a distillation of various influences including his contact in Paris with Symbolist poetry and the painting of Picasso and Matisse.*

A sinuously receding plain of water.

Still out of sight the sun
Bathes in its urns.

A colour of soft flesh passes across.
And suddenly she opens
The great calm of her eyes towards the bays.

The sunken shadow of the rocks dies.

Sweetness budding out from joyful hips,

True love is a gentle killing,

And I enjoy her
Suffused by the alabaster wing
Of an immobile morning.

## (3) MONTEROSSO AL MARE

### Eugenio Montale, *Mediterranean*, 1924

*Montale spent summers, from childhood to early adulthood, at a family villa at Monterosso. The sea in his sequence Mediterranean figures natural, ever-changing force as against human limitation.*

Ancient one, I am drunk with the voice
that escapes from your mouths when they lift open
like green bells and thrust back again,
backwards and fall away.
The house of my faraway summers
was at your side, you know,
there in the country where the sun broils
and mosquitoes cloud the air.
Today as then I turn to stone in your presence,
sea, but no longer worthy
– as I believe – of the solemn warning
of your breathing. You told me first of all
that the tiny ferment
of my heart was no more than an impulse
of yours, that in my depth of being was
your perilous law: to be immense and manifold
and hold as one:
and so empty myself of every foulness
as you do who dash upon the shores
among cork seaweed starfish
the unassailing rubbish of your void.

## (4) SAN REMO

### Italo Calvino, *The Road to San Giovanni*, 1962

*Calvino ponders, with characteristic self-reflexivity, the apparent gulf between his father's interests and his own. (Later he concludes that there is in fact a kinship between the one's passion for plants and growing things and the other's for words and writing.)*

I could recognize not a single plant or bird. The world of things was mute to me. The words that flowed and flowed inside my head weren't anchored to objects, but to emotions, fantasies, forebodings. And all it took was for a scrap of trampled newspaper to find its way beneath my feet and I would be engrossed in soaking up the writing on it, mutilated and unmentionable – names of theatres, actresses, vanities – and already my mind would be racing off, the sequence of images would go on for hours and hours as I walked silently behind my father, who might point to some leaves on the other side of a wall and say, 'Ypotoglaxia jasminifolia' (I'm inventing the names; I never learnt the real ones), 'Photophila wolfoides', he would say (I'm inventing; they were names of this sort), or 'Crotodendron indica', (of course I could perfectly well have looked up some real names, instead of inventing them, and maybe rediscovered what plants my father had actually been naming for me; but that would have been cheating, refusing to accept the loss that I inflicted on myself, the thousands of losses we inflict on ourselves and for which there is no making amends). (And yet, and yet, if I had written some real names of plants here it would have been a gesture of modesty and devotion on my part, finally resorting to that humble knowledge that my youth rejected in order to try my luck with other cards, unknown and treacherous, it would have been a way of making peace with my father, a demonstration of maturity, and yet I didn't do it, I indulged in this joke of invented names, this intended parody, sure sign that I am still resisting, arguing, sure sign that that morning march to San Giovanni is still going on, with its same discord, and that every morning of my life is still the morning when it's my turn to go with Father to San Giovanni.)

# Biographies and important works

CALVINO, Italo (1923–85), was born near Havana in Cuba. His mother was a botanist and his father a botanist and agronomist, to whose native San Remo the family returned in 1925. Calvino fought as a Communist partisan in 1943–5 and remained a member of the Communist party until he resigned in the aftermath of the suppression of the Hungarian rising of 1956. Between 1948 and 1984 he worked for the Turin publishing company Einaudi, which had published his 'neorealist' first novel Il sentiero dei nidi di ragni (The Path to the Nest of the Spiders), 1947, on the recommendation of Pavese (◊Piedmont). He lived in Paris during 1967–80 and then chiefly in Rome. His characteristic voice emerged in the trilogy of novels collected as I nostri antenati (Our Ancestors), 1960: the tone described by Kathryn Hume as 'mercurial, half detached but half involved, serious but never ponderous, ironically flirtatious, hilarious, desperate'. The events, settings and figures (Calvino distrusted both realist plotting and psychological 'character') in the trilogy are fantastic – the viscount cloven into good and bad halves, the tree-dwelling baron – but reflect the plight of the alienated modern citizen. Calvino's satirical insight relies often on the choice of an unexpected viewpoint, physical or mental: in *Marcovaldo ovvero le stagioni in città* (*Marcovaldo or the Seasons in the City*), 1963, the city is variously, comically and thought-provokingly transformed, its topography or society renegotiated, by snow, fog, or the innocence of the poor Marcovaldo and his dreams of country freedom. The many subsequent novels and stories continue Calvino's daring experiments with fantastic narrative, symbological rather than symbolic, often self-reflexive. As Hume points out, he loves symmetries but is also suspicious of them and of order in general; while some of the *Marcovaldo* stories come to a comic climax, more often their ending is slightly unexpected, off-key. *La strada di San Giovanni* (*The Road to San Giovanni*), 1962, republished posthumously in slightly revised form 1990, discusses his resistance to his father's love of order. While succeeding in expressing regret that father and son should thus have been divided, Calvino continues to enact his inevitable resistance in the free, digressive, questioning manner of the piece.

DICKENS, Charles (1812–70), was in Italy for nearly a year in 1844–5, travelling from Genoa to most of the other main cities as far south as Naples. *Pictures From Italy*, 1846, treats Italy and Italians with characteristic energy, humour, horror and enthusiasm. The emphasis is avowedly less on the paintings and statues which dominate many accounts of the time than on dramatic or romantic scenes and landscapes, strange, shocking or comic customs and incidents, picturesquely or pathetically decaying buildings. Satire is directed mainly at the perceived theatricality and insincerity of Roman Catholic observances. (This resulted in the withdrawal of Clarkson Stanfield, the intended illustrator of the book; Samuel Palmer replaced him, producing some appropriately lyrical landscape drawings.) Politically, *Pictures From Italy* is less forthright. 'Miseries and wrongs' are on the whole expected to speak for themselves, although the concluding section does blame them on 'years of neglect, oppression and misrule' and express a generalized hope that 'a noble people may be, one day, raised up from these ashes'.

Among the most memorable scenes in *Pictures* are an execution in Rome, where the sudden, instant drop of the head into a leather bag contrasts shockingly with the preceding detailed liveliness of the crowd, and the ascent, amid hot sulphurous smoke and red flames, to the brim of Vesuvius (Naples and Campania, Extract 8.)

MAZZINI, Giuseppe (1805–72), Genoese republican ideologist, founded the influential nationalist movement Giovine Italia (Young Italy) while in exile in France in 1831. Following a failed revolution in Savoy in 1833, Mazzini was condemned, in absentia, to death. In Switzerland in 1834 he launched Giovine Europa (Young Europe). In 1837 he settled in England, remaining until 1848 and returning later for extended periods. He was prominently involved, as a Tribune, in the abortive Roman Republic of 1849. He helped to plan failed insurrections in various

Italian cities during the 1850s, but saw instead the triumph of Cavour's monarchist ideal in the united Italy of 1861. Mazzini spent his last years in Italy, but discreetly since the 1833 death-sentence was never lifted. He died in Pisa.

Mazzini's ideas were the inspiration for much nationalist action and debate. He was also a prolific writer of political and literary essays and journalism and of works including *I doveri dell' uomo* (*The Duties of Man*), 1860, and *Note autobiografiche* (*Autobiographical Notes*), 1861–6, where he talks of the sacrifice involved in giving up for the good of the cause his dreams of writing plays and novels. Mazzini believed strongly in literature as 'a means, not an end', and was therefore implacably opposed to the idea of *l'art pour l'art*. Manzoni (◊Lombardy) was one of the authors of whom he most approved.

MONTALE, Eugenio (1896–1981), lived mostly in Genoa, apart from war service in 1917–18, until 1927. For a time he hoped to become a professional singer, a fact often linked with his stress on musicality in verse. He was director of the Vieusseux Library in Florence until in 1938 he was removed having refused to join the Fascist Party. From 1947 he lived in Milan, where he worked principally for the *Corriere della sera*, most fruitfully as music critic between the mid-1950s and late 1960s. In 1975 he was awarded the Nobel Prize for Literature.

Montale's aesthetic was defined in opposition to the rhetorical, politically committed work of Carducci (◊Emilia-Romagna) and D'Annunzio (◊Lombardy). He struggled against 'our heavy, polysyllabic language' to 'excavate' a new lyrical clarity. At the same time he admits that all language, like all things human, is limited and inflexible by comparison with a larger force like the sea of the sequence *Mediterraneo* in *Ossi di seppia* (*Cuttlefish Bones*), 1925. Here (see Extract 3) a cleansing process would result from acceptance that 'the tiny ferment/of my heart was no more than an impulse of yours'. But – given the difficulty of such acceptance – Montale's emphasis is usually more overtly personal than that of T.S. Eliot, with whom he has often been compared. A number of poems in *Le occasioni* (*The Occasions*), 1939 and *La bufera e altro* (*The Storm and Others*), 1956, are concerned with Clizia, a figure with many different functions – real Jewish woman, muse made flesh, Beatrice-figure, goddess, challenger, seer. During the 1970s, starting with *Satura: 1962–70* (*Miscellany: 1962–70*), 1971, Montale published several volumes in a more direct, less lyrical manner than the earlier collections. *Xenia*, in *Satura*, is a meditation on his dead wife. He tells her that his poetry of 'non-belonging' (*inappartenenza*, meaning that he is not identified with any group or movement) belongs to her if to anyone.

# EMILIA-ROMAGNA

'Bologna rises, dark and turreted into the clear winter sky, whilst glad sunshine gleams from the snow-capped hill above.'
*Giosuè Carducci,*
*In the Piazza of San Petronio*

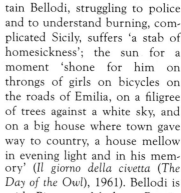

Leonardo Sciascia's (◊Sicily) Captain Bellodi, struggling to police and to understand burning, complicated Sicily, suffers 'a stab of homesickness'; the sun for a moment 'shone for him on throngs of girls on bicycles on the roads of Emilia, on a filigree of trees against a white sky, and on a big house where town gave way to country, a house mellow in evening light and in his memory' (*Il giorno della civetta* (*The Day of the Owl*), 1961). Bellodi is from **Parma**, one of the cities – with Piacenza, Modena, Reggio Emilia, and Bologna – strung along the Roman Via Aemilia, which ran from Milan to the sea at Rimini across a huge and famously fertile plain of cornfields, orchards and pastures. Such cities were, for J.A. Symonds◊, writing before industrialization somewhat blurred their edges, 'all like large country houses: walking out of their gates, you seem to be stepping from a door or window that opens on a trim and beautiful garden, where mulberry-tree is married to mulberry by festoons of vines, and where the maize and sunflower stand together in rows between patches of flax and hemp'.

North of the Roman road are the cities of Ferrara and Ravenna, now part of the same fertile plain thanks to the gradual drainage of the surrounding malarial marshes. Their earlier defensive separation helped make Ravenna a late Roman and Byzantine capital and goes some way to explaining the rise of Ferrara to local dominance under the house of Este between the 14th and 16th centuries.

**Bologna** has since the middle ages been noted for the two areas of expertise mentioned by John Evelyn (◊Lazio) in 1645: 'This town . . . is a famous University, situate in one of the richest spots of Europe for all sorts of provisions'. Students have included Dante (◊Florence), Petrarch (◊Veneto and North-East), Tasso◊, who was forced to flee after writing incautious lampoons on his learned seniors, and in

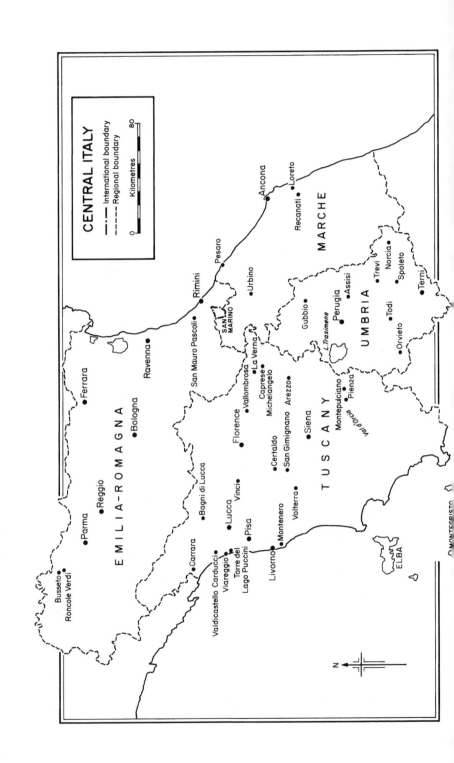

CENTRAL ITALY

- - - International boundary
- - - - Regional boundary

0     Kilometres     80

N

EMILIA-ROMAGNA

Busseto
Roncole Verdi
Parma
Reggio
Ferrara
Bologna
Ravenna
Carrara
Bagni di Lucca
San Mauro Pascoli
Rimini
SAN MARINO
Pesaro

Valdicastello Carducci
Viareggio
Torre del Lago Puccini
Lucca
Vinci
Pisa
Montenero
Livorno
Volterra

TUSCANY

Florence
Vallombrosa
La Verna
Caprese Michelangelo
Arezzo
Certaldo
San Gimignano
Siena
Montepulciano
Pienza
Val d'Orcia

Urbino

MARCHE

Ancona
Loreto
Recanati

UMBRIA

Gubbio
L. Trasimene
Perugia
Assisi
Todi
Orvieto
Trevi
Norcia
Spoleto
Terni

ELBA

MONTECRISTO

modern times Giorgio Bassani♭. From 1860 to 1904 the poet Giosuè Carducci was Professor of Italian Eloquence at Bologna, arriving as a young radical and retiring, a revered member of the establishment, to what is now his memorial museum, the **Casa di Carducci**, at 5 Viale Carducci. Writing in an increasingly industrialized city, and partly in reaction to his own reluctant conversion to monarchism, Carducci looked back nostalgically to the time of the medieval communes evoked by buildings like the city's main church, **San Petronio** (Extract 1). Nearby, in Piazza Porta di Ravegnana, are the most conspicuous of Carducci's towers caressed 'by the wings of long centuries', the **Torre degli Asinelli**, built in 1109–10, and the lower **Torre Garisenda**. Nearer, in the (restored) **Palazzo del Re Enzo**, is the destination of the 'Consuls with their conquered kings', or at least king: Enzo, King of Sardinia, captured at the battle of Fossalta in 1249, was confined here until his death in 1272.

Evelyn's 'provisions' included sausages and 'great quantities of Parmegiano cheese . . . which makes some of their shops perfume the streets with no agreeable smell'. Usually responses to the gastronomic capital *Bologna la grassa* have been more positive. Visitors at one time, however, came also to see the graceful, classicizing, often rather ethereal paintings of the 17th century Bolognese school, still well represented in the **Pinacoteca Nazionale**. Esteemed above all were the Carracci family and Guido Reni, who was long popular enough to be known, in the same fashion as Raphael or Titian, simply as 'Guido'. But tastes changed to the point where, in 1847, John Ruskin (♭Venice) could denounce Reni as insincere, the representative of 'a feeble and fallen school'. The ensuing century of neglect helped to remove Bologna from most travellers' itineraries.

**Parma** too, and its baptistery of pink Veronese marble, would surely have been celebrated more frequently if it had featured on the more usual modern tourist routes. Stendhal (♭Lombardy) does set *La Chartreuse de Parme* (*The Charterhouse of Parma*), 1839, here in name, but this Parma, with a huge citadel and high tower in which Fabrice is imprisoned and a Charterhouse to which he eventually withdraws, is clearly not meant for the real city. In fact, as A.E. Greaves argues in his book on Stendhal and Italy, Parma is chosen as the place for the ridiculous reactionary court of Ernest-Ranuce IV because real targets like the repressive regime of nearby Modena at the time could not be so openly satirized. (Parma's real ruler, Napoleon's widow Marie-Louise, was too negligible a political quantity to complain very loudly even if she had wanted to.)

The Roman road ended at the port of Ariminium, now the beach resort of **Rimini**. Augustus erected the arch (**Arco d'Augusto**, c.27 B.C.) at the junction of the Via Aemilia and the Via Flaminia. But the city's literary reputation is connected with the deeds and misfortunes of its medieval and renaissance Malatesta despots. In 1285 Giovanni

Malatesta killed his wife Francesca da Rimini and her lover, his brother Paolo, probably at the castle of **Gradara**, north-west of Pesaro; the tale is told by Francesca in Dante's *Inferno* (*Hell*), after 1309, (Extract 5). Sigismondo Malatesta (1417–68) was a rare combination, as the historian Jacob Burckhardt put it, of 'unscrupulousness, impiety, military skill and high culture'. He commissioned work from Pisanello, Piero della Francesca and Alberti and transformed an existing church into the **Tempio Malatestiano**, a boldly classical celebration of his own secular glory. For Ezra Pound (◊Tuscany), in *A Guide to Kulchur*, 1938, the Tempio is the emphatic statement of Sigismondo, the 'entire man' of his 'Malatesta Cantos'. It may be 'a jumble and a junk shop' but it 'registers a concept. There is no other single man's effort equally registered'.

North-west of Rimini, near the **Rubicone** – the river Rubicon which divided the Roman provinces of Italy and Cisalpine Gaul and which Julius Caesar illegally and proverbially crossed with his army in 49 B.C. – is **San Mauro Pascoli**, named after the poet Giovanni Pascoli◊ who was born there in 1855. In 1867 Pascoli's father, an estate manager, was murdered on the road from Cesena by a personal enemy who was never brought to justice; his mother died a year later. For the adult Pascoli, living elsewhere, the landscape around San Mauro became an image of the childhood that preceded these events, the lost idyll: there are jays in the elms and lustrous ducks on the ponds, whispering poplars, jasmine, mimosa; along the banks of the Rio Salto (a local stream) the child sees in imagination the bright breast-plates of the knights errant; always in the distance is 'the azure vision of San Marino' (*Rio Salto*, 1887; *Romagna*, 1897).

## FERRARA

Ludovico Ariosto◊, in *Orlando Furioso* (*Orlando Mad*), 1516–32, borrows a useful classical device whereby actual (or idealised) hindsight becomes poetic foresight. So Merlin can prophesy from the tomb that the warrior woman Bradamante will be the mother, by the heroic Ruggiero, of a race of dukes, marquises, 'mighty cavaliers/And captains', just princes under whose sway 'Mankind will see renewed the world of gold'. Prominent among them, of course, will be Ariosto's patrons Duke Alfonso I d'Este and his brother Cardinal Ippolito, and their father Duke Ercole I.

Ercole I (ruled 1471–1505) is celebrated by Ariosto as a soldier, drainer of marshes to set Ferrara in 'a fertile plain' (initiating a project which went on into modern times), and creator of 'More amplitude within new walls' – 'temples, palaces to make her fair/He'll build, and theatres, and many a square'. This 'amplitude' was the so-called *addizione ercolea* or Herculean extension of 1493–1503 by which the old city, vulnerable to attack and increasingly overcrowded (there were up to 30,000 inhabitants) was dramatically enlarged under the direction of the architect Biagio Rossetti. Many of the buildings have now been lost or transformed, but the broad avenues first established by the *addizione* remain a distinctive feature of Ferrara. Jacob Burckhardt hailed it in 1860 as the first piece of modern town-planning.

Ercole put his palaces, theatres and squares to good use. There were glorious entries and festivities, buildings draped in cloth-of-gold, the **Castello Estense** linked to the **Cathedral** by ramps for especially grand occasions, jousts and races (most Italian cities once had their equivalent of the Sienese *Palio*). There were also plays, mostly either in the great squares (the predecessors of the modern Piazza della Repubblica or Piazza Castello) or in the Gran Salone of the new ducal palace, a complex of buildings which, unlike the older Castello Estense to which it was connected, did not survive later 16th century fires and demolitions. It was under Ercole's aegis that many of the plays of Plautus and Terence were, beginning in 1486 with Plautus' *Menaechmi*, staged for the first time since antiquity not among scholars, but (in translation) for large audiences. Performances were given most often on festival occasions like the wedding of Ercole's daughter Isabella d'Este to the Marquis of Mantua in 1490 or the coming of Lucrezia Borgia at carnival-time in 1502 as wife of the future Alfonso I. In Lucrezia's case the welcome had to be impressive enough to satisfy – by report at least – her doting and dangerous father Pope Alexander VI as well as to indicate the honour of the house she was joining. There were processions, nightly banquets and entertainments, and productions of five comedies by Plautus (in Latin this time) which Isabella, visiting from Mantua, confessed to finding somewhat wearing; a performance length of five to six hours was achieved by the inclusion of spectacular descents in cloud machines and interludes of song, dance, and mock battles.

Alfonso I did not share his father's passion for plays. And understandably – his hold on power was precarious amid the shifting alliances of such larger powers as the Papacy, France, and Venice – he took a greater interest in actual warfare than the heroic romance version of Ariosto. He found him more useful, indeed, as regional governor, adviser, diplomat, and comrade in arms than as court poet. But the court remained fertile ground for poets and scholars. Ercole's immediate predecessors had built up an extensive library ranging from rare classical texts to popular romance, and the university had flourished since its foundation in 1442; its principal luminary, the humanist and Greek scholar Guarino of Verona (1374–1460), had helped to institute the tradition of learning at court. The Estensi, poetically inclined or not, found Ariosto's glorification (with occasional subtle hints at criticism) politically acceptable, but it was crucial too to the development of an *Orlando Furioso* in which past and present are continually counterpointed to ironic, comic or perspective-shifting effect.

Lucrezia Borgia, living in the present Castello (transformed a generation before from grim fortress complete with *sala di decapitazione* to habitable palace) was a good source of patronage and inspiration. For example she attracted from Pietro Bembo (◊Veneto and North-East) love sonnets, well-crafted letters and the dedication of *Gli asolani*. The myth of Lucrezia as wicked poisoner and serial adultress is partly the result of the nefarious deeds of her father and brother, partly a later male fantasy. Somewhat more innocently, male writers have made a fetish of Lucrezia's glowing golden hair: Bembo's heart winged its way, in courtly verse, into the 'silken hoard' and was trapped when she bound it; she sent him some tresses, which were later preserved with the Bembo correspondence in the Ambrosian Library in Milan, whence Byron stole a single hair in 1816. Théophile Gautier (◊Naples and Campania), recalling 'cette blonde Lucrèce' and Byron's enviable trophy, is aware that Lucrezia cannot have been the 'monster' of legend, but implies that this is rather a shame as he gazes at the Castello, where glorious excesses, poisonings and murders must have taken place during that lost time of Italian 'refinement and crime'.

Less lurid imaginings are possible at the quiet house and garden (now 67 Via Aristo) to which Ariosto retired from court distractions in the mid-1520s. Here he worked on the final version of *Orlando*, published in 1532. In the older (pre-*addizione ercolea*) part of the town, is the **Palazzo Paradiso** where he lived for a time in his youth and was buried in 1533. The tomb, with bust of the poet and trumpeting figure of Fame, is reached through the reading rooms of the **Biblioteca Ariostea**. Near the tomb valuable items from the library's collection are displayed, including autograph poems and letters by Torquato Tasso and by the Ferrarese playwright, story-teller and literary theorist Giambattista Giraldi Cinzio◊.

A sadder sight is **Tasso's Prison**, one of the dark, low-vaulted underground cells in what survives of the Ospedale Sant'Anna behind Corso Giovecca. (Admission can be obtained from the reception desk at the Conservatorio di Musica Girolamo Frescobaldi in Via Gaetano Previati.) Tasso, who suffered from recurrent fever, drank to excess, and was morbidly sensitive to any imagined slight, was incarcerated after some of his more violent outbursts at the court of Duke Alfonso II. He remained at the 'hospital' from 1579 to 1586. Soon afterwards, a romantic tradition developed that his madness, his imprisonment, or both, resulted from his presumption in falling in love with the Duke's sister Leonora (to whom he addressed some poems). As a figure of the misunderstood or alienated artist Tasso appealed powerfully to later writers including Goethe and Byron, who both came to see the cell. In fact it has long been clear that Tasso was confined here, if at all, only initially or in his 'madder' moods. But, embittered by the apparent lack of response to his pleading and threatening letters to the Duke, the court, and anyone who might intervene on his behalf, Tasso did suffer during those seven years at least a version of the 'Long years of outrage, calumny, and wrong; /Imputed madness, prison'd solitude,/ And the mind's canker in its savage mood' imagined in Byron's *The Lament of Tasso*, 1817.

In happier days, Tasso had pleased the court of Alfonso II (still the 'magnanimo Alfonso' of the first canto of his *Gerusalemme Liberata* (*Jerusalem Delivered*), completed in 1575). The high point of the festivities for Alfonso's wedding to Barbara of Austria in 1565 had been his entertainment *Il tempio d'Amore* (*The Temple of Love*), featuring artfully constructed pyramids, temples, rocks and forest and illuminated by 1000 huge candles. The Knights of Virtue and Honour, led by the Duke himself, proceeded through various tests and scenic wonders to the bright Temples of Love, Virtue and Honour. And in 1573 Tasso's subsequently much imitated pastoral play *Aminta* was performed, by the travelling company the Gelosi, at the (no longer extant) Belvedere palace on a small island in the River Po. Aspects of such plays and entertainments – love virtuous and base, matched and mismatched, heroic combat, frustrated or rewarded endeavour – nourished *Gerusalemme liberata*. This epic of the First Crusade, more concentrated and earnest than *Orlando Furioso*, appealed more to neo-classical tastes. But both poems, rooted in the culture of Ferrara, had a European following – sometimes overlapping, sometimes opposed – which lasted for centuries after the city itself, forfeit to the papacy at the death of Alfonso II without male heir in 1597, had lost its d'Este glory. (One branch of the family continued to rule at Modena.)

Centuries of relative obscurity followed. In 1786 Goethe (◊Naples and Campania) was in low spirits in this 'beautiful, depopulated city in the middle of a flat plain' once animated by a brilliant court. Dickens (◊Liguria), 60 years later, found it picturesquely deserted, with so much grass growing 'in the silent streets, that anyone might make hay there, literally, while the sun shines'. Among the inhabitants of this quieter city was a substantial Jewish community, originally welcomed by the Estensi and at least tolerated under papal rule. The ghetto, in the old quarter, was centred on Via Vignatagliata and Via Mazzini, the street of the synagogue of Giorgio Bassani's *Il giardino dei Finzi-Contini* (*The Garden of the Finzi-Continis*), 1962. Emancipation from the 1860s enabled many of Ferrara's Jews to assimilate, achieving professional positions (even membership of the Fascist party in some cases) and to move freely along the airy avenues of the *addizione* – Corso Giovecca, Viale Cavour and above all Corso Ercole I D'Este, leading, as in Bassani, 'straight as a die from the Castle to the Wall of the Angels, with dark, imposing dwelling-houses on either side . . . and, high in the distance, a backdrop of brick red, leafy green, and sky that seems to lead you into infinity'. Within the wall, at the end of the Corso, is the (fictional, unlike much of Bassani's Ferrara) estate of the Finzi-Contini, seemingly an enchanted land of its own, far from the past of the ghetto and, at first, from the threat posed by the racial laws promulgated in 1938, the first step on the road to internment and, from 1943, deportation to Germany. While the earlier Finzi-Contini and Alberto, the son who dies in 1942, have their grand memorial in the Hebrew Cemetery, Micòl Finzi-Contini and her parents have no known resting-place. (See Extract 3 and Lazio, Extract 1.)

## RAVENNA

Early in the fifth century the 'open country' of Italy became, as Edward Gibbon (◊Rome) puts it, 'covered with a deluge of barbarians'. Since 'the adjacent country, to the distance of many miles, was a deep and impassable morass', the Emperor Honorius, 'anxious only for his personal safety retired to the perpetual confinement' of Ravenna, which thus became the capital in turn of the last western emperors, the Ostrogothic kings of Italy, and the Exarchs or viceroys installed after the city's recapture by Belisarius, general of the eastern emperor Justinian and subject of Robert Graves's novel *Count Belisarius*, 1938.

Successive rulers expressed their power (often inseparable from their devotion) in the mosaic decoration of Ravenna's churches. The small domed **Mausoleum of Galla Placidia**, Honorius' sister, surges with fruit-trees, stags slaking their thirst at sacred founts, transfigured prophets. Theodoric of the Ostrogoths left his mark in the mosaics of **Sant' Apollinare Nuovo**, including representations of Classis – Augustus' port, from which the sea had already begun to retreat – and of his palace. (The current mosaics date from c. 550, early in the years of Byzantine rule, but are thought likely to resemble those of about fifty years earlier which they replaced.) Much more than the relatively sober mosaics, however, the huge stone **Mausoleum of Theodoric**, built outside the old walls to the north of the city, and the story – accurate or not – that a suit of golden armour was found there only to disappear again, suggest a mythic figure. Indeed he went on to feature in medieval heroic saga and romance, in Germany, as the mighty 'Dietrich von Bern' (i.e. from Verona, his other chief city). Less happily, the real Theodoric is remembered for putting to death his former counsellor, the philosopher Boethius◊.

In the mosaics of **San Vitale** Justinian, the empress Theodora and their courtiers stand confident and bejewelled. (The courtier who stands between the crowned and nimbused emperor and the cross-bearing archbishop Maximianus may be Belisarius.) **Sant' Apollinare in Classe** (the former Classis) and its mosaics also date from Justinian's reign (527–65). In the 19th century, when John Addington Symonds came to the church, it was still separated from the town by a 'vast fen', visited only hurriedly by the fever-fearing devout, and tended by an old monk 'left alone to sweep the marsh water from his church floor' while Christ sits enthroned and 'the saints around him glitter with their pitiless, uncompromising eyes and wooden gestures, as if 12 centuries had not passed over them, and they were nightmares only dreamed last night, and rooted in a sick man's memory' (*Sketches and Studies in Italy and Greece*, 1874).

The Byzantines lost most of their western outposts once more in the eighth century. Italy fragmented increasingly into city-states under nominal control of the Holy Roman Empire or, later, the rival jurisdiction of the Papacy, and Ravenna's pre-eminence, its great mosaic days, were over. But it re-enters literary history in the early 14th century with its rulers of the Da Polenta family, under whose protection the exiled Dante (◊Florence) lived for his last few years. As a result Ravenna has a literary trophy much coveted in Tuscany and elsewhere, **Dante's tomb**. His bones, originally buried in the church of San Francesco, were rediscovered and transferred to the present small neo-classical shrine in 1865.

Ravenna and the Romagna came under Venetian control and then, from 1512, papal. Byron (◊Venice), with his liberal sympathies and unorthodox lifestyle, proved something of an embarrassment to the papal authorities when he lived in Ravenna for much of 1820 and 1821. (Life was made easier, however, by his friendship with Count Giuseppe Alborghetti, second only to the Cardinal Legate in the government of the area.) Byron came to Ravenna because it was the home of Countess Teresa Guiccioli, his relationship with whom had begun in Venice; her elderly husband supported the political status quo, but her father and brother, the Counts Gamba, were keen reformists. Most of Byron's time in Ravenna was spent at **Palazzo Guiccioli**, at 54 Via Cavour. At first he lived on the upper floor. His liaison with the Countess – living below with her half-complaisant, half-suspicious husband – was conducted with the aid of servants watching the stairs in the best dramatic tradition. This was an improvement, at least, on the situation before he moved into the Palazzo, when he could see Teresa only in its 'great Saloon', 'so that,' he wrote to his friend Richard Belgrave Hoppner, 'if I come away with a Stiletto in my gizzard some fine afternoon – I shall not be astonished'. The Count contented himself with one or two angry outbursts only. Matters became simpler once, in July 1820, Teresa, granted a separation from her husband by the Pope, left the Palazzo to join her father.

Byron stayed on. During his residence in the Palazzo he wrote – mainly at night – productively, completing amongst much else three cantos of *Don Juan* and his satirical account of George III's arrival in heaven, *The Vision of Judgement*. (Against all justice, the King finally slips in while St Peter is distracted.) But he was also alert to local events. Through the Gamba connection he became involved with one of the *carbonaro* secret societies; he records in his Ravenna journal on 1 May 1821 how several months earlier, when revolution had been in the air, 'I had furbished up my arms – & got my apparatus ready for taking a turn with the Patriots – having my drawers full of their proclamations – oaths – & resolutions – & my lower rooms of their hidden weapons of most calibres'. The time had not been ripe for insurrection (a rebellion in Naples had foundered; Ravenna remained a papal city until 1860). The shots which Byron did hear fired in anger in Ravenna had come earlier, on the evening of 9 December 1820. The victim was Luigi Dal Pinto, commandant of the papal soldiers in Ravenna. Byron found him nearly dead, and had the body carried to his house (Extract 4). The brute fact of sudden death impressed him more than the political context. Although the 'weapons of most calibres' might have been used against the same Dal Pinto, Byron repeats his narrative in several letters and includes a stylized version of it in the fifth Canto of *Don Juan*, the occasion for reflections on the absurdity of the fact that one who had been 'The foremost in the charge or in the sally,/Should now be butchered in a civic alley'. With horrible and puzzling suddenness 'Five bits of lead,/Or three or two or one send very far'.

In July 1821 the Gambas were banished. Teresa reluctantly agreed to follow them to Florence. Byron, with less flattering reluctance ('It is awful work, this love, and prevents all a man's projects of good or glory') eventually left Ravenna at the end of October.

## OTHER LITERARY LANDMARKS

**Bologna**: the tomb of Giosuè Carducci◊ is in the **Cimitero della Certosa**.

**Bologna**: the oldest surviving building connected with the University is the 14th century **Collegio di Spagna**. The mid-16th-century **Archiginnasio** contains an anatomy theatre of 1637.

**Ferrara**: the **Palazzo dei Diamanti** or **Schifanoia** ('Banish Boredom') palace, known for its 15th century frescoes, was sometimes the venue for dramatic performances in the 16th century.

**Ferrara**: on the wall outside the **Castello Estense** in Corso Martiri della Libert are plaques in memory of the 11 Ferrarese citizens shot by Fascists on 15 November 1943. The killings are the subject of one of the *Cinque storie ferraresi* (*Five Stories of Ferrara*), 1956, by Giorgio Bassani◊.

**Reggio** was the birthplace of Ludovico Ariosto◊, who saluted it as 'smiling'. It was governed in 1487–94 by Ferrara's earlier courtier-poet Boiardo◊.

**Le Roncole**, now **Roncole Verdi**: birthplace of the opera-composer Giuseppe Verdi (1813–1901). Also near Busseto, at Sant'Agata di Villanova, is Villa Verdi, where he wrote and farmed from 1849.

# BOOKLIST

Ariosto, Ludovico, *Orlando Furioso (The Frenzy of Orlando): a Romantic Epic*, Barbara Reynolds, trans, Penguin, Harmondsworth, 1975. **Extract 2.**

Bassani, Giorgio, *The Garden of the Finzi-Continis* [1962], Isabel Quigly, trans, Quartet, London, 1974. **Extract 3.**

Bassani, Giorgio, *Five Stories of Ferrara* [1956], William Weaver, trans, Harcourt Brace Jovanovich, New York, 1971.

Brand, C.P., *Torquato Tasso: a Study of the Poet and his Contribution to English Literature*, Cambridge University Press, Cambridge, 1965.

Burckhardt, Jacob, *The Civilization of the Renaissance in Italy*, S.G.C. Middlemore, trans, Penguin, Harmondsworth, 1990.

Byron, George Gordon, Lord, '*Between Two Worlds': Byron's Letters and Journals Volume 7, 1820*, Leslie A. Marchand, ed, John Murray, London, 1977. **Extract 4**

Byron, George Gordon, Lord, *The Complete Poetical Works*, Jerome J. McGann, ed, Clarendon Press, Oxford, 1980–93.

Carducci, Giosuè, *Selected Verse*, David H. Higgins, ed and trans, Aris and Phillips, Warminster, 1994. **Extract 1.**

Dante Alighieri, *The Divine Comedy: Inferno*, Mark Musa, trans [1971], Penguin, Harmondsworth, 1984. **Extract 5.**

Evelyn, John, *The Diary of John Evelyn*, Guy de la Bédoyère, ed, Boydell, Woodbridge, 1995.

Greaves, A.E., *Stendhal's Italy: Themes of Political and Religious Satire*, Exeter University Press, Exeter, 1995.

Pascoli, Giovanni, *Selected Poems*, P.H. Horne, ed, Manchester University Press, Manchester, 1983. [Italian text with English introduction and notes].

Pound, Ezra, *A Guide to Kulchur* [1938], Peter Owen, London, 1952.

Radcliff-Umstead, Douglas, *The Exile Into Eternity: a Study of the Narrative Writings of Giorgio Bassani*, Associated University Presses, London and Toronto, and Fairleigh Dickinson University Press, Rutherford, 1987.

Stendhal (Henri Beyle), *The Charterhouse of Parma* [1839], C.K. Scott Moncrieff, trans, David Campbell, London, 1992.

Symonds, John Addington, *Sketches in Italy and Greece*, London, 1874.

Tasso, Torquato, *Jerusalem Delivered [1581]. The Edward Fairfax Translation*, Roberto Weiss, intr, Centaur Press, London, 1962.

# *Extracts*

## (1) BOLOGNA

### Giosuè Carducci,
### *In the Piazza of San Petronio*, 1877

*Carducci, at the centre of medieval Bologna, evokes its days as a free city commune in the 13th century. 'Conquered kings' refers particularly to the capture of King Enzo, son of the Emperor Frederick II, in 1249.*

Bologna rises, dark and turreted, into the clear winter sky,
whilst glad sunshine gleams from the snow-capped hill above.

It is that sweet time when the setting sun greets
the towers and your temple, saintly Petronius;

Those towers whose battlements the wings of long centuries caress,
and the solitary summit of your solemn shrine.

The sky reflects a cold adamantine light;
and the air like a silvery veil lies

Over the square, and softens the contours of the surrounding masses,
which the defending arms of our forefathers raised in dark stone.

The sun dawdles watchfully over high crests and gables, and plays its
slow, glad beams of purple light,

And appears to rouse the spirit of times past from the grey stone
and the dark vermilion brick;

And through the frozen air it arouses nostalgia for those
blazing Maytimes, for those warm, scented evenings,

When noble ladies would lead dances in the square
at the return of their Consuls with their conquered kings.

So the fleeting Muse smiles upon my verses, in which there lingers
still an empty yearning for the grace of ancient times.

## (2) FERRARA

### Ludovico Ariosto,
### *Orlando Furioso (Orlando Mad)*, 1516–32

*Ariosto, court poet of Alfonso I of Ferrara, draws on classical romance, and contemporary sources in his vast poem. Orlando*

(Charlemagne's paladin Roland) has just discovered that
Angelica, for whom and for whose love he has long quested,
has married a common soldier in the shepherd's house where he
is staying. Within a few stanzas he will descend into violent, tree-
uprooting, rock-hurling frenzy.

When he can give his sorrow fuller rein,
Fleeing all others, in his room alone,
The tears run streaming down his cheeks like rain.
Sigh follows upon sigh and groan on groan.
Fumbling and groping for his bed, in vain
He seeks relief; harder than any stone,
Sharper than nettles, is that downy nest
Whereon Orlando never can find rest.

Then in his travail suddenly he knows
That in this very bed on which he lies
His love has lain, and often, in the close
Embrace that nothing of herself denies.
No less abhorrence now Orlando shows
And no less quickly from that couch he flies
Than we may see a startled peasant leap
Who spies a snake where he lay down to sleep.

The bed, the house, the shepherd he now hated.
His one desire was but to get away.
Not for the moon, not for the dawn he waited,
Not for the streaks of white which herald day.
His arms, his horse he first appropriated
And where the forest's heart of darkness lay
Shrouded in densest foliage, he rode
And to his grief gave vent in solitude.

His tears, his groans, his sobbings never cease.
All night, all day, in anguish and in pain,
Fleeing all habitats, he finds no peace.
Lying unsheltered on the hard terrain,
He marvels at the fount his eyes release,
That such a living spring they should contain.
His sighing too an endless rhythm keeps
And to himself he muses as he weeps. . . .

'I am not he, I am not he I seem.
He who Orlando was is dead and gone,
Slain by his lady, so untrue to him,
By her ingratitude, alas, undone.
I am his spirit whom the Fates condemn
To suffer in this dread infernal zone,

No body, but a shadow which must rove,
A warning to all those who trust in love.'

## (3) FERRARA

### Giorgio Bassani,
### *The Garden of the Finzi-Continis*, 1962

*The narrator and Micòl, with whom he will later fall in love,
speak for the first time at the edge of her family's large estate
bounded by the 15th-century city walls. From the beginning of
the novel, the reader has known that she and most of the family
will die in the deportation of Italian Jews to Germany from
1943.*

How many years have gone by since that remote June afternoon? Over
thirty, and yet, if I shut my eyes, Micòl Finzi-Contini is still there,
looking over the garden wall, watching me, talking to me. She was little
more than a child in 1929, a thin fair 13-year-old with large light
magnetic eyes, and I a stuck-up, dandified, extremely middle-class
brat in short trousers, whom the first whiff of trouble at school was
enough to throw into the most childish despair. We stared at each
other. Above her the sky was blue, all of a piece, a warm, already
summer, sky without a trace of cloud. Nothing could change it, and
nothing has, in fact, changed it, at least in my memory.

'Well, d'you want to or don't you?' said Micòl.

'I . . . I'm not sure . . . ' I started to say, pointing to the wall. 'It
seems terribly high to me.'

'Because you haven't seen it properly,' she retorted impatiently.
'Look there, and there, and there,' and she pointed to make me see.
'There are masses of notches, and even a nail at the top. I stuck it in
myself.'

'Yes, there are footholds all right,' I murmured uncertainly, 'but . . . '

'Footholds!' she broke in at once, and burst out laughing, 'I call
them notches.'

'Well, you're wrong, because they're called footholds,' I said, acid
and obstinate. 'Anyone can see you've never been up a mountain.'

## (4) RAVENNA

### George Gordon, Lord Byron, letter to Thomas
### Moore, 9 December 1820

*In his response to the assassination of Luigi Dal Pinto, Byron
combines curiosity about and frustration with Italian ways,*

*human sympathy, horror at (and fascination by) the fact of sudden death, and acute self-awareness. To an extent he simply wants to show himself in a good light to his valued friend, the Irish poet Thomas Moore, but the probably not unjustified image of himself as a leader, taking charge as others founder, foreshadows Byron's departure from Italy to serve the cause of Greek independence three years later.*

I open my letter to tell you a fact, which will show you the state of this country better than I can. The commandant of the troops is *now* lying *dead* in my house. He was shot at a little past eight o' clock, about two hundred paces from my door. I was putting on my great-coat to visit Madame la Contessa G[uiccioli] when I heard the shot. On coming into the hall, I found all my servants on the balcony, exclaiming that a man was murdered. I immediately ran down, calling on Tita (the bravest of them) to follow me. The rest wanted to hinder us from going . . .

However, down we ran, and found him lying on his back, almost, if not quite, dead, with five wounds, one in the heart, two in the stomach, one in the finger, and the other in the arm. Some soldiers cocked their guns, and wanted to hinder me from passing. However, we passed, and I found Diego, the adjutant, crying over him like a child – a surgeon, who said nothing of his profession – a priest, sobbing a frightened prayer – and the commandant, all this time, on his back, on the hard, cold pavement, without light or assistance, or any thing around him but confusion and dismay.

As nobody could, or would, do any thing but howl and pray, and as no one would stir a finger to move him, for fear of consequences – I lost my patience – made my servant and a couple of the mob take up the body – sent two soldiers to the guard – despatched Diego to the Cardinal with the news, and had the commandant carried upstairs into my own quarter. But it was too late, he was gone – not at all disfigured – bled inwardly – not above an ounce or two came out.

I had him partly stripped – made the surgeon examine him, and examined him myself. He had been shot by cut balls or slugs. I felt one of the slugs, which had gone through him, all but the skin. Everybody conjectures why he was killed, but no one knows how. The gun was found close by him – an old gun, half filed down.

He only said, 'O Dio!' and 'Gesu' two or three times, and appeared to have suffered little. Poor fellow! he was a brave officer, but had made himself much disliked by the people. I knew him personally, and had met with him often at conversazioni and elsewhere. My house is full of soldiers, dragoons, doctors, priests, and all kinds of persons, – though I have now cleared it, and clapt sentinels at the doors. Tomorrow the body is to be moved. The town is in the greatest confusion, as you may suppose.

You are to know that, if I had not had the body moved, they would have left him there till morning in the street for fear of consequences. I would not choose to let even a dog die in such a manner, without succour: – and, as for consequences, I care for none in a duty.

Yours, &c.

P.S. The lieutenant on duty by the body is smoking his pipe with great composure. – A queer people this.

## (5) RIMINI

### Dante Alighieri, *Hell*, after 1309

*The poet, guided through Hell by Virgil ('your teacher'), meets Francesca da Rimini, who was murdered with her lover Paolo Malatesta by her husband, his brother Giovanni. Clearly Francesca's charms are intended to be perceived as dangerous, a point arguably reinforced by the extent to which readers' hearts have been won by her pained, intense tale of lovers bound for ever, blown relentlessly in the winds of Hell with Dido and others who sinned for love.*

When finally I spoke I sighed, 'Alas,
what sweet thoughts, and oh, how much desiring
brought these two down into this agony.'

And then I turned to them and tried to speak;
I said, 'Francesca, the torment that you suffer
Brings painful tears of pity to my eyes.

But tell me, in that time of your sweet sighing
how, and by what signs, did love allow you
to recognize your dubious desires?'

And she to me: 'There is no greater pain
than to remember, in our present grief,
past happiness (as well your teacher knows)!

But if your great desire is to learn
the very root of such a love as ours,
I shall tell you, but in words of flowing tears.

One day we read, to pass the time away,
of Lancelot, how he had fallen in love;
we were alone, innocent of suspicion.

Time and again our eyes were brought together
by the book we read; our faces flushed and paled.
To the moment of one line alone we yielded:

it was when we read about those longed-for lips
now being kissed by such a famous lover,
that this one (who shall never leave my side)

then kissed my mouth, and trembled as he did.
Our Galehot was the book and he who wrote it.
That day we read no further.' And all the while

the one of the two spirits spoke these words,
the other wept, in such a way that pity
blurred my senses; I swooned as though to die,

and fell to Hell's floor as a body, dead, falls.

# Biographies and important works

ARIOSTO, Ludovico (1474–1533), born in Reggio Emilia where his father, Niccolò, was constable of the castle, in about 1485 followed him to the ducal capital Ferrara, where Niccolò rose high in the service of Duke Ercole I. Ludovico, after attempting to read law at the university of Ferrara, followed the pursuit of letters (with parental blessing) until his father's death in 1500. He was in the service of Cardinal Ippolito d'Este, son of Duke Ercole, between 1503 and 1517 and then of Duke Alfonso I from 1518. He worked as diplomat, administrator and soldier, and was (miserably) governor of the remote and lawless Garfagnana region (1522–5). From 1528 he lived in retirement.

Ariosto began work on *Orlando furioso* (*Orlando Mad*) in about 1505; the three versions of the work appeared in 1516, 1521 and 1532. The material of this vast poem includes the madness of Orlando (the French Roland, 'One who so wise was held in former time') for love of the elusive Angelica and his eventual cure, the adventures of the Christian hero Rinaldo and the pagan Ruggiero who will convert and marry the warrior woman Bradamante, single combats and pitched battles, seduction and chaste love, the wiles of the wicked and sensual sorceress Alcina, and journeys through the known world and even to the moon (whither Astolfo must travel in order to bring back Orlando's wits). Its sources are also multiple; Boiardo's unfinished *Orlando innamorato* (*Orlando In Love*), 1483–95, had already begun the melding of the romance Matter of France – Charlemagne and his paladins – and the Arthurian Matter of Britain which Ariosto further shaped and complicated by drawing on a wide range of classical material. Ariosto develops the Virgilian dynastic perspective – Ruggiero and Bradamante as ancestors of the house of D'Este as Virgil's Aeneas is Augustus' ancestor – and as a result is able to counterpoint, politicize or ironize much of his material. (Another important context for the Christian/pagan battles of the poem is the Turkish threat to western Europe. Soon after its publication *Orlando furioso* became subject to detailed allegorical interpretation, and such meaning is certainly discernible at times, but on the whole the allegorical level is less obviously present than in Edmund Spenser's *The Faerie Queene*, 1590–6, for which it set a number of precedents. Ariosto's sudden, often tantalizing, deflating or comic, shifts of plot and perspective are also among the influences on Byron's manner in *Don Juan*.

Ariosto also wrote five comedies, of which the best known is *I suppositi* (*The Pretenders*), 1509.

BASSANI, Giorgio, born in 1916, is a Jewish Ferrarese novelist and journalist. His best known novels, published between 1956 and 1972, form collectively *Il romanzo di Ferrara* (*The Novel of Ferrara*), 1974. In these tales Bassani's major preoccupation is with loneliness and non-belonging and, pitted against them and the terrible events of the 1930s and 1940s, memory.

From near the beginning of *Il giardino dei Finzi-Contini* (*The Garden of the Finzi-Continis*, 1962) the reader knows that the independent Micòl Finzi-Contini will, together with her parents and grandmother, die in the deportation of Jews to Germany which began in 1943. This fact, emphasised continually by the division between the narrrator's present time and his and the Finzi-Continis' past, invests memory with particular significance and scenes like the early tennis-parties and walks in the garden with Micòl or, later, the painful ending of their relationship, with a quasi-mythical status. In the garden time sometimes appears to stand still, and indeed the Finzi-Continis, seemingly safe behind the walls of their estate, behave as if they are immune to the flux of time. (They have segregated themselves already and are less shocked by the racial laws of 1938 than assimilated Jews like the narrator's father.) Alberto's fatal illness is ignored for as long as possible. Micòl treasures the past, revisiting the 'sacred' places of her childhood when the narrator could be treated like a brother, or flirted with, with no expectation that they will enter an adult and future-oriented relationship. Finally the family domain, only partially open to outsiders, is preserved by one of them in the substance of the novel and dedicated, as if she were still alive, 'to Micòl'. Although the narrator is never called Giorgio in *Il giardino*, as in Vittorio de Sica's popular 1970 film, this is of course a deeply autobiographical novel. (Bassani himself found the film too sentimental and disliked its many alterations and failure to preserve the past/present dichotomy.)

BOETHIUS, Anicius Manlius Severinus (c.476–524), consul in 510 and head of the civil service under Theodoric the Ostrogoth, wrote many scholarly works, including commentaries on Aristotle and Plato, some of which survive. He was imprisoned on treason charges in 523 and executed at Pavia in 524. While in prison, he wrote his most famous work, *De Consolatione Philosophiae* (*The Consolation of Philosophy*), an urgent and wide-ranging dialogue between the author and Lady Philosophy. Her consolations are, roughly speaking, Stoic and Neoplatonic, although Boethius himself appears to have been a Christian. The *Consolation* was widely disseminated and translated in the medieval and Renaissance periods. In England its translators included Alfred the Great and Geoffrey Chaucer.

BOIARDO, Matteo Maria (1441–

94), Count of Scandiano (south of Reggio Emilia), whose family had long been in d'Este favour, was governor of Modena (1480–3) and Reggio Emilia (1487–94). His intricately plotted *Orlando innamorato* (*Orlando in Love*), 1495, introduced many of the situations, characters and techniques further exploited by Ariosto in *Orlando furioso*.

CARDUCCI, Giosuè (1835–1907), came from the Tuscan Maremma (he was born at Valdicastello and lived at Bolgheri and then at Castagneta) and often returned to the landscape which, he felt, inspired 'my proud spirit, my scornful song / and my heart where unsleeping love and hate reside' (*Traversando la Maremma Toscana, Crossing the Tuscan Maremma*). Carducci's father was a doctor whose radical pro-Risorgimento views forced the family to leave the area and settle in Florence in 1849. Carducci remained fiercely committed to the ideal of Italian unity. For a time he also shared his father's republicanism, but he came to accept the monarchy and was a friend of Queen Margherita, wife of Umberto I, from the late 1870s. From 1860 to 1904 he was Professor of Italian Eloquence at Bologna, and became closely identified with the city. His principal collections of verse were *Odi barbare* (*Barbarian Odes*), 1877–89 and *Rime nuove* (*New Poems*), 1861–87. In 1906 he was awarded the Nobel Prize for Literature.

Carducci came to prominence as a political poet, anticlerical and in favour of human progress and freedom of thought and expression with the energetically controversial *A Satana* (*To Satan*), 1865. His ideal of nature – that this, not the church, must be the great guiding force – informs his landscape poems. Yet his interest in ancient modes and metres makes him clas-

sical as much as Romantic. Classical Rome also matters to Carducci as the place where the roots of a modern Italian consciousness must primarily be sought, a point pursued in *Dinanzi alle Terme di Caracalla* (*At the Baths of Caracalla*) and *Alle fonti di Clitumno* (*At the Springs of Clitumnus*), 1876. The relative freedom of the medieval Italian communes also became a touchstone for him (see Extract 1).

GIRALDI CINZIO, Giambattista (1504–73), was born in Ferrara, where he was Professor of Rhetoric in 1541–62. 'Il Cinzio' and 'Cinthio' are forms of the name he uses in some of his poems, *Cynthius*. Giraldi's Senecan tragedy *L'Orbecche*, the first Italian vernacular tragedy actually to achieve performance, was seen in Ferrara in 1541. He was also a prolific writer of stories, gathered under the academic-sounding partly Greek title *Gli hecatommithi* (*The Hundred Stories*), 1565. The structure of the compilation is roughly that of Boccaccio's *Decameron* (◊Florence), but the emphasis is somewhat more consistently moralistic. It includes sources for a number of Giraldi's own plays and for Shakespeare's *Othello*, 1604 (directly) and *Measure for Measure*, 1604 (at one remove). Much of his important theoretical writing is contained in the *Discorso* on romance, comedy, and tragedy of 1554. Here he argues for *tragedia mista* ('mixed tragedy') in which good as well as bad characters get their just deserts, and for romance as a form of epic but not subject to rigidly Aristotelian ideas of unity. Aristotle and Horace are no infallible guide; after all, they knew neither 'our language nor our manner of composition'. The best guide for romance is, rather, Ariosto's◊ *Orlando furioso*.

GUARINI, Battista (1538–1612),

Ferrarese courtier, diplomat, playwright and dramatic theorist, of the same family as the humanist scholar Guarino of Verona (1374–1460). Guarini's play Il pastor fido (The Faithful Shepherd), 1590, was written in 1580–5 and first performed in 1595. Its pastoralism is indebted to Tasso's Aminta, but distinct from it particularly because Guarini's play is a tragicomedy. Responding to attacks on Il pastor, he defended the mixing of 'tragic and comic pleasure' partly on the then unfashionable grounds of truth to life (Compendio della poesia tragicomica (Compendium of Tragicomic Poetry), 1601.

PASCOLI, Giovanni (1855–1912), was born at San Mauro (now San Mauro Pascoli). He held various school and university posts before succeeding Carducci̯ as Professor of Italian Eloquence at Bologna in 1904. Having early lost five members of his close family, and given up his student belief in direct socialist action, Pascoli sought in his poetry the recovery of an ideal, sometimes mystic, country tranquillity. The collections Myricae (Tamerisks) and Canti di Castelvecchio (Songs of Castelvecchio) appeared in 1891 and 1903.

SYMONDS, John Addington (1840–93), English poet, translator, and author of a colourful History of the Renaissance in Italy, 1875–86, lived for long periods in Italy. The first volume of his popular Sketches in Italy and Greece appeared in 1874.

TASSO, Torquato (1544–95), born in Sorrento, was the son of the poet Bernardo Tasso. He studied law at Padua and Bologna. His first published venture into heroic romance was Rinaldo, 1562. In Ferrara his entertainment for Alfonso II's wedding, Il tempio d'Amore (The Temple

of Love) was performed in 1565 and Aminta, a pastoral play derived from both classical and vernacular sources and telling the tale of the lovelorn Aminta and his 'cruel fair' Silvia, in 1573. The Duke, officially Tasso's patron from 1572, first ordered the temperamental poet's confinement in 1577. Tasso fled Ferrara and wandered to several other courts before returning in 1579. Further violent outbursts led to his incarceration until he was finally released into the care of the Duke of Mantua in 1586. Gerusalemme liberata (Jerusalem Delivered), completed in. 1575 but not to the satisfaction of the tormentedly scrupulous author, was published against his will in 1581. He later produced a revised version, La Gerusalemme reconquistata (Jerusalem Reconquered), 1593. Tasso's other late works include Discorsi del poema eroico (Discourses on the Heroic Poem), 1594. His last years were spent mainly as a guest in various courts, monasteries, and lodgings in Mantua, Florence, Naples and Rome. At the time of his death in Rome Pope Clement VIII had apparently agreed to crown him poet on the Capitol as Petrarch (◊Veneto and North-East) had been crowned in 1341.

Gerusalemme liberata responds to 16th century Italian theorists' demand for a Christian epic. Homer and Virgil are important models for Tasso's poem of the capture of the Holy Sepulchre by the heroic capitano Goffredo and his knights (some historical, some fictional) in the First Crusade. But the attempts of Hell and its African and oriental agents to frustrate the crusaders' efforts give ample opportunity, also, for the inclusion of romance matter – knights are, for example, temporarily led astray by love or enchantment. Rinaldo (who figures as legendary forebear of the Estensi) temporarily falls victim to the pagan Armida in her garden of delights where (in Edward Fairfax's 1600 translation, somewhat free but still truest to the spirit of the original) 'Her breasts were naked, for the day was hot,/ Her locks unbound wav'd in the wanton wind'. Armida and her garden are a major source of Acrasia and her 'Bower of Bliss' in Edmund Spenser's *The Faerie Queene*. The passage in which Tancredi mortally wounds an adversary whom he recognizes too late as his beloved Clorinda and baptizes her as she dies also acquired the status of an archetype. It was set as a dramatic cantata, *Il combattimento di Tancredi e Clorinda*, by Claudio Monteverdi in 1624. More generally, Tasso's Christian epic was a useful example to John Milton in *Paradise Lost*, 1667. Even during the poet's lifetime, however, there was fierce debate between the rival adherents of the inventive and various Ariosto and the more classically purposeful Tasso; the debate remained familiar to educated readers until the mid-19th century.

# FLORENCE

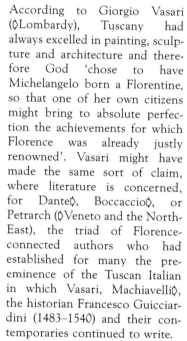

'This was the preparation for a new sort of bonfire – the Burning of Vanities. Hidden in the interior of the pyramid was a plentiful store of dry fuel and gunpowder; and on the last day of the festival, at evening, the pile of vanities was to be set ablaze to the sound of trumpets, and the ugly old Carnival was to tumble into the flames amid the songs of reforming triumph.'
*George Eliot, Romola*

According to Giorgio Vasari (◊Lombardy), Tuscany had always excelled in painting, sculpture and architecture and therefore God 'chose to have Michelangelo born a Florentine, so that one of her own citizens might bring to absolute perfection the achievements for which Florence was already justly renowned'. Vasari might have made the same sort of claim, where literature is concerned, for Dante◊, Boccaccio◊, or Petrarch (◊Veneto and the North-East), the triad of Florence-connected authors who had established for many the pre-eminence of the Tuscan Italian in which Vasari, Machiavelli◊, the historian Francesco Guicciardini (1483–1540) and their contemporaries continued to write.

Dante had been distinctly less sanguine about life in the city which exiled him. Florence has become so great, he sourly observes in *Inferno* (*Hell*, after 1309), that it beats its wings over land and sea and its name is also very well known in Hell. By the late 13th century Florence had emerged as a powerful and wealthy centre for banking and trade (especially in textiles), but was riven by faction, violence, and corruption. Dante finds an impressive tally of Florentine thieves, killers, traitors, embezzlers and sexual transgressors to fill places in the appropriate infernal circles. Once, Dante has his more comfortably placed great-great-grandfather the crusader Cacciaguida claim in *Paradiso* (*Heaven*, c.1320), things had been different: in the 12th century the city was peaceful; embroidered gowns, high dowries and opulent interior decoration were unknown, women tended their spindles and children or told the family tales of the heroic past. Everyone lived 'within the circle' of the monastic church of the **Badia Fiorentina** (later much altered), near which Dante was born in 1265, perhaps on the site of the present **Casa di Dante** museum. (Cacciaguida also mentions the **Baptistry**, still in Dante's time the central sacred and civic building, the house of one of the city's patron Saints, John the Baptist.)

Whether or not there is any truth in this idealised picture, Dante's Florence seems to have been a more violent place than Cacciaguida's. This was above all because of the struggle between the Guelfs and Ghibellines, the complexities and inconsistencies of which have often vexed not only its victims but those trying to summarise it. On the whole the Guelfs supported the Pope and were drawn from the merchant class, while the more aristocratic Ghibellines supported the Holy Roman Emperor, regarded as successor to the Roman emperors. The Guelfs gained ascendancy in Florence in 1267 but themselves, in the mid-1290s, split into fierce rival groups known as the Whites and the Blacks, led by the Donati and Cerchi families. The Blacks were more anti-imperial and wanted a socially narrower elite than the Whites, but the groups seem to have been based more often on clan loyalties than on politics or class.

Dante, prominent in government and associated with the Whites, was banished when the Blacks seized control in 1301. But he soon loosened his ties with the Whites, and was prepared to accept the protection of Ghibelline leaders like Can Grande della Scala of Verona. For Dante the papal-imperial contest was the great issue confronting the church and the world, besides which the details of Florentine faction dwindled into insignificance. That *The Divine Comedy* is not a simple factional work – Ghibellines, Blacks and Whites are distributed fairly evenly through its realms – accelerated its acceptance, after Dante's death, as the defining poem of Florence. In the second half of the 14th century ownership of manuscript copies of *The Divine Comedy* was common in the merchant class, and the civic authorities paid for public lectures expounding its doctrine. Dante's image could be admired in prominent places: painted among the Blessed in Nardo di Cione's Last Judgement (Strozzi Chapel, **Santa Maria Novella**, 1350s–60s), for instance, or, later, holding his great work, which sheds its light on Florence, in Domenico di Michelino's picture for the **Duomo** (1496). (A rather more human, more quietly reflective figure in a fresco by Giotto in the chapel of the **Palazzo del Bargello** has also been plausibly claimed as Dante.) Dante was securely launched as an archetypal figure, many of whose features are present in Boccaccio's biography of the early 1350s: a man formidably learned, often abstracted, 'his gait grave and gentle, and ever clad in most seemly apparel . . . his face long, his nose aquiline, and his eyes rather large than small', his expression 'ever melancholy and thoughtful', his life's work proceeding from love of Beatrice (read less allegorically than by many early commentators).

Twenty-seven years after Dante's death the Black Death of 1348 checked the growth and confidence of Florence in a way that internecine conflict had failed to. Between a third and a half of the population perished, including Boccaccio's father and step-mother. The introduction to *Il decamerone* (*The Decameron*), 1348–51, describes the plague (mixing first-hand observation with some details from an eighth century chronicle). The streets are full of dead and dying, corpses are packed without ceremony into mass graves, houses have been abandoned, and no magistrates are left to stop criminals from going openly about their business. There would be weeping everywhere 'if there were anyone left to weep'. Some try to combat the plague by reclusive and temperate living. Others decide that:

> 'the surest remedy to a disease of this order was to drink their fill, have a good time, sing to their hearts' content . . . and make light of all that was going on . . . Day and night would find them in one tavern or another, soaking up the booze like sponges, and carousing all the more in other people's houses the moment word got out that that's where the fun was to be had.'

Boccaccio's seven young women and three young men meet, instead, in the Filippo di Strozzi chapel of the spacious Dominican church of **Santa Maria Novella**, where they sketch a civilised plan for ten days' peaceful recreation in the hills near Florence. The tales (Extract 1) they will tell will not be penitential; for the most part they will have less in common with the Heaven and closely Dante-based Hell which Nardo di Cione would soon paint for the Strozzi chapel than with the realistic, if gracefully arranged figures in Domenico Ghirlandaio's 1480s frescoes for the same church's Cappella Maggiore. The subjects of the stories range from noble sacrifice to ribald practical joke. They function not as the traditional reproof of sinners who have brought divine visitation on themselves but as therapy for survivors.

The city gradually recovered from the Black Death, and its oligarchic system of government glided gradually, in the early 15th century, into rule by the Medici family. The Medici were cultural as well as political patrons: Cosimo, effectively ruler from 1434, keenly collected ancient manuscripts and had them copied (beginning the collection housed since 1532 in the Biblioteca Laurenziana at **San Lorenzo**), was a patron of architecture (Michelozzo's **Palazzo Medici**, later Medici-Riccardi, was begun in 1444) and sculpture, and advanced scholars including the neo-Platonist philosopher Marsilio Ficino. Knowing Cosimo, acute reasoner, wise and strong governor, was, Ficino declared, as important for him as reading Plato; the Greek 'showed me the idea of courage' once while 'Cosimo showed it every day'. Cosimo's son Piero 'the Gouty' was interested in painting, most famously commissioning for the chapel of Palazzo Medici, during his father's lifetime, Benozzo Gozzoli's fresco of the Procession of the Magi (with the kings, the ranks of their red-hatted Florentine retinue, and stylized rocky paths and tall trees). Like many of his descendants he was also a collector of 'those little objects, coins and cameos' which, as J.R. Hale says, 'were both precious in themselves and, to the sensitive ear, transmitters of the pulse which had given life to the manners and ideas of antiquity'.

Piero's son and (1469–92) successor was Lorenzo the Magnificent◊, almost certainly the crowned and gold-adorned young magus on a white horse in Gozzoli's fresco. (Later, more realistic Florentine images of the black-haired, crumpled-featured, always slightly ironic or wry-looking Lorenzo include one in a fresco by Domenico Ghirlandaio in the Sassetti chapel of **Santa Trinità**. His death-mask is at **Palazzo Medici-Riccardi**.) Under his aegis Ficino, Angelo Poliziano◊, and Giovanni Pico◊, Count of Mirandola, one of the most progressive and controversial thinkers of the age, met at the **Villa Medicea** in **Careggi**, or at Ficino's house nearby, as an informal but serious-minded Platonic Academy. In this country retreat of the Medici (which now belongs to the city's main hospital) Lorenzo was, in Samuel Taylor Coleridge's excited but not wholly unjustified imaginings, 'wont to discourse with Ficino, Politian, and the princely Mirandola on the Ideas of Will, God, and Immortality' (*The Statesman's Manual*, 1816).

The Florentine Neo-Platonists sought a synthesis between classical, biblical, mystical and modern inspiration. Some of them also expressed themselves more simply in vernacular love-sonnets and poems and songs for the many festivals – seasonal, civic, or Medicean – in the squares of Florence. Lorenzo himself wrote poems in Tuscan in fulfilment of his passionate conviction that it was intrinsically as various and adaptable as Latin or Greek. (It was also perhaps politically advantageous to associate the Medici with the culturally powerful Tuscan triad of Dante, Petrarch, and Boccaccio.) But there is nothing coldly theoretical about Lorenzo's song of fleeting youth for the carnival of 1490 (Extract 5) or Poliziano's most sung and recited lyric for the *Calendimaggio*, the May Day celebration in which flowering may branches were paraded. It begins, from an opening line traditional to the festival, and with untranslatable enthusiasm:

> *'Ben venga maggio*
> *e 'l gonfalon selvaggio!*
> *Ben venga primavera*
> *che vuol l'uom s'innamori'*

('Welcome is May – or the may-branch – and the forest – or wild – banner! Welcome is Spring, that makes man fall in love').

The Medici continued to dominate Florence, with republican interludes in 1494–1512 and 1527–31, until 1737. From 1569 they were

Grand Dukes of Tuscany. At the **Palazzo Pitti** and the **Uffizi** they built up the extensive art collections which form the basis of the modern museums. In 1743 the last of the Medici, Anna Maria, left all the family property, including the paintings, statues, and galleries, to the new line of Grand Dukes of the house of Lorraine, on condition that the collections were kept intact and not removed, since they were 'for the ornament of the state, for the benefit of the people, and to induce the curiosity of foreigners'. Curiosity was successfully induced, and the art treasures bulked increasingly large in the Florentine diaries and books of Grand Tourists and their humbler successors.

It has often been felt, indeed, that Florence is a city of art treasures and tombs only, a place for looking back, for reassurance from the Old Masters. But the Florence-connected poems of Robert Browning◊ in *Men and Women*, 1855, suggest some of the ways in which the present can engage in productive dialogue with the past rather than passively accepting it. Browning explores the imperfect, the unfinished, the fleshly: Giotto leaving his **Campanile** 'still to finish', thus cherished more than the facile perfection of the circle he drew with one stroke to demonstrate his skill (*Old Pictures in Florence*). In *The Statue and the Bust* Grand Duke Ferdinando has Giovanni Bologna 'John of Douay' portray him on horseback 'here aloft,/Alive, as the crafty sculptor can,/In the very square I have crossed so oft' – the equestrian statue in **Piazza Santissima Annunziata** – but thus commemorates not ducal boldness but missed opportunity. Out of purely worldly considerations, he failed to fulfil his desire for the lady who captivated him when he looked up from the square to see her leaning from a window of what is now the **Palazzo Budini-Gattai**, and she too failed to act until, as her youth faded, she had Luca della Robbia make a bust of her to look down on the square. (The bust, unlike the statue, is fictional.) There is an implicit contrast with the bolder conduct which led Browning and Elizabeth Barrett to marry and come together to Florence. In *Fra Lippo Lippi* (Extract 2) the painter is rebuked by some for painting flesh and blood figures rather than spiritual, ethereal ones which, like Fra Angelico's, will lift men over 'perishable clay', but cannot resist doing so any more than he can resist the call of the flesh in the shape of 'sportive ladies' and 'whiffs of song'. Similarly mixing earthiness and high aspiration, Browning on the whole shares Lippo's belief that 'This world . . . means intensely, and means good: /To find its meaning is my meat and drink.'

By Browning's time Florence was the home of a large English and American community. The Brownings were among the hosts of such shorter term but industrious visitors as Nathaniel Hawthorne (◊Rome), who wrote a copious notebook account of his four months in Florence in the summer of 1858. (The full text was first published in *The French and Italian Notebooks*, 1980.) Perhaps his favourite activity here was to gaze long and hard at sculpture, whether on repeated visits to the studio of Hiram Powers, an American long resident in Florence, or to the Venus de' Medici at the Uffizi. (At first sight of the Venus, Hawthorne felt 'a kind of tenderness for her; an affection, not as if she were one woman, but all womankind in one', and this remained his usual impression even if occasionally she palled and seemed 'little more than any other piece of yellowish-white marble'.) In the Medici Chapel at **San Lorenzo** he was a little uncertain how to respond to the figures of Day, Night, Dawn, and Dusk; like other works by Michelangelo (◊Rome), 'they sprawl, and fling their limbs abroad with adventurous freedom', but their purpose is unclear – the sculptor has 'put his allegorical progeny here only for lack of other house-room'. But Hawthorne has no doubts about the statue, above Dawn and Dusk, of Lorenzo de' Medici, Duke of Urbino (d. 1528), the one work 'grand enough to vindicate for' Michelangelo 'all the genius that the world gave him credit for':

'after looking at it a little while, the spectator ceases to think of it as a marble statue; it comes to life, and you see that this princely figure is brooding over some great design, which, when he has arranged it in his own mind, the world will be fain to execute for him. . . . This statue is one of the things I look at with highest enjoyment, but also with grief and impatience, because I feel that I do not come at all which it involves, and that by-and-by I must go away and leave it forever. . . . It is a shame for me to write about such a great work, and leave out everything that really characterizes it; its naturalness, for example, as if it came out of the marble of its own accord, with all its grandeur hanging heavily about it, and sat down there beneath its weight. I cannot describe it. It is like trying to stop the ghost of Hamlet's father by crossing a spear before it.'

Such wrestling with sculptural meaning was continued in *The Marble Faun*, 1860.

Permanent residents did not, of course, spend their lives in churches and galleries. The British in particular did what they could to make Florence like home, as Iris Origo (◊Tuscany) remembered in her autobiography *Images and Shadows*, 1970:

'The English Church in Via La Marmora, Maquay's Bank in Via Tornabuoni, the Anglo-American stores in the Via Cavour . . . and, for the young people, the Tennis Club at the Cascine – these were their focal points. If they lived in a Florentine *palazzo* it was at once transformed – in spite of its great stone fireplaces, and brick or marble floors – into a drawing-room in South Kensington: chintz curtains, framed water-colours, silver rose-bowls and library books, a fragrance of home-made scones and of freshly made tea ('But no Italian will warm the tea-pot properly, my dear').'

E.M. Forster◊, travelling to Italy for the first time in 1901 (the year before Origo's birth), found England equally difficult to escape in the restraining company of his mother and the other guests at the Pension Simi, on the first floor at 2 Lungarno alle Grazie (now part of the Jennings Riccioli), fictionalized as the Pension Bertolini in *A Room With a View*, 1908. Signora Bertolini is a cockney, Lucy Honeychurch's fellow guests (all English) include a clergyman and two 'little old ladies', and there are portraits of Queen Victoria and Lord Tennyson on the wall. Lucy, thanks mainly to the Emersons – less conventional Bertolini guests – an unexpected kiss, and the spirit of Italy, will in the end make good her escape from stultifying Englishness. Forster himself felt that Italy was beginning to 'thaw' his northernness, but fulfilment was more difficult for an Edwardian man forced to hide his homosexuality and his frustration with his mother and himself.

Largely unknown to the foreign community, Florentine intellectual life was flourishing in the early 20th century, as it had not for generations, in the lively debates and controversies associated with such periodicals and reviews as *La Voce* (*The Voice*) and the early work of Aldo Palazzeschi◊. And close by the famous buildings and English tea-shops the poorer natives of Florence continued to live and work. Vasco Pratolini◊ was born into a poor family at 1b, Via de' Magazzini, near Piazza della Signoria, in 1913, and later moved with his grandmother to Via del Corno, even closer to the Palazzo Vecchio (a fact which went some way towards consoling her for moving out of the old place where she had heard the Palazzo's bells chime the hours every day for 30 years). Pratolini's novels are often set in these and similar streets, with their cramped accommodation smelling of cats and oil and horse-dung, in the 1920s and 1930s. Whether here or in more respectable quarters of Florence (Extract 6), Pratolini is good at evoking the city often ignored by its foreign rhapsodists – dairy bars, cinemas, billiard clubs – and those who frequent it: café workers, a blacksmith, newspaper vendors, maids, policemen.

## SANTA CROCE

The Franciscan church of Santa Croce, established on an earlier foundation in the 1290s, was from the first regarded as a statement of Florence's earthly glory as well as a space in which to preach the message of St. Francis (◊Umbria and Marche) to large congregations. And from the 15th century it housed a Florentine, and then increasingly an Italian, pantheon of the great deceased. The earlier tombs and monuments include those of Leonardo Bruni (1373–1444), humanist scholar, republican apologist, and chancellor of Florence, portrayed holding his *Historiae Florentini Populi* (*Chronicles of the Florentine People*), 1415–44, and of the artist Lorenzo Ghiberti (1378–1455), who was responsible for the east and north bronze doors of the Baptistery. The tomb of Michelangelo (◊Rome) by Vasari (◊Lombardy) is in the south aisle. Monuments to the more controversial Machiavelli◊, in the south aisle, and Galileo Galilei (1564–1642), in the north, were added only in the 18th century. (Burial in the church had been forbidden Galileo's body from 1642 to 1737. During his lifetime he had been more acceptable to the Protestant John Milton than to the Vatican; Milton recalled in his defence of free expression, *Areopagitica*, 1644, his visit to 'the famous Galileo, grown old a prisoner to the Inquisition, for thinking in astronomy otherwise than the Franciscan and Dominican licensers thought'. And in Book One of *Paradise Lost*, 1667, Satan's shield is like the moon which Galileo viewed 'through optic glass'.)

In the 19th century, with its Westminster Abbey status well established, Santa Croce became the burial place of the composer Cherubini (1760–1840), the Piedmontese poet and dramatist Vittorio Alfieri (1749–1803), with a notable monument by Canova, and Alfieri's lover the Countess of Albany (1753–1824), wife of Charles Stuart the Young Pretender and centre of a literary salon at the **Palazzo Masetti** (2 Lungarno Corsini). Among her guests were Chateaubriand, Stendhal (◊Lombardy), and the young poet Ugo Foscolo◊. Foscolo's remains eventually came to Santa Croce in 1871 from England, where he had died in political exile in 1827; he had meditated on the tombs of his great predecessors here in *Dei sepolcri* (*On Sepulchres*), 1807. But there are also some notable absentees in the form, as Byron (◊Venice) puts it in Canto Four of *Childe Harold's Pilgrimage*, 1818, of 'the all Etruscan [i.e. Tuscan] three': Dante◊ is buried in Ravenna, Petrarch (◊Veneto and North-East) at Arquà, and Boccaccio◊ at Certaldo. A memorial to Dante was added in 1829, and in 1865, with much civic and national pageantry (Florence was the capital of Italy at the time), the large statue outside the church was unveiled on the occasion of the sixth centenary of his birth.

Walking round such a temple of greatness can be a rather sterile experience. In E.M. Forster's *A Room With a View*, 1908 (Extract 4) Lucy Honeychurch, deprived of her Baedeker's guide, doesn't know what she 'ought' to admire. Children mistake Machiavelli for a saint or fall on the upturned toes of an 'odious' bishop. And Rev. Eager lecturing his 'earnest congregation' on the Giotto frescoes in the Peruzzi Chapel takes a reverential Ruskin-derived attitude that provokes Mr Emerson's outburst 'Built by faith indeed! That simply means the workmen weren't paid properly. . . . Look at that fat man in blue [St John ascending]! He must weigh as much as I do, and he is shooting into the sky like an air-balloon'.

Outside, **Piazza Santa Croce** has been used for less melancholy ceremonies than the funerals of the great or the tours of Mr Eager.

Poliziano◊ wrote his *La giostra* (*The Joust*), 1475–8, after a tourney had been held here, in 1475, to celebrate the establishment of a league between Florence and the chief Italian powers. The jousting was won by Giuliano, brother of Lorenzo the Magnificent, wearing silver armour made by the painter Verrocchio and the colours of his (safely married) lady Simonetta Cattaneo Vespucci. Poliziano's unfinished poem tells the story of the idealised love of the hunter Giulio for a beautiful nymph, idealised all the more perhaps because Simonetta died, to the general grief, at some point in the composition of the poem in 1476. It was the assassination of Giuliano in the Pazzi conspiracy of 1478, however, which stopped further work on *La giostra*. (The conspirators, with covert papal backing, attempted to kill both brothers as they attended a service at the Duomo, but Lorenzo escaped with a slight wound to the neck and rushed to safety through the bronze doors of the sacristy.) The poem was to have described and allegorized Giuliano's jousting prowess, but got no further than part of the vision in which Venus inspired him to take up arms.

*La giostra* did, however, have lasting influence. It was one of the many literary and iconographic sources of Botticelli's *La Primavera* and *The Birth of Venus* now in the **Uffizi**. (Botticelli had designed Giuliano's standard for the joust, showing Simonetta as Pallas Athena, and the *Primavera* was commissioned by Lorenzo's cousin Lorenzo di Pierfrancesco di Medici.) Simonetta, like Flora in the *Primavera*, is a fair-skinned nymph, her garment ornamented with flowers, and 'in her movement she is regally mild, her glance alone could quiet a tempest'; Cupid goes to Venus' realm 'where every Grace delights, where Beauty weaves a garland of flowers about her hair, where lascivious Zephyr flies behind Flora and decks the green grass with flowers'. And here too a bas-relief depicts the birth of Venus:

> 'a young woman with non-human countenance is carried on a conch-shell, wafted to shore by playful zephyrs . . . the sky and the elements laughing about her; the Hours treading the beach in white garments, the breeze curling their loosened and flowing hair; their faces not one, not different, as befits sisters.'

Such scenes, whether written or painted, are affected by the Platonic (or syncretic Christian-Platonist) ideal of Love expounded most persuasively by Ficino◊. Their fascination results from the combination of such transcendental beliefs with the transient and immediate: Botticelli's serene Flora was the frightened Chloris who flees the lust of Zephyrus; she wears a dress whose flowers look painted rather than woven, suggesting an origin in some festival (perhaps, as Charles Dempsey and others have said, the Spring *Calendimaggio*), yet lasts, as festive painted cloth and festivals did not, in *La Primavera*; the Graces dance and Venus beckons, yet are still, in stasis.

## PIAZZA DELLA SIGNORIA AND THE PALAZZO VECCHIO

In the 1490s Fra Girolamo Savonarola (1452–98) exerted more influ-ence over the Florentines than anybody else ever has. This charismatic Prior of San Marco preached with terrifying power, prophesied the French invasion of 1494, which he interpreted as a scourge of God, and was fiercely opposed to worldly frivolity. He used the **Piazza della Signoria**, site of many a carnival and *festa*, for his Bonfire of the Vanities as described by George Eliot in *Romola*, 1862–3 (Extract 3). Savonarola dominated the restored republican Florence for several years after the flight of Lorenzo's sons in 1494, but, as some of his prophecies rang less true and more skilled political rivals inside and outside the city intrigued against him, he lost his grip on power. (Amid the more serene spirituality of the frescoes by Fra Angelico of half a century before it is not easy to imagine the priory of **San Marco** in the turbulent days of 1497, when Savonarola's opponents besieged it with stone-throwing machines and fought their way in against determined resistance from the monks.) He had defied a summons to Rome and a ban on his preaching by Pope Alexander VI (Rodrigo Borgia, a prelate whose self-indulgence contrasted markedly with Savonarola's asceti-cism and who needed to remove him for political reasons) and was therefore excommunicated in June 1497. In 1498 he was arrested and condemned to death. He and two of his chief disciples were hanged, and their bodies then burnt, in the Piazza where once the Vanities had blazed. But the memory of the fearsome preacher was not easily eradicated. For instance Michelangelo, as a very old man in the 1550s, could still, according to his biographer Ascanio Condivi, remember the spine-chilling tone of Savonarola's voice.

Florence continued a republic, but a more secular one, until the return of the Medici in 1512. During this period Michelangelo's David (1504) was erected outside the republic's headquarters in Palazzo della Signoria as a declaration against tyrants. (The statue now in place is a copy. The original is in the **Accademia**.) And inside the palace Niccolò Machiavelli, later the theorist of tyrannies and republics, worked as Second Chancellor. It was after his fall from office, torture, and imprisonment in 1512–13 that he distilled his experience of statecraft and close knowledge of Roman history into the controversially prac-tical conclusions of *Il principe* (*The Prince*), 1513. (This and his later works were written on his estate, seven miles from Florence, at **Sant'Andrea in Percussina** (Extract 7), in a house, still standing, known as the Albergaccio from the nearby *albergo* or inn.)

In some ways the later Medici fulfilled Machiavelli's precepts for the successful prince. They heavily fortified Florence, as much in order to keep those within the city under control as to defend it from attack; Cosimo I, ruler of Florence from 1537 and elevated as the first Grand Duke of Tuscany in 1569, was a sombre figure who crushed dissent, skilfully freed himself of the domination of the Emperor Charles V, and decorated the Palazzo Vecchio – especially the **Salone dei Cinquecento** – with images of his family and their deeds. Cosimo's equestrian statue by Giovanni Bologna, commissioned by his son Ferdinando I (1595), is another confident statement of power. But in the popular imagination such rulers inhabited a world not of cool absolutism but of scandalous sexual intrigue and ingeniously managed assassinations: of villainous stage Machiavels rather than the real Machiavelli. Legend had it that Cosimo I committed incest with his daughters and murdered one of his sons. The murder of Cosimo's predecessor Alessandro in 1537 was remembered with sordid interest: his kinsman and fellow-debauchee, the melancholic Lorenzino or Lorenzaccio de' Medici, had lured him to his house with the prospect of a receptive woman before stabbing him with the aid of a hired assassin and fleeing with a deeply bitten hand. Such conduct was, northern Europe generally believed, typical of Renaissance Italy. But by emphasising the killer's troubled, part-lapsed republican idealism, Alfred de Musset was able to base on this story one of the most psychologically interesting plays of the 19th century, *Lorenzaccio*, 1834.

## CASA GUIDI

In 1860 Robert Browning found a cheap, old book in the Piazza San Lorenzo market, jumbled with worn picture-frames, 'Modern chalk-drawings, studies from the nude,/Samples of stone, jet, breccia, porphyry', faded tapestries, and copies of Dumas fils' *La Dame aux camélias*, Horace for schools, and 'the Life, Death, Miracles of Saint Somebody.' He bought it and, reading as he walked, made his way home to Casa Guidi, crossing the Arno by Ponte Santa Trinità.

This account of the 'old yellow book' – the records of a Roman murder trial of 1698 which became the source of Browning's long poem *The Ring and the Book*, 1868–9 – suggests the compactness, the imaginative manageability, of Florence. Casa Guidi, where (in six rooms on the *piano nobile*) he and Elizabeth Barrett Browning lived for much of the time between 1847 and her death there in 1861, was conveniently near the Pitti palace and the **Boboli Gardens**, and not far from the river. The house, long an empty, melancholy place, has now been splendidly restored by the Browning Institute of New York. The drawing room has been furnished and decorated as far as possible to recreate it as painted for Browning by George Mignaty just after his wife's death.

In Casa Guidi much of Browning's *Men and Women* and Barrett Browning's *Aurora Leigh* were written (the former in the 'small sitting room', the latter in the drawing room). *Casa Guidi Windows*, 1848–51, Barrett Browning's vigorous poetic contribution to the Risorgimento cause, revolves around her view of a procession celebrating Grand

Duke Leopoldo II's granting the citizens the right to form a civil guard – a small concession but, she hoped, a step in the direction of fuller liberty. (Part Two expresses bitter disappointment at the reduction of liberty which actually soon followed.) *Casa Guidi Windows* pits present against past more insistently than do Robert Browning's Italian poems: certainly the past must be learnt from, but poets' 'cadenced tears' will not help Italy free herself from foreign or tyrannical domination; for too long she has been the 'impassioned nympholept' of her own past, forgetting:

> 'How one clear word would draw an avalanche
> Of living sons around her, to succeed
> The vanished generations.'

Elizabeth Barrett Browning died at Casa Guidi, in Robert's arms, on 29 June 1861. Because of her unswerving commitment to the Risorgimento she was much honoured in Italy; the exterior of Casa Guidi still bears an inscription in which 'Grateful Florence' remembers the poet whose work 'forged a golden link between Italy and England'.

## OTHER LITERARY LANDMARKS

**Cimitero Protestante** (or English Cemetery), Piazza Donatello: tombs of Elizabeth Barrett Browning◊, the poet Arthur Hugh Clough (1819–61), the writer in verse and prose Walter Savage Landor (1775–1864) and the novelist and travel-writer Frances (Fanny) Trollope (1780–1863), mother of Anthony.

**Doney's Café**, Via Tornabuoni: a meeting-place for such expatriates as Stendhal (◊Lombardy), Gautier (◊Naples and Campania), and Ralph Waldo Emerson (1803–82).

**Loggia dei Lanzi**, Piazza della Signoria: the dramatic vicissitudes involved in casting *Perseus Trampling Medusa* (1545) are the subject of Cellini's (◊Rome) *Autobiography*, II.73–8.

**Palazzo Bianca Cappello**: house, at 26 Via Santo Spirito, built by Grand Duke Francesco I (ruled 1574–87) for his Venetian mistress and then wife, a version of whose story is told in Thomas Middleton's tragedy *Women Beware Women*, c. 1621–2.

**San Marco**: tomb slabs of Poliziano◊ and Pico della Mirandola◊

**Santa Maria Novella**: in a Ghirlandaio fresco (Cappella Tournabuoni) humanists Ficino◊, Cristoforo Landino (1424–98), Poliziano◊, and Gentile Becchi are portrayed.

**Santa Trinità**: in the Sassetti Chapel fresco Poliziano◊ and Luigi Pulci (1432–84), author of the comic epic *Il Morgante* (*Morgante*), 1483, are shown ascending the stairs with their pupils, the sons of Lorenzo the Magnificent.

**Via Guicciardini**: at no. 22, opposite the Pitti Palace, Fyodor Dostoevsky finished *The Idiot* in 1868–9.

**Via Romana**: at no. 43 Claire Clairmont (1798–1879) lived in her later years, in circumstances which inspired Henry James's (◊Venice) *The Aspern Papers*, 1888.

**Villa di Poggio Gherardo**: often suggested as the setting of some of the story-telling in Boccaccio's◊ *Decameron*.

**Villino Trollope**, Piazza dell'Indipendenza: Fanny Trollope lived here with her elder son Thomas Adolphus (1810–92).

# BOOKLIST

Beauman, Nicola, *Morgan: a Biography of E.M. Forster*, Hodder and Stoughton, London, 1993.

Boccaccio, Giovanni, *The Decameron* [1348–51], Guido Waldman, trans; Jonathan Usher, ed, Oxford University Press, Oxford and New York, 1993. **Extract 1**.

Browning, Elizabeth Barrett, *The Works*, Karen Hill, ed, Wordsworth Editions, Ware, 1994.

Browning, Robert, *The Poems*, John Pettigrew and Thomas J. Collins, eds, Penguin, Harmondsworth, 1993. **Extract 2**.

Caesar, Michael, ed, *Dante: the Critical Heritage, 1314–1870*, Routledge, London and New York, 1989.

Dante Alighieri, *The Divine Comedy* [c. 1309–20], Mark Musa, trans, Penguin, Harmondsworth, 1984–6.

Dempsey, Charles, *The Portrayal of Love: Botticelli's 'Primavera' and Humanistic Culture at the Time of Lorenzo the Magnificent*, Princeton University Press, Princeton, 1992.

Eliot, George, *Romola* [1863], Andrew Brown, ed, Clarendon Press, Oxford, 1993. Includes detailed information on Eliot's sources, her visits to Florence, and the city in the 15th century. **Extract 3**.

Forster, E.M., *A Room With a View* [1908], Oliver Stallybrass, ed,

Penguin, Harmondsworth, 1978. **Extract 4**.

Hale, J.R., *Florence and the Medici: the Pattern of Control*, Thames and Hudson, London, 1977.

Hawthorne, Nathaniel, *The French and Italian Notebooks*, Thomas Woodson ed, Ohio State University Press, Columbus, 1980.

Hibbert, Christopher, *Florence: the Biography of a City*, Viking/Penguin, London, 1993.

Machiavelli, Niccolò, *The Literary Works of Machiavelli: Mandragola, Clizia, a Dialogue on Language, Belfagor. With Selections from the Private Correspondence*, J.R. Hale, ed and trans, Greenwood Press, Westport, CT, 1979. **Extract 7**.

Medici, Lorenzo de', *Selected Poems and Prose*, Jon Thiem, ed and trans, Pennsylvania University Press, 1991. **Extract 5**.

Medici, Lorenzo de', *Selected Writings with an English Verse Translation of the Rappresentazione di San Giovanni e Paolo*, Corinna Salvadori, ed, Foundation for Italian Studies, Dublin, 1992.

Origo, Iris, *Images and Shadows: a Part of a Life*, John Murray, London, 1970.

Pico della Mirandola, Giovanni, *Oration on the Dignity of Man* [1486], Elizabeth Livermore Forbes, trans, in *The Renaissance Philosophy of Man*, Ernst Cassirer,

*Booklist continued*

Paul Oskar Kristeller, and John Herman Randall, Jr., eds, University of Chicago Press, Chicago, 1948.

Poliziano, Angelo, *The Stanze*, David Quint, trans, University of Massachusetts Press, Amherst, 1979. (Includes *The Joust*).

Pratolini, Vasco, *Family Chronicle* [1947], Martha King, trans,

Quartet Books, London, 1991/ Italica Books, New York, 1988. **Extract 6.**

Skinner, Quentin, *Machiavelli*, Oxford University Press, Oxford, 1981.

Vasari, Giorgio, *Lives of the Artists* [1568], George Bull, trans, 2 vols, Penguin, Harmondsworth, 1987.

Wallace, David, *Giovanni Boccaccio: the Decameron*, Cambridge University Press, Cambridge, 1991.

# Extracts

## (1) FLORENCE

### Giovanni Boccaccio,
### *The Decameron* (c. 1348–51), ninth day, second story

*The tales of The Decameron are told by seven young women and three young men seeking respite in the country from the sorrows and dangers of plague-stricken Florence. The whole work, ranging from tales of love and loss to farcical stories like the one told here by Elissa, has often been seen as a 'human comedy' analogous to Dante's Divine Comedy.*

They knocked on her door and when she answered they said ; 'Quick, Reverend Mother, get up! We've caught Isabetta with a young man in her cell.'

That night the abbess had a priest for company . . . so she leapt out of bed and dressed in the dark as best she could. When she reached for her veil (they call it a psaltery because of its shape) what she grabbed hold of were the priest's breeches. Short of time, she flung the garment on her head in place of her veil, quite unawares, and out she strode, hastily closing the door behind her as she cried: 'Where is this miscreant?' And with the other nuns, who were so keyed up to catch Isabetta red-handed that they never even noticed what the abbess had on her head, she reached the cell door and, with the others' help, drove it crashing to the floor. In they surged and found the lovers hugging each other in bed and so stunned at this irruption they just didn't react. . . .

The abbess took her seat in the chapter house and in the presence of all the nuns, whose eyes were fastened upon the guilty party, she addressed her in the most opprobrious terms ever used against a woman: she was a woman, she said, whose disgusting and scandalous conduct would defile the good name, the holiness, and honour of the convent if it ever got out. And she accompanied her diatribe with the most solemn threats.

The culprit kept silent; she hung her head, shamefaced, quite lost for words, so that people began to feel a bit sorry for her. The abbess piled up her invective, until Isabetta looked up and noticed what the lady had on her head – the leggings with their ties were hanging down on either side of her face. Drawing the right inference, she recovered her composure at once and said, 'Reverend Mother, pray God help you tie your bonnet-strings, then do tell me what is on your mind.'

'What bonnet-strings, you whore?' snapped the abbess, who had failed to grasp her meaning. 'Do you have the impudence to bandy words with me? Do you think what you have done is a laughing matter?'

Isabetta, however, repeated what she had just said: 'Do please, Reverend Mother, tie your bonnet-strings, then say to me what you will.' At this, several of the nuns turned to look at the abbess and she herself raised her hands to her head. Now they all realized what Isabetta had been talking about.

The abbess therefore . . . quite changed her tune: she began speaking along very different lines, asserting how impossible it was to resist the lusts of the flesh. Each one, therefore, was to feel free to take her pleasure when it offered, just as they had been doing on the sly. So she released the young woman and went back to bed with her priest, while Isabetta returned to her lover's arms.

## (2) FLORENCE

### Robert Browning, *Fra Lippo Lippi*, 1855

*Fra Lippo (Filippo) Lippi (c.1406–69) painted rather more naturalistically than many of his predecessors. According to Vasari (◊Lombardy), Browning's source, Lippo was as respon-sive to the flesh in his life as in his art. (In the poem he outlines a philosophy of the search for meaning in, rather than pious rejection of, the world.) In the present extract, he has left the Medici Palace, where he is working for Cosimo de' Medici on a picture of St Jerome, and is being questioned by the watch.*

What, brother Lippo's doings, up and down,
You know them and they take you? like enough!

I saw the proper twinkle in your eye -
'Tell you, I liked your looks at very first.
Let's sit and set things straight now, hip to haunch.
Here's spring come, and the nights one makes up bands
To roam the town and sing out carnival,
And I've been three weeks shut within my mew,
A-painting for the great man, saints and saints
And saints again. I could not paint all night –
Ouf! I leaned out of window for fresh air.
There came a hurry of feet and little feet,
A sweep of lute-strings, laughs, and whifts of song, –
*Flower o' the broom,*
*Take away love, and our earth is a tomb!*
*Flower o' the quince,*
*I let Lisa go, and what good in life since?*
*Flower o' the thyme* – and so on. Round they went.
Scarce had they turned the corner when a titter
Like the skipping of rabbits by moonlight, – three slim shapes,
And a face that looked up . . . zooks, sir, flesh and blood,
That's all I'm made of! Into shreds it went,
Curtain and counterpane and coverlet,
All the bed-furniture – a dozen knots,
There was a ladder! Down I let myself,
Hands and feet, scrambling somehow, and so dropped,
And after them. I came up with the fun
Hard by Saint Laurence, hail fellow, well met, –
*Flower o' the rose,*
*If I've been merry, what matter who knows?*
And so as I was stealing back again
To get to bed and have a bit of sleep
Ere I rise up tomorrow and go work
On Jerome knocking at his poor old breast
With his great round stone to subdue the flesh,
You snap me o' the sudden.

## (3) FLORENCE

### George Eliot, *Romola*, 1862–3

*The heroine of this novel set in the 1490s has been much
influenced by the powerfully charismatic reformer Fra Girolamo
Savonarola, but comes increasingly to share Eliot's ambivalence
towards him. His Bonfire of the Vanities in the Piazza della
Signoria is, like many features of the book, drawn with meticu-
lous care from contemporary sources.*

She chose to go through the great Piazza that she might take a first survey of that unparalleled sight there while she was still alone. Entering it from the south, she saw something monstrous and many-coloured in the shape of a pyramid, or, rather, like a huge fir-tree, 60 feet high, with shelves on the branches, widening and widening towards the base till they reached a circumference of 80 yards. The Piazza was full of life: slight young figures, in white garments, with olive wreaths on their heads, were moving to and fro about the base of the pyramidal tree, carrying baskets full of bright-coloured things; and maturer forms, some in the monastic frock, some in the loose tunics and dark-red caps of artists, were helping and examining, or else retreating to various points in the distance to survey the wondrous whole; while a considerable group, amongst whom Romola recognized Piero di Cosimo, standing on the steps of Orgagna's Loggia, seemed to be keeping aloof in discontent and scorn.

Approaching nearer, she paused to look at the multifarious objects ranged in gradation from the base to the summit of the pyramid. There were tapestries and brocades of immodest design, pictures and sculptures held too likely to incite to vice; there were boards and tables for all sorts of games, playing-cards along with the blocks for printing them, dice, and other apparatus for gambling; there were worldly music-books, and musical instruments in all the pretty varieties of lute, drum, cymbal, and trumpet; there were masks and masquerading dresses used in the old carnival shows; there were handsome copies of Ovid, Boccaccio, Petrarca, Pulci, and other books of a vain or impure sort; there were all the implements of feminine vanity – rouge-pots, false hair, mirrors, perfumes, powders, and transparent veils intended to provoke inquisitive glances: lastly, at the very summit, there was the unflattering effigy of a probably mythical Venetian merchant, who was understood to have offered a heavy sum for this collection of marketable abominations, and, soaring above him in surpassing ugliness, the symbolic figure of the old debauched Carnival.

This was the preparation for a new sort of bonfire – the Burning of Vanities. Hidden in the interior of the pyramid was a plentiful store of dry fuel and gunpowder; and on this last day of the festival, at evening, the pile of vanities was to be set ablaze to the sound of trumpets, and the ugly old Carnival was to tumble into the flames amid the songs of reformimg triumph.

## (4) FLORENCE

### E.M. Forster, *A Room With a View*, 1908

*Lucy Honeychurch is alone in Santa Croce, without either a Baedeker's guide or a chaperone. The novel traces her movement*

*from thinking, or believing that she should think, as she has been
told, to a more natural response. Mr Emerson, who shocks others
by always saying what he feels to be true, is one of the main
agents of the change.*

Of course it must be a wonderful building. But how like a barn! And
how very cold! Of course, it contained frescoes by Giotto, in the
presence of whose tactile values she was capable of feeling what was
proper. But who was to tell her which they were? She walked about
disdainfully, unwilling to be enthusiastic over monuments of uncertain authorship or date. There was no one even to tell her which, of all
the sepulchral slabs that paved the nave and transepts, was the one that
was really beautiful, the one that had been most praised by Mr
Ruskin.

Then the pernicious charm of Italy worked on her, and, instead of
acquiring information, she began to be happy. She puzzled out the
Italian notices – the notice that forbade people to introduce dogs into
the church – the notice that prayed people, in the interests of health,
not to spit. She watched the tourists; their noses were as red as their
Baedekers, so cold was Santa Croce. She beheld the horrid fate that
overtook three Papists – two he-babies and a she-baby – who began
their career by sousing each other with the Holy Water, and then
proceeded to the Machiavelli memorial, dripping but hallowed.
Advancing towards it very slowly and from immense distances, they
touched the stone with their fingers, with their handkerchiefs, with
their heads, and then retreated. What could this mean? They did it
again and again. Then Lucy realized that they had mistaken Machiavelli for some saint, and by continual contact with his shrine were
hoping to acquire virtue. Punishment followed quickly. The smallest
he-baby stumbled over one of the sepulchral slabs so much admired
by Mr Ruskin and entangled his feet in the features of a recumbent
bishop. Protestant as she was, Lucy darted forward. She was too late.
He fell heavily upon the bishop's upturned toes.

'Hateful bishop!' exclaimed the voice of old Mr Emerson, who had
darted forward also. 'Hard in life, hard in death. Go out into the
sunshine, little boy, and kiss your hand to the sun, for that is where
you ought to be. Intolerable bishop!'

## (5) FLORENCE

### Lorenzo de' Medici ('The Magnificent'),
### *The Triumph of Bacchus and Ariadne*, 1490

*The Florentine leader wrote poems for both private and public
occasions. This piece is associated with the carnival of 1490.*

How lovely is youth in its allure,
Which ever swiftly flies away!
Let all who want to, now be gay:
About tomorrow no one's sure.

Here are Bacchus, Ariadne,
For one another all afire:
Because time flies and plays us false,
They always yield to their desire.
These nymphs of theirs and other folk
Are merry every single day.
Let all who want to, now be gay:
About tomorrow no one's sure.

Those who love these pretty nymphs
Are little satyrs, free of cares,
Who in the grottoes and the glades
Have laid for them a hundred snares.
By Bacchus warmed and now aroused
They skip and pass the time away.
Let all who want to, now be gay:
About tomorrow no one's sure.

These nymphs fall gladly for the ruses
That the satyrs execute:
Who can avoid the lure of Love
Except some rude, unfeeling brute?
So now among themselves they mingle,
Playing and singing all the day.
Let all who want to, now be gay:
About tomorrow no one's sure.

Behind the rest, that heavy sack
Astride a jackass is Silenus,
Old and drunk and ever jocund,
Long on years but not on leanness.
Although he cannot sit up straight,
He's full of cheer and laughs away.
Let all who want to, now be gay:
About tomorrow no one's sure.

And last of all appears King Midas:
All that he touches turns to gold.
But if it does not make him happy,
What is the use of wealth untold?
What sweetness will he ever taste,
Who has a thirst he can't allay?
Let all who want to, now be gay:

About tomorrow no one's sure.

Now listen well to what I say,
That none may count on what's to come.
Let men and women, young and old,
Today be glad and have some fun.
Let's cast aside all gloomy thoughts
And have perpetual holiday.
Let all who want to, now be gay:
About tomorrow no one's sure.

Among you lasses and young lovers
Long live Bacchus and Desire!
Now let us pipe and dance and sing,
Our hearts consumed with sweetest fire!
Away with suffering and sorrow!
Let what is fated have its way.
Let all who want to, now be gay:
About tomorrow no one's sure.

## (6) FLORENCE

### Vasco Pratolini, *Family Chronicle,* 1947

*In this autobiographical novel the narrator and his younger
brother, Ferruccio, have been brought up in markedly different
social settings. In the light of Ferruccio's early death, the details
of the brothers' tentative, gradually deepening contact with each
other as young men take on a special, intimate significance.*

I lived on Via Ricasoli, next to the safety exit of the movie house
'Modernissimo'. It was late in the evening, perhaps nine o'clock.
Across the street, the globe of a dairy bar was lighted; from the
illuminated second floor came dance music. It was still cold and the
moon and stars were out. At the end of the street, directly in front of
us, the dome and apse of Santa Maria del Fiore [the Duomo] were
framed. We passed the building of the local newspaper, *La Nazione*,
and turned into the Piazza del Duomo.

'How did you get my address?' I asked.

'I asked at the Registry Office!' You were smiling.

'Do you feel like a real supper?'

'In the evening I usually eat lightly. We could eat something standing
up at 'Becatelli'.'

You were really different from what I had always thought; you were
a friend; I took you by the arm.

The place was almost deserted. Giovanni Becatelli sat at the cashier's desk with his listless air. Two customers stood eating from their plates at the marble counter. Sitting at the only table were the newspaper vendor of Piazza Vittorio and his wife, both fat and perhaps suffering from dropsy, and the old tie salesman who had pains in his arms and legs.

'Do you come here often?' I asked you.

'The owner's son was my friend from school.'

Giovanni brightened upon seeing us enter; at first he didn't know we were together.

'Ciao,' he said to you. How come you're still out at this hour?'

You were a little embarrassed, but you recovered your natural reserve. 'I'm with my brother,' you said.

Giovanni shook his head, and he too, like your friends, said, 'Since when is he your brother?'

'Since we were born,' I said.

We had to show him our identification cards to convince him. We ate a bowl of pasta and a sandwich. You drank a sweet white wine.

## (7) Sant'Andrea in Percussina

### Niccolò Machiavelli, letter to Francesco Vettori, 10 December 1513

*Machiavelli, a senior official of the Florentine republic, withdrew to his estate at Sant'Andrea on his release from imprisonment by the restored regime of the Medici. Here he wrote his books, including* The Prince, *which he initially hoped would help him to win the favour of the new rulers; this letter is, no doubt, as much a witty and well crafted piece of self-presentation as a literal 'day in the life of Machiavelli'.*

When I leave the wood I go to a spring and on from there with a book under my arm, Dante or Petrarch, or one of the minor poets, Tibullus, Ovid or someone like that, to a *uccellare* [bird-snare] which I have. I read of their amorous passions and their loves; I remember my own – and for a while these reflections make me happy. Then I move on along the road, to the inn, talking to passers-by, asking news of the places they come from, hearing about this and that, and observing the various tastes and fancies of mankind. This brings me to lunch time, when I and my brood eat such food as this poor farm and my slender patrimony provides. When I have eaten, I go back to the inn, where I usually find the landlord, a butcher, a miller and a couple of bakers. With these I act the rustic for the rest of the day, playing at *cricca* and *tric-trac,* which lead to a thousand squabbles and countless slanging-matches – our fights are usually over a farthing but we can be heard shouting none the less from San Casciano. So, trapped among this vermin I rub the mould from my wits and work off the sense of being so cruelly treated by Fate – content to be driven on along this road if only to watch for her to show some sign of shame.

When evening comes, I return home and go into my study. On the threshold I strip off my muddy, sweaty, workday clothes, and put on the robes of court and palace, and in this graver dress I enter the antique courts of the ancients and am welcomed by them, and there I taste the food that alone is mine, and for which I was born. And there I make bold to speak to them and ask the motives of their actions, and they, in their humanity, reply to me. And for the space of four hours I forget the world, remember no vexation, fear poverty no more, tremble no more at death: I pass indeed into their world. And as Dante says that there can be no understanding without the memory retaining what it has heard, I have written down what I have gained from their conversation, and composed a small work *De principatibus*, where I dive as deep as I can into ideas about this subject, discussing the nature of princely rule, the forms it takes, how these are acquired, how they are maintained, why they are lost.

# Biographies and important works

BOCCACCIO, Giovanni (1313–75), was born either in Florence or at Certaldo in the Val d'Elsa. In 1327 he moved to Naples with his father, the representative of the great Florentine banking company of the Bardi. It was his father's high connections which enabled Boccaccio to move in the courtly circles whose culture informs much of his early work. After a period working for the bank and then studying canon law, Boccaccio persuaded his father (who, perhaps to his relief, left Naples in 1332) to let him dedicate himself to literature. Among his Neapolitan works are the prose romance *Il Filocolo* (*Filocolo*), c.1336, the verse romance *Il Filostrato* (*Filostrato*), c.1338, and the epic poem *Teseida* (*The Book of Theseus*), 1340–1. (These last two works were the principal sources of Chaucer's *Troilus and Criseyde* and *The Knight's Tale*.)

Boccaccio's Fiammetta ('Little Flame'), often mentioned or invoked by him, was traditionally identified with Maria d'Aquino, an illegitimate (and quite probably non-existent) daughter of King Robert the Wise of Naples; she is now generally agreed to be a poetic construct. She functions most often as a stylized representation of love, its hopes and delusions. But in the *Elegia di Madonna Fiammetta* (*Elegy of Lady Fiammetta*), 1343–4, there is a more 'realistic' psychological insight which has led to the work's being regarded as a novel before its time. The insight results above all from the fact that, unusually, the woman

herself narrates her adulterous love
for Panfilo, her desertion by him
and her attempted suicide. All this
is, of course, filtered through a
male author, but we come much
closer to a female viewpoint than
is ever the case with Dante's Beatrice or Petrarch's Laura.

In 1340 or 1341 Boccaccio
returned to Florence as a result of
family financial problems and the
more general economic crisis of
the 1340s. Here he compiled *Il decamerone* (*The Decameron*), c. 1348–
51. The title is derived from the
Greek *deka hemeron*, 'of ten days';
each of the ten well-born and soci-
able young Florentines, seven
female and one male, tells ten stories, one each day. The tales thus
introduced come from a great variety of sources – classical, folk,
romance; there are bawdy *fabliaux*,
explorations of pathos and suffering, settings for clever quips and
retorts, anecdotes about the earlier
Florentine notables Giotto and
Guido Cavalcanti.

*The Decameron* has frequently
been read as a delightful, often
ribald and outrageous, collection
of stories. But the framing narrative
ensures that, in context, it is rather
more than this. The license, including the freedom of both the female
narrators and the women whose
stories are told, is afforded by the
special context of the plague, by the
narrators' carefully established
respectability, and by the clarity of
structure which the frame provides.
There is a movement from examples of vice at the beginning to
examples of noble conduct at the
end. The daily monarchs prescribe
themes for their fellow narrators:
the Fourth Day, for example, concentrates on people whose love has
ended unhappily (from the noble
Ghismunda, who drinks poison
from a chalice containing the heart
of her lover, murdered by her
incestuously-inclined father, to the

villainous Brother Alberto, a cheat
in love who is eventually cheated
himself). The Fifth Day concentrates on those who are unfortunate at first but achieve happiness
in the end, the Eighth on the decep-
tions men and women practise on
each other.

*The Decameron* has been a useful
quarry for other artists: the main
plot of Shakespeare's *All's Well
That Ends Well*, c.1603, derives
from the English translation of a
French version of the tale of Giletta
and Beltram (III.9) and Keats drew
on the story of Lisabetta, who
grows basil over the head of her
murdered lover, in *Isabella, or the
Pot of Basil*, 1820; Pasolini's (◊Lazio)
free film adaptation of *The Decameron*, with some new stories
added, appeared in 1971.

After *The Decameron* Boccaccio
wrote more often in Latin than in
Italian, chiefly under the influence
of his friend Petrarch (◊Veneto and
North-East), although he did also
encourage him to preserve and
value the vernacular works, which
were to become models of Tuscan
literary usage and style from the
15th century onwards. Boccaccio's
encyclopaedic *Genealogia Deorum
Gentilium* (*Genealogies of the Gentile
Gods*), c.1350–60 with later revi-
sions, is an early and important
contribution to the humanist campaign to make classical texts and
learning available. Late works in
Italian include the *Trattatello in
laude di Dante* (*Treatise in Praise of
Dante*), c. 1351–60, and (in a very
different vein from the *Elegy of
Lady Fiammetta*) the satirical anti-
feminist *Corbaccio* c. 1365. In
1373–4 Boccaccio lectured on *The
Divine Comedy* in Florence, and in
1375 died at Certaldo.

BARRETT BROWNING, Eliza-
beth (1806–61), published poetry
from her early teens onwards,
often on classical, religious, and

philosophical themes. She was a fairly well known poet by the time she started to correspond with Robert Browning in 1845. They married, strongly against her father's will, in September 1846. The love poems of *Sonnets from the Portuguese* (in *Poems*, 1850) date from this period. The Brownings lived mainly in Italy from then until Barrett Browning's death in 1861, first in Pisa and then, from 1847, in Florence. Her most important works are *Casa Guidi Windows*, 1851, and the long 'novel in verse' *Aurora Leigh*, 1856. *Aurora Leigh* is a first-person account, in nine books, of Aurora's early childhood in Tuscany, her less happy time in England under the care of her rigidly upright aunt, her making her way as a writer, and her relationship with her cousin Romney Leigh. *Aurora* examines the plight of women and the role of artists in mid-Victorian society. It champions and demonstrates writing on modern issues – 'this live, throbbing age,/That brawls, cheats, maddens, calculates, aspires' – against the moats, drawbridges, 'togas and the picturesque' of much contemporary poetry, and does so in inventively various, often colloquial language. Italy, where the poem begins and reaches its climax, functions as the site and symbol of independence, freedom of choice, freedom from restriction, joy.

BROWNING, Robert (1812–89), first travelled in Italy in 1838, and lived there following his marriage to Elizabeth Barrett for much of the period 1846–61, chiefly in Florence. From 1878 he was again a regular visitor to Italy, especially to Venice, where he died in December 1889. Italy is a recurrent theme or setting in poems from *Sordello*, 1840, to *Asolando*, 1889. Browning was sympathetic to the movement for Italian unification, if rather more detached about it than his wife; 'The Italian in England' (*Dramatic Romances and Lyrics*, 1845), spoken by an exiled opponent of Austrian rule, is the most direct verse expression of his sympathies, and was praised by Mazzini (◊Liguria). More often the poems use or celebrate the landscape – the 'castle, precipice-encurled,/In a gash of the wind-grieved Apennine' of 'De Gustibus' or 'The yellowing fennel, run to seed/There, branching from the brickwork's cleft' of 'Two in the Campagna' (both in *Men and Women*, 1855) – or explore psychology through the dramatic monologues of Italian historical or quasi-historical figures like the vain and sinister Duke of Ferrara in 'My Last Duchess' (*Dramatic Lyrics*, 1842) and the painters Fra Lippo Lippi and Andrea del Sarto (*Men and Women*).

One of Browning's main interests is in 'the dangerous edge of things./The honest thief, the tender murderer, /The superstitious atheist' ('Bishop Blougram's Apology', in *Men and Women*). This theme is developed more extensively in *The Ring and the Book*, 1868–9, founded on the trial papers concerning the Roman Count Guido Franceschini's murder of his young wife Pompilia and her parents in 1698. The truth becomes clear only after each main protagonist has spoken his or her monologue; the divided views of the people of Rome, and the Pope's thoughts on the difficulty of passing judgement, are also introduced.

The more personal significance of Italy in Browning's work is perhaps best summed up in 'By the Fireside' (*Men and Women*), where actual and mental landscapes continually merge and intersect. The ageing speaker, reading a 'great wise book' of Greek by the fireside, journeys through imaginative frames or arches of branch-work until 'we slope to Italy at last/And youth, by green degrees'. The remembered details of woodland, crumbling bridge and ruined chapel, at first apparently descriptive only, gradually prepare the way for an epiphanic moment of love between the walkers in which 'The sights we saw and the sounds we heard,/The lights and the shades made up a spell/Till the trouble grew and stirred'.

DANTE ALIGHIERI (1265–1321), was born into an established but not especially prosperous or powerful Florentine Guelf family. His education included a period at the University of Bologna. In 1289 he fought at the battle of Campaldino, in which the Guelfs decisively defeated the Ghibellines of Arezzo. In the mid-1290s he entered public life, being elected to high office as *priore* for June-August 1300. He was banished when the 'Black' Guelfs wrested control of Florence from the 'Whites'. In exile he became decreasingly identified with the Whites and their attempts to regain power; his political position was complex, but his most solid belief was that temporal power throughout Italy should be the Emperor's, as spiritual power the Pope's. One of Dante's main protectors in the years after leaving the city was Can Grande della Scala, lord of Verona and a Ghibelline leader. Dante travelled widely in Italy, and probably to Paris, often on diplomatic missions for his various protectors. He lived mostly in Ravenna from 1317, and died there.

Dante began his literary career in the 1280s as, with his friend Guido Cavalcanti (c.1240–1300), a leading practitioner of the love-poetry later called *dolce stil nuovo* ('sweet new style'). *La vita nuova* (*The New Life*), c.1292–4), arranges 31 earlier poems and provides them with an

alleged autobiographical context in the prose narrative of the story of his love for Beatrice: his falling in love with her when he was nine and she a little younger, his joy in her 'natural dignity and admirable bearing', her greeting once given and later denied, her death, and his return after some straying to pure dedication to the one who now 'in glory gazes upon the countenance of God'. (Beatrice was Bice or Beatrice Portinari (d.1290), daughter of Folco Portinari and wife of Simone de' Bardi.) *La vita* is, as Steve Ellis puts it, 'a fervent, mystical and esoteric working of the *fin amour* [courtly love] tradition into a Christian context in which Beatrice becomes the vehicle of divine grace and of Dante's salvation.' It is also important for its sophisticated and influential use of the vernacular, which Dante championed – in Latin, the language necessary for any case that needed weighty discussion at this time – in *De vulgari eloquentia* (*On Vernacular Eloquence*), c. 1303–4.

At the end of *La vita nuova* the author, encouraged by a 'miraculous vision', expresses the desire to write of Beatrice 'that which has never been written of any other woman'. The desire will be consummated in *La divina commedia* (*The Divine Comedy*), c.1309–20, called by Dante himself simply *La commedia*). Here Beatrice, in Heaven, has taken pity on Dante and sends the poet Virgil, dweller in the Limbo of virtuous pagans at the edge of Hell, to be his physical and moral guide, out of the dark wood in which Dante finds himself lost and despairing 'Nel mezzo del cammin di nostra vita' ('in the middle of our life's journey'), down through the successively lower and more horrific circles of Hell to the pit and up the mount of Purgatory whence Beatrice herself leads him through an increasingly visionary and light-filled Heaven. These three realms, drawn from a range of Christian and pagan traditions and realised in precise and carefully chosen detail, form a comprehensively ordered system. Hell works on the principle of *contrapasso*, derived like much of Dante's theology from Saint Thomas Aquinas, by which for instance Bertran de Born, for setting Henry II of England's son Henry against his father and so cutting a natural bond, must carry his head parted from his body. Steve Ellis writes of the 'passionate symmetry' of Dante's imagination. There are appointed places in the appropriate level of Hell, Purgatory, or Heaven, for Dante's contemporaries and predecessors, good and bad popes and princes, for Satan in the pit chewing Judas and Brutus (killer of Caesar and so enemy of the imperial idea) and for the Virgin Mary and Saint Francis in the Empyrean.

The experience of reading *The Divine Comedy* is, however, less predictable or mechanical than explanation of its system may suggest. (Flexibility is much assisted by Dante's use – the first – of *terza rima*, where eleven-syllable lines rhyme a b a  b c b  c d c.) The Dante of the poem starts from despair and confusion, needs to ask many questions, feels grief and compassion for many of the sufferers in Hell, makes clear that he is prone to the pride, anger, and lust which penitents in Purgatory remember, and is reminded by Beatrice of his all too human lapses from the divine love which she should inspire. His enlightenment – his move, with the reader, from instinctive sympathy for sufferers in Hell like Francesca da Rimini towards Heaven's perspective – is gradual.

Dante's posthumous reputation was not unmixed. His Thomist theology soon came to seem old-fashioned. To some of Petrarch's (◊Veneto and North-East) followers the verse seemed lacking in grace, elegance, and the classical culture which now came to dominate the world of letters. The main resurgence in his popularity came in the late 18th and 19th century, when he was co-opted as a patriotic Italian by the Risorgimento movement and took up his position as founder of Italian literature in the new literary histories. But it is clear that Dante has never lacked readers. Among 20th century authors Ezra Pound (◊Tuscany) and T.S. Eliot make pervasive use of incidents and quotations from Dante. (Eliot's dedication of *The Waste Land* to Pound as *il miglior fabbro*, 'the better craftsman', aptly quotes one poet on another – Guido Guinicelli on Arnaut Daniel – in *Purgatorio* xxvi.)

ELIOT, George (1819–80), was the name used by Mary Ann or Marian Evans. Most of her novels, including *Middlemarch* (1871–2), deal with society and personal relationships in Victorian England. *Romola* (1862–3) is set in Florence mostly in the years between the expulsion of Piero de' Medici in 1494 and the execution of Fra Girolamo Savonarola in 1498. Eliot, like many writers of 19th century historical fiction, researched her period in minute detail, reading contemporary chronicles, documents, and literature as well as visiting the Florentine sites extensively in 1860 and 1861. Fictional characters mingle with such real citizens as the shrewd Machiavelli and the eccentric painter Piero di Cosimo. *Romola* appeared in monthly instalments in *The Cornhill Magazine*, illustrated with equal passion for historical verisimilitude by Frederick Leighton. Few readers have disagreed with the verdict of *The*

*Westminster Review* in October 1863 that the 'background ... somewhat oppresses the human interest of the tale, and in its ultimate impression affects us like a mediaeval painted window, in which the action has to be disentangled from the blaze of colour and overwhelming accessories'. The author, however, thought highly of the work.

Romola's story, like those of several of the protagonists of Eliot's English novels, is concerned with an unhappy marriage which leads eventually to moral and personal growth. Her husband is the handsome, plausible, and self-indulgent Greek/Italian Tito Melema, a double-dealer in love as in politics. One of Romola's other most important relationships is with Savonarola, whose disciple she for a time becomes. It is in the portrayal of Savonarola that Eliot's research and conviction are most effectively combined – his is 'the struggle of a mind possessed by a never silent hunger after purity and simplicity, yet caught in a tangle of egoistic demands, false ideas, and difficult outward conditions, that made simplicity impossible'. He is one of several father-figures in the novel whom Romola eventually comes to do without, but for all his flaws – as in Florence for many years after his death – Savonarola's personal charisma, terrifying sermons, and 'burning indignation at the sight of wrong' are not to be forgotten.

FICINO, Marsilio (1433–99), Florentine Neo-Platonist philosopher, from an early age patronized by the Medici. In 1462 Cosimo de' Medici gave him a house near the Medici villa at Careggi, where he was one of the earliest members of the informal 'Platonic Academy'. By 1469 Ficino had largely completed his translation of Plato into Latin. As published in 1484, this major work did much to establish Plato (with, or often rather than, Aristotle) as the most authoritative of ancient philosophers. He also worked on the ancient neo-Platonists, and published *Theologia Platonica de immortalitate animarum* (*Platonic Theology on the Immortality of Souls*), 1485. Ficino, unlike earlier theologians, regards Platonic doctrine as itself divinely inspired; 'its revival is necessary in order that the Christian religion may be confirmed and rendered sufficiently rational to satisfy the sceptical and atheistical minds of the age' (Josephine A. Burrows). One of the central beliefs advanced in his commentaries on Plato was in the idea of 'Platonic Love' – human love as a preparation for the love of God. Readers of the commentaries later included Ronsard, Spenser, and Milton.

FORSTER, E.M. (1879–1970), toured Italy in 1901–2. In *The Story of a Panic*, 1904, and his first novel *Where Angels Fear to Tread*, 1905, Italy is the home of natural, primitive, and often dangerous forces. To some extent this remains true in *A Room With a View*, 1908, where the murder in Piazza della Signoria gives Lucy her first inkling that Italy will affect her more deeply than photographs of works of art or her Baedeker's guide. Italy becomes a vehicle of spontaneity: Lucy and George Emerson, whom she thinks she should disapprove of, kiss amid the violets of Fiesole; back in England, the memory and spirit of Italy (in coalition with Mr Emerson's eccentric wisdom) work to defeat social convention and to re-unite Lucy and George, who can now return to Florence to hear the Arno symbolically 'bearing down the snows of winter into the Mediterranean'. Such fulfilment in defiance of Edwardian convention, like that glimpsed more briefly by some of the characters in *Where Angels Fear To Tread*, was tantalisingly attractive to Forster as an undeclared homosexual.

*A Room With a View* is both social comedy and search for the natural or transcendent in human relations. (The much-quoted injunction 'only connect' occurs in Forster's *Howards End*, 1910.) Perhaps as a result of this combination it has been adapted for radio and television and, in 1985, a film by Merchant/Ivory.

FOSCOLO, Ugo (1778–1827), was born on the island of Zante or Zakynthos, of a Greek mother and a Venetian father. He first came to Italy in 1793. He served, at first enthusiastically, with Napoleonic armies in Italy and France between 1797 and 1806. Opposed both to the authoritarian French regime in Italy and the Austrian rule which succeeded it, he fled abroad, first to Switzerland in 1813 and then, in 1816, to England, where he died in poverty brought on by unfortunate investments and an extravagant lifestyle. Among Foscolo's most notable works are the epistolary novel of love and politics *Le ultime lettere di Jacopo Ortis* (*The Last Letters of Jacopo Ortis*), 1798–1802 and the sonnet 'A Zacinto' ('To Zante'), 1803. In the longer poem *Dei sepolcri* (*On Tombs*), 1807, protest at the French edict against individual memorial inscriptions and burial within cities leads to reflections on tombs' significance, both personal and national, to the living.

MACHIAVELLI, Niccolò (1469–1527), born in Florence, was second chancellor of the Florentine republic from 1498. He led important embassies to Louis XII of France, the Emperor Maximilian, and Cesare Borgia, the bold, ruthless, and at the time highly successful son of Pope Alexander VI. (Both Borgia's boldness in obtaining power and glory and his lack of foresight in letting them slip from his grasp make him a useful subject of discussion for Machiavelli in *Il principe*.) In 1512 Machiavelli lost office on the restoration of the Medici, and in 1513, wrongly suspected of conspiracy, was arrested and tortured before being released in a general amnesty. The works he wrote in retirement at Sant'Andrea in Percussina were aimed in part at obtaining employment under the new regime. No appointment was forthcoming, but in 1520, through the influence of his friend Filippo Strozzi with Cardinal Giulio de' Medici (later Pope Clement VII), he was commissioned to write his *Istorie fiorentine* (*Florentine Histories*), 1525, where of necessity he steers carefully between his own radical views and what his patron wishes to hear. At Sant'Andrea he also wrote *Il principe* (*The Prince*), 1513, the reflections on the nature of republics in *Discorsi sopra la prima deca di Tito Livio* (*Discourses on the First Ten Books of Titus Livius* c.1514–19, the comedy *La Mandragola* (*Mandragola*), c.1518, a fast-moving and often acerbic story of the gulling of an old lawyer by his young wife and her lover), and *L'arte della guerra* (*The Art of War*), 1521.

Machiavelli's political works are informed by deep immersion in ancient history, the experience and observation of 15 years' statecraft, and a keenness not merely to repeat conventional views. *Il principe*, intended partly as advice to the new rulers of Florence, is the most original and controversial of these works. Where earlier treatises on monarchy had laid emphasis on the need to act in accordance with moral and religious scruples and in a manner likely to win the subjects' love, Machiavelli counselled that all means were acceptable in the establishment and maintaining of a principate. It is more important to be feared than loved. The successful prince must be prepared to use both cunning and, particularly at the beginning of his rule, force: to be both a fox and a lion. Such beliefs, and the distortions of them which rapidly occurred, resulted in England in the creation of the stage 'Machiavel': in Shakespeare's *Henry VI, Part Three*, 1592, the future Richard III will 'put the murderous Machiavel to school' and Marlowe's *The Jew of Malta*, c.1592, is introduced by the murderous Nick Machevill who 'count[s] religion but a childish toy.' (Machiavelli's first name conveniently reinforced the tradition of calling the Devil Old Nick.) The reality of *Il principe* was, as readers including Francis Bacon were aware, very different. In language as in thought it is remarkably lucid, intelligent, and honest.

MEDICI, Lorenzo de' (1449–92), later called 'Il Magnifico' – the Magnificent – received a thorough humanist education from teachers including Marsilio Ficino◊. He undertook several diplomatic missions for his father Piero 'the Gouty' before succeeding him as virtual ruler of Florence and head of the Medici bank in 1469. His skill and luck in foreign policy maintained Florentine independence from the larger Italian powers and helped delay the intervention of France until after his death.

Lorenzo wrote, in addition to some two thousand letters, much and various verse, some of which he introduced, vigorously asserting the pre-eminence of Tuscan language and literature, in *Comento de' miei sonetti* (*Commentary on My Sonnets*), c.1490–2. As well as

courtly sonnets he produced festival songs, religious poems and drama, and parodies.

PALAZZESCHI, Aldo (1885–1974), born in Florence as Aldo Giurlani, early produced several volumes of verse. He was briefly associated with Futurism, but was too much attracted to irony, parody, and genre-breaking to remain for long associated with any one school or movement. Of his radically experimental early prose works the most remarkable is *Il codice di Perelà* (translated as *The Man of Smoke*), 1911, which, using a wide range of parodic and improvised styles, relays the fantastic and satirical story of the ubiquitous man of smoke; *Il Doge* (*The Doge*), 1967, is a late return to a similar manner. *Sorelle Materassi* (*The Materassi Sisters*), 1934, is ostensibly more orthodox but is concerned, again, with the effect on others of someone markedly 'different'. Here a young man materially ruins but physically and spiritually rejuvenates his two aunts and their servant. Palazzeschi's interest in difference is intimately related to his position as a homosexual in early 20th century Italy.

PICO DELLA MIRANDOLA, Count Giovanni (1463–94), was one of the most eclectic readers and independent thinkers of the Renaissance, versed in a a wide range of philosophical and theological material in Hebrew, Arabic, Greek, and Latin. He attended the universities of Bologna, Ferrara, Paris and Padua, and was a frequent visitor to Florence, becoming associated with the 'Platonic Academy', from 1479. In 1486 he issued, in Rome, 900 theses or truths, challenging other scholars to debate them with him in public the following year. But a commission set up by Pope Innocent VIII condemned 13 of the theses as heretical; Pico fled to France, where he was imprisoned, but released partly through the intercession of Lorenzo the Magnificent. His *Oratio*, later known as *Oratio de hominis dignitate* (*Oration on the Dignity of Man*), 1486, had been intended as an opening speech for the proposed disputation. Its early sections argue eloquently the protean power of human beings, who can become beasts, enslaved to their appetites, or ascend in spirit to the level of the angels: 'Who would not admire this our chameleon?' An *Apologia* (1487) dedicated to Lorenzo, defends the theses and incorporates much of the *Oratio*; the theses themselves were published as *Conclusiones* in the edition of Pico's work by his nephew (1495–6). Shocking though his ideas seemed to some traditionalists, Pico saw them as supporting rather than undermining Christian belief. At the end of his life he became a close friend of Savonarola, and in 1493 joined him in the Dominican order.

POLIZIANO, Angelo (1454–94), Angelo Ambrogini took his humanist surname from Mons Politianus, the Latin name of his birthplace, Montepulciano. In English he is often known as Politian. A precocious classical scholar, he translated Books II-V of Homer's *Iliad* into Latin hexameters between 1469 and 1475 and was befriended by Ficino. From 1473 he was a companion of Lorenzo de' Medici and subsequently his secretary and tutor to his sons. In 1480 he was appointed Professor of Latin and Greek Eloquence at the Studio (university) of Florence, where he lectured on a wide range of classical authors. His *Miscellanea* (1489) long remained an important textbook of editorial technique. Today, however, Poliziano is read

mainly as an author of Italian verse, including dance and carnival lyrics fairly similar to those of Lorenzo, the more ambitious *La giostra* (*The Joust*), 1475–8 – an unfinished attempt to write an Italian poem in the manner of classical epic – and the dialogues of *La favola di Orfeo* (*The Fable of Orpheus*), 1480, the prototype of Italian pastoral drama in the following century. Like his friend Pico della Mirandola, at the end of his life Poliziano was associated with Savonarola.

PRATOLINI, Vasco (1913–91), was born into a working-class family in Florence. Having taken various jobs, he decided at the age of 18 to embark on a programme of intensive study, supporting himself on the meagre wages earned from tasks like undertaking research for university students. In the short term this led to illness brought on by malnutrition, but also laid the foundations for Pratolini's career as a journalist, translator, and novelist. In his early twenties he supported the Fascists, but soon became their opponent. In Florence in 1938–9, with the poet Alfonso Gatto (1909–76), he edited the journal *Campo di Marte* (*The Field of Mars*), until its suppression by the authorities. Pratolini then moved to Rome, serving in the Resistance there in 1943–4, and was again based in Rome from 1951. *Cronaca familiare* (*Family Chronicle*), 1947, the story of his relationship with his younger brother, is the most closely autobiographical of the novels: he declares in a foreword that 'This book is not a work of the imagination. It is the author's conversation with his dead brother . . . He has the remorse of having barely understood his brother's spirituality, and too late. These pages are therefore offered as an inadequate atonement'. The insistent addressing of the book to the dead Ferruccio – the countless repetitions of *tu*, 'you' – embodies a yearning to bridge the gaps of class, early disharmony, and death between the two brothers, to understand Ferruccio and to grasp the different significance for each of the loss of their mother. A film version of *Cronaca familiare*, with a cast headed by Marcello Mastroianni, was directed by Valerio Zurlini in 1962.

Other novels by Pratolini have broader social agenda, but remain rooted in the poor quarters of Florence where he grew up. Among the most interesting are *Cronache di poveri amanti* (*Tales of Poor Lovers*), 1947, with its large cast of workers of Via del Corno under Fascist rule, *Le ragazze di San Frediano* (*The Girls of San Frediano*), 1949, and the later trilogy *Una storia italiana* (*An Italian Story*), 1955–66.

# TUSCANY

'The lofty, gloomy houses are adorned with lamps, brightly coloured tapestries are hanging from all the windows, almost covering the grey, decaying walls, and lovely girls' faces are looking out above them, so fresh and blooming that I perceive it is life itself which has invited beauty and youth to help celebrate the marriage-feast with death.'
Heinrich Heine,
The Town of Lucca

To the Florentine essayist Giovanni Papini◊ Tuscany was a 'grey, bare, circumscribed region' compared with more exotic southern climes: 'well suited to sensitive natures, to the hermit mind', a place where 'one is conscious of the skeleton of stone beneath the green sod, where the great, dark, lonely hills rise suddenly as if threatening the peaceful valleys at their base' (Un uomo finito (A Man – Finished), 1912). Such (comparative) austerity has been suggested as one reason for the particular appeal of Tuscany to northern Europeans. But this is not, of course, the only landscape in the region or the only attitude to it. When Robert Browning (◊Florence) in By the Fireside, 1855, forays into countryside partly imaginary but partly Tuscan, a completely different range of colours from Papini's is introduced. Here lovers walk among 'rose-flesh mushrooms' and coral-nippled toadstools in the early November hours that:

> 'crimson the creeper's leaf across
> Like a splash of blood, intense, abrupt,
> O'er a shield else gold from rim to boss.'

In the north are the marble mountains of Carrara (whose quarries were used by Michelangelo (◊Rome) and Henry Moore), in the west the balze – strange eroded rock formations – of Volterra, in the far south the Val d'Orcia, part barren, part cultivated, the land, 'without mercy, without shade' in summer and buffeted by the north wind in winter, of Iris Origo's◊ *War in the Val d'Orcia*, 1947 (Extract 5).

The cities set in or near these landscapes – most obviously the once separate states of Florence, Pisa, Lucca, and Siena – also have their own very distinctive styles in architecture and painting, although the smaller cities do not share Florence's native literary tradition. Foreigners have, however, gravitated to them and written about them, or about **Livorno**, the main port of arrival and departure. Among those who came here in search of sunlight and warm air was the consumptive and asthmatic Tobias Smollett◊, who lived at the end of his life at **Montenero**, several miles south of the centre of Livorno, overlooking the sea in 'a most romantic and salutary situation', and was buried in the **British Cemetery** (59 Via Verdi) in 1771.

Shelley (◊Rome) lived at Montenero during the summer and autumn of 1819, writing much of his verse-drama *The Cenci* and the political poem *The Mask of Anarchy* in the large-windowed tower of Villa Valsovano where, Mary Shelley later said in a note to the play, often 'the dazzling sunlight and heat made it almost intolerable to every other; but Shelley basked in both'. (In the 20th century 'basking' became more fashionable and took place especially on the beaches of **Viareggio**). And it was from Livorno that Shelley, his friend Edward Williams and their boat-boy Charles Vivian sailed on their fatal journey of 8 July 1822. They were last seen, off Viareggio, in mountainous seas which presumably exhilarated Shelley, lover of boats, waves, and 'the steep sky's commotion' (*Ode to the West Wind*, 1819); apparently he refused an offer of help by the captain of a fishing-boat. Then, according to the captain, the English party were begged by speaking-trumpet 'for God's sake reef your sails or you are lost', Williams tried to obey, and Shelley angrily seized his arm to prevent him. The bodies were washed ashore, in pitiable state, ten days later. Edward John Trelawny, adventurer, unreliable biographer and autobiographer, and friend of Shelley, organised the cremation on the beach at **Il Gombo** with Byron and others in attendance. Trelawny maintained, perhaps with more mythic than factual accuracy, that 'the heart remained entire' (*Records of Shelley, Byron, and the Author*, 1858). Shelley's ashes were later buried in the Protestant Cemetery in Rome.

## SIENA

The Palio is 'a particularly brutal kind of horse-race. It all goes on in the square with a parade of flag-wavers in medieval costume, knights in armour – all the delights of the Middle Ages without the stink and the fear of plague'. This is the opinion of Haverford Downs in John Mortimer's (◊Umbria and Marche) *Summer's Lease*, 1988. Always ready with what he is happy to regard as a well-worded opinion, Haverford has not in fact been to the definitive Sienese event. This

time, however, he finds himself part of the family expedition. The
**Piazza del Campo** is indeed, as he predicted, 'packed'. But, with
characteristic 'nerve', he manages, through a chance meeting with an
ex-schoolfriend of his daughter, to get the whole party into an apartment with a view of the square. To the characters the noisy and rapid
race itself is not very important, but in passing Mortimer indicates
some of the traditional Sienese passion for it. Aristocrats are prepared
to be friendly with mere dentists for the sake of a good view. The
supporters of the victorious jockey of the Hedgehog *contrada* or parish
storm onto the course and the owner of the apartment, an Ostrich
man, is 'cock-a-hoop' when the Dragon endures the disgrace of coming second, for the Ostrich has hated the Dragon since the Middle
Ages.

Siena is usually calmer. But even with no Palio in progress Virginia
Woolf found that (here as elsewhere) 'the thought evaporates, runs
hither and thither' in 'the vast tunnelled arched stone town, swarmed
over by chattering shrieking children' (*Diary*, 13 May 1933). Woolf's
sensitivity to, and ability to write about, the difficulty of writing is
characteristic. Henry James (◊Venice), during his second Italian
sojourn in 1873, had fewer qualms. He was already alert to the aesthetic and associative nuances of place as he reflected on the **Palazzo
Pubblico** and square as seen by moonlight (Extract 4) and with simpler
enthusiasm described the Cathedral at morning: its 'fantastic and
luxuriant' semi-oriental facade and its interior 'concert of relieved
and dispersed glooms' (*Italian Hours*, 1909).

Saint Catherine of Siena◊ lived in a humbler part of the town. As
Caterina Benincasa she was born in 1347 at the house and work-place
of her father, a dyer, now the **Casa di Santa Caterina**. After her death
and her canonization in 1461 the house became a grander place with
the addition of frescoes and a loggia and the conversion of rooms into
oratories. One of these occupies the site of Catherine's bedroom. 'In
this little room', recalled her friend and disciple (originally her spiritual adviser) Raimondo of Capua 'were revived the ancient deeds of
the holy fathers of Egypt' [the early monks and hermits of the desert],
about whom, miraculously, Caterina had never been told (*Vita Sanctae
Catherinae Senensis* (*The Life of Saint Catherine of Siena*), c. 1380).
According to Raymond she fasted continuously, eating nothing but
raw herbs for much of her life, deprived herself of sleep (when she did
rest she used a stone, still displayed, for a pillow), and spent her time
in vigils and meditation. But after the age of 16 she also went out of the
house to work with the poor and diseased in the streets and hospices
of Siena. Later she was involved in the more complex human affairs of
the papacy in Rome and elsewhere, but she remained strongly associated with the city of her birth. Catherine's head is preserved in a
reliquary in the church of **San Domenico**.

Catherine was canonized by a less ascetic church leader, Pope Pius

II, who, as Enea Silvio Piccolomini⟩ wrote secular literature in Latin and had become bishop of Siena in 1450. The most tangible Sienese reminder of Pius' varied career and interests is Pinturicchio's frescoed account of his life (1502–9), commissioned by his nephew Francesco Piccolomini (Pope Pius III) in the **Libreria Piccolomini** (reached from the left-hand aisle of the cathedral). Henry James began the day here, he recalled many years later, in 'charmed homage to Pinturicchio, coolest and freshest and signally youngest' of painters. Under his brush the adventures and achievements of the 'most profanely literary of Pontiffs and last of would-be Crusaders . . . smooth themselves out for us very much to the tune of the "stories" told by some fine old man of the world, at the restful end of his life, to the cluster of his grandchildren'.

## PISA

In the 12th century Pisa was a major naval and mercantile power and the home of a distinctive architectural style. The 'Campo dei Miracoli' (officially called Piazza del Duomo) commemorates both the pride of this period and its more spiritual emphases. As Aldous Huxley⟩ puts it in *Those Barren Leaves*, 1925:

> 'Islanded in their grassy meadow within the battlemented walls, the white church, the white arcaded tower miraculously poised on the verge of falling, the round white baptistery seemed to meditate in solitude of ancient glories – Pisan dominion, Pisan arts and thoughts – of the mysteries of religion, of inscrutable fate and unfathomed godhead, of the insignificance and the grandeur of man.'

The more pragmatic novelist Tobias Smollett, in *Travels Through France and Italy*, 1766, had admired the cathedral for its 'massy pillars of porphyry, granite, jasper' and yellow and green ('verde antico') marble.

Smollett, like many travellers, found Pisa a restful place. In particular, the 'spacious corridor' of memorials around the **Camposanto Monumentale** (originally built in the 13th century to enclose 43 tons of soil from the Hill of Golgotha) seemed to him 'a noble walk for a contemplative philosopher'. Pisa's long period of decline from worldly glories had begun with its loss of dominance at sea to Genoa, signalled most decisively in the battle of Meloria in 1284 and the carrying off by the Genoans of the harbour chains in 1342. (Eventually returned in the 19th century, they are now in the Camposanto.) Count Ugolino della Gherardesca was blamed for the disaster of Meloria and imprisoned by his former ally, Archbishop Ruggieri degli Ubaldini. Ugolino suffers in the Ninth Circle of Dante's Hell (Extract 2), but the archbishop's place is even lower because he starved to death not only the count but four innocent members of his family. They died in the tower, thereafter called the 'Torre della Fama' (Hunger Tower), which was later incorporated in the 17th-century **Palazzo dell' Orologio**. The horror of this incident remained in the minds of many later writers. Most, including Ezra Pound◊ in *The Pisan Cantos*, 1948, understand Dante to say (modern commentators disagree) that Ugolino, the last of the prisoners to die, resorts to cannibalism.

Pound wrote much of *The Pisan Cantos* while detained in somewhat more humane circumstances, in 1945, at the American Disciplinary Training Centre just outside the city at Metato. It was from here that he was flown home to America to face treason charges resulting from his close association with Fascism. He briefly images the camp and the nearby road (from Viareggio to Pisa):

> 'and there was a smell of mint under the tent flaps
> especially after the rain
> and a white ox on the road towards Pisa
> as if facing the tower.'

Earlier poets had remained in Pisa voluntarily. Quiet though much of the city was, the presence of a major university encouraged by the Grand Dukes of Tuscany did provide some social and intellectual life, especially on the north bank of the Arno. Giacomo Leopardi (◊Umbria and Marche) wondered, in 1827, at hearing 'ten or twenty languages spoken, while brilliant sunshine lights up the gilding of the cafés, the shops full of frivolities, and the windows of the palaces and houses'. (One of the cafés of the day has survived: **Caffè dell' Ussero**, in Lungarno Pacinotti.) A few years before, Byron (◊Venice) had lived (1821–2) in the **Palazzo Toscanelli** (then called Palazzo Lanfranchi) on Lungarno Mediceo. The building now houses archives, but the attractive golden-yellow marble front remains relatively unchanged. (The lease had been organised by Shelley (◊Rome), himself living at Tre Palazzi Chiesa, roughly opposite on the south bank.) Here Byron completed several cantos of *Don Juan*, written, according to Leigh Hunt◊, at night with the aid of gin and water. In the mornings, Hunt remembered in *Lord Byron and Some of his Contemporaries*, 1828:

> 'He breakfasted; read; lounged about, singing an air, generally out of Rossini, and in a swaggering style, though in a voice at once small and veiled; then took a bath, and was dressed; and coming down-stairs, was heard, still singing, in the court-yard, out of which the garden ascended at the back of the house. . . . My study, a little room in a corner, with an orange-tree peeping in at the window, looked upon this court-yard.'

## LUCCA

Medieval Lucca was a seat of power and influence, a capital of the Lombard dukes, briefly subjugated by Pisa in the 14th century but not, unlike Pisa and most other Tuscan cities, absorbed by Florence. Napoleon gave it to his sister Elisa in 1799; it remained a separate state until it passed to the Grand Duchy of Tuscany in 1847. With its ramparts and gardens Lucca offers a refuge from less intimate Florence.

The churches of Lucca had a profound effect on John Ruskin (◊Venice) as he intensively pondered, drew, and described them in almost daily letters to his parents in 1845. **San Frediano** is 'all glorious dark arches and columns – covered with holy frescoes – and gemmed gold pictures on blue grounds'. San Michele in Foro, more precisely, has a facade inventively ornamented with scenes of hunting:

> 'little Nimrods with short legs and long lances – blowing tremen-dous trumpets – and with dogs which appear running up and down the round arches like flies, heads uppermost – and game of all descriptions – boars chiefly, but stags, tapirs, griffins and dragons – and indescribably innumerable, all cut out in hard green porphyry, and inlaid in the marble.'

(In 1858–66 the facade was extensively restored or, as far as Ruskin was concerned, 'destroyed'). It was the Romanesque style, here and in the **cathedral of San Martino**, which most often excited him to characteristic extremes of enthusiasm, but he was also fascinated by the later (1408, by Jacopo della Quercia) recumbent effigy of Ilaria del Carretto in the north transept of the cathedral. Each evening, as 'the rose tints leave the clouds', he would spend a quarter of an hour with Ilaria, who lies:

> 'on a simple pillow, with a hound at her feet. Her dress is of the simplest middle age character, folding closely over the bosom, and tight to the arms, clasped about the neck. Round her head is a circular fillet, with three star shaped flowers. From under this the hair falls like that of the Magdalene, its undulation *just* felt as it touches the cheek, and no more . . . The cast of the drapery, for *severe natural* simplicity and perfect grace, I never saw equalled, nor the fall of the hands – you expect every instant, or rather you seem to see every instant, the last sinking into death. There is no decoration nor work about it, not even enough for protection – you may stand beside it leaning on the pillow, and watching the twilight fade over the sweet, dead lips and arched eyes in their sealed close.'

On later visits the resemblance which Ruskin saw to Rose La Touche, a young woman who had refused his proposal of marriage, made it difficult to draw Ilaria: she is too like 'some peepies that ain't dead but are of stone', he wrote to Joan Severn in August 1874. But in 1845 the one damper on his enthusiasm was his exasperation at the neglect (or worse) of the medieval monuments by the Lucchesi, who, a vein of robust xenophobia helped him to believe, 'seem bad enough for anything'.

Some years earlier Heinrich Heine, in the Lucca section of his *Reisebilder* (*Travel Pictures*), 1826–31, had taken a more quizzical look at the churches and what was going on in and around them (partly in his memory, not a little in his imagination). His narrator, attending mass in the cathedral with a mocking irreverent English lady and a devout Italian one, finds the cathedral 'a simple, handsome church, its coloured marble facade decorated with those short columns built on top of one another, that look so comically dismal'. The sermon is given by 'a big, burly monk whose ancient Roman face with its bold, commanding air was in remarkable contrast to his coarse habit, so that the man looked like an emperor of poverty'. Many of his colleagues, in a splendid variety of costumes long familiar 'thanks to the efforts of our theatre director', are to be seen in procession on festival days when the usually deathly streets of Lucca are decked out and crowded as if an entire population has risen from the grave 'to mimic life in the maddest of masquerades' (Extract 1).

## SAN GIMIGNANO AND VOLTERRA

E.M. Forster's Monteriano in *Where Angels Fear to Tread*, 1905, is based loosely on San Gimignano, whose preserved medieval towers and streets he saw briefly in 1902. In the novel Philip Herriton, even though he arrives in high irritation to sort out his sister-in-law's improvident marriage to a young native, and driven in 'what is suitably termed a *legno* – a piece of wood', does not fail to notice how from a distance the brown city of Monteriano and its towers 'seemed to float in isolation between trees and sky, like some fantastic ship city of a dream' or how on the way up the hill there are small trees 'whose stems stood in violets as rocks stand in the summer sea . . . The cart-ruts were channels, the hollows lagoons; even the dry white margin of the road was splashed, like a causeway soon to be submerged under the advancing tide of spring'. Philip's Englishness, however, is only briefly to be submerged. At the opera (Extract 3) and for other brief moments he manages to shed some of the inhibitions which contribute to the misunderstandings and unhappiness between English and Italians in the book. But from the beginning there have been indications that Italy may be less simply romantic or perfidious than the characters assume. For instance Gino, the man Philip has come to confront, is the son of a dentist: 'A dentist in fairyland! False teeth and laughing gas and the tilting chair at a place which knew the Etruscan League . . . and the Middle Ages, all fighting and holiness, and the

Renaissance, all fighting and beauty!' (Probably Philip would have found more convincingly Italian the early 14th century poet known as Folgore (Splendour) da San Gimignano◊, although he spoils the division between medieval and Renaissance by having engaged both in fighting and, through verbal miniatures of a courtly, elegant life, the pursuit of beauty.)

**Volterra** more obviously 'knew the Etruscan League'. As Velathri it was a large (spreading further down the hill than Volterra) and important city whose main gate, the **Porta all' Arco**, has survived in only partly modified form. D.H. Lawrence (◊Sardinia) scrutinized 'the deep old gateway, almost a tunnel, with the outer arch facing the desolate country on the skew' in the last chapter of *Etruscan Places*, 1932. It has 'that peculiar weighty richness of ancient things; and three dark heads, now worn featureless, reach out curiously and inquiringly . . . to gaze from the city and into the deep hollow of the world beyond'. The Romans restored the arch and built their fine **Theatre** north of the Etruscan walls. Much of the medieval city survives. But there remains a sense of difference, of set-apartness, about Volterra on its windy bluff, 'a sort of inland island, still curiously isolated, and grim', which Lawrence at least would like to associate with the Etruscan presence. The surroundings are another element in this feeling: the wilderness through which Lord Hovenden's car mounts towards Volterra in *Those Barren Leaves*, 1925, by Lawrence's contemporary Aldous Huxley◊, the 'bare, unfertile hills, between whose yellowing grasses showed a white and ghastly soil', the 'infernal aspect' of the 'parched hills and waterless gulleys, like the undulations of a petrified ocean' which 'expanded interminably round them'. Volterra is 'the capital of this strange hell'.

## OTHER LITERARY LANDMARKS

**Arezzo**: Casa di Vasari, 55 Via XX Settembre, is the house frescoed and decorated by Giorgio Vasari (◊Lombardy) for himself in the 1540s.

**Arezzo**: Casa Petrarca, 28 Via dell' Orto, is the (rebuilt) birthplace of Petrarch (◊Veneto and North-East).

**Caprese Michelangelo**: Michelangelo (◊Rome) was born here, probably in the Palazzo Pretorio.

**Bagni di Lucca**: spa stayed in by writers including Heine◊ and Shelley (◊Rome) – plaque at 141 Viale Umberto. The Anglo-French novelist Ouida (1839–1908) is buried in the Protestant cemetery.

**Certaldo**: Boccaccio (◊Florence) was probably born here. In his last years he led a quiet, scholarly life at the (reconstructed) Casa di Boccaccio. He is buried in the church of Santi Michele e Iacopo.

**Elba**: island of Napoleon's first exile in 1814–15. His house in

Portoferraio is now the Museo Napoleonico dei Mulini. He also lived at the Villa Napoleone di San Martino.

**La Verna**: monastery on the site where St Francis (◊Umbria and Marche) received the Stigmata in 1224.

**Lucca**: small museum in the birthplace of the composer Giacomo Puccini (1858–1924), 30 Via di Poggio.

**Montegufoni**: medieval castle (not open to the public) bought by Sir George Sitwell in 1909, the home of his son the writer Sir Osbert Sitwell (1892–1969).

**Montepulciano**: a plaque at 5 Via Poliziano marks the birthplace of Angelo Poliziano (◊Florence).

**Montecristo**: the small island (not visitable) where Edmond Dantès finds treasure in *Le Comte de Monte-Cristo* (*The Count of Montecristo*), 1844–6, by Alexandre Dumas *père*.

**Pienza**: birthplace (as Corsignano) of Enea Silvio Piccolomini◊. As Pope Pius II he had it rebuilt as an (unfinished) ideal Renaissance city.

**Pisa**: museum and library at the Domus Mazziniana, 72 Via Mazzini, where the Risorgimento thinker and activist (◊Liguria) died in 1872.

**Siena**: the Loggia del Papa, Via di Pantasseto, was built for Pope Pius II (Enea Silvia Piccolomini◊) in 1462. The state archives in Palazzo Piccolomini (52 Via Banchi di Sotto) display some of his manuscripts and Boccaccio's (◊Florence) will.

**Torre del Lago Puccini**: house and tomb of Giacomo Puccini.

**Valdicastello Carducci**: museum in the birthplace of Carducci (◊Emilia-Romagna).

**Vallombrosa**: in John Milton's *Paradise Lost*, 1667, the fallen angels lie 'Thick as autumnal leaves that strew the brooks/In Vallombrosa, where the Etrurian shades/High overarch'd embower'. A plaque marks the house where, according to tradition, Milton stayed in 1638.

**Vinci**: in the castle is a Museo Leonardiano; the birthplace of Leonardo da Vinci (◊Lombardy) is close by at Anchiano.

# BOOKLIST

Beauman, Nicola, *Morgan: a Biography of E.M. Forster*, Hodder and Stoughton, London, 1993.

St Catherine of Siena, *I, Catherine: Selected Writings of Saint Catherine of Siena*, Kenelm Foster and Mary John Ronayne OP, trans, Collins, London, 1980.

Clegg, Jeanne, and Paul Tucker, *Ruskin in Tuscany*, Ruskin Gallery, Collection of the Guild of St George, Sheffield, and Lund Humphries, London, 1993.

Dante Alighieri, *The Divine Comedy*, Mark Musa, trans, Penguin, Harmondsworth, 1984–6. **Extract 2.**

*Booklist continued*

Forster, E.M., *Where Angels Fear to Tread* [1905], Penguin, Harmondsworth, 1976. **Extract 3**.

Heine, Heinrich, *Selected Prose*, Ritchie Robertson, trans, Penguin, London, 1993. **Extract 1**.

Huxley, Aldous, *Those Barren Leaves* [1925], David Bradshaw, intr, Flamingo, London, 1994.

James, Henry, *Italian Hours* [1909], Tamara Follini, intr, Century Hutchinson, London, 1986. **Extract 4**.

Mitchell, R.J., *The Laurels and the Tiara: Pope Pius II 1458–1464*, Harvill, London, 1962.

Origo, Iris, *War in Val d'Orcia: a Diary* [1947], John Murray, London, 1984. **Extract 5**.

Papini, Giovanni, *A Man – Finished* [1912], Mary Pritchard Agnetti, trans, Hodder and Stoughton, London, 1924.

Piccolomini, Enea Silvio, *Memoirs of a Renaissance Pope: the Commentaries of Pius II*, Florence A. Gragg, trans, and Leona C. Gabel, ed, George Allen and Unwin, London, 1960.

Pound, Ezra, *The Cantos*, Faber, London, 1987.

Blessed Raymond of Capua, *The Life of Saint Catherine of Siena*, George Lamb, trans, Harvill Press, London, 1960.

Woolf, Virginia, *The Diary of Virginia Woolf*, Anne Olivier Bell, ed, Penguin, Harmondsworth, 1979–85.

# Extracts

## (1) LUCCA

### Heinrich Heine, *The Town of Lucca*, 1831

*In one of his idiosyncratic Travel Pictures, a mixture of travel-writing, fiction, philosophising and satire, Heine explores decay, festivity, and the various manifestations of the Roman Catholic church in Lucca.*

The whole town was as silent as the grave, everything was so colourless and motionless, the sunlight played on the roofs like gilded tinsel on the head of a corpse, tendrils of ivy hung down here and there, like dried-up green tears, from the windows of a ruinous house, the gleam of mildew and the fearful mouldering of death could be sensed everywhere, the town seemed only the ghost of a town, a stone spectre in broad daylight. I searched for a long time in vain for the trace of a living being. All I remember is that a beggar was lying asleep, with his palm outstretched, outside an old palazzo. I also remember seeing a monk, at the upper window of a blackish, decaying little house, with his red neck and his fleshy bald head protruding far out of his brown habit and beside him could be seen a naked female with a full bosom; down below I saw a little boy entering the half-open front door, dressed as an Abbate in black, and carrying in both hands a huge, fat-bellied wine-bottle. At that moment a faint, ironic bell rang nearby, and the novellas of Boccaccio chuckled slyly in my memory. These sounds, however, could not quite dispel the strange horror that gripped my soul. Its power was perhaps strengthened by the warm, bright sunshine that lit the sinister building; and I perceived that ghosts are still more terrifying when they throw off the dark mantle of light and appear in the clear light of noonday.

Returning to Lucca now, a week later, how astonished I was by the changed appearance of the town! 'What is this?' I cried, as lights dazzled my eyes and crowds surged through the alleyways. 'Has an entire population risen from its grave as a nocturnal ghost, to mimic life in the maddest of masquerades? The lofty, gloomy houses are adorned with lamps, brightly coloured tapestries are hanging from all the windows, almost covering the grey, decaying walls, and lovely girls' faces are looking out above them, so fresh and blooming that I perceive it is life itself which has invited beauty and youth to help celebrate its marriage-feast with death.' Indeed, it was a living festival of the dead; I do not know what it is called in the calendar, but at any rate it must have been the day when some patient martyr was flayed, for I later saw a holy skull and a few additional bones, adorned with flowers and jewels, being carried about to nuptial music. It was a beautiful procession.

At its head walked the Capuchins, who were distinguished from the other monks by their long beards, and formed, as it were, the sappers in this army of faith. They were followed by Capuchins without beards . . . These in turn were followed by habits of different colours, black, white, yellow, striped, and by three-cornered hats worn low over the eyes, in short, by all the monastic costumes with which we have long been familiar, thanks to the efforts of our theatre director.

## (2) PISA

### Dante Alighieri, *Hell* (after 1309)

*In 1288 Count Ugolino della Gherardesca was imprisoned on treason charges by his former ally Archbishop Ruggieri degli Ubaldini. Ugolino was starved to death with four other members of his family. (In reality two sons and two grandsons, the younger aged about 15; Dante makes them all young sons.) The count pauses in his continual gnawing at the archbishop's head to tell his story. His last words here probably mean not that he finally gave way to cannibalism, but simply that he died of hunger.*

'And then they awoke. It was around the time
they usually brought our food to us. But now
each one of us was full of dread from dreaming;

then from below I heard them driving nails
into the dreadful tower's door; with that,
I stared in silence at my flesh and blood.

I did not weep, I turned to stone inside;
they wept, and my little Anselmuccio spoke:
"What is it, father? Why do you look that way?"

For them I held my tears back, saying nothing,
all of that day, and then all of that night,
until another sun shone on the world.

A meagre ray of sunlight found its way
to the misery of our cell, and I could see
myself reflected four times in their faces.

I bit my hands in anguish. And my children,
who thought that hunger made me bite my hands,
were quick to draw up closer to me, saying:

"O father, you would make us suffer less,
if you would feed on us: you were the one
who gave us this sad flesh; you take it from us!"

I calmed myself to make them less unhappy.
That day we sat in silence, and the next day.
O pitiless earth! You should have swallowed us!

The fourth day came, and it was on that day
my Gaddo fell prostrate before my feet,
crying: "Why don't you help me? Why, my father?"

There he died. Just as you see me here,
I saw the other three fall one by one,
as the fifth day and the sixth day passed. And I,

by then gone blind, groped over their dead bodies.
Though they were dead, two days I called their names.
Then hunger proved more powerful than grief.'

He spoke these words; then, glaring down in rage,
attacked again the live skull with his teeth
sharp as a dog's, and as fit for grinding bones.

## (3) SAN GIMIGNANO

### E.M. Forster,
### *Where Angels Fear to Tread*, 1905

*Three English visitors on a misguided mission to 'rescue' a baby
from its Italian father after the death of the English mother have
come to Monteriano, a town famous for its medieval towers and
based partly on San Gimignano. They decide, half against their
better judgement, to go to a production of Donizetti's Lucia di
Lammermoor. (It was in fact in Florence that Forster had seen
the opera in May 1903.)*

The chorus of Scotch retainers burst into cry. The audience accompanied with tappings and drummings, swaying in the melody like corn
in the wind. Harriet, though she did not care for music, knew how to
listen to it. She uttered an acid 'Shish!'

'Shut it,' whispered her brother.

'We must make a stand from the beginning. They're talking.'

'It is tiresome,' murmured Miss Abbott; 'but perhaps it isn't for us
to interfere.'

Harriet shook her head and shished again. The people were quiet,
not because it is wrong to talk during a chorus, but because it is
natural to be civil to a visitor. For a little time she kept the whole
house in order, and could smile at her brother complacently.

Her success annoyed him. He had grasped the principle of opera in
Italy – it aims not at illusion but at entertainment – and he did not
want this great evening-party to turn into a prayer-meeting. But soon
the boxes began to fill, and Harriet's power was over. Families greeted
each other across the auditorium. People in the pit hailed their brothers and sons in the chorus, and told them how well they were singing.
When Lucia appeared by the fountain there was loud applause, and
cries of 'Welcome to Monteriano!'

'Ridiculous babies!' said Harriet, settling down in her stall. . . .

Lucia began to sing, and there was a moment's silence. She was stout
and ugly; but her voice was still beautiful, and as she sang the theatre
murmured like a hive of happy bees. All through the coloratura she
was accompanied by sighs, and its top note was drowned in a shout of
universal joy.

So the opera proceeded. The singers drew inspiration from the
audience, and the two great sextettes were rendered not unworthily.
Miss Abbott fell into the spirit of the thing. She, too, chatted and
laughed and applauded and encored, and rejoiced in the existence of
beauty. As for Philip, he forgot himself as well as his mission. He was
not even an enthusiastic visitor. For he had been in this place always. It
was his home.

## (4) SIENA

### Henry James, *Italian Hours*, 1909

*James, then a little known journalist and short-story writer, describes his first experience of the Piazza del Campo in 1873.*

I arrived late in the evening, by the light of a magnificent moon, and while a couple of benignantly-mumbling old crones were making up my bed at the inn strolled forth in quest of a first impression. Five minutes brought me to where I might gather it unhindered as it bloomed in the white moonshine. . . . The waiting scene was in the shape of a shallow horse-shoe – as the untravelled reader who has turned over his friends' portfolios will respectfully remember; or, better, of a bow in which the high wide face of the Palazzo Pubblico forms the cord and everything else the arc. It was void of any human presence which could figure to me the current year; so that, the moonshine assisting, I had half-an-hour's infinite vision of mediaeval Italy. The Piazza being built on the side of a hill – or rather, as I believe science affirms, in the cup of a volcanic crater – the vast pavement converges downwards in slanting radiations of stone, the spokes of a great wheel, to a point directly before the Palazzo, which may mark the hub, though it is nothing more ornamental than the mouth of a drain. The great monument stands on the lower side and might seem, in spite of its goodly mass and its embattled cornice, to be rather defiantly out-countenanced by vast private constructions occupying the opposite eminence. This *might* be, without the extraordinary dignity of the architectural gesture with which the huge high-shouldered pile asserts itself.

On the firm edge of the palace, from bracketed base to grey-capped summit against the sky, there grows a tall slim tower which soars and soars till it has given notice of the city's greatness over the blue mountains that mark the horizon. It rises as slender and straight as a pennoned lance planted on the steel-shod toe of a mounted knight, and keeps all to itself in the blue air, far above the changing fashions of the market, the proud consciousness of a rare arrogance once built into it. This beautiful tower, the finest thing in Siena and, in its rigid fashion, as permanently fine thus as a really handsome nose on a face of no matter what accumulated age, figures there still as a Declaration of Independence besides which such an affair as ours, thrown off at Philadelphia, appears to have scarce done more than helplessly give way to time. Our Independence has become a dependence on a thousand such dreadful things as the incorrupt declaration of Siena strikes us as looking for ever straight over the level of.

## (5) Val d'Orcia

### Iris Origo, *War in the Val d'Orcia*, 1947

*The author introduces her journal of life in 1943–4 on the La
Foce estate, near Montepulciano, in a once barren area which
she and her husband had transformed by intensive farming since
their arrival in 1924.*

The following are the conditions under which this diary has been
written:

We live on a large farm in southern Tuscany – 12 miles from the
station and five from the nearest village. The country is wild and
lonely: the climate harsh. Our house stands on a hillside, looking
down over a wide and beautiful valley, beyond which rises Monte
Amiata, wooded with chestnuts and beeches. Nearer by, on this side
of the valley, lie slopes of cultivated land: wheat, olives and vines, but
among them still stand some ridges of dust-coloured clay hillocks –
the *creti senesi* – as bare and colourless as elephants' backs, as
mountains of the moon. The wide river-bed in the valley holds a
rushing stream in the rainy season, but during the summer a mere
trickle, in a wide desert of stones. And then, when the wheat ripens
and the alfalfa has been cut, the last patches of green disappear from
the landscape. The whole valley becomes dust-coloured – a land
without mercy, without shade. If you sit under an olive-tree you
are not shaded; the leaves are like little flickering tongues of fire.
At evening and dawn the distant hills are misty and blue, but under
one's feet the dry earth is hard. The cry of the cicadas shrills in the
noonday. One can only wait – anxiously, thirstily – for the September rains, when the whole countryside comes to life again. Then the
vintage comes, the ox-carts are piled high with purple and yellow
grapes. The farm-houses and the trees around them are hung with
the last vestiges of the harvest: the orange cobs of the Indian corn,
hanging to dry, gay and fantastic as a Russian ballet décor. Then
there is the autumn ploughing, and one last harvest before the
winter: that of the olives. The fruits turn from green to red, from
red to the ripeness of dark purple; they are gathered and pressed,
and pressed again; their oil is stored in great jars, fit for Ali Baba,
and their kernels serve us for fuel. And now we wait for the winter,
and with it comes the north wind, the *tramontana*, sweeping across
the bare uplands. It drives the farmer indoors; it buffeted and
tore the escaping prisoners of war and partisans until they had per-
force to take shelter, for months on end, in the stables of the farm.

# Biographies and important works

CATHERINE OF SIENA, SAINT. Caterina Benincasi (1347–80), was the last of the 25 children of a Siena dyer. At the age of six she experienced the first of her visions, and at 16, having overcome much family opposition, she joined the Dominican lay order of the Mantellate. In Siena she undertook various charitable works and led a life of continual abstinence and austerity. She developed a considerable degree of influence, both spiritual and political, over her contemporaries, mediating between the Pope and the Florentines and even, in 1376–7, playing a major role in persuading Pope Gregory XI to bring the papacy back from Avignon to Rome. She died in Rome and was buried in the Dominican church of Santa Maria sopra Minerva, but her head was soon removed to become a precious relic at San Domenico in Siena. She was canonized in 1461, and in 1939 joined St Francis as patron saint of Italy.

381 of Catherine's letters have survived. Often conversational in tone (they were mostly dictated to her followers), they deliver counsel and fearless reprimand, express the divine love, and show an intense interest in people's well-being. Her most important theological work is the *Dialogo della divina provvidenza* (*Dialogue of Divine Providence*), 1378.

FOLGORE DA SAN GIMIGNANO (d. after 1332) – 'Splendour of San Gimignano' – was born Giacomo di Michele. He is known to have served as a footsoldier against Pistoia in 1305. His 32 sonnets, influenced to a degree by earlier Provençal troubadour verse, date from c.1309–17; the most well known of them profess to show a 'noble band' of Siena how to pass each month of the year in an appropriately refined and courtly manner and have thus excited comparison with French Books of Hours.

HEINE, Heinrich (1797–1856), a German Jew, was baptized as a Christian in 1825 in the hope of obtaining career advantages. After an abortive start in business he had studied at the universities of Bonn, Göttingen and Berlin. He travelled in Germany, England and, in 1828, northern Italy, before settling in France in 1831. His most popular work was the lyric poetry of the *Buch der Lieder* (*Book of Songs*), 1827. The four volumes of *Reiserbilder* (*Travel Pictures*) appeared between 1826 and 1831. These sketches are not so much accounts of travel as allusive, often whimsical meditations on various topics, often encouraged by encounters with fictional or semi-fictional characters and held loosely together by a sense of place; the most evident source is the novels of Laurence Sterne. *The Town of Lucca*, in the fourth volume, 1831, wanders around the subject of religion, with the narrator by turns interested in and exasperated by both the irreverence of Lady Matilda and the simple piety of Francesca.

HUNT, Leigh (1784–1859), liberal essayist, poet, and editor, came to Pisa in 1822 at the invitation of Shelley (◊Rome), who persuaded Byron (◊Venice) to publish *The Vision of Judgement* in Hunt's *The Liberal* (1822). He remained in Italy with his family, amid his habitual financial difficulties, until 1825. Hunt's works include *The Story of Rimini*, 1816, a poem inspired by Paolo and Francesca in Dante's *Inferno*, and the play *A Legend of Florence*, 1840.

HUXLEY, Aldous (1894–1963), author of *Brave New World*, 1932, lived in Italy for several periods in the 1920s and 1930s. *Those Barren Leaves*, 1925, includes satire on various English social types. An expedition in which Lord Hovenden's fast driving exhilarates his intended wife and appals his earnest socialist would-be mentor Mr Falx gives Huxley the opportunity briefly to describe many Italian cities and landscapes. More developed accounts of the Palio at Siena, Sabbioneta, and Piero della Francesca's *Resurrection* at Sansepolcro ('the best picture in the world') are included in *Along the Road: Notes and Essays of a Tourist*, 1925.

ORIGO, Iris (1902–88), of moneyed Anglo-American parentage, lived in Italy for most of her life. Her mother Lady Sybil Cutting (caricatured as Lilian Aldwinkle by Aldous Huxley in *Those Barren Leaves*) owned the Villa Medici, built for Cosimo de' Medici, in Fiesole. With her husband Marchese Antonio Origo, Iris Origo lived on the farm estate of La Foce in the Val d'Orcia from 1924, introducing intensive cultivation to a formerly barren area. During 1943–4, when

the Val d'Orcia occupied a vital strategic position, she sheltered or helped, at considerable personal risk, both escaped British prisoners-of-war and children made homeless by British bombing. These experiences are recorded, in matter-of-fact but compassionate manner, in *War in the Val d'Orcia: a Diary*, 1947. Origo wrote a number of other books on Italian subjects including *The Last Attachment: the Story of Byron and Teresa Guiccioli*, 1949; *The Merchant of Prato: Francesco di Marco Datini*, 1957, a life of the best known citizen of 14th century Prato; and a biography of Leopardi (◊Umbria and Marche). Her autobiography, *Images and Shadows: a Part of a Life*, 1970, includes further material on life at La Foce and on the Anglo-Florentine milieu of her youth.

PAPINI, Giovanni (1881–1956), was a Florentine essayist, journalist, and poet, who took up a variety of different intellectual positions in quick succession: briefly an anarchist, then a 'pragmatist', for a time after 1913 he was a futurist inspired by Marinetti (◊Venice). After the First World War Papini became a religious conservative and nationalist, winning favour under the Fascists. His *Un uomo finito*, (A Man – Finished), 1912, is an autobiographical account of an earlier spiritual journey ending in a 'return to the land'.

PICCOLOMINI, Enea Silvio (1405–64), was known as a poet and man of letters (often under his Latin name Aeneas Sylvius) long before he was elected as Pope Pius II in 1458. All his work is in Latin. In the early 1440s he was attached to the court of Frederick III of Germany and was subsequently secretary to Pope Eugenius IV, Bishop of Trieste from 1447 and of Siena from 1450. As Pope he maintained an interest in literature, campaigned vigorously for a new crusade against the Turks, and was involved in the partially completed project to transform his birthplace, originally called Corsignano, into his ideal city of Pienza (from 'Pius').

The most readable works of Aeneas Sylvius are his *Historia de duobus amantibus*, 1444 (*Story of Two Lovers*), an uninhibited Boccaccian tale of illicit love and its aftermath, and the *Commentarii*, 1464 (*Commentaries*), a detailed account of politics during his reign as Pope diversified by (often rather conventional) descriptions of his travels in Italy and of such events as the boat-races he organized on Lake Bolsena. Such secular activities helped to make Piccolomini something of a bugbear for the Reformation and the Counter-Reformation.

POUND, Ezra (1885–1972), lived in Venice in 1908 and at Rapallo from 1924. He sympathised with Fascism and broadcast from Rome during the Second World War. Held at Pisa in 1945, he was sent for trial in Washington, DC, but judged mentally unfit and remained at a Hospital for the Criminally Insane until 1958. On his release he returned to Italy. He died in Venice.

Among the many sources and materials drawn on in Pound's multi-layered work are Chinese, Provençal and medieval Italian poetry, including Dante and Guido Cavalcanti. The first three *Cantos* appeared in 1917 and the remaining one hundred and fourteen gradually between 1925 and 1970. *The Pisan Cantos*, 1948, are (amongst other things) a visionary, fragmentary attempt to understand the position in which he finds himself. Pound's often eccentric, often stimulating prose utterances include *ABC of Reading*, 1934, and *A Guide to Kulchur*, 1938.

# UMBRIA AND THE MARCHE

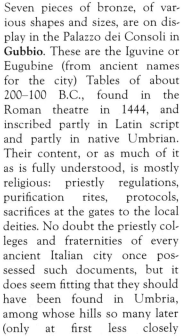

' . . . it seemed more like a city than a mere palace. For he adorned it not only with the usual objects, such as silver vases, wall-hangings of the richest cloth of gold, silk and other similar material, but also with countless antique statues of marble and bronze, with rare pictures, and with every kind of musical instrument.'
*Castiglione,*
*The Book of the Courtier*

Seven pieces of bronze, of various shapes and sizes, are on display in the Palazzo dei Consoli in **Gubbio**. These are the Iguvine or Eugubine (from ancient names for the city) Tables of about 200–100 B.C., found in the Roman theatre in 1444, and inscribed partly in Latin script and partly in native Umbrian. Their content, or as much of it as is fully understood, is mostly religious: priestly regulations, purification rites, protocols, sacrifices at the gates to the local deities. No doubt the priestly colleges and fraternities of every ancient Italian city once possessed such documents, but it does seem fitting that they should have been found in Umbria, among whose hills so many later (only at first less closely regulated) religious movements flourished.

Spiritual activity was especially lively in the 13th century. There was a strong community of Cathars in the valley of **Spoleto** and the message of St. Francis of Assisi, who shared their renunciation of worldly goods but not their rejection of the created world, was defined partly in opposition or reaction to theirs. Umbria abounds in Franciscan stories, many of them gathered in the *Fioretti* (*Little Flowers of St Francis*), by the friar Ugolino di Monte Santa Maria (c. 1260–1342). At Gubbio for instance the saint tamed a fierce human-devouring wolf, addressing it courteously as 'Brother Wolf' and winning its pledge to stop eating the townsfolk who, in response, were to provide it with food. (Mutuality is the usual stress of such stories, as of Francis' own teaching.) Francis' doctrine and his example as author of the vernacular *Cantico di Frate Sole* (*Canticle of Brother Sun*), 1224–6, inspired, later in the century, the passionate devotional poems of a Franciscan from another hill-town of central Umbria, Iacopone da Todi◊. Further south the cathedral on the high rock of **Orvieto** was begun in 1290.

The natural attractions of Umbria include not only such hills but celebrated waters. The **Cascata delle Marmore** near Terni was a spectacle beloved of topographical artists in the age of the picturesque. Byron (◊Venice), who visited the falls briefly in 1817, describes the roaring, cleaving

> 'fall of waters! rapid as the light
> The flashing mass foams shaking the abyss;
> The hell of waters! where they howl and hiss,
> And boil in endless torture'

in *Childe Harold's Pilgrimage*, Canto Four, 1818. He also pauses for the calmer **Fonti del Clitunno** near Trevi, much admired by classical poets including Propertius◊, who speaks of hunting 'Where Clitumnus roofs his beautiful streams with his/Own grove, and the waters lave the snow-bright cattle'. Giosuè Carducci (◊Emilia-Romagna) meditated more grandiloquently on Mother Italy by the springs and the snow-white bull-calves, watched from the surrounding mountains by stately, grave, green Umbria herself. Beside the usually peaceful waters of **Lake Trasimene** occurred the bloody rout of the Roman legions ambushed between the hills and the northern shore (some distance further north than now) by Hannibal in 217 B.C. Livy (◊Rome) claims that the fighting was so fierce that the combatants failed to notice an earthquake. The battle took place near Tuoro sul Trasimeno; the presumed site can be observed from a series of viewing platforms. In the vicinity of Sanguineto and Monte Sanguigno some of the dead were buried: 'A name of blood, from that day's sanguine rain' as Byron puts it in *Childe Harold*. More recently the carnage at Trasimene, together with political murder in medieval **Perugia**, have been used to counterpoint more modern psychological cruelties and menaces in Barry Unsworth's novel of expatriates in Umbria *After Hannibal*, 1996.

To the north and west of Umbria are the Marche (in English the Marches, called after the three Marches into which this church-ruled area was divided in the 11th century). The secular emphasis of Renaissance **Urbino** dominates the region's literary reputation, but there was, as in Umbria, much religious activity also. At **Loreto**, most evidently, the large sanctuary built from 1468 onwards shelters the Casa Santa (the house of the Virgin Mary, miraculously transported from Nazareth).

Conspicuous among the pilgrims to Loreto in 1796 was Count Monaldo Leopardi of **Recanati**, who with other loyal citizens of the papal Marche came to implore the Virgin to defeat the forces of General Bonaparte. The count, unlike many of his less single-minded compatriots, refused to go to the windows of **Palazzo Leopardi** in 1797 to see the Frenchman, now victorious in spite of the prayers, ride through Recanati. He was conservative in politics and religion, as was his considerably more formidable and austere wife Countess Adelaide. Their son, the poet Giacomo Leopardi, born in the Palazzo and discouraged for as long as possible from leaving Recanati, came into bitter conflict with them. He came to feel acutely the provinciality and philistinism of the Marche (Extract 2), but was often homesick once he had seized the freedom to wander in larger and more cultured cities. At Palazzo Leopardi one can visit the four peaceful rooms which still house the magnificent library in which the poet spent the years of his youth in 'mad and desperate study' which helped to undermine further his fragile health but also prepared the ground for his philosophical verse and prose. Count Monaldo's vast and miscellaneous collection of books acquired by purchase, inheritance and donation was, in one of his more sympathetic gestures, officially open to the citizens of Recanati from 1812. (According to Giacomo, nobody came.)

## ASSISI

Ancient Assisi is known chiefly from Propertius'◊ reference to 'climbing Asis' as his native town and from the **Temple of Minerva** (converted into the church of Santa Maria). This was the first complete classical building seen by Goethe (◊Naples and Campania), who in 1786 admired the architect's 'logical procedure' in this 'modest temple, just right for such a small town'.

Goethe had walked determinedly past the double basilica of San Francesco to his long-awaited temple: 'I turned away in distaste from the enormous substructure of the two churches on my left, which are built one on top of the other, like a Babylonian tower, and are the resting place of St. Francis'. Goethe came to Assisi before the growth of interest in medieval art in the 19th century. But already most visits were organized around the churches and chapels which the early biographers and collectors of legends had helped to associate indelibly with the significant spiritual events in the life of the most popular of saints.

One of the first of these events took place at the then dilapidated church of **San Damiano**, south of Assisi. Here, Francis' biographer Saint Bonaventure◊ records in his *Legenda maior* (*Greater Life*), c.1260–3, the young Francesco di Bernardone heard a voice calling three times from the crucifix 'Francis, repair my house. You see it is falling.' He set about providing for the repair of San Damiano and other local churches, realizing only later that he had been called to reform or 'repair' the whole institution of the church. At San Damiano in 1212 Francis received Chiara Offreduccio, the Saint Clare whose life and legend became closely entwined with his. At the convent of San Damiano for forty years she headed the order dedicated to poverty and obedience who would become known as the 'Poor Clares', governed by her Rule, the first such to be composed by a woman. (In 1257 they moved to a more central symbolic site, the basilica of **Santa Chiara**, where Clare's body is displayed in the crypt and the crucifix which spoke to Francis in the Oratorio del Crocifisso.)

While the Poor Clares became an enclosed order, like most other contemporary female orders, Francis and his early followers moved frequently, preaching, praying, living in small groups on meagre alms. For a time they lived in rudimentary huts around the small chapel of the **Porziuncola**, down the hill from Assisi. He was anxious not to set an example of comfortable accommodation for the brothers yet to come; but the Porziuncola itself was encased, in the late 16th century, by the capacious domed pilgrim-church of **Santa Maria degli Angeli**. The **Eremo delle Carceri**, Francis' hermitage in the woods up the hill from the town, is more peaceful. Here, later legend says, he preached to the birds.

When he knew he was dying, he had himself carried down to the Porziuncola area. His earthly life was ending, Bonaventure happily notes, where his spiritual life had begun. He spent his last days in praise, says his earliest biographer Thomas of Celano in the so-called *First Life of St. Francis*, 1228, singing his *Cantico di Frate Sole* (*Canticle of Brother Sun*), 1224–6 (Extract 1) and adding to it the last lines which 'exhorted death itself, terrible and hateful to all, to give praise'.

Francis died on 3 October 1226 in the cell of the Porziuncola now called the Cappella del Transito. For some hours, on his instructions, the body was left naked on the bare earth before burial. He was canonized less than two years later. In 1230 his remains were translated, in their surviving stone coffin, from San Giorgio (a church later absorbed by Santa Chiara) to the Lower Church of the new **Basilica of San Francesco**. This would become, with the completion of the Upper Church in the early 1250s, Goethe's 'Babylonian tower', for some a betrayal of the saint's faith in poverty and humility, for others a statement of his resulting spiritual glory. The frescoes of San Francesco, particularly those in the Upper Church by a group probably including Giotto, and inspired by the writing of Bonaventure and oral tradition, provided the definitive sequence of Franciscan images: the voice from the crucifix, the Stigmata (the wounds of the crucified Christ received by Francis at La Verna in Tuscany), the saint preaching to the Sultan, the Pope, and the birds, his death and the mourning of the sisters at San Damiano. The basilica and frescoes were seriously damaged in the earthquakes of September 1997.

# URBINO

'On the slopes of the Apennines, almost in the centre of Italy towards the Adriatic, is situated, as everyone knows, the little city of Urbino'. So says Castiglione), early in *Il cortegiano* (*The Book of the Courtier*), 1528, the book of courtly debates on courtliness (Extract 3) which made Urbino renowned throughout western Europe in the 16th century and beyond. The debates (idealised versions of those the characters, real noblemen and noblewomen present in Urbino in 1507, could have had) take place in the Sala delle Veglie of the palace built in the mid-15th century by Duke Federico da Montefeltro. Castiglione, having remembered Federico's 'prudence, humanity, justice, generosity and unconquerable spirit' and incomparable military ability, turns to his no less notable house, which he 'built on the rugged site of Urbino' and furnished:

> 'so well and appropriately that it seemed more like a city than a mere palace. For he adorned it not only with the usual objects, such as silver vases, wall-hangings of the richest cloth of gold, silk and other similar material, but also with countless antique statues of marble and bronze, with rare pictures, and with every kind of musical instrument; nor would he tolerate anything that was not most rare and outstanding.'

Moreover he collected fine books in Greek, Latin, and Hebrew and adorned them with gold and silver, 'believing that they were the crowning glory of his great palace'. Federico's manuscripts eventually passed to the Vatican Library, but the room where he kept and read them, his **Studiolo**, survives intact, glowing with inlaid panels (*intarsie*) which represent, in deceptively convincing perspective, open cupboards, a squirrel, armour, books, an hour-glass, and alpine scenery. The armour and the books, as in the palace's portrait of the Duke reading and encased in steel by Justus of Ghent, are a favourite combination.

Federico's court painter was Raphael's father, Giovanni Santi (d.1494), whose house (57 Via Raffaello) can be visited; the palace's space, proportion and harmony are often credited as an influence on Raphael's work. Piero della Francesca (c.1410/20–92) also painted for Duke Federico. His portraits of the Duke – 'broken nose, warts and all' as *The Oxford Dictionary of Art* puts it – and Duchess Battista Sforza are now in the Uffizi in Florence, but the palace retains Piero's *Flagellation of Christ*, the enigmatic work whose apparently casual violence so absorbs the protagonist of John Mortimer's novel *Summer's Lease*, 1988 (Extract 4).

For Castiglione, Urbino retained more intimate meanings than for those coming to look at the much-praised architecture and paintings. His was not a fantasy court but an idealised one, and one element in his book is nostalgia for 1507 and its people, many of them dead, including Duchess Elisabetta Gonzaga (wife of Federico's son Guido-baldo, ailing in the book, dead in 1508). The fourth book of *Il corte-giano*, added 15 years later, ends with a scene where, poignantly, time is for a while vanquished or forgotten: so absorbed are the courtiers in discussing divine love and beauty that they do not notice that it is dawn. At last the windows towards the hills are opened and they see the dawn 'with the beauty and colour of a rose, and all the stars had been scattered, save only [aptly for the debate just ended] the lovely mistress of heaven, Venus, who guards the confines of night and day'. There is a delicate but cold breeze and birds sing joyously 'among the murmuring woods' as all take leave of the Duchess and agree to meet again at evening.

## OTHER LITERARY LANDMARKS

**Ancona**: Arch of the emperor Trajan (ruled AD 98–117), described by Hester Piozzi (◊Piedmont) as 'white as his virtue, shining as his char-acter, and durable as his fame'.

**Norcia**: here in about 480 was born St. Benedict, author of the Benedictine Rule and founder of the monastery of Montecassino (south-east of Rome).

**Pesaro**: museum in the birthplace (34 Via Rossini) of the composer Gioacchino Rossini (1792–1868).

**Spoleto**: Fra Filippo Lippi (see Florence, Extract 2) frescoed the apse of the Cathedral in 1467–9, probably including himself, in monk's habit, as one of the figures in the Dormition of the Virgin. Lippi died soon after completing the work; his tomb is in the left transept.

**Todi**: Iacopone da Todi◊ is buried in the church of San Fortunato and commemorated by a statue in Piazza Umberto I.

### BOOKLIST

Bradford, Ernle, *Hannibal*, Mac-millan, London, 1981.

Burke, Peter, *The Fortunes of the Courtier: the European Reception of Castiglione's Cortegiano*, Polity Press, Cambridge, 1995.

Byron, George Gordon, Lord, *Poe-tical Works*, Jerome J. McGann,

ed, Clarendon Press, Oxford, 1980–93.

Castiglione, Baldassare, *The Book of the Courtier* [1528], George Bull, trans, Penguin, Harmonds-worth, 1967. **Extract 3**.

Chilvers, Ian, Harold Osborne and Dennis Farr, eds, *The Oxford*

*Booklist continued*

Dictionary of Art, Oxford University Press, Oxford and New York, 1988.

*Francis and Clare: the Complete Works*, Regis J. Armstrong and Ignatius C. Brady, trans, SPCK, London, 1982. **Extract 1**.

*Saint Francis of Assisi: Writings and Early Biographies: English Omnibus of the Sources for the Life of St. Francis*, Marion A. Habig, ed, SPCK, London and Franciscan Herald Press, Chicago, 1979.

Leopardi, Count Giacomo, *A Leopardi Reader*, Ottavio M. Casale, ed and trans, University of Illinois Press, Urbana, Chicago and London, 1981. **Extract 2**.

Mortimer, John, *Summer's Lease*, Penguin, London, 1988. **Extract 4**.

Origo, Iris, *Leopardi: a Study in Solitude*, Hamish Hamilton, London, 1953.

Propertius, *The Poems*, Guy Lee, trans, Clarendon Press, Oxford, 1994.

Unsworth, Barry, *After Hannibal*, Hamish Hamilton, London, 1996.

# *Extracts*

## (1) Assisi

### St. Francis of Assisi, Canticle of Brother Sun, 1224–6

*Francis' hymn was intended to be sung, and English translation can only imperfectly render the simple but resonant praise of the 'Altissimu, onnipotente, bon Signore' through his creation.*

Most High, all-powerful, good Lord,
Yours are the praises, the glory, the honour, and all blessing.
To You alone, Most High, do they belong,
and no man is worthy to mention Your name.
Praised be You, my Lord, with all your creatures,
especially Sir Brother Sun,
Who is the day and through whom You give us light.
And he is beautiful and radiant with great splendour;
and bears a likeness of You, Most High One.
Praised be You, my Lord, through Sister Moon and the stars,
in heaven You formed them clear and precious and beautiful.
Praised be You, my Lord, through Brother Wind,
and through the air, cloudy and serene, and every kind of weather
through which You give sustenance to your creatures.

Praised be You, my Lord, through Sister Water,
which is very useful and humble and precious and chaste.
Praised be You, my Lord, through Brother Fire,
through whom You light the night
and he is beautiful and playful and robust and strong.
Praised be You, my Lord, through our Sister Mother Earth,
who sustains and governs us,
and who produces varied fruits with coloured flowers and herb.
Praised be You, my Lord, through those who give pardon for Your
Love and bear infirmity and tribulation.
Blessed are those who endure in peace
for by You, Most High, they shall be crowned.
Praised be You, my Lord, through our Sister Bodily Death,
from whom no living man can escape.
Woe to those who die in mortal sin.
Blessed are those whom death shall find in Your most holy will,
for the second death shall do them no harm.
Praise and bless my Lord and give Him thanks
and serve Him with great humility.

## (2) RECANATI

### Count Giacomo Leopardi,
### letter to Pietro Giordani, 30 April 1817

*Leopardi, aged 18, replies with some exasperation to Giordani's
defence of Recanati. The poet soon began to find his parents
irksome as well as his birthplace; his father wrote that one
should take interest in, and feel loyalty to, 'only that morsel of
the earth in which one is born and spends one's life'.*

It's all very well to say that Plutarch loved his Chaeronea and Alfieri
his Asti. They loved them but did not live there. So I too shall love my
birthplace when I am far away from it; meanwhile, I say I hate it
because I am in it, since this poor town is guilty only of not having
offered me one good thing besides my family. It is sweet and beautiful
to remember the place where one has spent his childhood. Yet it is too
easy to say: 'Here you were born and here Providence wants you to
stay.' Say to a sick man, 'If you try to heal yourself, you are fighting
Providence,' or to a poor man, 'If you try to improve your lot, you are
questioning Providence.' . . .

Do you really believe that the Marches and southern Italy are like
Romagna and northern Italy? There the word 'literature' is often
heard. There they have papers, academies, discussion groups, and
bookshops in great number. Gentlemen read a little. Ignorance is for

the masses, who wouldn't be the masses without it. But many try to study and many fancy themselves poets and philosophers; they may not really be such but they at least try. . . . Here, my dear sir, everything is dead, everything is foolishness and stupidity. Foreigners are amazed at this silence, this universal sleep. Literature is a sound unheard of. The names of Parini, Alfieri, Monti, Tasso, and Ariosto have to be explained. There is no one who wants to be something else, not a one for whom the name of ignorant seems strange. They call each other that sincerely and know they speak the truth. Do you think a great mind would be esteemed here? As a pearl in a dung-heap. . . . Indeed, I will tell you without any boasting that our library has no equal in the province and only two inferiors. On the door it is written that this library is for citizens too and all are welcome. Now how many do you think frequent it? Never a one.

## (3) URBINO

### Baldassare Castiglione, The Book of the Courtier, 1528

*Count Ludovico da Canossa defines for the court of Urbino the virtue of* sprezzatura - *'not placing value in' - or nonchalance. For at least a century this concept was highly influential not only in Italy but throughout western and northern Europe.*

I have discovered a universal rule which seems to apply more than any other in all human actions or words: namely, to steer away from affectation at all costs, as if it were a rough and dangerous reef, and (to use a perhaps novel word for it) to practise in all things a certain nonchalance which conceals all artistry and makes whatever one says or does seem uncontrived and effortless. I am sure that grace springs especially from this, since everyone knows how difficult it is to accomplish some unusual feat perfectly, and so facility in such things excites the greatest wonder; whereas, in contrast, to labour at what one is doing and, as we say, to make bones over it, shows an extreme lack of grace and causes everything, whatever its worth, to be discounted. So we can truthfully say that true art is what does not seem to be art; and the most important thing is to conceal it, because if it is revealed this discredits a man completely and ruins his reputation. . . .

Whatever action [nonchalance] accompanies, no matter how trivial it is, it not only reveals the skill of the person doing it but also very often causes it to be considered far greater than it really is. This is because it makes the onlookers believe that a man who performs well with so much facility must possess even greater skill than he does, and that if he took great pains and effort he would perform even better. To give other examples, consider a man using weapons, and about to throw a dart or handle a sword or other weapon. If, without thinking about it, he casually takes up a position at the ready, so naturally that it seems as if his whole body assumes the right posture without any strain, then even if he does nothing more he demonstrates that he is in complete command of what he is doing. Similarly in dancing, a single step, a single unforced and graceful movement of the body, at once demonstrates the skill of the dancer. When a musician is singing and utters a single word ending in a group of notes with a sweet cadence, and with such ease that it seems effortless, that touch alone proves that he is capable of far more than he is doing. Then, again, in painting, a single line which is not laboured, a single brush stroke made with ease, in such a way that it seems the hand is completing the line by itself without any effort or guidance, clearly reveals the excellence of the artist, about whose competence everyone will then make his own judgement. The same happens in almost every other thing.

## (4) Urbino

### John Mortimer, *Summer's Lease*, 1988

*Molly Pargeter, renting a villa in English-filled 'Chiantishire' with her family, follows the 'Piero della Francesca trail' from Arezzo to Urbino. At the same time she pursues her investigation into the affairs of the mysterious owner of her villa, Buck Kettering, and, connectedly, finds the unfathomableness and danger of human relationships crystallized in Piero's 'Flagellation'.*

With one hand on his hip . . . the young Lord of Urbino stands, barefoot and serene, between two evil counsellors. What are they plotting, discussing, arguing about? What terrible and irrevocable decisions they may have come to, no one can tell. What is certain is that they are far too involved in their own concerns to notice the act of cruelty which is casually, almost elegantly, taking place at the remote end of the building. Christ is standing, an impassive, white figure against a white column. The arms of the flagellators are raised gracefully. Pontius Pilate in a hat with a long peak is watching with detachment. It was the picture Molly had in her mind all the holiday and the one that she had come so far to see. All the books she had read told her that its importance lay in its effect on what the architecture of the Ducal Palace was going to be, on the perfect balance of its forms and its special harmony. Molly was interested, far more interested, in the mysterious involvement of groups of people in their own awful concerns. They can be together, she thought, by the same walls, on the same floor and know nothing of each other's lives. They can commit terrible acts quietly, casually, at the other end of a room and nobody seems to notice. Of the things she felt she had to do that day, looking at the picture was the most exciting and the most alarming. She shivered a little as she stood before it, and the Tapscotts hurried away to 'knock off the Raphaels, before the place closes'. She stood on alone, in front of the picture, half expecting Buck Kettering to step out of the shadows and explain it to her. She stood for a long time but nobody came and she decided to go on to the final stage of her journey.

# Biographies and important works

BONAVENTURE or Bonaventura, Saint (1221–74), born at Bagnoreggio near Orvieto, was Minister General of the Franciscan order from 1257. He was opposed to the Spirituals, the more extreme ascetic and anti-intellectual wing of the Franciscan movement, and his *Legenda maior* (*Greater Life*), c.1260–3, was in part an attempt to restore unity to the divided groups. Here Bonaventure draws heavily on the life of St Francis by Thomas of Celano, but writes in a more lyrical and mystical vein. The *Legenda minor* (*Lesser Life*) is a more concentrated version of the larger work. (Both versions were intended mainly to be read aloud in the friaries.) Among Bonaventure's other writings are an exposition of the Rule of Francis and the works of mystical theology which led to his designation as the 'Seraphic Doctor'. He was canonized in 1482.

CASTIGLIONE, Count Baldassare or Baldesar (1478–1529), a Mantuan nobleman, served the courts of Milan, Mantua, and, between 1504 and 1515, Urbino. (He was sent on diplomatic missions to Rome and other parts of Italy and to England.) He was papal ambassador in Spain (1524–9).

*Il cortegiano* (*The Book of the Courtier*), 1528, was written around 1513–18 and revised in the early 1520s. It takes the form of a dialogue (following the precedent of Plato, Cicero, and more immediately of his friend Pietro Bembo (◊Veneto) supposed to take place on four successive evenings in the court of Urbino in 1507. The speakers or characters have the names, opinions, and – at least in part – relationships of real courtiers either attached to the court of Urbino or lingering there after the visit of Pope Julius II. One speaker advances a case which is frequently interrupted but always delivered with the quality of *grazia* (grace) which courtiers must bring to all their actions. The related quality which has attracted most interest in readers of *Il cortegiano* is *sprezzatura* ('not placing value on'), the art of nonchalance, of appearing to act with effortless grace and skill. Castiglione's work, highly educated and carefully planned but conversational, rarely prescriptive or didactic, is itself an example of *sprezzatura* in writing. Other topics considered are appropriate courtly language (the literary Tuscan of Petrarch and Boccaccio's time or something more modern and less Tuscan), the relative merits of painting and sculpture, the necessary accomplishments and manner of the female courtier and whether she is the equal of the male, and how the courtier can best serve the prince. Peter Burke, reflecting recently on Castiglione's contexts, says that 'he helped to adapt humanism [born in the by then mostly defunct city-republics] to the world of the court, and the court to the world of humanism'; more urgently, as absolute monarchy became more widespread and gunpowder robbed the nobility of their military functions and values, *Il cortegiano* was 'an attempt to redefine the identity of the Italian nobles at a time when their traditional roles were under threat'. The book was at its most popular in the 16th and early 17th century, when there were about 62 Italian editions and many translations into the languages of western and northern Europe. The relatively open dialogue, allowing debate, contradiction, and playfulness, was most often read, instead, as a handbook for courtly conduct.

FRANCIS OF ASSISI, Saint (1181/2–1226), was the son of a successful linen merchant of Assisi, Pietro di Bernardone. The process of his conversion began during and after a period as a prisoner of war in Perugia in 1204. Visions and an increasing commitment to the ascetic life issued in his renunciation of any claim to his family's wealth in 1207. By 1209 he was the leader of a group of disciples. In 1210 his Rule was personally sanctioned by Pope Innocent III. The Franciscan order spread rapidly through Europe during the saint's lifetime; he attempted to press even beyond Europe, preaching before the Sultan in Egypt in 1219. He received the Stigmata, according to his early followers, in

1224. He was canonized in 1228.

The *Cantico di Frate Sole* (*Canticle of Brother Sun*), 1224–6, written in Umbrian Italian with its surviving elements of Latin, is one of the earliest known Italian vernacular texts. Here Francis concentrates on the elements and the heavenly bodies, elsewhere (and in the early lives and legends) more often on animals. These too are brothers and sisters with whom, under God, there should be a respectful, mutual relationship. This has been one element in Francis' modern appeal. (In 1980 Pope John Paul II made him patron saint of ecology.) In the 13th century it was an attitude to the creation which won orthodox approval as a refutation of the Cathar heretics' belief in the evil of the material world.

IACOPONE DA TODI (1236–1306), one of the ascetic Franciscan Spirituals, for a time excommunicated and imprisoned for his opposition to Pope Boniface VIII in the 1290s, is known for his many *laude* (praise songs) and as possible author of the popular Latin devotional poem the *Stabat Mater*. One of his most intense yet witty poems is *Come è somma sapienza essere reputato pazzo per l'amore di Cristo* (*How It is the Height of Wisdom To Be Thought Mad For the Love of Christ*): greater philosophy than this 'has yet to be seen in Paris'.

LEOPARDI, Count Giacomo (1798–1837), born in Recanati, spent most of his youth in intensive study and writing. Throughout his life he was chronically ill. He was angered, however, by any suggestion that this simply explained away his pessimistic philosophy. Increasingly he reacted against the provincialism of the town and then against the ethical and religious conservatism of his parents. Eventually he was able to spend some months in Rome in 1822–3 but was mostly disappointed by its cultural life. He spent much of 1825–7 somewhat more contentedly in Bologna, Florence, and Pisa. After the lonely '16 months of horrible night' of his last period in Recanati, Leopardi returned, with the financial aid of friends and, for the first time, his disapproving mother, to Florence. Here he lived mostly with his patient friend Antonio Ranieri, to whose home town, Naples, they moved in 1833.

In all these places, with occasional intermissions caused by ill-health, Leopardi continued to write. His *Zibaldone di pensieri* (*Notebook of Thoughts*), 1817–32 – manuscript reflections on topics including philosophy and literature from Homer to Voltaire – runs to 4,526 pages. The other most important prose work is the ironical *Operette morali* (*Little Moral Works*), 1827. But Leopardi is known chiefly for the poems gathered in *Canti* (*Songs*), 1831, 1845, and especially 'A Silvia' ('To Sylvia'), 1828, a lyrical address to a dead girl whose loss of expectation becomes the speaker's; *Il tramonto della luna* (*The Setting of the Moon*), 1836, where the dark landscape abandoned by the moon suggests human isolation and mortality; and *La ginestra, o il fiore del deserto* (*Broom, or the Desert Flower*), 1836. *Broom* looks more extensively at the illusions which prevent people from seeing Nature as a cruel stepmother only; it is perhaps in this view, part of his ruthless exclusion of religious or quasi-religious solutions, that Leopardi differs most obviously from other Romantics. There is, however, a possibility of consolation for the 'noble man' who can honestly look the truth in the face, blame nature and not his fellows, and embrace them in deep fraternal love. The pessimism of Leopardi's early work gives way gradually, in the late poems, to 'a stubborn positive belief in man's ability to move with relative grace in a world where the odds are against him' (Ottavio M. Casale).

MORTIMER, John (born 1923). A barrister, playwright, and novelist, Mortimer is the author of works including the Rumpole stories and *A Voyage Round My Father*. *Summer's Lease*, 1988, set in the 'Chiantishire' of British holidaymakers and expatriates, combines mild social satire and a detective story. Molly Pargeter, determined to track down Buck Kettering, the owner of the villa she is renting, and to unravel various local corruption scandals which he seems to be connected with, learns something about herself and her relationships in the process. She follows the 'Piero della Francesca trail' in fulfilment both of a long-held ambition and as a result of fascination with (and clues leading towards) her fellow Piero-enthusiast Kettering. Among the other characters are Molly's old but incorrigible father Haverford Downs, who fancies himself as a wit, a 'shocker' and a womanizer; Mortimer displays his gift for parody in Haverford's self-satisfied, gossipy 'Jottings' despatched from Italy to the weekly *Informer*. There are also some Italians, seen as they appear to the English: a woman seeking revenge for her lover's murder, an icily sophisticated *baronessa*, an old prince terrified of spiders and *omosessuali*, a Communist priest and, glimpsed more briefly, a bank assistant 'whose face was a mask of disappointment nobly borne and from whose carmined lips dangled a cigarette miraculously balancing a tube of ash.'

PROPERTIUS, Sextus (c. 50 B.C.– c. 20 A.D.) was born in or near Assisi (the Roman Asisium or, at least in his poems, Asis). He spent most of his life in Rome, where he was a friend of Ovid (◊Abruzzo) and a member of the circle of Maecenas. The text, arrangement, and date of his poems is often uncertain, since they have survived in no manuscript earlier than 1200. Most of the poems analyse the nature of the subject's tempestuous love for Cynthia (based in some sense on a real woman called Hostia) and are remarkable for their varied use of mythology as a heightened equivalent to his own emotional state. One of the most affecting poems is spoken by Cynthia's ghost, combining a degree of recrimination with gentle humour, continued love, and a request for an inscribed and ivy-free tomb.

THOMAS OF CELANO (c.1185–c.1160) was a Franciscan friar commissioned by Pope Gregory IX to write what has become known as the *First Life of St. Francis*, 1228. Further biographical details and accounts of further miracles were added in the *Second Life*, 1246–7. Thomas also wrote a life of St. Clare of Assisi, c.1255.

# ROME

'The Thermae of Caracalla
. . . consist of six
enormous chambers,
above 200 feet in height, and
each enclosing a vast space
like that of a field. There
are in addition a number
of towers and labyrinthine
recesses hidden and woven
over by the wild growth of
weeds and ivy.'
*Percy Bysshe Shelley in a letter
to Thomas Love Peacock*

Edward Gibbon◊ was at once
intoxicated by Rome, the physical manifestation of his reading,
in 1764:

'My temper is not very sus-
ceptible of enthusiasm, and
the enthusiasm which I do
not feel I have ever scorned
to affect. But at the distance
of 25 years, I can neither forget nor express the strong
emotions which agitated my
mind as I first approached
and entered the eternal
City. After a sleepless night
I trod with a lofty step the
ruins of the Forum; each
memorable spot where
Romulus stood, or Tully
[Marcus Tullius Cicero◊] spoke, or Caesar fell was at once present
to my eye; and several days of intoxication were lost or employed
before I could descend to a cool and minute investigation.'

Even with such investigation, however, it is rarely easy to find absolutely for certain where the events described in Roman history and
literature occurred. This is mainly because of the continually developing, physically and imaginatively palimpsestic nature of the city: in
Gibbon's time the Forum Romanum, where Cicero spoke, was largely buried beneath the *Campo vaccino* – the 'cow field'; much has
now been excavated and the livestock was long ago removed, but
paintings and engravings have kept the more rural Forum a familiar
image. The spot where Caesar fell – in the Theatre of Pompey – was
more efficiently buried under Palazzo Righetti in Via di Grottapinta
in the 15th century, but was continually recreated in places far from
Rome: 'How many ages hence/Shall this our lofty scene be acted
over/In states unborn and accents yet unknown?' Cassius asks in

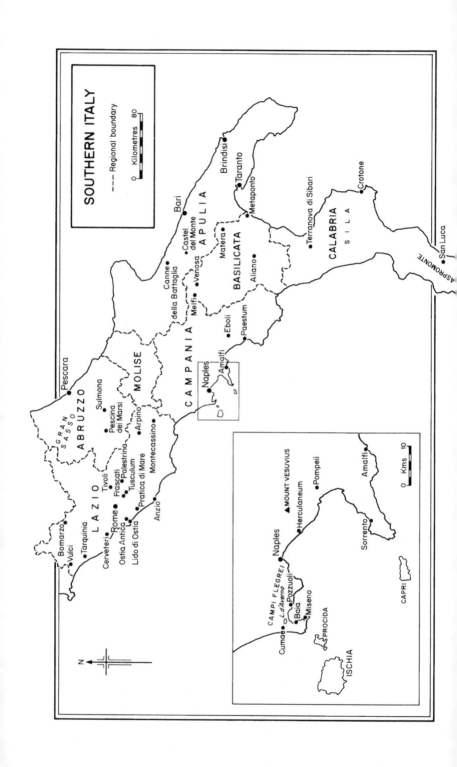

SOUTHERN ITALY

--- Regional boundary

0 Kilometres 80

N

**LAZIO**

Bomarzo
Vulci
Tarquinia
Cerveteri
Rome
Ostia Antica
Lido di Ostia
Anzio
Frascati
Tusculum
Palestrina
Pratica di Mare
Tivoli
Montecassino
Arpino
Pescina dei Marsi
Sulmona
Pescara

**ABRUZZO**

GRAN SASSO

**MOLISE**

**CAMPANIA**

Naples
Amalfi
Eboli
Paestum
Melfi
Venosa
Canne della Battaglia
Castel del Monte
Bari

**APULIA**

Brindisi
Taranto
Metaponto

**BASILICATA**

Matera
Aliano
Terranova di Sibari
Crotone

**CALABRIA**

SILA

ASPROMONTE

San Luca

---

0 Kms 10

▲MOUNT VESUVIUS

Naples
Herculaneum
Pompeii
Amalfi
Sorrento
CAPRI

CAMPI FLEGREI
Cumae
L. d'Averno
Pozzuoli
Baia
Miseno
PROCIDA
ISCHIA

Shakespeare's *Julius Caesar*, 1599–1600, and goes some distance towards answering his apparently rhetorical question by speaking English.

'Each memorable spot where Romulus stood' is the terrain of legend, the early Rome whose endurance, stern consistency, and purity, were retailed by writers like Livy◊ to a more morally complicated present: Lucretia the innocent victim of rape who preferred suicide to living with any hint of dishonour (Extract 6), Lucius Junius Brutus who, revenging her, expelled the kings and subsequently, unflinchingly loyal to the Republic, executed his own sons as traitors to it; Mucius Scaevola who thrust his hand into the fire and burnt it off to demonstrate to his captor, King Lars Porsenna, how much a Roman dared 'do and suffer' and so won his freedom and the astonished Porsenna's withdrawal of his forces; the soldier Marcus Curtius who, when an oracle said that Rome's chief strength must be thrown into an abyss which had opened in the Forum before it would close up, rode unhesitatingly into it to meet his death and save his country. (The traditional site of the abyss is marked as in ancient times by a fig, a vine, and an olive-tree, now in a railed area near the Column of Phocas in the Forum.) These stories remained vital long after the small city-state of Rome had become the empire and then collapsed: as Ian Donaldson says in his study of the legend of Lucretia, such tales of sacrifice are 'celebrated and scrutinized in Christian art and literature with something of the same intensity as are the deaths of the Christian saints and martyrs, and even Christ himself'.

Roman ruins, like Roman tales, were gradually inscribed with new meanings. Even in dwindling medieval Rome, where lawless noblemen menaced each other from their towers (the surviving **Torre delle Milizie** near Trajan's Market, for instance), pilgrims sometimes paused to admire the remains of ancient splendour as well as the relics and resting-places of the early saints. Some time in the 12th century, when there was a general reawakening of interest in antiquity, an Englishman, Master Gregorius, probably visiting the city on ecclesiastical business, wrote his brief but enthusiastic *Narracio de mirabilibus urbis Romae* (*The Marvels of Rome*). Gregory observes, like many before and since, that ruins 'teach us clearly that all temporal things will soon pass away, especially as Rome, the epitome of earthly glory, languishes and declines so much every day'. But he is eager to report on the earthly glory: he is much impressed by the equestrian statue of Marcus Aurelius on the Capitoline Hill (now in the Capitoline Museum) and the various theories about the rider's identity; by the figures, actually Castor and Pollux (now on the Capitol) who are said to represent 'the first mathematicians, to whom horses were assigned because of the quickness of their intellects'; and by the columns so large that 'no one can throw a pebble as high as their capitals' at the **Baths of Diocletian** (part of the *frigidarium* of which would be adapted by Michelangelo and his successors as the lofty and spacious **Santa Maria degli Angeli**).

Two centuries later Petrarch (◊Veneto and North-East), a visitor more deeply versed in ancient life and letters, looked out over the ruins from the roof of the Baths – 'no other place affords such a wide view, such brisk air, such silence and longed-for solitude' (*Epistulae familiares* (*Familiar Letters*), 1337–41). This seemed to Petrarch and his learned guide Giovanni Colonna di San Vito, uncle of his patron Cardinal Giovanni Colonna, an ideal place to forget private and public affairs and range in conversation – as their eyes ranged across the crumbling remains – over philosophy, ancient and modern history, and 'the origin of the liberal and mechanic arts'. Petrarch yearned for the idealised ancient city where such ideas were widely discussed not only on quiet rooftops but in many a villa and hall. In the 1340s this longing for old Rome seemed about to be fulfilled as Petrarch was crowned poet laureate on the Capitol and sent letters declaring his support for Cola di Rienzo, his more colourful, unstable fellow enthusiast, who subdued the city's warring aristocrats to rule for two brief periods as 'Tribune' of the Roman people. Cola, whose high-handed rule – more that of a dictator than a tribune – alienated his original supporters, was eventually killed near the steps leading up to Santa Maria d'Aracoeli, where his statue now stands. (Other memorials include a now rarely read novel by Edward Bulwer-Lytton, *Rienzi, or the Last of the Tribunes*, 1835, and Wagner's early opera of heroic nationalism *Rienzi*, 1842.) Petrarch's ideals, however, centred less exclusively on the city itself, had more lasting influence. He did not need the ruins, much though they inspired him, to go on reviving the ancient glories by editing and disseminating Latin texts and his own Latin poems, propounding that 'rebirth' which was about, so strikingly, to affect Italian and European life.

In Rome the Renaissance was facilitated by the growth of Papal power, status, and riches in the late 15th and early 16th century. The city famous for its past was transformed into one known also for the splendour of its innumerable palaces and churches. Renaissance humanism allowed classical and Christian motifs to blend in the decoration of these buildings – Raphael (1483–1520) excelled equally in painting madonnas, *The School of Athens* for the **Stanza della Segnatura** in the Vatican, or the triumphantly pagan *Galatea* for the **Palazzo Farnesina**. As far as Protestant and Counter-Reformation reformers and later generations were concerned, the two worlds mingled too easily: the fictional, but not entirely implausible, dying prelate in Robert Browning's (◊Florence) 'The Bishop Orders his Tomb at Saint Praxed's Church', 1845, wants both 'the Saviour at his sermon on the mount' and 'one Pan/Ready to twitch the Nymph's last garment off' for the bas-relief of his tomb. By the end of the poem it is clear that the bishop's sons – he stops calling them 'nephews' – are unlikely to oblige with a magnificent monument of basalt and 'peach-blossom marble all, the rare, the ripe/As fresh-poured red wine of a mighty pulse'. As Browning may wish his reader to be aware, there is no tomb at all like this in the real **Santa Prassede** (a church, near Santa Maria Maggiore, where in fact pre-Renaissance elements predominate, most excitingly in the vaulted Chapel of San Zeno with its luminous ninth-century mosaics of Christ and the saints).

The mood of Rome darkened after the brutal sack of the city by German Lutheran troops in 1527. There were fewer brazen bishops and carefree Galateas. Michelangelo's◊ Sistine *Last Judgement* (1536–41) was felt to express the temper of this age as his *Creation* (1508–12) had expressed the glorious days of Pope Julius II, patron of arts, winner of battles, gatherer and dispenser of riches. But – as Michelangelo's later work continued to attest – the Popes were soon building again on the grand scale, partly at least in order to advance the Counter-Reformation.

Protestants became, perhaps rightly, cautious about going to Rome. One of those who did venture into the city in 1587 was the future English ambassador in Venice, Sir Henry Wotton (1568–1639), but he took the precaution of disguising himself as a German Catholic, 'as light in my mind as in my apparel', with 'a mighty blue feather' in his hat. But by the mid-17th century the climate of mutual suspicion had eased somewhat. The diarist John Evelyn (◊Lazio), of royalist persuasion but not so fervidly that he wanted to fight in the English Civil Wars, arrived in 1644 to find the Baroque in full flower. Gianlorenzo Bernini had twenty years earlier produced such dramatic sculptures as *Apollo and Daphne* and the *Abduction of Proserpina* (now in the **Galleria Borghese**), was famous for his work at St Peter's and the fountain in **Piazza Navona** (the obelisk on Evelyn's 'stupenduous [sic] artificial rock') and was about to embark on the *Ecstasy of St Teresa* in **Santa Maria della Vittoria**. Just before Evelyn's visit, he was told, Bernini had staged 'a public opera (for so they call shows of that kind) wherein he painted the scenes, cut the statues, invented the engines, composed the music, writ the comedy, and built the theatre'.

Such wonders were admired by Evelyn and others from cultures visually more sober than Bernini's Rome. But there is often a certain ambivalence when the wonders are specifically Catholic. The sermons at St Peter's at Easter 1645 are acceptably 'full of Italian eloquence and action', but a parade of flagellants to the accompaniment of dismal chanting by monks and friars makes 'altogether a horrible and indeed heathenish pomp'. Kissing the papal toe ('that is, his embroidered slipper') in the Vatican Consistory, Evelyn seems at once impressed and embarrassed, feeling he ought to condemn such goings on for the record, but not quite able to. At the **Catacombs of San Calisto** he notes without further comment the finding of phials of dried blood, lachrymatories, and skeletons which turn to dust when touched. As a

polite outsider he is more delicate in his treatment of religious practices and personnel than some Romans. The satirical sayings attached
to the base of **Pasquino**, the battered remains of an ancient statue in
Piazza Pasquino, south of Piazza Navona, allowed the safest outlet for
discontent or perhaps simply for irritation with the Pope in the city of
the popes, the priests in the city where everyone seems to be a priest.
One of Pasquino's most remembered Latin utterances concerned the
pillaging by Pope Urban VIII Barberini of ancient bronze roofing from
the portico of the **Pantheon** for cannons at Castel Sant' Angelo and
Bernini's baldacchino in St Peter's: *Quod non fecerunt barbari / Fecerunt
Barberini* ('What the barbarians did not do, the Barberini did').

Another of Urban's projects, the **Palazzo Barberini**, was completed
by Bernini in 1633. From 1856, as the home of the American sculptor
William Wetmore Story (1819–95), it became a centre of the now
vigorously flourishing expatriate community. Henry James (◊Venice)
was persuaded by Story's family to undertake the somewhat laborious
task of putting together a biography from the large body of his surviving papers and correspondence. In the resulting *William Wetmore Story
and His Friends*, 1903, James devotes some space to recreating the
ambience of the palazzo, which from outside 'faces you . . . with the
assurance of some great natural fact', and where Story and his family
occupied 'a voluminous apartment of the second floor'. Here they
entertained Elizabeth Gaskell, the Brownings (◊Florence), Hawthorne◊
and many others and, providing James with his most satisfying literary
anecdote, hosted a children's party where after Hans Christian Andersen 'had read out to his young friends *The Ugly Duckling*, Browning
struck up with the *Pied Piper*; which led to the formation of a grand
march through the spacious Barberini apartment, with Story doing his
best on a flute in default of bagpipes'.

Such indoor splendours and doings needed, as Rome expanded in
the 19th century, to be complemented by time spent in the city's green
places. In the **Villa Borghese** gardens Count Donatello, Hawthorne's
'wild, sweet, playful, rustic creature' in *The Marble Faun*, 1860, strays
among ilex, stone-pines, cypresses and large daisies in 'scenery . . .
such as arrays itself in the imagination, when we read the beautiful old
myths, and fancy a brighter sky, a softer turf, a more picturesque
arrangement of venerable trees, than we find in the rude and untrained
landscapes of the Western world'. But this sense of removedness from
the city proper makes the area also, in literature at least, a place for sad
lovers' trysts and undesired encounters. Soon after dancing with
Donatello and pelting him with flowers, Hawthorne's Miriam is alone
in the garden face to face with the unavoidable man from her past. In
Matilde Serao's (◊Naples) *La conquista di Roma* (*The Conquest of Rome*),
1885, Francesco Sangiorgio, the politician whose ambition founders
mostly as a result of unreciprocated love, strolls unhappily with his
beloved Angelica on the deserted **Pincio** above the green mass of the

Villa Borghese and the carnival crowds in the city. Daisy, in Henry James's (◊Venice) *Daisy Miller*, 1879, walks more conspicuously with Giovanelli on the Pincio, causing much social awkwardness for the narrator Winterbourne.

Less wealthy settlers in Rome, who increased in number when the city became capital of Italy in 1871 – the seat of government and its many branches, the necessary destination of suppliants, representatives, people seeking fame and fortune – came upon a new and less than ideal world. Serao's Sangiorgio, arriving for the first time as a deputy for Basilicata, expecting marvels, wonders as his train reaches the station 'Where was Rome, then?' The crowd pushes and shoves, the railway staff ignore him in favour of more important top-hatted and tailcoated passengers. Stones and rubbish from rebuilding work are around, and the demolition programme stops him reaching the Forum. Old Rome is no more inspiring than new: the majesty of the Colosseum is rather dimmed by 'the dirty light of a rainy day' and Sangiorgio can only pretend to admire **Trajan's Forum**, 'where the mutilated pillars serve for tree-trunks, that great burial-place for dead cats, that great dwelling-place for stray cats'. Full of ambition, Sangiorgio wants a wider arena in which to be acclaimed; he will succeed only temporarily, partly because, as a cynical fellow deputy explains, Rome's strength, power and loftiness 'is lodged in an almost divine attribute – indifference':

> 'You may make a stir – howl, rave, set fire to your house and your books, and dance on the ruins – Rome will take no note of it. It is the city to which all have come, and where all have fallen: why should it be concerned with you, an infinitesimal atom, passing across the scene so quickly?'

Individuality is easily lost in the big city. In the dark stairwells of the chilly and dirty tenements women in particular, as the narrator of Sibilla Aleramo's◊ *Una donna* (*A Woman*), 1906, discovers, are in danger of losing their personal identity (Extract 1). In less desperate situations, however, individuals often rejoice in mass urban living: *Fellini's Roma* (1972) opens with a celebration of noise and movement converging on Rome; Alberto Moravia's◊ *La romana* (*The Woman of Rome*), 1947, more usually concerned with interior monologue and sexual relations, at one point has its protagonist Adriana take her mother back on their old walk along **Via Nazionale**, past 'the furriers, shoe-makers, stationers, jewellers, watch-makers, book-sellers, florists, drapers, toy-shops, ironmongers, milliners, hosiers, glove-shops, cafés, cinemas, banks; here were the lighted windows of the big buildings, with people moving about the rooms or working at desks', and electric signs, newspaper kiosks, chestnut-sellers, beggars. (Adriana's way of participating in all the activity is to go into a shop and steal her mother a head-scarf.)

Moravia himself (born in 1907) grew up in the quieter streets of the residential area east of the Villa Borghese gardens, in what he remembered as an island of 'middle-class tranquillity'. (Among his earliest recollections of this respectable world was one of his mother's black straw hat – topped by birds' nests, cherries, or bunches of flowers – when she kissed him before going out to the opera.) But for Romans of Moravia's generation experience of less restful settings was inevitable. Life in Rome was at its worst in 1943–4, when it was occupied by the German army. There were food shortages and Allied bombing. Anti-Jewish laws were enforced, leading to the death of around 7000–8000 Jews from central and northern Italy, mostly deported to Auschwitz and Belsen. The worst violence in Rome was the massacre of 335 Roman civilians (about a hundred of them Jews) at the **Ardeatine Caves**, near the Catacombs, on 24 March 1944, in reprisal for the killing of 32 SS men by resistance fighters. (The memorial and grave of the massacre victims is the **Mausoleo delle Fosse Ardeatine**, Via Ardeatina.) There is some evidence (cited by Richard Lamb) that General Kesselring also considered blowing up three poor districts of Rome, San Lorenzo, Tiburtino, and Testaccio, having removed their inhabitants to concentration camps. These suburbs are among the places lived in, precariously, by Ida and her small son Useppe, result of rape by a passing German soldier, in Elsa Morante's◊ long novel *La storia* (*History: a Novel*), 1974. The half-Jewish Ida escapes arrest but suffers in many of the ways likely for a struggling mother in Rome in 1944. In the last months of German occupation frightened people cowered in the air-raid shelters or 'the labyrinthine basements of the great monuments', while:

> 'the daily news of the round-ups, torture, and slaughter circulated through the neighbourhoods like death-rattle echoes without any possible response. It was known that, just outside the city's girdle of walls, ineptly buried in mined ditches and caves, numberless bodies were thrown to decompose . . . And the crowd avoided speaking of their unquiet, shapeless presence, except in some evasive murmurs. Every contact and every substance gave off a funereal, prison stench; dry in the dust, damp in the rain.'

Criticism of the ostensibly more civilised Fascist Rome which preceded these extreme conditions can afford to be more subtle. Carlo Emilio Gadda◊ in *Quer pasticciaccio de Via Merulana* (*That Awful Mess on Via Merulana*), 1957 (Extract 3) makes the city of 1927 the home of involved and tentacular corruption and further rebels against its deceptive orderliness in his bizarre, unpredictable, 'baroque' use of language. The distinctive city he creates is one of an extraordinary range of real and fictive 20th-century Romes: the Via Merulana with its solid, concealing facades (now, however, a busier and livelier street than in Gadda's time); the fashionable studio-built version of Via

Veneto in Federico Fellini's *La dolce vita* of 1960 (subsequently imitated, Fellini claimed, by Via Veneto itself); or the alleys, derelict
buildings, and scrub-land in Pier Paolo Pasolini's (◊Lazio) *Ragazzi di
vita* (*The Ragazzi*), 1955, where 'silently, between banks that stank like
a urinal in the sun, the Tiber flowed as yellow as if it were casting up
all the garbage it was freighted with'.

## THE CAPITOLINE HILL

The **Capitoline hill** (**Campidoglio**) was the fortress and sacred centre
of early Rome. Here, according to Livy◊, the men digging the foundations for the Temple of Capitoline Jupiter found 'a human head, its
features intact', which was an omen that this place 'was to be the
citadel of the empire and the head of the world' (whence the name,
from *caput*, head); here, as the Gauls clambered up the rocky slopes
one night in 390 B.C., the Romans, just in time, were alerted to their
peril by the cackling and wing-clapping of Juno's sacred geese. The
Capitol was crucial to Roman identity, a fact reflected by the frequent,
often urgent references to it ('To the Capitol!' and the like) in Shakespeare's *Coriolanus*, set in Rome's small, precarious, new Republic not
long after the expulsion of the kings. (It is again an important marker
for the later Romans of *Julius Caesar*.)

The temple on the hill was the destination of triumph, where
victorious generals, having ridden up the Sacra Via through the
Forum, would sacrifice to the gods. Therefore Petrarch (◊Veneto
and North-East) declared as emphatically as possible his allegiance
to the ideal of Rome when in a solemn ceremony on Easter Day
1341, he was crowned with laurel on the Capitol (in the audience
chamber of the **Palazzo del Senatore**, subsequently much restruc-
tured). Ancient triumphers had worn crowns of laurel while poets
and other notables had been content with oak; a proudly laurelled
Petrarch both proclaimed devotion to his Laura's tree and claimed
kinship with the men most honoured by Rome. Later, in *I trionfi* (*The
Triumphs*), c.1356–74, he would help to transform the ancient victory
parade into a symbol of inner or metaphorical conquest.

Externally, the Capitol lost its Roman appearance in the Middle
Ages. But inside the **Museo Capitolino** and the **Palazzo dei Conser-
vatori** it retains important collections of ancient sculpture. The Capitoline collection recurs in the writings of 19th century visitors to
Rome. In Room One is the Dying Gaul, long thought of as the Dying
Gladiator: Byron's (◊Venice) noble figure 'Butcher'd to make a Roman
holiday' (*Childe Harold's Pilgrimage*, Canto Four, 1818). In the same
room is the resting satyr used by Nathaniel Hawthorne◊ in *The Marble
Faun*, 1860 – 'the sportive and frisky thing' somehow made marble,
and kept neither animal nor human only, 'and yet no monster, but a
being in whom both races meet, on friendly ground' and who, like

Count Donatello who so resembles it, might possibly 'be educated through the medium of his emotions; so that the coarser, animal portion of his nature might eventually be thrown into the background, though never utterly expelled'. The effect of the sculptures more generally is, for Henry James (◊Venice) in *The Portrait of a Lady*, 1881, an influence of 'noble quietude; which . . . slowly drops on the spirit the large white mantle of peace' (Extract 4).

Pious legend records that it was close to the Capitoline Museum, in what became the church of **Santa Maria d'Aracoeli** (on the site of the Temple of Juno Moneta and near that of Capitoline Jupiter), that Christianity laid its first claim to Rome. As the Tiburtine Sibyl prophesied the advent of the king of kings to the earthly monarch Augustus, he saw a vision of the Virgin standing on an altar and heard a voice proclaiming it 'the altar of the Son of God'. In consequence, Augustus built here the *Ara Coeli* ('Altar of Heaven'; the present altar is 13th century). And here, recalled Edward Gibbon◊, for whom Christianity had much to do with the weakening and collapse of Rome's empire, 'on the 15th of October, 1764, as I sat musing amidst the ruins of the Capitol, while the barefooted friars were singing vespers in the Temple of Jupiter . . . the idea of writing the decline and fall of the city first started to my mind'.

## THE FORUM ROMANUM

It is difficult to hold in the mind a single image of the Forum. Here and there stand pillars and reconstructed buildings, and the substantial arches adorned with scenes of glory; around them extends a mass, at first sight very confusing, of ruins, bricks and numbered lumps of marble, modern plaques, areas still being excavated, and amidst it all shrubs and pines, the rippling dance of oleanders in the wind, dust perhaps blowing up around a brown or grey cemented temple-base like – the walker seeking ancient things might fancy – sacrificial smoke. There are views of nearby churches and the treed higher ground of the Palatine Hill.

Such richness or confusion results from the densely packed nature of an area where buildings of different periods overlap and sometimes overlay each other. Among the relics (repeatedly rebuilt, however) of half-legendary days are the circular **Temple of Vesta** where the sacred flame was continually tended by the Vestal Virgins, and the **Regia** where the holy king Numa Pompilius was supposed to have lived in the late 8th and early 7th centuries B.C. Numa, introducer of the cult of Vesta to Rome, features in the legends as the principal founder of such early religious rites as the progress through the city of the 12 Salii, or Leaping Priests, of Mars, 'chanting their hymns to the triple beat of their ritual dance'. Livy◊ in *Ab urbe condita* (*From the Foundation of the City*), 29 B.C.>, says that Numa won people to love of the gods by the 'marvellous tale' that he met the goddess Egeria at night to receive guidance on the establishment of rites and appointment of priests.

Later the Forum was as much a civic, business and political centre as a religious. Politically one of its most important occasions was on 8 November 63 B.C., when at the **Temple of Jupiter Stator** (the remains of which lie somewhere near the foot of the Palatine hill) the Senate assembled to debate the increasing threat of a *coup d'état* by the disaffected patrician Lucius Sergius Catilina. Marcus Tullius Cicero◊, most eloquent of Roman orators (having taken the precaution of placing armed guards around the building) turned his formidable skills on Catiline himself, audaciously present in an attempt to show his good intentions:

> 'What a scandalous commentary on our age and its standards! For the Senate knows all these things [i.e. evidence of the intended coup]. The consul [Cicero] sees them being done. And yet this man still lives! Lives? He walks right into the Senate. He joins in our national debates – watches and marks and notes down with his gaze each one of us he plots to assassinate.'

The offender left Rome soon afterwards. Cicero went on to deliver an even more vituperative second *In Catilinam* speech and, thanks not only to his persuasive skills but to an effective intelligence-network, was able to arrest and sentence to death five of Catiline's senatorial co-conspirators. They were strangled in the **Tullianum**, the grim underground chamber which formed part of what later became known as the Mamertine Prison, and which survives as the chapel of **San Pietro in Carcere**, beneath San Giuseppe dei Falegnami. This was also the destination of most important triumphal captives. It was 'about 12 feet below ground, enclosed all round by walls and roofed by a vault of stone. Its filthy condition, darkness, and foul smell give it a loathsome and terrifying air', reports the Republican historian Sallust in *Catilinae coniuratio* (*The Conspiracy of Catiline*), c. 44–40 B.C. This lower chamber is still damp and claustrophobic. Only St Peter and St Paul among ancient prisoners seem to have come out of the Tullianum alive: they converted their keepers and baptised them in a spring which appeared miraculously. The water and the column to which the saints were chained are shown. In the larger upper chamber are two plaques remembering those who did perish here: one for martyrs of the church, the other for victims of Roman triumph or dissension – Jugurtha, King of Numidia (d.104 B.C.), Vercingetorix the leader of the Gauls against Caesar (d.46 B.C.), Simon Ben Giora leader of the Jewish insurrection (d.71 A.D.), the emperor Tiberius' disgraced favourite Sejanus (d.31 A.D.) and 'many others, unknown or less famous, who perished in the whirlpools of human hatreds and human events'.

Catiline, more fortunate than his executed supporters, died in battle against Rome early in 62 B.C. at Pistoia. Cicero was convinced that he had, as he perhaps understandably never tired of reminding people, saved the Republic. But within 15 years his old opponent Gaius Julius Caesar had become sole ruler. For a brief period in the months after Caesar's assassination in 44 B.C. Cicero became in effect head of state and, still hoping for the recovery of the Republic, directed his last orations sternly against Mark Antony. In 43 B.C. Cicero was murdered on Antony's instructions, and his head and hands nailed up on the **Rostra** – the platform in the Forum from which he had often spoken. (The Rostra, from which the Roman people were addressed, long stood in front of the Senate's traditional meeting-place, the **Curia**, but were moved further forward to the position of the present remains either by Caesar or soon after his death.)

From the Rostra Antony had spoken some equivalent of 'Friends, Romans, countrymen . . . ' and read out Caesar's will. A myth was being inaugurated; Brutus would be consigned to deepest Hell by Dante (◊Florence), exalted by good republicans, repeatedly re-examined in performances of *Julius Caesar*. The site of Caesar's funeral pyre in the Forum is marked by the surviving base of the altar of the **Temple of Caesar**, erected in 29 B.C. Caesar had become a god, *Divus Iulius*. The historian Suetonius, lover of omens and anecdotes, says that there was heavenly help at the cremation, perhaps from the twins Castor and Pollux:

> 'Two divine forms . . . suddenly appeared, javelin in hand and sword at thigh, and set fire to the couch with torches. Immediately the spectators assisted the blaze by heaping on it dry branches and the judges' chairs, and the court benches, with whatever else came to hand. Thereupon the musicians and masked professional mourners, who had walked in the funeral train wearing the robes that he had himself worn at his four triumphs, tore these in pieces and flung them on the flames – to which veterans who had assisted at his triumphs added the arms they had then borne. Many women in the audience similarly sacrificed their jewellery together with their children's golden buttons and embroidered tunics.'

Then the new cycle of violence began, as the crowd ran with brands from the pyre to burn down the assassins' houses. Plutarch (◊Sicily), followed by Shakespeare in *Julius Caesar*, says that they happened upon Cinna the poet and tore him to pieces because he was the namesake of Cinna the conspirator. Shakespeare's mob are eager to kill him whoever he is: if he is a poet not a conspirator 'tear him for his bad verses' all the same.

Peace was not fully restored until Octavian – Shakespeare's Octavius Caesar – defeated Antony and Cleopatra to become 'the universal landlord' (*Antony and Cleopatra*, 1606–7). He was accorded the surname Augustus – 'reverend', 'majestic' – in 27 B.C., and erected and restored buildings majestically enough to be able to claim to have found Rome brick and left it marble. Tradition has him, however, enjoying the fruits of peace in a relatively unassuming house on the **Palatine Hill**. (The **Domus Augustana** developed into a grander palace under his successors.) Here, it is said, he would recline while listening to Virgil (◊Naples and Campania) and Horace◊ reading their poems in the company of their discerning patron Maecenas.

Down in the Forum bloodshed became infrequent, but poets and other mortals did not always find peace. In one of his *Sermones* (*Satires*), Horace narrates an irritating encounter on the Sacra Via with 'a fellow I knew only by name' who, hoping to worm his way into Maecenas' circle, insists that he has time to accompany the poet wherever he wants to go. Until at last the bore is seized upon by an opponent in a law-case, Horace seems doomed to suffer the fate an old fortune-teller once foretold him: he will die not by poison, the sword, bad lungs or gout, but worn out by a chatterbox; 'let him avoid all gasbags on reaching man's estate'. More than a century of business, bustle, coups and corruption later, Juvenal, a more aggressive satirist, rendered in *Saturae* (*Satires*), c. A.D. 110–128, a Rome full not only of bores but of thugs, collapsing tenement blocks, and sexual perversion. The only solution, argues a friend in *Satire* Three (Extract 5) is to leave.

## THE COLOSSEUM; THE BATHS OF CARACALLA

Modern tourists admire the sunlit stone, and their predecessors gathered flowers, in the amphitheatre where ill-protected gladiators duelled to the death, big cats tore Christians to pieces, and the crowd shouted for more blood. This extreme contrast, the building's still extreme size, and the shape – an arena excites expectation that shows or happenings will fill the centre – together help to account for the talismanic power of the Colosseum. Byron (◊Venice), whose meditations in the moonlight in *Childe Harold's Pilgrimage*, Canto Four, 1818 and *Manfred*, 1817, enhanced this power for several generations of visitors and readers, finds the Colosseum a 'long-explored but still exhaustless mine / Of contemplation'. It is the haunt of some 'dread power / Nameless, yet thus omnipotent'.

In some cases the over-familiarity of Byron's lines was in fact inhibiting. In *The Marble Faun*, 1860, Nathaniel Hawthorne◊ has 'a party of English or Americans' 'paying the inevitable visit by moonlight, and exalting themselves with raptures that were Byron's, not their own'. But Hawthorne senses a similar 'dread power' when he chooses to set here the scene before the murder of Miriam's mysterious follower. The sculptor Kenyon speaks somewhat whimsically, but aptly in view of what is to come, of the contrast between a Colosseum 'really built for us' artists and its original purpose of allowing '80,000 persons . . .

squeezed together, row above row, to see their fellow-creatures torn by lions and tigers limb from limb'. Raising the theme of contrition which will dominate the rest of *The Marble Faun*, Kenyon continues 'Fancy a nightly assemblage of 80,000 melancholy and remorseful ghosts, looking down from those tiers of broken arches, striving to repent of the savage pleasures which they once enjoyed, but still longing to enjoy them over again!' Here, allegedly, countless terrifying spirits had appeared to Benvenuto Cellini and a necromancer of his acquaintance (*Vita* (*Autobiography*), 1558–62).

Hawthorne brought to the ruins the ambivalence of much American literature of this time about the old world. Rome is a resource for sculptors and painters, an inescapable fact, but its past weighs heavy on the present: it is a place of melancholy, decay, death and guilt as well as picturesqueness. It is a dangerous place for sons and daughters of the new world like the eponymous characters in Henry James's *Daisy Miller*, 1878, and *Roderick Hudson*, 1875. Daisy dies of 'Roman fever' after a final socially and medically improvident exposure to scandal and the night air in the Colosseum. Roderick wants to climb a fragmentary wall of the arena to pick a radiant blue flower in a last bid to prove his strength and decisiveness to Christina Light, but fails in this attempt as in most others.

Ruins can be rendered imaginatively safer if they are in some way transformed or transfigured: by Byronic moonlight, perhaps, or by the flowering vegetation which Shelley describes wreathing, incorporating, almost expanding the **Baths of Caracalla** (Extract 9); or by a nationalist or mystical sense of regenerative potency in the symbols of old Rome, as for Mussolini or less crudely for Giosuè Carducci (◊Emilia-Romagna) who in *Dinanzi alle Terme di Caracalla* (*At the Baths of Caracalla*), 1877, salutes the goddess Roma who is not dead but sleeping, albeit unnoticed by trivial moderns like the green-eye-shaded British tourist peering in her book to find the Roman walls or the passing peasant whistling sombrely through his beard.

## THE SISTINE CHAPEL AND ST PETER'S

Giorgio Vasari in *The Lives of the Artists* (1550, enlarged 1568) promoted Michelangelo's work as the summit of human achievement. The Sistine ceiling (1508–12) and Last Judgement (1536–41) are peaks in Vasari's narrative of what he perceived as the progress of the artist and of art in general. Michelangelo acquires quasi-divine power, indeed, as Vasari blurs the distinction between God's creation and the artist's: on the Sistine ceiling God 'stretches out his right hand towards Adam, a figure whose beauty, pose, and contours are such that it seems to have been fashioned that very moment by the first and supreme Creator rather than by the drawing and brush of a mortal man'. God divides light from darkness, 'self-sustained with arms outstretched, in a revelation of love and creative power' and, Vasari proclaims, the ceiling has itself been 'a veritable beacon to our art, . . . restoring light to a world that for centuries has been plunged into darkness'.

The Last Judgement is evidently more appropriate to the sombre atmosphere of Rome in the years after the sack of 1527. Here, says Vasari, Michelangelo:

> 'imagined to himself all the terror of those days and he repre-sented, for the greater punishment of those who have not lived well, the entire Passion of Jesus Christ. . . . We see the seated figure of Christ turning towards the damned His stern and terri-ble countenance in order to curse them; and in great fear Our Lady draws her mantle around her as she hears and sees such tremendous desolation.'

The glory of creation was not always so evident to the producer himself. In a sonnet on painting the ceiling Michelangelo evokes the physical contortions necessary to perform this feat: the belly and chin change places, the body is bent like a Syrian bow. The poems more widely explore the frustrations and failures of love and creation. In old age Michelangelo doubts the very value of painting and sculpture, which once he sought to make 'an idol or a king' (Extract 7), for 'the soul that turns to God again', turns to Vasari's 'first and supreme Creator'.

Michelangelo's employers were sometimes less high-minded. Pope Julius II, who bullied the reluctant sculptor into decorating the Sistine ceiling, wanted it as a tribute to his personal glory as much as God's, and threatened once to throw him off his own scaffolding if the work didn't progress more swiftly. (Soon afterwards an apology and pre-sents were forthcoming.) But perhaps the end result moved Julius to devotion as well as self-gratification; the overbearing Pope Paul III, who virtually forced Michelangelo to work on the Sistine Last Judge-ment, did apparently fall to his knees before it to pray God not to charge him with his sins on that final day.

Whatever their response to papal splendours and foibles, visitors have proceeded, since Michelangelo's time, to the Sistine Chapel, the Vatican Museum, and St Peter's. Opinions are expected of them, as by Gilbert Osmond – a character with an ego at least as large as that of any Renaissance pope – of Isabel Archer in Henry James's (◊Venice) *The Portrait of a Lady,* 1881:

> '"It's very large and very bright," she contented herself with replying.
> "It's too large; it makes one feel like an atom."
> "Isn't that the right way to feel in the greatest of human temples?" she asked with rather a liking for her phrase.

"I suppose it's the right way to feel everywhere, when one *is* nobody. But I like it in a church as little as anywhere else."'

St Peter's has been the tomb and architectural project of popes, announced by Bernini's colonnade, surmounted by Michelangelo's dome and containing works as various as his early Pietà, the 13th-century St Peter with his much-kissed foot, and Bernini's extravagant Baroque baldacchino (1633) over the apostle's tomb, described by John Evelyn (◊Lazio) as 'a thing of that art, vastness, and magnificence, as is beyond all that man's industry has produced of the kind'. Such a place demands an opinion or an emotional response – prayer, poetry, irritation, Isabel's 'conception of greatness' which 'rose and dizzily rose' when she first 'found herself beneath the far-arching dome and saw the light drizzle down through the air thickened with incense and with the reflections of marble and gilt, of mosaic and bronze'.

## CASTEL SANT' ANGELO

The Castel Sant'Angelo is a firm reminder of papal power. Benvenuto Cellini◊, the goldsmith, sculptor, and autobiographer of the artist as hero, gives a racy, splendidly immodest account of his activities as a gunner defending the fortress and Pope Clement VII when most of Rome had already fallen during the sack of 1527. His was the shot, he tells us, which killed the enemy general, Charles of Bourbon, and he could have blown to pieces most of the other leaders had it not been objected that without them the marauding soldiers would be even more difficult to control. More expectedly for a goldsmith he was also told to remove the papal jewels from their gold settings, sew the jewels into Clement's robes, and melt the gold down, prior to the Pope's escape along the (extant) covered way leading from the Bastion of San Martino to the Vatican.

Wrongly accused of having stolen the gold, Cellini found himself back in the Castel Sant'Angelo, now as a prisoner, in 1538. He had made many enemies as a result of papal favour, the tempestuous nature which had led him more than once to stab an opponent to death in the streets of Rome, and perhaps also because of his cavalier attitude to the truth (which in the autobiography, however, can be explained almost convincingly as a feature of the genre – the hero's life). While those more and less favourably disposed to him intrigued to have him freed or executed or forgotten about, he remained a prisoner high in the keep of the castle. Eventually – or so he tells us – with the aid of sheets cut into strips, a purloined pair of pincers, sentries who turned a blind eye, fervent prayer, and his native ingeniousness, he succeeded in lowering himself from the roof in two stages. With a broken leg and bleeding hands which he had to bathe in his own urine he crawled, fighting off dogs, until he could persuade a water-carrier to take him on his back to Saint Peter's, and then crawled on until rescued by the well-disposed Cardinal Cornaro. Soon, however, he was back in prison, expecting death at the subsequently demolished Tor di Nona on the Tiber, and then transferred back to the Castel Sant'Angelo. This time Cellini was consigned to one of the **Prigione storiche** (historic cells), down the staircase from the Cortile di Alessandro VI. Traditionally the last cell was his. Here he was saved from attempted suicide by divine intervention and beheld radiant, consoling dream-visions of a beautiful young man and of the sun which from the depths of his cell he longed to see. In 1539 he was released and restored to favour. Other inmates of the Prigione storiche were Beatrice Cenci (executed for parricide in 1599, the subject of Shelley's◊ *The Cenci*) and the philosopher Giordano Bruno, burnt at the stake after a seven-year heresy trial in 1600.

## The Keats-Shelley Memorial House; The Protestant Cemetery

In November 1820 the English poet John Keats◊, dying of tuberculosis, moved with his loyal friend the painter Joseph Severn into the *pensione* which is now the Keats-Shelley Memorial House. This contains a fine collection of books, paintings, and objects connected with Keats, Shelley◊ (including Severn's posthumous picture of him at the Baths of Caracalla), and Byron, who lived opposite the house at 66 Piazza di Spagna earlier in 1820. Generations of visitors to the small room in which Keats died on 23 February 1821, aged 25, have looked out at the view of the palm-trees and the crowds on the **Spanish Steps** and felt the contrast with the agonising suffering of the last weeks of what Keats called, in his last letter, his 'posthumous existence'. Keats' life-mask, his death-mask, and Severn's sketch of him at 3.00 a.m. on 28 January – 'drawn to keep me awake – a deadly sweat was on him' – are to be seen in the room.

Keats is buried in the older and more spacious part of the Protestant Cemetery near the ancient **Pyramid of Caius Cestius**, a peaceful place of trees and grass, originally, as Shelley describes it in the preface to his elegy on Keats *Adonais*, 1821, 'an open space among the ruins, covered in winter with violets and daisies'. Keats' tombstone bears his melancholy claim that he was one – unrecognized, sensitive to hostile criticism – 'whose name was writ in water'. But the faithful Severn (who returned to Rome as British Consul in 1860–72 and died there in 1879), lived long enough, we are reminded by the inscription on the stone next to his friend's, to see him 'numbered among the Immortal Poets of England'. (Keats had written to his brother and sister-in-law in

October 1818 that 'I think I shall be among the English poets after my death'.)

'It might make one in love with death, to think that one should be buried in so sweet a place', continues Shelley's preface. (When he first saw it in 1818, however, he pressed the thought further in a letter to his friend Peacock: given such beauty 'one might, if one were to die, desire the sleep [the dead] seem to sleep. Such is the human mind and so it peoples with its wishes vacancy and oblivion'.) After Shelley's own death in 1822 his ashes were buried at the top of the sloping newer part of the cemetery beneath an inscription which includes, from *The Tempest*, the lines:

> 'Nothing of him that doth fade,
> But doth suffer a sea-change
> Into something rich and strange.'

This alludes to his drowning, appropriately salutes the seas and waters of his poems, and suggests an early confidence in Shelley's circle that he was not one 'whose name was writ in water'. The tomb was designed by Shelley's friend and unreliable biographer Edward John Trelawny (1792–1881), who was buried next to him. Also in the new cemetery (fuller than the old but still calmly meditative among its oleanders and umbrella-pines) are the graves of John Addington Symonds (◊Emilia-Romagna), the novelist R.M. Ballantyne (1825–94), author of *The Coral Island*), the sculptor William Wetmore Story (1819–95), and Antonio Gramsci (◊Sardinia).

## OTHER LITERARY LANDMARKS

**Caffè Greco**: café, at 86 Via Condotti, founded in 1760 and patronised by a long list of artists in Rome including Goethe (◊Naples and Campania), Stendhal (◊Lombardy), Leopardi (◊Umbria and Marche), Nikolai Gogol, Liszt, Wagner, Mark Twain, and Hans Christian Andersen.

**Campo dei Fiori**: statue (1887) of Giordano Bruno, burnt at the stake here in 1600.

**Capitoline Hill**: the Tarpeian Rock, from which traitors to the Roman Republic were hurled to their deaths, was probably at the south-west corner of the hill. The name comes from the Tarpeia who, legend has it, treacherously let the Sabines into the fortress on the hill.

**Domine Quo Vadis**: church marking the point on the Via Appia Antica at which Jesus appeared to St Peter, causing him to return to Rome where he was martyred – the subject of Henryk Sienkiewicz's novel *Quo Vadis?*, 1896, and the epic MGM film of 1951.

**Palatine Hill**: somewhere at the foot of the hill was the Lupercal, the cave where Romulus and Remus were suckled by a wolf. Plutarch

(◊Sicily) says that in the fertility rite of Lupercalia young patricians ran naked and struck people with 'shaggy thongs'. Barren women like Calpurnia in *Julius Caesar* might, if struck, 'shake off their sterile curse'.

**Palazzo Cenci**: the 'vast and gloomy pile of feudal architecture' where Shelley◊ set much of the first three acts of *The Cenci*.

**Santa Maria Maggiore**: church renowned for its mosaics and 'the sense it gives you . . . of having been prayed in for several centuries by an endlessly curious and complex society' (Henry James).

**Trevi Fountain**: the scene of a famous encounter between Corinne and Lord Nelvil, their faces reflected by moonlight in the water, in Anne-Louise-Germaine de Staël's *Corinne, ou l'Italie*, 1807.

# BOOKLIST

Aleramo, Sibilla, A Woman [1906], Rosalind Delmar, trans, Virago, London, 1979. **Extract 1.**

Banti, Anna, Artemisia [1947], Shirley D'Ardia Caracciolo, trans, University of Nebraska Press, Lincoln and London, 1988. **Extract 2.**

Browning, Robert, The Poems, John Pettigrew and Thomas J. Collins, eds, Penguin, Harmondsworth, 1993.

Cellini, Benvenuto, The Autobiography, George Bull, trans, Folio Society, London, 1966.

Selected Political Speeches of Cicero, Michael Grant, trans, Penguin, Harmondsworth, 1969.

Donaldson, Ian, The Rapes of Lucretia: a Myth and its Transformations, Clarendon Press, Oxford, 1982.

Evelyn, John, The Diary of John Evelyn, Guy de la Bédoyère, ed, Boydell, Woodbridge, 1995.

Gadda, Carlo Emilio, That Awful Mess on Via Merulana [1957], William Weaver, trans, introduction by Italo Calvino, Quartet Books, London, 1985. **Extract 3.**

Gibbon, Edward, The History of the Decline and Fall of the Roman Empire [1776–88], David Womersley, ed, Allen Lane, Penguin, London, 1994.

Gibbon, Edward, Memoirs of My Life [1796], Betty Radice, ed, Penguin, Harmondsworth, 1984.

Gregorius, Master, The Marvels of Rome, John Osborne, trans, Pontifical Institute of Mediaeval Studies, Toronto, 1987.

Hibbert, Christopher, Rome: the Biography of a City, Penguin, London, 1987.

Horace: Satires and Epistles. Persius: Satires, Niall Rudd, trans, Harmondsworth, Penguin, 1979.

Holmes, Richard, Shelley: the Pursuit, Penguin, Harmondsworth, and Viking Penguin, New York, 1987.

James, Henry, Daisy Miller [1879] and Other Stories, Jean Gooder, ed, Oxford University Press, Oxford, 1985.

James, Henry, The Portrait of a Lady [1881], Geoffrey Moore and Patricia Crick, ed, Penguin, Harmondsworth, 1984. **Extract 4.**

*Booklist continued*

James, Henry, *Roderick Hudson* [1875], Geoffrey Moore and Patricia Crick, ed, Penguin, Harmondsworth, 1986.

Juvenal, *The Satires* [c.110–128], Niall Rudd, trans, introduction and notes by William Barr, Clarendon Press, Oxford, 1991. **Extract 5**.

Lamb, Richard, *War in Italy 1943–1945: a Brutal Story*, John Murray, London, 1993.

Livy [Titus Livius], *The History of Early Rome* [29 B.C.>], Aubrey de Sélincourt, trans, Penguin, Harmondsworth, 1960. **Extract 6**.

Livy [Titus Livius], *Rome and Italy: Books VI-X of The History of Rome from its Foundation*, Betty Radice, trans, Penguin, Harmondsworth, 1982.

*The Marvels of Rome*, Francis Morgan Nicholls, trans, Ellis and Elvey, London, 1889.

Michelangelo Buonarotti, *The Sonnets of Michelangelo*, Elizabeth Jennings trans, Carcanet Press, Manchester, 1987. **Extract 7**.

Morante, Elsa, *History: a Novel*, William Weaver, trans, Penguin, Harmondsworth, 1980, Alfred Knopf, Inc. (USA), 1977.

Moravia, Antonio, *The Woman of Rome* [1947], Lydia Holland, trans, Granada, London, 1984. **Extract 8**.

Petrarca, Francesco, *Letters from Petrarch*, Morris Bishop, trans, Indiana University Press, Bloomington and London, 1967.

Rawson, Elizabeth, *Cicero: a Portrait*, Cornell University Press, Ithaca, N.Y., 1983.

Serao, Matilde, *The Conquest of Rome* [1885], Ann Caesar, ed, Pickering and Chatto, London, 1991.

*The Letters of Percy Bysshe Shelley*, Frederick L. Jones, ed, 2 vols, Clarendon Press, Oxford, 1964. **Extract 9**.

Gaius Suetonius Tranquillus, *The Twelve Caesars* [c.115–130 A.D.], Robert Graves, trans, revised and expanded by Michael Grant, Penguin, Harmondsworth, 1980.

Wood, Sharon, *Woman as Object: Language and Gender in the Work of Alberto Moravia*, Pluto, London, 1990.

# *Extracts*

## (1) ROME

### Sibilla Aleramo, *A Woman*, 1906

*The narrator, closely reflecting the author's own experiences, feels trapped by marriage to a disloyal and violent man and by motherhood. (Ibsen's* A Doll's House, *1879, is one of the book's explicit inspirations.) While still living with her husband, she is briefly able to work in the expanding industrial city, where she comes across women whose sufferings are more extreme and more difficult to resolve than her own.*

My new friend took me to the district of San Lorenzo one day. It made my blood run cold. I wanted simply to destroy it, all of it. When had I ever felt like this before? Outside fierce sunshine scorched the street. In the distance the Tiburtine hills rose up like a haven of peace. But no sun penetrated the tenements we entered. Dark stairwells flecked with damp rose up before us. At every floor we came to badly-lit corridors where half-dressed women gathered to watch us, their filthy blouses barely covering their breasts. They stared at us, hostile, and they terrified me because they had experienced depths of horror of which I knew nothing. In raucous voices they told us about sickness, births, lock-outs, accidents. They asked for nothing; they accepted everything. A fair-haired little girl came down the stairs, her cheeks still rosy, her smile still innocent. Then she disappeared. Foul smells emanated from the open doorways; the entire building echoed with shrill voices, shouting, complaining . . .

Back in the street I suddenly glimpsed once more that peaceful countryside on the horizon. I wanted desperately to escape to its meadows and streams. I wanted to forget the fact that there were human beings – beings like me, like my son, like the saintly woman who had taken me there – who lived in rags in rooms with hardly any ventilation, chilled to the bone, ignorant of the reasons for their pitiless confinement to such hovels.

My duty lay here. I was convinced that I could throw myself into the thick of life and confront the monstrous reality. . . . I wanted to show this place to all those who admired Rome's palaces, who lingered beside her fountains, who gathered at the theatre in the evenings, who crowded together to watch a prince walk by or witness the unveiling of a useless statue. And if, after seeing it, they were still able to ignore such misery I would gladly give the signal to destroy them all!

## (2) ROME

### Anna Banti, *Artemisia*, 1947

*Banti's novel concerns the 17th-century painter Artemisia Gentileschi, a woman attempting to express her individuality in a male-oriented society. Her memory of rape by a fellow artist has become gradually 'a mere curiosity devoid of emotion' and she is able to enjoy a short period of unusual stability when she lives for a time with her husband Antonio Stiattesi and his extended family.*

'Goodnight, Francesco,' she says, getting up and arranging on her shoulders the Spanish mantilla that Antonio gave her. She leaps into the carriage with a nimble sense of adventure, a lady travelling incognito.

In the hired carriage that bounces over the stones and potholes she opens her eyes wide: darkness as they charge down the steep hill, then an ever-increasing number of torches and footmen, lights in roadside shrines, lamps of cautious wayfarers. But she feels safe and when she gets out at the marquis's gate (ten yards from the cellar opening) she is merry as a masker and takes pleasure in her regal passage through the room where the Stiattesis eat, sleep and carouse, often 10 or 15 of them at a time. She does not care that Mariuccia says, 'Here's that wh – Artemisia.' Once the door of her room is closed, nothing can annoy her. Fine if Antonio is back, fine if he's not. Alone, she sings as she undresses, sometimes with clowning, theatrical gestures. She turns the key in the lock, nibbles on bread and walnuts, almond cake, dried chestnuts. Then when everything is quiet, when the talk on the other side of the door has ceased, she opens her trunk and takes out paper and charcoal. Just as before she draws by lamplight, but now she feels rejuvenated, carefree, getting up now and then to chew on a dry fig and peep out of the high window that looks onto the marquis's courtyard. The horses, noisily clattering their shod hooves and rearing upright before passing through the gateway, brush the grill on her window with their enormous mouths. The footmen are shouting, the torches are smoking, the red garb and florid face of a cardinal flicker like embers in the shadows at the bottom of the main stairs, while his retinue swoop down to hold up his train. And Artemisia throws herself down onto her floor-level bed to rest.

## (3) ROME

### Carlo Emilio Gadda,
### *That Awful Mess on Via Merulana*, 1957

*Ostensibly a detective novel,* That Awful Mess, *set in 1927, probes the essentially hedonistic morality of a Fascist society in which almost all the characters, rather than a single murderer, are implicated. Gadda's style, playing with dialect, convoluted structures, digression and parody, reacts against the conventions of that society and its still imperfect successors.*

In his wisdom and in his Molisan poverty, Officer Ingravallo, who seemed to live on silence and sleep under the jungle of that black mop, shiny as pitch and curly as astrakhan lamb, in his wisdom, he sometimes interrupted this silence and this sleep to enunciate some theoretical idea (a general idea, that is) on the affairs of men, and of women. At first sight, or rather on first hearing, these seemed banalities. They weren't banalities. And so, those rapid declarations, which crackled on his lips like the sudden illumination of a sulphur match, were revived in the ears of people at a distance of hours, or of months, from their enunciation: as if after a mysterious period of incubation. 'That's right!' the person in question admitted, 'That's exactly what Ingravallo said to me.' He sustained, among other things, that unforeseen catastrophes are never the consequence or the effect, if you prefer, of a single motive, of *a* cause singular; but they are rather like a whirlpool, a cyclonic point of depression in the consciousness of the world, towards which a whole multitude of converging causes have combined. He also used words like knot or tangle or muddle, or *gnommero*, which in Roman dialect means skein. But the legal term, 'the motive, the motives,' escaped his lips by preference, though as if against his will. The opinion that we must 'reform within ourselves the meaning of the category of cause,' as handed down by the philosophers from Aristotle to Immanuel Kant, and replace cause with causes, was for him a central, persistent opinion, almost a fixation, which melted from his fleshy, but rather white lips, where the stub of a spent cigarette seemed, dangling from one corner, to accompany the somnolence of his gaze and the quasi-grin, half-bitter, half-sceptical, in which through 'old' habit he would fix the lower half of his face beneath that sleep of his forehead and eyelids and that pitchy black of his mop. This was how, exactly how, he defined 'his' crimes. 'When they call me . . . Sure. If they call *me*, you can be sure that there's trouble: some mess, some *gliuommero* to untangle,' he would say, garbling his Italian with the dialects of Naples and the Molise.

# (4) ROME

## Henry James, *The Portrait of a Lady*, 1881

*Isabel Archer, between conversations with a rejected suitor and a potential one, reflects in the Capitoline Gallery. In several of James' novels Rome and its monuments are the setting for encounters between American freshness, boldness or naïveté and the complex, inscrutable, and often dangerous old world.*

They shook hands, and he left her alone in the glorious room, among the shining antique marbles. She sat down in the centre of the circle of these presences, regarding them vaguely, resting her eyes on their beautiful blank faces; listening, as it were, to their eternal silence. It is impossible, in Rome at least, to look long at a great company of Greek sculptures without feeling the effect of their noble quietude; which, as with a high door closed for the ceremony, slowly drops on the spirit the large white mantle of peace. I say in Rome especially, because the Roman air is an exquisite medium for such impressions. The golden sunshine mingles with them, the deep stillness of the past, so vivid yet, though it is nothing but a void full of names, seems to throw a solemn spell upon them. The blinds were partly closed in the windows of the Capitol, and a clear, warm shadow rested on the figures and made them more mildly human. Isabel sat there a long time, under the charm of their motionless grace, wondering to what, of their experience, their absent eyes were open, and how, to our ears, their alien lips would sound. The dark red walls of the room threw them into relief; the polished marble floor reflected their beauty. She had seen them all before, but her enjoyment repeated itself, and it was all the greater because she was glad again, for the time, to be alone. At last, however, her attention lapsed, drawn off by a deeper tide of life. An occasional tourist came in, stopped and stared a moment at the Dying Gladiator, and then passed out of the other door, creaking over the smooth pavement. At the end of half an hour Gilbert Osmond reappeared, apparently in advance of his companions. He strolled towards her slowly, with his hands behind him, and his usual inquiring, yet not quite appealing smile.

# (5) ROME

## Juvenal, *Satire 3*, 110–128 A.D.

*Umbricius, a man leaving Rome for good, tells his friend why, giving Juvenal the opportunity to voice wide-ranging criticism of a Rome full of noise, corruption, and Greeks. 'The emperor Drusus' is thought to refer to Claudius (ruled A.D. 41–54), proverbially prone to sleepiness; 'Corbulo' is the famously strong and successful general, Gnaeus Domitus Corbulo (d.66 A.D.).*

Here most invalids die from lack of sleep (but the illness
itself is caused by food which lies there undigested
on a feverish stomach); who ever obtained a good night's rest
in rented lodgings? It costs a fortune to sleep in the city.
That's the root of the trouble. The coming and going of waggons
in the narrow winding streets, the yells at a halted herd,
would banish sleep from even a seal or the emperor Drusus.
If duty calls, as the crowd falls back, the rich man passes
quickly above their faces in a large Liburnian galley,
reading or writing or taking a nap as he speeds along.
(The closed windows of a litter can make the occupant drowsy.)
Yet he'll arrive before us. As we hurry along we are blocked
by a wave in front; behind, a massive mulitude crushes
my pelvis; *he* digs in with an elbow, *he* with a hard-wood
pole; then *he* hits my head with a beam, and *he* with a wine-jar.
My legs are caked with mud; from every side I am trampled
by giant feet; a soldier stamps on my toe with his hob-nails.

Look at all that smoke; a crowd is having a picnic.
A hundred guests, each with a portable kitchen behind him.
Corbulo could hardly carry such enormous utensils,
so many things on his head, as that unfortunate slave-boy,
who keeps his head erect and fans the flame as he runs.
Freshly mended tunics are ripped; a giant fir-tree
on a swaying cart comes bearing down; another waggon
carries a pine; they nod overhead and threaten the people.
For if the axle transporting Ligurian marble collapses,
tipping its mountainous load down on the hordes beneath,
what is left of their bodies? Who can locate their limbs
or bones?

# (6) ROME

### Livy, *From the Foundation of the City,* 29 B.C. onwards

*The story of Lucretia's rape by Tarquin and of the consequent expulsion of the kings by Brutus was one of the legends through which Romans defined their identity. To a degree Lucretia stands for violated Roman liberty. But the more personal and psychological aspects of the story continued to be explored in later centuries by artists including Titian, Shakespeare, and Benjamin Britten.*

When all was quiet, he drew his sword and made his way to Lucretia's room determined to rape her. She was asleep. Laying his left hand on her breast, 'Lucretia,' he whispered, 'not a sound! I am Sextus Tarquinius. I am armed – if you utter a word, I will kill you.' Lucretia opened her eyes in terror; death was imminent, no help at hand. Sextus urged his love, begged her to submit, pleaded, threatened, used every weapon that might conquer a woman's heart. But all in vain; not even the fear of death could bend her will. 'If death will not move you,' Sextus cried, 'dishonour shall. I will kill you first, then cut the throat of a slave and lay his naked body by your side. Will they not believe you have been caught in adultery with a servant – and paid the price?' Even the most resolute chastity could not have stood against this dreadful threat.

Lucretia yielded. Sextus enjoyed her, and rode away, proud of his success.

[She sent for her father and husband and their two trusted friends.] They found Lucretia sitting in her room, in deep distress. Tears rose to her eyes as they entered, and to her husband's question, 'Is it well with you?' she answered 'No. What can be well with a woman who has lost her honour? In your bed, Collatinus, is the impress of another man. My body only has been violated. My heart is innocent, and death shall be my witness. Give me your solemn promise that the adulterer shall be punished – he is Sextus Tarquinius. He it is who last night came as my enemy disguised as my guest, and took his pleasure of me. That pleasure will be my death – and his, too, if you are men.'

The promise was given. One after another they tried to comfort her. They told her she was helpless, and therefore innocent; that he alone was guilty. It was the mind, they said, that sinned, not the body: without intention there could never be guilt.

'What is due to *him*,' Lucretia said, 'is for you to decide. As for me I am innocent of fault, but I will take my punishment. Never shall Lucretia provide a precedent for unchaste women to escape what they deserve.' With these words she drew a knife from under her robe, drove it into her heart, and fell forward, dead.

Her father and husband were overwhelmed with grief. While they stood weeping, helplessly, Brutus drew the bloody knife from Lucretia's body, and holding it before him cried: 'By this girl's blood – none more chaste till a tyrant wronged her – and by the gods, I swear that with sword and fire, and whatever else can lend strength to my arm, I will pursue Lucius Tarquinius the Proud, his wicked wife, and all his children, and never again will I let them or any other man be King in Rome.'

## (7) ROME

### Michelangelo Buonarotti,
### sonnet sent to Giorgio Vasari, September 1554

*This poem was written (in several versions) between 1552 and 1554, when Michelangelo was in his late seventies, after his last works as a painter and almost his last as a sculptor. (He remained highly active as architect at St Peter's.) Art, rejected here, often figures or ensures some kind of immortality in the earlier poems. The two deaths referred to are the actual death of the body and the further 'death' of the soul in damnation. This translation is by the poet Elizabeth Jennings.*

Already now my life has run its course,
And, like a fragile boat on a rough sea,
I reach the place where everyone must cross
And give account of life's activity.

Now I know well it was a fantasy
That made me think art could be made into
An idol or a king. Though all men do

This, they do it half unwillingly.

The loving thoughts, so happy and so vain,
Are finished now. A double death comes near -
The one is sure, the other is a threat.

Painting and sculpture cannot any more
Quieten the soul that turns to God again,
To God who, on the cross, for us was set.


## (8) ROME

### Alberto Moravia, *The Woman of Rome*, 1947

*Moravia uses the first person narrative of his novel to explore the relationship between individual consciousness and external fact. What at first Adriana thinks is distress caused by her profession as a prostitute in fact results from the more general malaise of being alive, of being one of the many who, seemingly unaffected by the 'absurd, ineffable anguish' of their lives, go around 'playing sincerely their insincere parts'.*

I used to shudder uncontrollably, feeling my hair stand on end, and suddenly the walls of my flat, the city and even the world seemed to vanish, leaving me suspended in dark, empty, endless space – suspended, what's more, in the same clothes, with the same memories, name and profession. A girl called Adriana suspended against nothingness. Nothingness seemed to me something terrible, solemn and incomprehensible, and the saddest aspect of the whole matter was my meeting this nothingness with the manners and outward appearance I bore in the evening when I used to meet Gisella in the confectioner's, where she waited for me. I find no consolation in the idea that other people also acted and moved in just as futile and inadequate a way as I did when faced with this nothingness, within this nothingness, surrounded by this nothingness. I was only amazed at their not noticing it, or not making their observations known, not referring more often to it, as usually happens when many people all at once discover the same fact.

At these times I used to throw myself on to my knees and pray, perhaps more through a habit contracted in childhood than from a conscious will. But I did not use the words of the usual prayers, which seemed too long for my sudden mood. I used to throw myself on to my knees so violently that my legs hurt for some days afterwards, and used to pray aloud in a voice filled with despair, saying: 'Christ have mercy upon me,' just these few words. It was not really a prayer but a magic formula which I thought might dispel my anguish and bring me back to reality. After having cried out impulsively in this way, with all my strength, I remained for some time with my face in my hands, utterly absorbed. At last I used to become aware that my mind was a blank, that I was bored, that I was the same Adriana as ever, that I was in my own room; I touched my body half-astonished at finding it whole, and getting up from my knees I slipped into bed. I felt very tired and aching all over, as if I had fallen down a rocky slope, and I went to sleep immediately.

# (9) ROME

## Percy Bysshe Shelley, letter to Thomas Love Peacock, 23 March 1819

*The combination of ruined architecture and vegetable growth at the Baths of Caracalla was important in the genesis and writing – mostly here – of* Prometheus Unbound, 1820. *While 'power and imperialism', as Shelley's biographer Richard Holmes says, were destroyed, 'the forces of human love and freedom, and of Nature, which he regarded as allies, did in the end reassert themselves, just as the beautiful and innocent white blossoms of the laurustinus covered over the desolation of Caracalla'.*

The Thermæ of Caracalla . . . consist of six enormous chambers, above 200 feet in height, and each enclosing a vast space like that of a field. There are in addition a number of towers and labyrinthine recesses hidden and woven over by the wild growth of weeds and ivy. Never was any desolation more sublime and lovely. The perpendicular wall of ruin is cloven into steep ravines filled with flowering shrubs whose thick twisted roots are knotted in the rifts of the stones. At every step the aerial pinnacles of shattered stone group into new combinations of effect, and tower above the lofty yet level walls, as the distant mountains change their aspect to one rapidly travelling along the plain. The perpendicular walls . . . surround green and level spaces of lawn, on which some elms have grown, and which are interrupted towards their skirts by masses of the fallen ruin overtwined with the broad leaves of creeping weeds. The blue sky canopies it, and is as the everlasting roof of these enormous halls. But the most interesting effect remains. In one of the buttresses which supports an immense and lofty arch . . . are the crumbling remains of an antique winding staircase, whose sides are open in many places to the precipice. This you ascend, and arrive on the summit of these piles. Here grow on every side thick entangled wildernesses of myrtle and the myrtelus and bay and the flowering laurustinus whose white blossoms are just developed, the wild fig and a thousand nameless plants sown by the wandering winds. These woods are intersected on every side by paths, like sheep tracks through the copse wood of steep mountains, which wind to every part of these immense labyrinths. . . . Come to Rome. It is a scene by which expression is overpowered: which words cannot convey.

# Biographies and important works

ALERAMO, Sibilla, was the name taken by Rina Pierangeli Faccio (1876–1960), novelist and journalist born in Alessandria. At 16 she married a man who had seduced her probably in the hope of succeeding to her father's position as a factory manager. Her husband was unfaithful, sexually demanding, and violent. Increasingly interested in the ideal of women's emancipation, she eventually left her husband and, much more reluctantly, her child. *Una donna* (*A Woman*), 1906, Aleramo's best-known novel, is closely related to her own story. Born into a patriarchal structure, the narrator at first adores her free-thinking intellectual father, only later discovering that he is betraying her mother, driving her to madness and attempted suicide. The daughter had regarded her as a negligible figure; 'Why do we idealise sacrifice in mothers?' she later asks. 'Who gave us this inhuman idea that mothers should negate their own wishes and desires?' The repetition of this pattern in the narrator's own marriage helps her to see that she is writing not only about a particular woman's pain but about the suffering and dilemmas of women of the period more generally. Personal relationships, the stuff of Aleramo's novel, must be established on a freer basis before more general reform – of the laws which deprived women of property rights and custody of children, for instance – can be achieved.

*Una donna* was a seminal work in early 20th century feminism and women's writing. At one point Aleramo challenges the orthodoxies of Italian literature written by men: why do the poets write about Beatrice and Laura instead of 'the women they lived with, who bore their children', who acted as their domestic servants? The book was frowned on or obscured during the highly conservative Fascist years, but again became popular in the women's movement and elsewhere from the 1960s onwards. (Aleramo herself held various political allegiances before emerging as a Communist after the Second World War.)

BANTI, Anna, is the pseudonym of Lucia Lopresti Longhi (1895–1985), born in Florence, who lived in Rome until 1934 and later again in Florence. Many of Lopresti's books are on 17th century and other painting; in 1924 she married the art historian Roberto Longhi. She was literary editor of the journal *Paragone* from 1950 and also edited the art section following her husband's death in 1970. She began to publish short stories under the name Anna Banti in 1937. Her first novel, *Sette lune* (*Seven Moons*), 1941, announced the continuing central theme of her fiction: the difficulty and anguish faced by women attempting to fulfil their potential in an uncomprehending, patriarchal society.

*Artemisia*, 1947, is inspired by what is known of the life of the painter Artemisia Gentileschi (c.1593-c.1652) who was raped by her fellow artist Agostino Tassi (tried for the crime but acquitted) in Rome in 1612 and later worked and taught in Naples, France, and England. The first version of Banti's book was destroyed with her house during air-raids on Florence in 1944. Re-writing *Artemisia* became an integral part of the new version; recreating the book is intimately connected with the need to unearth Artemisia's story, buried once by the passing of three centuries and then again by the bombing. Narrator and character become closely linked: the original *Artemisia* was intended to alleviate Artemisia's grief at the loss – through rape – of her original freedom, and if the book is lost she remains, in a sense, violated, not given back her freedom or individuality. In the new version the narrator attempts to repair these losses, engaging often in dialogue with Artemisia, questioning her, involving her, even trying to tell her of her own war-time griefs. Banti acknowledges, however, that it is finally impossible to reconstruct the thoughts and emotions of three hundred years ago, and partly for this reason the novel does not provide any straightforward history and analysis of Artemisia's life. Instead facts are treated allusively, indirectly, with much left unsaid, to be deduced from interior monologue or from description. Among the impressions which filter through are those of the protagonist's relationships with her withdrawn, art-dedicated father and with the daughter, Porziella, who shuns her affection. One of the main difficulties in their relationship is Artemisia's unorthodox position as a teacher of art in a city (Naples at this point)

of male artists. There is no recognised role-model for Porziella to follow: her mother is not a princess, peasant, tradeswoman, saint or – whatever some say – courtesan.

*Judith Decapitating Holophernes*, the painting by Artemisia Gentileschi most used in the novel, survives in two versions in the Uffizi, Florence (damaged in the 1993 bombing) and the Capodimonte museum, Naples. Among Banti's later novels *La camicia bruciata* (*The Burnt Shirt*), 1973, explores the unhappy lot of the wives of the last two Medici Grand Dukes of Tuscany.

CELLINI, Benvenuto (1500–71), Florentine goldsmith and sculptor, worked in Rome in the 1520s and 1530s, at the court of François I of France in 1540–5, and then mainly in Florence. He began his *Vita* (*Autobiography*) in 1558 and abandoned it some time after 1562; it was eventually published in 1728. Fact, fiction, self-justification, and technical information mingle in a narrative shaped by sources including saints' lives and *novelle*. The story reaches dramatic climaxes with the Sack of Rome in 1527, the author's escape from Castel Sant' Angelo in 1538, and the casting, amid great difficulties, of his most famous work, the bronze *Perseus* of 1557. In 1838 Hector Berlioz based an opera on Cellini's operatic life.

CICERO, Marcus Tullius (106–43 B.C.), born at Arpinum (Arpino), studied law in Rome and, later, philosophy in Athens and Rhodes. He became rapidly established as an advocate and orator, particularly after his successful exposure of the corrupt Sicilian governor Verres in 70 B.C. Having proceeded through the administrative offices of quaestor, aedile, and praetor, he became consul for 63 at, as with the other appointments, the earliest allowable age. His success against the Catilinarian conspiracy was the main achievement of his consulship. In 58–57 he was temporarily banished by his political enemies on the grounds that the Catilinarians had been executed without trial. (This had been authorized by an emergency decree of the Senate.) A supporter of Pompey and republicanism and opponent of Caesar, Cicero increasingly lost influence as the Roman republic foundered, and turned increasingly to philosophical and literary composition. After Caesar's assassination he delivered, in 44–43, the 14 *Philippics* (named after the Athenian orator Demosthenes' speeches against Philip II of Macedonia) against Mark Antony. As a result he was proscribed by Antony and murdered in December 43.

An unusually large proportion of Cicero's work has survived, including most of his forensic speeches. Based on, but not bound by, Greek models, they range from cool analysis to the 'thundering, sparkling, totally one-sided vituperation' (Michael Grant) of the first *Contra Catilinam* (*Against Catiline*), 63 B.C. The speeches as we have them are to some extent literary productions, 'written up' accounts by Cicero of what he actually said, but clearly give at least something of the flavour of the originals. He also wrote treatises on oratory, philosophical works including *Tusculanae disputationes* (*The Tusculan Disputations*), 44, a broadly Stoic discussion of the conditions for human happiness, written in an exceptionally lyrical, urgent, personal style, and many letters, most interestingly those to his friend Titus Pomponius Atticus.

Cicero's influence on prose writing between late Roman times and the 18th century was greater than that of any other classical author. His complex but clear sentence-construction became a model – to be followed and reacted against – particularly in Renaissance Europe. Also widely read from the early middle ages was the *Somnium Scipionis* (*The Dream of Scipio*), a fragment of a longer work, where Scipio Aemilianus learns, in a dream-vision, of the reward for virtue in the next life.

GADDA, Carlo Emilio (1893–1973), born in Milan, worked as an engineer until 1935, travelling extensively abroad and in Italy. He wrote short stories, essays, and the novels *Quer pasticciaccio brutto de via Merulana* (*That Awful Mess on Via Merulana*), 1957 and *La cognizione del dolore* (*Acquainted With Grief*), 1963–70. *La cognizione*, first worked on in 1938–41, evokes, somewhat in the manner of James Joyce, the tortured relationship between a mother and the troubled survivor of her two sons, Gonzalo, in the land of 'Madragàl', which is evidently Italy, and in the province of 'Nea Keltiké' (Lombardy) in particular. The novel is full of Gadda's usual linguistic play, half-serious literary references, and digressions. When he was described as 'baroque', Gadda replied that the world was baroque and he merely 'perceived and portrayed its baroqueness'.

*Quer pasticciaccio* (partly published in 1946) concerns the investigation of a murder in 1927 but, as Italo Calvino (◊Liguria) points out in his introduction, the murder story is gradually forgotten; Gadda wants not to find solutions but to depict 'the seething cauldron of life, the infinite stratification of reality, the inextricable tangle of knowledge'. It is a novel 'stretched out of shape from within by the excessive richness of the material and the intensity with which the author charges it'.

GIBBON, Edward (1737–94), travelled in Italy in 1764–5 because 'according to the law of custom and perhaps of reason, foreign travel completes the education of an English gentleman'. Following his inspiration on the Capitol there intervened 'several avocations', much reading, and the expansion of the project from Rome's decay to that of the whole empire, before the publication of *The History of the Decline and Fall of the Roman Empire*, 1776–88. This monumental but elegantly and often incisively expressed work surveys events between the reign of Trajan (98–117) and the fall of Constantinople in 1453. Gibbon's *Memoirs*, a version of which was published posthumously in 1796, survive in six variant drafts. They include accounts of his Italian journey and of the genesis and completion of his 'laborious work'.

HAWTHORNE, Nathaniel (1804–64), was American consul at Liverpool in 1853–7 and lived in Italy during 1857–9. His *French and Italian Notebooks*, not published in full until 1980, contain detailed accounts of places, sculpture, and, often most interestingly, people. Material used in *The Marble Faun*, 1860, often appears in an earlier form in the notebooks.

To some extent the highly particularised setting of *The Marble Faun* attempts simply to re-create Hawthorne's Roman impressions; Roman objects and places, he claimed, 'cannot easily be kept from flowing out upon the page'. But the city also provides atmosphere, imagery and symbols for this novel of mysterious suffering, guilt, and redemption. The Catacombs and the Tarpeian Rock are perhaps the most obvious exam-

ples of symbolic settings and, more subtly, the palimpsestic city as a whole is a place which refuses easy moral judgements; with 'all the weary and dreary Past . . . piled upon the back of the Present' it contrasts with modern American certainties. This is one of the reasons why, although one can attempt to summarize the novel as a tale of moral progress in which the once carefree, faun-like Donatello learns to take responsibility for his actions and Miriam is, connectedly, purged and healed, an element of mystery remains. Miriam's dark hair and dark depths, so insisted on for so long, are not easily forgotten, closed off in a conclusion; some of the characters both remain deeply suspicious of Catholicism and find relief in temporary collaboration with it. Like Henry James (◊Venice), but in a more intense, symbolic, sometimes emotionally troubled mode, Hawthorne reflects on the complicating, enriching, and guilt-creating encounter between the old world and the new.

JUVENAL – Decimus Junius Juvenalis (c.A.D. 60–c.136) – was born at Aquinum (Aquino). He was possibly (but the evidence is very slim) banished for causing offence to a favourite of the capricious and dangerous emperor Domitian. His *Saturae* (*Satires*), c.110–28, date from the safer times of Trajan and Hadrian but still find vices and people in plenty to attack: merit goes unrewarded while the rich, the sexually perverted, and the interloping Greeks rule the roost. Satire 6 is an exercise in savage misogyny. Satire 3 portrays the physical collapse and moral corruption of urban Rome, setting the precedent for many later attacks on city-life; Samuel Johnson's *London*, 1738, is based on it. (Johnson's *The Vanity of Human Wishes*, 1749, adapts Satire 10.)

'Invective' is a word frequently used in discussion of Juvenal. His aggression has been habitually contrasted with Horace's mellower, more urbane approach to satire: John Dryden, one of the English poets most influenced by Juvenal's example, said that Horace's 'urbanity, that is, his good manners, are to be commended, but his wit is faint; and his salt . . . almost insipid. Juvenal is of a more vigorous and masculine wit . . . He treats his subject home: his spleen is raised, and he raises mine; he drives his reader along with him' (A Discourse Concerning . . . Satire, 1693).

HORACE – Quintus Horatius Flaccus (65–8 B.C.), born at Venosa in Apulia, studied in Rome and Athens and then fought for the republicans (led by Brutus) in the civil war of 44–42 B.C. He was pardoned by the victorious triumvirs, but recovered financial security only with the aid of the influential Gaius Maecenas, whom he met through his fellow poet Virgil (◊Naples and Campania). Maecenas' most substantial gift to the poet was a villa (lost or unidentified) in the Sabine Hills.

Horace is best known for his Odes (books one to three, 23 B.C.; book four, 13 B.C.), on a wide variety of themes from politics to country life and the joys of wine. These were the poems which later generations most imitated and most admired for their urbanity. The Sermones (Satires), 30 B.C., Epistles (c.22–16 B.C.), and Ars Poetica, c.18 B.C., are broadly similar in tone.

LIVY is the English name for Titus Livius (59 B.C.-A.D. 17), little more of whom is known than that he was born in Patavium (now Padua) and spent most of his adult life in Rome. Roughly a quarter of his history Ab urbe condita (From the Foundation of the City), begun in 29 B.C., has survived. It includes many of the stories which later Europeans would re-tell, translate, hold up as examples, or paint: Romulus and Remus, the Rape of Lucretia, the expulsion of the Tarquins and establishment of the Republic by the first Brutus, Horatius' defence of the bridge (the inspiration of Lord Macaulay's once much-recited poem 'Horatius' in Lays of Ancient Rome, 1842), the battles against Hannibal. Livy's declared aim is to contribute 'not, I hope, ignobly' to 'the labour of putting on record the story of the greatest nation in the world'. He will contrast the early heroic days of Rome with the decadence of later times.

Like other ancient historians Livy is interested more in moral or imaginative truth than in verifiable facts – which, for the earliest times were not, besides, available.

Livy's sympathies were evidently republican, but he was on good terms with Augustus, and with the future Emperor Claudius. (He appears as a minor character in Robert Graves's I Claudius, 1934.)

MICHELANGELO BUONAROTTI (1475–1564), from Caprese – now Caprese Michelangelo – near Sansepolcro, enjoyed the patronage, and lived in the household, of Lorenzo the Magnificent (◊Florence)in his mid-teens. Much of his tempestuous but successful career as sculptor, painter, and architect was spent in the service, frequently discontinuous or frustrating, of successive Popes. Often referred to as 'the divine' following the frescoing of the ceiling of the Sistine Chapel (1508–12), Michelangelo, like Leonardo da Vinci (◊Florence) and Raphaël, partook of or was responsible for a remarkable rise in the status of the artist. The Lives of the Artists of Giorgio

Vasari (◊Lombardy) was important to this process, and to the establishment of the paradigm of the artist as moody, inspired Michelangelesque figure.

Michelangelo began to write poetry, as far as is known, in about 1504. Most of the poems date from after 1515, and especially from the 1530s to 1550s. Many of them are sonnets, a number of which are addressed to Tommaso de' Cavalieri (c.1509–87), a young nobleman with whom he fell in love in 1532, or to his close friend Vittoria Colonna (1490–1547), a Roman noblewoman whom he met in 1536 and by whose religious poems he was significantly influenced. Often the poems explore, or at least gesture towards, the dilemma of a homosexual whose moral beliefs conflict with his sexuality. Related to this dilemma is a more general struggle between the earthly and the spiritual, with art sometimes regarded as having power to transcend mortality – to show people in a thousand years' time how beautiful Vittoria was, for instance. In some of the later poems, however (see Extract 7) art has no such power.

Michelangelo's work as sculptor and painter sometimes touches the poems directly, as in his semi-serious account of painting the Sistine ceiling while 'bent like a Syrian bow'. The art has often been compared not to the artist's own verse but – for sublimity, grandeur of conception, boldness of execution – to Dante's. As Vasari points out, the Sistine Last Judgement, in addition to the wider parallels with *The Divine Comedy*, takes from it (*Inferno*, Canto Three), Charon 'in an attitude of frenzy . . . striking with his oar the souls being dragged into his bark by the demons'. For Elizabeth Jennings, introducing her translation of the sonnets, both there and in the sculpture 'the

dominating feature is vehement energy, an energy which is mastered by a longing for order'.

MORANTE, Elsa (1912–85), was born in Rome and lived there for the rest of her life. She was half-Jewish. Her family were middle-class but poor. In 1936 she met, and in 1941 married, the more privileged Alberto Moravia◊. (They separated twenty years later.) Morante's novels are *Menzogna e sortilegia* (*The House of Lies*), 1948, *L'isola di Arturo* (*Arturo's Island*), 1957, *La storia* (*History: a Novel*), 1974, and *Aracoeli* (*Aracoeli*), 1982. She also published short stories, poetry, and children's books.

The first two novels are lyrical explorations of memories, fantasies, and the shock of their encounter with actual circumstances. *History*, more traditional in structure, looks more bleakly, in the context of Useppe's short life, at the random intrusion of history into the affairs of the individual. Morante sub-titled the novel 'a scandal which has lasted 2000 years' and conceived it as equally poem, accusation, and prayer. A film version, directed by Luigi Comencini, was released in 1986.

MORAVIA, Alberto (1907–90), was born Alberto Pincherle into a wealthy bourgeois Roman family, of a Jewish father and Christian mother. Between the ages of nine and 17 he suffered from bone tuberculosis. As a result he had the opportunity for the eclectic reading – Dostoyevsky, Shakespeare, Rimbaud, Joyce – which, he felt, made him receptive to diverse interests and milieux in a way untypical of his class and time. As early as 1925 Moravia began *Gli indifferenti* (*The Time of Indifference*), 1929, a novel of sexual insecurity and the gap between individual consciousness and external reality; he was fond of pointing out that it long preceded such more explicitly existentialist works as Sartre's *La Nausée* of 1939 and Camus' *L'Étranger* of 1942. Among the most successful of his many novels of the 60 years after *Gli indifferenti* are *La romana* (*The Woman of Rome*), 1947, *La noia* (*The Empty Canvas*), 1960, and *1934*, 1982. Sexuality, the alienated individual, and the emptiness of Fascist and bourgeois society are the themes to which Moravia most often returns.

*La romana* is a first-person account by Adriana, a working-class girl who becomes a prostitute in 1930s Rome. It at first excited controversy because of its subject-matter and the disconcertingly 'innocent' interest which the narrator takes in herself and her own motives and feelings, and later, in some feminist criticism, for Moravia's presumptuous use of the first person. There has also been debate over Adriana's unrealistic use of 'correct literary style'. Moravia justifies this as a way of doing her 'the same service the public letter-writers perform when they interpret and commit to paper on the street corners the unformulated sentiments of illiterate servant-maids'. In fact the 'literariness' of the style varies, increasing markedly, as Sharon Wood points out, when Adriana reflects on her position; the resulting conflict in narrative functions helps to make *La romana* a text 'of linguistic disruption and ideological paradox'.

Adriana's acceptance of herself and her destiny is explained by the author, in a French interview, as the most elementary form of existentialism: a refusal to make moral and ideological judgements in spite of the immediate post-war pressure to do so, a more optimistic, holistic, and characteristically Italian version of existentialism

than the pre-war gloom of Sartre and Heidegger.

*Racconti romani* (*Roman Tales*), 1954 and *Nuovi racconti romani* (*New Roman Tales*), 1959, offer further sketches of Roman lives – incidents involving plumbers, servants, caretakers, thugs and others – from a less innocent and often funnier perspective.

SHELLEY, Percy Bysshe (1792–1822), lived in Italy – mainly at Bagni di Lucca, Naples, Rome, Livorno, and Pisa – with his second wife Mary Wollstonecraft Shelley and her step-sister Claire Clairmont, from 1818 until his death in the Gulf of Spezia in 1822. During these years Shelley wrote most of his important works, including *Prometheus Unbound*, 1820, and *The Defence of Poetry* (written 1821, published 1840). Italian landscape and seascape are described, or inform the imagery, in *Ode to the West Wind*, 1819, *Lines Written Among the Euganean Hills*, 1818, *Julian and Maddalo*, 1818, and many other poems. In a different vein, he composed in 1819 *The Cenci*, a powerful verse drama (much influenced by Shakespeare and his contemporaries) on the murder by Beatrice Cenci of her incestuous, arrogant father in 1598. Beatrice, Shelley says in his preface, 'was evidently a most gentle and amiable being . . . violently thwarted from her nature by the necessity of circumstance and opinion'. To 'present to the reader all the feelings of those who once acted' this story – as he attempts to – 'would be as a light to make apparent some of the most dark and secret caverns of the human heart'. The death of Keats in Rome in 1821 prompted Shelley's elegy *Adonais*.

Shelley, since boyhood a radical idealist and atheist, continued to concern himself with English politics during his Italian years, and was also keenly interested in revolutionary movements and attempts in Italy, Spain, and Greece. His comments on Italian society are found mainly in his letters; he writes to Thomas Love Peacock in April 1819, for instance, about the clanking of the chains of fettered criminals engaged in forced labour in St Peter's Square amid the 'musical dashing of fountains', azure beauty of the sky and magnificence of the architecture, as 'the emblem of Italy: moral degradation contrasted with the glory of nature and the arts'.

# LAZIO

'We took coach, and went 15 miles out of the city to Frascati, formerly Tusculanum, a villa of Cardinal Aldobrandini, built for a country house, but surpassing, in my opinion, the most delicious places I ever beheld for its situation, elegance, plentiful water, groves, ascents, and prospects.'
*John Evelyn, Diary*

The Roman Campagna – the plain between the Sabine mountains and the sea – has been changed almost beyond recognition by drainage, rapidly expanding human habitation, and the banishment of malaria. In the 19th century it was still a vast, wild area of grasses, the 'endless fleece/Of feathery grasses everywhere' of (Robert Browning's (◊Florence) *Two in the Campagna*, 1855), streams, and ruined ancient tombs and villas. Occasionally a shepherd was to be seen, a figure somewhere between the Arcadian contemplatives in the landscapes of Claude and Poussin and the 'villainous-looking' character 'with matted hair all over his face, and himself wrapped to the chin in a frowzy brown mantle' described by Dickens (◊Liguria) in *Pictures from Italy*, 1846. (William Beckford (◊Lombardy) had found the sheep themselves black and 'ill-favoured'; grazing near a 'ruined sepulchre' they, like the shepherds' huts 'propped up with broken pedestals and marble friezes', contributed to the general sense of desolation.)

The Campagna was (as the threat from brigands gradually decreased, and at times and seasons free from malaria) a place for contemplation – perhaps for trying, with Browning's speaker, to attach a recurrent, unfixable train of thought to the yellowing fennel 'branching from the brickwork's cleft, / Some old tomb's ruin' and to follow it to where 'one small orange cup amassed/ Five beetles, – blind and green they grope among the honey-meal'. The thought, and the near-fulfilment in the speaker's relationship, cannot be held, passing on like a thistle-ball, like the 'everlasting wash of air' of the Campagna:

'Only I discern –

209

Infinite passion, and the pain
Of human hearts that yearn.'

Tivoli and the higher, cooler Alban Hills, above the city and Campagna, have since ancient times been favoured retreats for reflection or enjoyment. Horace (◊Rome), Propertius (◊Umbria and Marche), and Maecenas (◊Rome) had villas somewhere in Tibur (ancient Tivoli), and it was later much favoured by one of the more meditative of monarchs, Hadrian. His **Villa Adriana** was built in 118–28 A.D., downhill from Tibur, as an extensive but somewhat more private retreat, with theatres, halls, baths, pools, a famous library, architectural tributes to Egypt and Greece, memorials to Hadrian's drowned beloved Antinous, and one final quiet place of withdrawal on the island in the Teatro Marittimo. For Marguerite Yourcenar, whose historical novel *Les Mémoires d' Hadrien* (*The Memoirs of Hadrian*), was published in 1951, the villa expresses the emperor's desire for rest and intimacy, unostentatious luxury, and the combined pleasures of art and nature – the work of a 'rich amateur'.

One of the first to excavate at Villa Adriana was Cardinal Ippolito d'Este, who in 1550 began in Tivoli itself the **Villa d'Este** (continued by other members of the family), whose waterfalls, fountains, mythological statuary, and tree-lined paths became as popular with painters and travellers as Tivoli's natural cliffs and cascades. At Villa d'Este in May 1645 John Evelyn◊ admired 'sweet and delicious gardens', 'pyramids of water', the hydraulic organ (visible but no longer operational) and artificial birdsong; he found similar delights in the gardens and water-theatre of Villa Aldobrandini at **Frascati** (Extract 2), in the Alban Hills.

Ancient Rome is rarely far away in these approaches to the city. In Evelyn's time the Villa d'Este and its gardens were full of Roman statues, Villa d'Adriana preserves imperial tastes, Browning's Campagna with its crumbling fragments is 'Rome's ghost since her decease'. Much less is to be seen or heard of the other nearby tribes eventually absorbed or subjugated by the early Romans. Their literature and most of their history are lost; the archaeological evidence for the pre-Roman period is scanty; the written evidence is Roman. The Sabines (living to the north-east of Rome) occur in Livy's (◊Rome) story of *The Rape of the Sabine Women*, where the fusion of neighbouring peoples is explained in terms of Romulus' men forcibly acquiring the women they needed to perpetuate the race and maintain the city. The Volsci (south-east of Rome) are known almost exclusively as the recurrent enemy in Plutarch's and Shakespeare's story of Coriolanus. The dearth of knowledge licenses artists' and directors' imaginings to an extent rarely possible with the familiar Rome: Rubens' robustly voluptuous Sabine women, Aufidius the stage Volscian (in *Coriolanus*) who can be anything from shaggy and hirsute in tartan to trim and lithe in leather.

The Etruscans (to the north of Rome) are at once more known and more enigmatic than the other ethnic groups: enigmatic partly by virtue of not being easily labelled, not Romans, not Greek colonists, not speakers of a Latin-related or even Indo-European language. (While some progress has been made in deciphering Etruscan, it is still much less fully understood than other ancient tongues.) Roman literature includes Etruscan villains who culminate in Sextus Tarquinius, but is also respectful towards Etruscan religious practices and especially that of the *haruspex* or diviner. The most distinctive tomb statues and paintings (to be seen especially in Rome at the **Villa Giulia** Etruscan museum and at **Cerveteri** and **Tarquinia**) are quite different from either Greek or Roman art. Known to us for only a century and a half, contextualized on the whole by no surviving literature, they are less limited by our preconceptions. Figures dance with sacred or profane energy or both. They smile, but in expression of exactly what emotion seems unknowable; 'the women with the conical head-dress', says D.H. Lawrence at the necropolis of Tarquinia, 'how strangely they lean forward, with caresses we no longer know!' (*Etruscan Places*, published posthumously in 1932). Lawrence makes them figures in one of his most attractive and characteristic myths: the vital, sensuous, natural non-Romans whom he had compared in his poem *Cypresses*, 1920, to the supple, dark-flame-like trees. At Tarquinia he observes dolphins, dancers, leopards, banqueters, and discerns 'a sense of the quick ripple of life', 'a quiet flow of touch' in opposition to the mere 'contact of surfaces, and juxtaposition of objects' in most art and most life; instead of outlining or drawing figures, the true Etruscan artist paints 'the flowing contour where the body suddenly leaves off, upon the atmosphere', for he sees 'living things surging from their own centre to their own surface'.

The narrator of Giorgio Bassani's *Il Giardino dei Finzi-Contini*, (*The Garden of the Finzi-Contini*), 1962 (Extract 1), finds the Etruscans of Cerveteri more down-to-earth, more simply human in their desire to place in their tombs 'not only their dead, but everything that made life beautiful and desirable'. The sheltered, reposeful conical mounds are in sad contrast with the unknown fate of the bodies of his deported fellow Jews.

The expansive, peaceful, grassy ruins of Ostia (**Ostia Antica**), once the port of Rome but now several miles inland, have a simpler appeal for visitors. Modern Romans mostly prefer, however, to go on until they reach the present littoral at **Lido di Ostia**, whose crowded, noisy beaches provide one of the settings, at once vital and sordid, for Pier Paolo Pasolini's novel of post-war Rome *Ragazzi di vita* (*The Ragazzi*), 1955 (Extract 3). On 2 November 1975 Pasolini was murdered near the sea-front. There is a memorial to him in Piazza Anco Marzio.

## OTHER LITERARY LANDMARKS

**Anzio**: ruins of ancient Antium, city of the Volsci, where parts of Shakespeare's *Coriolanus* are set. Months of heavy fighting followed the Allied landings at Anzio in January 1944.

**Arpino**: near Soria, the birthplace of Cicero (◊Rome). Ruins here may be those of his villa.

**Bomarzo**: the many fantastic mythological and other statues in the 16th century Parco dei Mostri include a colossal figure of Ariosto's (◊Emilia-Romagna) mad Orlando.

**Montecassino**: the abbey, re-built after its destruction in 1944, where Saint Benedict (c.480–c.547) composed his Rule.

**Palestrina**: Roman and earlier hill-town, the 'cool Praeneste' of Horace (◊Rome), *Odes* III.iv. The composer Giovanni Pierluigi da Palestrina (c.1524-94) was born in Vicolo Pierluigi.

**Pratica di Mare**: ancient Lavinium, founded, according to legend, by Aeneas.

**Tusculum**: remains, near Frascati, of the town where Cicero had a (not certainly identified) villa. This is the setting of *Tusculanae disputationes* (*The Tuscan Disputations*), 45 B.C.

**Vulci**: sparse remains of the Etruscan city, described by D.H. Lawrence (◊Sardinia) in *Etruscan Places*, 1932.

# BOOKLIST

Giorgio Bassani, *The Garden of the Finzi-Continis* [1962], Isabel Quigly, trans, Quartet Books, London, 1974. **Extract 1**.

Beckford, William, *The Grand Tour of William Beckford: Selections from Dreams, Waking Thoughts and Incidents* [1783], Elizabeth Mavor, ed, Penguin, Harmondsworth, 1986.

Browning, Robert, *The Poems*, John Pettigrew and Thomas J. Collins, eds, Penguin, Harmondsworth, 1993.

Evelyn, John, *The Diary of John Evelyn*, Guy de la Bédoyère, ed, Boydell, Woodbridge, 1995. **Extract 2**.

*D.H. Lawrence and Italy: Twilight in Italy, Sea and Sardinia, Etruscan*

*Places*, Anthony Burgess, intr, Penguin, Harmondsworth, 1985.

Lawrence, D.H., *Selected Poems*, Mara Kalnins, ed, Dent, London, 1992.

Livy, *The History of Early Rome*, [29 B.C.>], Aubrey de Sélincourt, trans, Penguin, Harmondsworth, 1960.

Pier Paolo Pasolini, *The Ragazzi* [1955], Emile Capouya, trans, Paladin, Grafton Books, London, 1989. **Extract 3**.

Yourcenar, Marguerite, *Memoirs of Hadrian [1951] and Reflections on the Composition of Memoirs of Hadrian*, Grace Frick and Marguerite Yourcenar, trans, Penguin, Harmondsworth, 1986.

# *Extracts*

## (1) CERVETERI

### Giorgio Bassani,
### *The Garden of the Finzi-Contini*, 1962

*In the prologue to the novel, in 1957, the narrator visits the Etruscan necropolis and thinks about the imposing Finzi-Contini family tomb in the Jewish cemetery at Ferrara. Like the Etruscan tombs it promises repose, yet this has been pitifully denied in the unknown fate of the bodies of his friends, the four Finzi-Contini deported to Germany in the autumn of 1943.*

*A nine-year-old girl, Giannina, has just been questioning her father's view that old tombs are any less gloomy than recent ones.*

'Well, of course, people who've just died are nearer to us, so we love them more,' he said. 'You see, the Etruscans have been dead for such ages . . . that it's as if they'd never lived, as if they'd *always* been dead.'

'But now you've said that,' she said gently, 'you've made me think the Etruscans did actually live, you know, and I love them as much as everyone else.'

Our visit to the necropolis, I remember, was wrapped round in the remarkable tenderness of what she had said. It was Giannina who made us ready to understand. It was she, the youngest, who in a way led us on.

We went inside the most important tomb, the one that belonged to the noble Matutina family: a low underground hall with 20 funeral beds arranged around as many niches in the tufa walls, and decorated with closely packed polychrome plaster casts of the beloved, trusted objects of everyday life: stoppers, ropes, hatchets, shears, spades, knives, bows, arrows, even hunting dogs and marsh birds. And meantime, I had cheerfully abandoned my last philological scruples, and was trying to imagine concretely what their frequent visits to this suburban cemetery can have meant to the late Etruscans of Cerveteri, the Etruscans of the time after the Roman conquest.

They would come from their nearby homes, probably on foot – I imagined – family troupes of young people like those we had met just now in the road, pairs of lovers or friends, or else alone; just as today, in Italian villages, the cemetery gate is still the place where the evening stroll is bound to end. They came among the cone-shaped tombs, which are solid and heavy as the bunkers the German soldiers strewed vainly all over Europe during this last war (gradually, through the centuries, the iron cart-wheels have cut two parallel furrows in the paved road that crosses the cemetery from one end to the other):

tombs that, even inside, obviously resembled the fortress-houses of the living. The world changed, admittedly – they must have said to themselves – it was no longer what it once had been, when Etruria, with its confederation of free aristocratic city-states, dominated nearly the whole of the Italic peninsula. New civilisations, rougher and more plebeian, but stronger and more warlike as well, now held sway. But what did it matter?

Once inside the cemetery where each of them owned a second home, and in it the bed on which he would soon be laid to rest with his fathers, eternity must no longer have seemed an illusion, a fairy-tale, a priests' promise. Let the future overturn the world, if it cared to; but there, whatever happened, in that small space sacred to the family dead; in the heart of those tombs where they had the foresight to take, not only their dead, but everything that made life beautiful and desirable; in that sheltered, well defended corner of the earth, there at least nothing would change, and their thoughts, their madness, still hovered round the conical mounds covered in coarse grass after 25 centuries.

# (2) FRASCATI

## John Evelyn, *Diary,* 5 May 1645

*Evelyn delights in the Baroque theatricality of the park at Villa Aldobrandini: he is pleased above all with the 'devices' or 'surprising inventions' which make possible the scenic and aural effects. Ancient Tusculum, where Cicero (◊Rome) lived at the 'Tusculanum' villa, was actually a few miles from Frascati.*

We took coach, and went 15 miles out of the city to Frascati, formerly Tusculanum, a villa of Cardinal Aldobrandini, built for a country house, but surpassing, in my opinion, the most delicious places I ever beheld for its situation, elegance, plentiful water, groves, ascents, and prospects. Just behind the palace (which is of excellent architecture) in the centre of the enclosure rises a high hill or mountain all over clad with tall wood, and so formed by nature as if it had been cut out by art, from the summit whereof falls a cascade, seeming rather a great river than a stream precipitating into a large theatre of water, representing an exact and perfect rainbow when the sun shines out. Under this is made an artificial grot, wherein are curious rocks, hydraulic organs, and all sorts of singing birds moving and chirping by force of the water, with several other pageants and surprising inventions. In the centre of one of these rooms rises a copper ball that continually dances about three foot above the pavement by virtue of a wind conveyed secretly to a hole beneath it; with many other devices to wet the unwary spectators, so that one can hardly step without wetting to the skin. In one of these theatres of water is an Atlas spouting up the stream to a very great height; and another monster makes a terrible roaring with a horn; but above all, the representation of a storm is the most natural, with such fury of rain, wind, and thunder, as one would imagine oneself in some extreme tempest. The garden has excellent walks and shady groves, abundance of rare fruit, oranges, lemons etc. and the goodly prospect of Rome, above all description, so as I do not wonder that Cicero and others have celebrated the place with such encomiums.

## (3) OSTIA

### Pier Paolo Pasolini, *The Ragazzi*, 1955

*Pasolini's first novel is set in the poor, coarse, violent but vital suburbs of Rome, whose seaside resort is Lido di Ostia.*

Nadia was stretched out on the sand, motionless, her face full of hatred for the sun, the wind, the sea, and all those people who had come to the beach like an army of flies on a cleared table. Thousands of them . . . lying alongside dozens of bathhouses, some on their backs, some on their bellies – but those were mostly old people. As for the young ones, the males, wearing drooping drawers or else tight trunks that showed off what was underneath, and the females, those show-offs, in tight, tight swimming suits with their hair streaming – all of them were walking up and down ceaselessly, as if they had nervous tics. They were calling to one another, yelling, shrieking, playing practical jokes, playing games, going in and out of the bathhouses, calling to the attendants. There was even a band of young boys from Trastevere, wearing Mexican hats and playing accordion, guitar, and maracas in front of the bathhouse; and their sambas blended with the rumbas on the Marechiaro loudspeaker, reverberating off the sea. Nadia was lying there amid all that racket, wearing a black bathing suit, and showing a lot of hair, black as the devil's, in sweaty coils under her arms, and the hair of her head was also coal-black, and her eyes were glaring murderously.

She was in her forties, a big woman, with firm breasts and thighs that looked like links of sausage, pumped up hard. She was in a rage because she was sick of that crowd of fresh-air fiends, and ocean bathing was not for her. She'd already done all the bathing she was going to do that morning in Mattonato, in Sor'Anita's bathtub.

# Biographies and important works

EVELYN, John (1620–1706), a Surrey gentleman, travelled in the Netherlands in 1641 and spent much of 1643–7 in France and Italy, partly in order to avoid the English Civil War and its aftermath. His *Diary*, first published in 1818, covers the years 1640–1706 and was written up from earlier notes chiefly in 1660 and 1680–4. (After 1684 events are recorded more immediately). Evelyn's account of his European tour is concerned with paintings, architecture, 'cabinets of rarities', gardens, fortifications, and anything else which can satisfy his tireless curiosity. In pursuit of this aim he was a founder member of the Royal Society in 1662 and wrote various works including *Sylva or a Discourse of Forest Trees*, 1664.

PASOLINI, Pier Paolo (1922–75), was born in Bologna. He spent part of his childhood and early adulthood in his mother's native Casarsa, in the Friuli region of north-eastern Italy. His early volumes of verse make creative use of Friulan dialect. From the beginning one of his main interests was in the poor and marginalized, their language, and their roots in an idealised pre-industrial past, belief in which complicated his relationship with the post-war communist party. (See *Le ceneri di Gramsci* (*The Ashes of Gramsci*), 1957.) Pasolini moved from rural Friuli to Rome in 1950 in the wake of a sex scandal. In the capital he was freer to explore both his homosexuality and different modes of writing. His first novel, *Ragazzi di vita* (*The Ragazzi*), 1955, renders the violent, temperamentally and linguistically explosive, sordid but vital world of the dilapidated suburbs of Rome. Theft, card-sharping, prostitution and murder are commonplace, and the boy Riccetto, once compassionate, learns in the end only that he has 'got to look out for Riccetto' – for number one. *Una vita violenta* (*A Violent Life*), 1959, has a similar setting, as have some of Pasolini's early films, beginning with *Accattone* (*Beggar*), 1961. Sexually explicit and politically embarrassing – shanty-towns did not accord with Christian Democratic governments' assertions about the growing prosperity of the new Italy – Pasolini's work was often the subject of censorship and legal proceedings. An attempt to prosecute *Ragazzi di vita* as pornography failed in 1956. Among the later most controversial works were the three films inspired by Boccaccio's *Decameron*, Chaucer's *Canterbury Tales*, and the *Arabian Nights*, the 'Trilogy of Life' (1970–4). Pasolini continued to publish poetry, stories, and translations and adaptations for the theatre, but felt that cinema was 'the direct language of reality'. He was murdered at Lido di Ostia in 1975.

# Naples and Campania

'In the distance appeared some huge quadrilateral masses, and when we finally reached them, we were at first uncertain whether we were driving through rocks or ruins. Then we recognised what they were, the remains of temples, monuments to a once glorious city.'
Goethe, *Italian Journey*

In 63 B.C. Cicero (◊Rome) argued forcefully against the division of Campania into private landholdings: 'the one most beautiful estate of the Roman people, the source of your wealth, an adornment in peacetime, a support in war ... the granary of your legions – will you allow this to perish?' Southern Italy in general was important to the Romans for reasons both practical and aesthetic, and the two were combined in the conquest or absorption, in the fourth to third centuries B.C., of the many prosperous Greek colonies like Cumae (founded mainly by the Euboeans in about 750–700 B.C.). There were those who regarded Greek culture as decadent and effeminate and dismissed Hellenized Romans with the insulting diminutive 'Graeculi', but they seem to have been in a minority. Most of the Greek towns were allowed, even encouraged, to retain their Greek language and identity. They benefited from the more general Roman compulsion to emulate, celebrate, or learn from Greece: statues were copied or imitated, orators trained in Athens or Rhodes, and almost all the Latin literature which has survived draws extensively on Greek models.

Virgil◊, who lived in or near Naples for much of his adult life, rivals, echoes, salutes or varies Homer almost at every turn in his national epic *Aeneis* (*The Aeneid*), 29–19 B.C. For instance Homer's tale of Troy is completed as Aeneas tells Dido the story of the Wooden Horse and Aeneas' subsequent wanderings often echo those of Odysseus. Aeneas, who flees from the Greeks at the fall of Troy, defeats them or at least gains equivalent status not by fighting them but by Latinizing, equalling or refining their exploits. And at the same time the

Romans who descend from Aeneas, and for whom the poem is written, are given roots as deep and distinguished as those of the Greeks.

So when the Roman forefather Aeneas makes his first Italian landfall near the Greek town of **Cumae**, he is establishing his credentials. Cumae is particularly important to Virgil because it had been, since the late seventh century B.C., the home of a famous Sibyl (Extract 1). Her large rock-cut grotto or *antrum* survives, including her arched inner chamber, the Holy of Holies in which the hero is instructed on how to enter the underworld at nearby **Lake Avernus** (Averno). Later Roman Cumae is also the probable setting of 'Trimalchio's Feast', the main extant section of Petronius Arbiter's◊ riotous, ribald *Satyricon*. Trimalchio's Sibyl has declined sadly since Aeneas' day: he claims to have seen her 'hanging in a flask; and when the boys cried at her "Sibyl, Sibyl, what do you want?" "I would that I were dead," she used to answer.'

Long before the excavation of the Sibyl's grotto in 1939, the temples at **Paestum** (Pesto), on a then marshy and malarial plain south of Salerno, stood as a reminder of Greek culture before its assimilation by Rome. Here, at one of the southernmost points of the usual Grand Tour, visitors immersed in Roman art and its Renaissance and later derivatives came upon something strange and unfamiliar, impressive and perhaps a little chilling, to be described in much the same terms as the monuments of Egypt: Dickens's 'awful [awe-inspiring] structures . . . standing yet, erect in lonely majesty, upon the wild, malaria-blighted plain' (*Pictures From Italy*, 1846), or what seem to Goethe at first 'crowded masses of stumpy conical columns', understandable only with some effort, a rewarding call for the exercise of the historical sense (*Italian Journey*, 1816–17, Extract 6).

## NAPLES

Homeric legend was adapted to tell how, when Odysseus escaped the deadly lure of the sirens' song by having himself bound to the mast while his followers rowed with their ears plugged, the siren Parthenope was so frustrated that she drowned herself in the Bay of Naples. Parthenope became an alternative name for the city of Neapolis, founded from Cumae in about 650–600 B.C.; **Sorrento** (the Roman Surrentum) may have some etymological connection with sirens. (Norman Douglas (◊Abruzzo and South) used *Siren Land* as the title of a collection of musings on the history and legends of the area in 1911.) The idea of dangerous charm persisted in the traditional ironic responses to the proverbial 'See Naples and die' and the contrast frequently made between the calm beauties of the Bay and the menacing presence of Vesuvius.

The city of Parthenope's most notable literary connection is with Virgil◊. Tradition states that his tomb bore his own simple summing-up

'Mantua gave me life, Calabria took it, now Naples holds me: I sang of flocks, farms, and heroes'. (He died at Brindisi – then in Calabria, now in Apulia – soon after landing there on the way home from a visit to Greece.) The site of the actual tomb, said to have been between Naples and Pozzuoli, has long been lost, but since the 14th century a Roman stone structure at **Mergellina**, now part of Naples, has been known as 'Virgil's Tomb'. This mausoleum with niches for ten cinerary urns, the sort of tomb known from its shape as a *columbarium* – dovecot – is above the Parco Virgiliano, where the remains of another great Italian poet, Leopardi (◊Umbria and Marche), were reburied in 1939.

Virgil lived on in Neapolitan popular tradition as the governor and magician 'Master Virgil', who built the two tunnels (really feats of imperial Roman engineering) beneath the hill of **Posilippo**, and the island **Castel dell' Ovo**, somewhere within which he suspended or concealed an egg (*uovo*) in a glass vessel. If the egg broke, the castle would collapse. In another version, he balanced the whole city on an egg. A more literary legend is associated with the so-called Villa di Virgilio or Palazzo degli Spiriti near Posilippo, where on nights of full moon Virgil's ghost sings verses from *The Aeneid* and accompanies himself on the lyre.

Naples, with its natural beauties, classical renown, and commercially and culturally advantageous location, remained an important centre under the successive medieval rulers of southern Italy – Byzantines, Normans, Angevins and Aragonians. It was under the Angevins – the family of Charles of Anjou, brother of Louis IX of France (St Louis) – that Naples was first the centre of a more or less permanent court, giving it the capital status which so strongly appealed to the Grand Tourists of later centuries. At court scholarship and the arts prospered particularly during the reign (1309–43) of Robert of Anjou. Robert himself was characterized as the *re saggio* – not only a 'sage' in the modern sense but a king of active virtuous wisdom. He wrote theological and moral treatises and cultivated a reputation for both learning and courtesy. (Some, however, accused him of parsimony and Dante – ranged against him politically – dismissed him in *Paradiso* (*Heaven*) as a king fit only for writing sermons.) The imposing location of his principal dwelling, the **Castel Nuovo** (built by his grandfather Charles of Anjou), reflects a general move to develop the harbours and expand the city towards them. Here Petrarch (◊Veneto and North-East) came in 1340 to obtain the king's approval of his laureate crowning (which he insisted, in spite of royal persuasions, must take place in Rome). He was examined for three days 'from noon to night' by one 'illustrious in letters as well as in rank, the only monarch of our time who loved learning and virtue'. The backdrop to some of their discussions may have been the frescoes, now long lost, which Robert had commissioned in 1329–31 from Giotto, the greatest visual artist of the day. Boccaccio (◊Florence), living in Naples between about 1327 and 1341 and highly connected at court, must also have known the castle and the frescoes.

Robert's more active pastimes included jousting, a custom much influenced by the French heritage and connections of the House of Anjou. Between January and May 1337 alone he took part in six tourneys, lavish occasions like those referred to by the speaker of Boccaccio's *Elegia di Madonna Fiammetta* (*Elegy of Lady Fiammetta*, 1343–4), in which ladies gather on important holidays, decked in their precious jewels and dressed like queens, to watch their knights clash to the encouragement of 'cheering voices . . . the ringing of bells, with the sounds of all kinds of instruments, and with the flapping of mantles that covered horses and men'. More direct encounters between the sexes were possible in church; Boccaccio's Panfilo and Fiammetta meet among the young, fashion-conscious courtiers who frequent **San Lorenzo Maggiore**. But their story, especially as told from the woman's point of view in the *Elegia*, takes them beyond the fine clothes and amorous glances of that milieu to the brief joy and long anguish of an obsessive and finally unrequited passion.

Robert the Wise died at the Castel Nuovo in 1343 and was buried in the church he had founded with his wife Sancia in 1310, Santa Chiara. His large tomb, beyond the high altar, includes an effigy in which he wears the habit of his favourite order, the Franciscans. Life at court became more complicated and dangerous during the troubled reign of the granddaughter who succeeded him, Giovanna I. She was, it seems, responsible for the murder of her first husband Andrea of Hungary in 1345, but probably did not, as legend claims, enjoy and then fiendishly dispose of countless lovers. One of the most popular locations for her devilish deeds is the **Castel Capuano**, probably because one of the lovers of the more certainly libidinous Giovanna II (d. 1435) was murdered here.

The Angevin dynasty finally expired when Alfonso I the Magnanimous, of the house of Aragon, supplanted King René in 1442. The new king's victorious entry into Naples was commemorated after 1455 by the addition to the refurbished Castel Nuovo of the splendid triumphal arch, replete with decoration both classical and gothic, which remains one of the more striking signs of the early Renaissance in the city. In literature, the works of Jacopo Sannazaro̓ were the most influential product of the High Renaissance court of Alfonso's successors. His romance *Arcadia* (written 1480–5 and circulated in manuscript before publication in 1501) is, as its translator Ralph Nash puts it, 'shrewdly eclectic', interweaving 'poetry with prose, ancient with modern, Christian with classical'. The hero Sincero sojourns among the swains of Arcadia, but cannot forget his love for the Naples he must at last return to, its harbour, the grand circuit of the walls, 'the fruitful mountain set above the city' – the Vomero and/or Capodimonte – and the festivities and tournaments. Sannazaro is buried at

Mergellina at the church of **Santa Maria del Parto**. He designed for himself a tomb which, like his work, mingles the pagan and the Christian. There are statues of Pan, Neptune, St James, and St Nazaro, and the inscription (composed by a love-poet and future cardinal, Pietro Bembo (◊Veneto and North-East) celebrates a closeness to Virgil which is both literal – his reputed tomb is nearby – and poetic.

Naples was, traditionally, the final destination of the Grand Tour. Some of the main features which attracted northern vsitors were summed up by the diarist John Evelyn (◊Lazio) in 1645:

> The very Winter here is a Summer, ever fruitful, so that in the middle of February we had melons, cherries, apricots, and many other sorts of fruit. The building of the city is for the size the most magnificent of any in Europe, the streets exceeding large, well paved, having many vaults and conveyances under them for the sullage, which renders them very sweet and clean even in the midst of winter. To it belongeth more than 3000 churches and monasteries, and those the best built and adorned of any in Italy. They greatly affect the Spanish gravity in their habit; delight in good horses; the streets are full of gallants on horseback, in coaches and sedans. The women are generally well-featured but excessively libidinous. The country people so jovial and addicted to music, that the very husbandmen almost universally play on the guitar, singing and composing songs in praise of their sweethearts, and will commonly go to the field with their fiddle; they are merry, witty, and genial, all which I attribute to the excellent quality of the air.

Most notable among Evelyn's 'exceeding large' streets was the Via Toledo (now Via Roma), the broad thoroughfare built by Don Pedro de Toledo, Spanish viceroy 1532–54. The **Palazzo Reale**, begun in 1600, replaced the smaller and grimmer Castel Nuovo. It was the palace of the viceroys and then of the Kings of the House of Bourbon (or, in Italy, Borbone) who ruled from 1734. Later in the 1730s the Borboni began to build new palaces south of Naples at **Portici** – now part of the university – and on the heights of **Capodimonte**, now Naples' most important art gallery. Further from the city, near Capua, the palace and park of **Caserta** (1752–74) were constructed on a lavish scale designed to remind people of Versailles. And royalty as well as opera could be watched at the **Teatro San Carlo**, built in 1737–8, where in 1780 William Beckford (◊Lombardy) attended a 'grand illumination' in which 'six rows of boxes blazed with tapers', their light concealing for some time 'the vast numbers of ugly beings, in gold and silver raiment, peeping out'.

In the early 19th century, after the interlude of French rule under Napoleon's brother Joseph Bonaparte and brother-in-law Joachim Murat, the pleasurable Naples of the northern tourists had something of a renaissance. The San Carlo, burnt down in 1816, was rebuilt in grand neoclassical style in 1817 and was an important venue for the operas of Rossini, Bellini, and their successors. On the calm Bay at night in August 1824 Marguerite, Countess of Blessington watched the elderly King Ferdinand, who usually figured in travellers' accounts as a homely, unlettered, rather coarse figure, do courteous honour to Napoleon's widow, the ex-empress Marie-Louise: against a backdrop of the white colonnades and dark foliage of the city, sleeping Vesuvius, and 'the vine-crowned height of the Vomero', music poured from 'a gilded barge, to which countless lamps were attached, giving it, when seen at a distance, the appearance of a vast shell of topaz, floating on a sea of sapphire'. The elderly king himself steered the Empress's barge like some 'hoary Neptune'. A few years before this show Samuel Rogers◊, the prosperous English poet, was enjoying snow-water and lemon at the best stall in the Toledo, music at the Cathedral for the feast of Our Lady of Loreto, and 'that azure bloom on the sea.' To complete the idyll, Rogers (like Goethe before him) refuted on the spot claims that the city was full of people doing nothing; the *lazzaroni* are 'a noisy, gay and harmless race', living hand to mouth but not idly. They crowd the quays and streets, selling fish and fruit and 'offering their little services on every occasion'. Dickens (◊Liguria) in 1844 responded with gusto to 'all Naples . . . out of doors, and tearing to and fro in carriages' (*Pictures from Italy*, 1846).

But as in earlier periods and as in any large city there was an uglier side to life in Naples in the 19th century. There was political repression, as the Borboni faced rebellions like the *carbonari* rising of 1820–1. The dying John Keats was outraged to see armed soldiers posted on either side of the proscenium arch in the Teatro San Carlo in 1820. Violence in the streets was taken for granted: in 1818 Shelley (◊Rome) saw a young man stabbed to death soon after his arrival, was laughed at for his horror and indignation by a Calabrian priest with whom he was travelling, and noted, in a letter to his friend Peacock, how 'external nature in these delightful regions contrasts with and compensates for the deformity and degradation of humanity'. And as the city continued to expand, the poverty of many of its inhabitants became more difficult to ignore or gloss over. A century and a half before debate about the British national lottery, Dickens worried about the way the Neapolitan version made the poor poorer. (Such was the degree of addiction, according to a tale he claims to have heard, that one typically superstitious native rushed up to a dying man thrown by a runaway horse and pleaded 'If you have one gasp of breath left, mention your age for Heaven's sake, that I may play that number in the lottery'.)

Foreigners' declining affection for Naples was much exacerbated by its ceasing to be a capital city. With the overthrow of the Borboni in 1860 the sense of vitality and coherence was, to a degree, lost. This was not simply because there were no longer diplomats to entertain and be entertained by, no longer a royal family to watch, intrigue against, and gossip about but, more seriously, because rule from Turin and then from Rome brought with it considerable financial disadvantages. Heavy taxes were imposed, the huge gold reserve of the Bank of Naples was seized by the Piedmontese regime in 1860, and Neapolitans then and later concluded that SPQR (Senatus Populusque Romanus) in fact stands for *Sono porchi, questi Romani* ('They're pigs, these Romans'). Rich foreigners decreased in numbers, and the new breed of Cook's tourists were not encouraged by their guide-books to visit the southern metropolis. Augustus Hare, whose detailed guides to France and Italy were much used in the late 19th and early 20th century, expresses his mingled affection for and irritation with the natives – 'insouciant and idle, good-natured and thieving . . . always laughing, except if thwarted, when they will stab their best friend without a pang' (*Cities of Southern Italy*, 1883). Officials are mostly corrupt, aristocrats idle, and even the food is suspect: earlier travellers had enthused about the simple joys of oranges and macaroni whereas now 'the horrible condiment called pizza (made of dough baked with garlic, rancid bacon, and strong cheese) is esteemed a feast'.

In the late 19th century there were large-scale building projects designed to modernize the city. Not only was some of the redevelopment aesthetically displeasing to visitors like George Gissing◊ (Extract 4), but it was little calculated to improve conditions for the poor. The novelist Matilde Serao◊ was the most eloquent opponent of the *sventramento*. She had recently moved to Rome when, in 1884, Naples was struck by a cholera epidemic, the fifth since 1860. The prime minister, Agostino Depretis, having seen for himself the dark alleys and decaying tenements of the city, proclaimed the need to gut Naples (*bisogna sventrare Napoli*). This became a well known phrase partly because of Serao's passionate, articulate and well-informed response to it in the first essay of *Il ventre di Napoli* (*The Belly of Naples*), 1884: does Depretis really deceive himself that three or four new streets will be enough to make much difference? In many parts of the city there are wells full of rubbish and dead animals and buildings where people, at least three or four to a room, cook in the attic and eat, sleep and die in the bedroom. There are streets full of wretched, angry, unemployed women. If the health and the moral well-being of the poor are to be restored, if they are to be taught how to live – 'they know how to die, as you've seen' – and that somebody cares about them enough to want to save them, 'it will not be enough to gut Naples: it will need to be almost completely rebuilt'.

Another problem which the Risorgimento did nothing to allay was the increasing strangle-hold of the Camorra, the Neapolitan counterpart of the Mafia. (A *camorra* was originally a short jacket worn by hired *bravi* in the days of Spanish rule. The organization started in the city's prisons in the early 19th century.) Camorra activities were a staple of the city's popular literature by the end of the century. Salvatore Di Giacomo's◊ short story 'Pasquino', 1893, tells of the bloody fate of a young *camorrista*, slim, elegant, thought by his evening gambling-cronies to have 'a good heart, a pretty mistress and money in his purse' but living at night a sordid life in the city's 'deserted squares and . . . lurid *vicoli* [alleys]', avoiding the police and rival gangsters and bullying the prostitutes he controls. In the absence of effective and incorruptible local and national government the organisation continued to expand its power in the 20th century. It flourished triumphantly in the chaotic period of food shortages, enforced prostitution, German advance and withdrawal, and Allied take-over in 1943–4 which has been graphically described by Norman Lewis◊ in *Naples '44*, 1978 (Extract 5), and by Curzio Malaparte◊ in *La pelle* (*The Skin*), 1950. One of the most interesting works with a Camorra setting is Eduardo De Filippo's◊ play *Il Sindaco del Rione Sanità* (*The Local Authority*), 1960, where Antonio Barracano, a feared and respected Camorra patriarch, faces complicated moral dilemmas – and risks and finally loses his life – as the man expected to dispense justice not only among his followers but in all local affairs, even quarrels over money in other people's families.

De Filippo, prolific playwright and actor, was the most popular Neapolitan theatre artist between 1945 and his death in 1984. His best known plays, among them *Napoli milionaria*, 1945, and *Filumena Marturano* (Extract 3), 1946, are written in what his translator Carlo Ardito describes as 'a natural mix of Italian and easily accessible Neapolitan' and explore both serious issues and their comic potential. The plays, still much performed, continue, like much writing from or about Naples, to celebrate laughter and vitality in the midst of crisis, on the brink of Vesuvius. Severe problems have continued, among them the aftermath of the unexpected cholera epidemic of 1973, the first since 1910, and the major earthquake of 1980. Today there are perhaps fewer rhapsodies about the blue Bay than there used to be. But the noisy streets can still become, as for the American anthropologist Thomas Belmonte, 'a brilliantly coloured frieze depicting a grand, if raucous *Commedia*'.

## CAMPANIA

Even when not thinking of cholera or the Camorra, writers on Naples have been aware of a sense of precariousness, of dangerous or endangered beauty, sirens and Vesuvius. Goethe◊, descending from the volcano into the sunset, meditated on the contrast of 'the Terrible beside the Beautiful' and concluded that 'the Neapolitan would certainly be a different creature if he did not feel himself wedged between God and the Devil'. Around Vesuvius, and further encouraging such reflections, are the abundant traces of past towns, past lives, most famously at **Herculaneum** (Ercolano; excavated gradually after 1738) and **Pompeii** (after 1748).

Travellers came usually with a developed second-hand knowledge of the buried cities. Many had been familiar since their school-days with the Younger Pliny's account of the great eruption of A.D. 79 (Extract 9). The Pompeiian style in painting and interior decoration spread far with the aid of such publications as the *Antichità di Ercolano*, brought out by the Accademia ercolanese di archeologia between 1757 and 1792 and the British antiquarian Sir William Gell's *Pompeiana* of 1817–32. In literature, the once-buried cities owed their fame above all to Edward Bulwer-Lytton's◊ *The Last Days of Pompeii*, 1834. This provided not only a popular melodramatic story of love and intrigue set piquantly against the background of a doomed Pompeii, but a wealth of detail which appealed to the growing taste for archaeological verisimilitude on the page, the stage and the canvas. So the hero, Glaucus, lives in a building which the reader can actually visit: the so-called **House of the Tragic Poet**, which 'You enter by a narrow vestibule, on the floor of which is the image of a dog in mosaic, with the well-known "Cave canem" – or "Beware the dog" . . . Advancing up the vestibule you enter an atrium, that when first discovered was rich with paintings . . . now transplanted to the Neapolitan Museum . . . ' Many other houses are described in minute detail, as is the amphitheatre and (no longer extant, but to be imagined on good scholarly authority) its 'awning (or *velaria*) . . . woven of the whitest Apulian wool, and variegated with broad stripes of crimson'.

Lytton also used the **Villa Diomedes**, named after the merchant Arrius Diomedes who was once believed, on the strength of a nearby inscription, to have owned it. During the excavation of this villa in 1771–4 a number of bodies of victims of the eruption were discovered, including the skeleton of a young woman the shape of whose breast had been preserved by hardened sand; we last see Arrius Diomedes' daughter, the fashionable Julia, among those retreating to the cellar. The partly-preserved young woman (who at some later date finally crumbled away) is also the inspiration of Théophile Gautier's◊ briefer and more melancholy time-warp tale of Arria Marcella (Extract 7). Gautier, while he shares something of Lytton's passion for archaeological detail, exploits the paradoxes of the well-preserved but dead city to more disturbing effect. His lovers, separated by 1800 years, are allowed at best a fleeting fulfilment, not the lasting bliss of Lytton's idealised Glaucus and Ione. Marcella is, briefly, living flesh and blood to Gautier's Octavien, but when he touches her bare arm it is deathly cold. So too the life of Pompeii has been preserved by the materials which destroyed it.

Giacomo Leopardi (◊Umbria and Marche), who spent the last few years of his life in Campania, reacted more philosophically to the remains of Pompeii in the poem *La ginestra, o il fiore del deserto* (*Broom, or the Flower of the Desert*), 1836. Lytton and Gautier attempt lovingly to recreate the ancient world where for Leopardi things ancient and modern demonstrate equally that human aspirations come to nothing. Pompeii is now merely a skeleton, dug up out of greed or piety, and Vesuvius continues to threaten 'the ruins scattered round' and anyone who attempts to scrape a living from the scorched soil. The 'gentle broom', whose 'fragrant thickets/Make beautiful this spoiled and wasted land' will also soon be swallowed up by the 'subterranean fire', but, unlike man, will accept its appointed end, 'not obstinate beneath/The rod of fate', not thinking its 'feeble stock immortal,/Made so by destiny or by' itself. Human beings can, however, once purged of such illusions, hold firmly to the fraternal love which is all that is left to them. (Leopardi wrote the poem at the porticoed neoclassical house thereafter called **Villa della Ginestra** on the slopes of Vesuvius – now among other houses – above Torre del Greco.)

Vesuvius itself was much ascended, painted and written about. It was often seen as menacing or, in the late 18th and early 19th century, solemn and sublime. During a period of 'slight' eruption in 1818, Shelley (◊Rome) went up to the summit and found there an irregular plain 'riven into ghastly chasms, and heaped up with great tumuli of stones and cinders and enormous rocks blackened and calcined'; he was especially excited by the crackling, creeping lava which in one place, gushing over a high crag, formed 'a cataract of quivering fire'. Dickens (◊Liguria), if with characteristic touches of humour, registers some similar impressions (Extract 8).

There are also traces of volcanic activity further west, near Pozzuoli. The **Solfatara** crater, named after the sulphurous gases it emits, used sometimes to be claimed as an influence on Hell in *Paradise Lost*. (Milton was in Naples in 1638.) The area of the **Campi Flegrei** (Phlegraean Fields) more generally is a traditional part of the visitor's itinerary, providing the title and some of the material for *Campi Phlegraei*, 1776, by Sir William Hamilton◊, British ambassador in Naples between 1764 and 1800, tireless guide, antiquary and volcanologist. Only a few miles away – wedged between God and the Devil again, in Goethe's terminology – is the coast at **Baia**, as Baiae a favourite watering-place of Roman emperors (Hadrian died here, Nero had his mother murdered nearby, and Caligula built a bridge of boats from Baia to Pozzuoli). The ancient remains, partly underwater, were used by Shelley in the quiet interlude of the third section of 'Ode to the West Wind' to characterize:

> 'The blue Mediterranean, where he lay,
> Lulled by the coil of his Crystalline streams,
> Beside a pumice isle in Baiae's bay,

And saw in sleep old palaces and towers
Quivering within the wave's intenser day.'

Nearly five hundred years earlier Boccaccio's Fiammetta rode and
hunted on 'the rocky coast of Baia high above the seashore', 'surrounded by the most lovely mountains thick with trees and vineyards'.
The beaches and gardens are full of young people dancing and singing
love-songs. Her husband hopes that all this, together with trips to
Cumae and Miseno, will cure her extreme melancholy. But the therapy
fails because, unknown to him, she is pining for her absent lover and
can only remember 'I was here with Panfilo, and here he said this, and
here we did that.'

## CAPRI

The emperor Tiberius caused many deaths and much unhappiness
during his reign (A.D. 14–37), but there is little evidence for the
crimes, debauchery, and perversions which, Roman gossips and historians were eager to assert, filled the days and nights of his old age on
Capri. Gaius Suetonius Tranquillus, in *De vita Caesarum* (*The Twelve
Caesars*), c. 115–130, reports orgies of eating and drinking (followed by
promotion for the emperor's bibulous companions) and how he built
'a private sporting-house' – somewhere, presumably, in what are now
the expansive ruins of the **Palazzo di Tiberio** or Villa Jovis – where
girls and young men who specialised in 'unnatural practices . . . would
perform before him in groups of three, to excite his waning passions'.
Obscene paintings and statues and 'erotic manuals from Elephantis in
Egypt' were available as prompts. Tiberius 'furthermore devised little
nooks of lechery in the woods and glades of the island, and had boys
and girls dressed up as Pans and nymphs posted in front of caverns or
grottoes'; the island became known as 'Caprineum' 'because of his
goatish antics'. Some perversions 'are almost too vile to discuss, much
less believe', but of course Suetonius happily goes on to record them:
paedophilia, assaults, protesting or refusing partners driven to suicide.

Tiberius was attracted to Capri by the seclusion then guaranteed by
its sheer coastline and mountainous interior. Reputedly he made good
use of the cliffs. Now as in Suetonius' time 'they still show the place at
the cliff top where Tiberius used to watch his victims being thrown
into the sea' – the **Salto di Tiberio** near the Villa Jovis.

On the ruins of another of Tiberius' villas, near **Anacapri**, the
fashionable Swedish doctor Axel Munthe (1857–1949) built the **Villa
San Michele**. He lovingly describes it, with its mosaic floors, antiquities (some found on site), and high views from the surrounding loggias,
pergolas, and terraces, in *The Story of San Michele*, 1929. Meanwhile,
mostly down in the town of Capri, a more sizeable community of
literary expatriates flourished, often seizing their pleasures more

urgently. Their social and sexual affairs – too tame for Suetonius, perhaps, but complicated and entertaining – feature, thinly disguised, in Sir Compton Mackenzie's novels *Vestal Fire*, 1927, and *Extraordinary Women*, 1928. D.H. Lawrence (◊Sardinia) knew Mackenzie and other members of the community like Norman Douglas (◊Abruzzo, Calabria, and South-East) on the island in 1920. He caricatured Douglas, with his 'wicked whimsicality' and less amiable drinking habits and pretensions, as James Argyle in *Aaron's Rod*, 1922; Mackenzie he liked 'as a man, but not as an influence', and Capri he grew 'very sick of', for, he wrote to his friend Catherine Carswell, 'it is a stewpot of semi-literary cats'. Nevertheless several generations of readers went on enjoying – semi-literary or not – Norman Douglas' novel *South Wind*, 1917, a celebration of how a hedonistic life on the Capri-like island of Nepenthe can 'open the moral pores'.

## OTHER LITERARY LANDMARKS

**Amalfi**: setting of John Webster's *The Duchess of Malfi*, 1612–13.

**Caudine Forks**: ravine, near Arienzo (north-east of Naples), the possible site of the defeat and shaming of a Roman army by the Samnites in 321 B.C., recorded by Livy (◊Rome).

**Ischia**: island celebrated in the poem *Ischia – For Brian Howard*, by W.H. Auden, who rented a house at Forio from 1948. Henrik Ibsen completed the first three acts of *Peer Gynt* at Villa Ibsen, Casamicciola Terme, in the summer of 1867. (Ibsen's Casamicciola, however, was mostly destroyed by the earthquake of 1883.)

**Miseno**: harbour and promontory. The promontory was said to be the burial place of Aeneas' trumpeter Misenus (see Virgil◊, *The Aeneid*). Near the harbour are the remains of a villa lived in by the general and seven times consul Caius Marius (157–86 B.C.) and then by Lucius Licinius Lucullus (d. 57 or 56 B.C.), an ex-general who became a by-word for luxury and feasting, mostly through Plutarch's (◊Sicily) *Life of Lucullus*.

**Naples**: tomb, at the Cimitero Nuovo, of Francesco De Sanctis (1817–83), teacher, education minister, and one of the most important critics and historians of Italian literature.

**Naples**: tomb, at the Girolamini church (also called San Filippo Neri) of the great philosopher and jurist Giambattista Vico (1668–1744).

**Naples**: the Palazzo Filmarino, where Vico had taught, contained the home and library of Benedetto Croce (1866–1952), writer on philosophy, literature, and history, senator, and respected opponent of Fascism. In 1947 Croce founded, on the same premises, the Istituto Italiano per gli Studi Storici (Historical Studies).

**Procida**: island setting of Alphonse de Lamartine's love-story *Graziella*, 1852.

# BOOKLIST

Beckford, William, *The Grand Tour of William Beckford: Selections from 'Dreams, Waking Thoughts and Incidents'*, Elizabeth Mavor, ed, Penguin, Harmondsworth, 1986.

Belmonte, Thomas, *The Broken Fountain*, Columbia University Press, New York, 1979.

Blessington, Marguerite, Countess of, *Lady Blessington at Naples*, Edith Clay, ed, Hamish Hamilton, London, 1979.

Boccaccio, Giovanni, *The Elegy of Lady Fiammetta*, Mariangela Causa-Steindler and Thomas Mauch, trans, University of Chicago Press, London and Chicago, 1990. **Extract 2**.

Boyle, Nicholas, *Goethe: the Poet and his Age. Vol. 1: the Poetry of Desire (1749–1790)*, Clarendon Press, Oxford, 1991.

Bulwer-Lytton, Edward, *The Last Days of Pompeii*, Sidgwick and Jackson, London, 1979.

Campbell, James L., Sr., *Edward Bulwer-Lytton*, Twayne Books, G.K. Hall, Boston, MA, 1986.

Dickens, Charles, *Pictures from Italy* [1846], David Paroissien, ed, Robinson, London, 1989; Ecco Press, New York, 1988. **Extract 8**.

De Filippo, Eduardo, *Four Plays: the Local Authority, Grand Magic, Filumena Marturano*, Carlo Ardito, trans; *Napoli Milionaria*, adapted by Peter Tinniswood, Methuen Drama, London, 1992. **Extract 3**.

Di Giacomo, Salvatore, 'Pasquino', Constance Hutton, trans, in *Italian Regional Tales of the Nineteenth Century*, Archibald Colquhoun and Neville Rogers, ed, Oxford University Press, London, 1961.

Douglas, Norman, *Siren Land* [1911], Mark Holloway, intr, Penguin, Harmondsworth, 1983.

Douglas, Norman, *South Wind* [1917], Secker and Warburg, London, 1979.

Gissing, George, *By the Ionian Sea* [1900], Marlboro/Northwestern, Evanston, 1996. **Extract 4**.

Goethe, Johann Wolfgang (von), *Italian Journey [1786–1788]* [1816–17], W.H. Auden and Elizabeth Mayer, trans, Penguin Books, Harmondsworth, 1970. **Extract 6**.

Hare, Augustus J.C., *Cities of Southern Italy*, St. Clair Baddeley, ed, Heinemann, London, 1911.

Kidwell, Carol, *Sannazaro and Arcadia*, Gerald Duckworth, London, 1993.

D.H. Lawrence, *The Letters of D.H. Lawrence: vol. 3, 1916–21*, James T. Boulton and Andrew Robertson, ed, Cambridge University Press, Cambridge, 1984.

Leopardi, Count Giacomo, *A Leopardi Reader*, Ottavio M. Casale, ed and trans, University of Illinois Press, Urbana, Chicago, London, 1981.

Lewis, Norman, *Naples '44*, Collins, London, 1978. **Extract 5**.

Malaparte, Curzio, *The Skin* [1950], David Moore, trans, Hamilton, Stafford, 1964.

Money, James, *Capri: an Island of Pleasure*, Hamish Hamilton, London, 1986.

Munthe, Axel, *The Story of San Michele*, Tim Burnett, intr, Folio Society, London, 1991.

Petronius Arbiter, *The Satyricon*, J.P. Sullivan, trans, Penguin, Harmondsworth, 1977.

*Booklist continued*

Pliny, *The Letters of the Younger Pliny*, Betty Radice, trans, Penguin Books, Harmondsworth, 1963. **Extract 9**.

Rogers, Samuel, *The Italian Journal*, J.R. Hale, ed, Faber, London, 1956.

Sannazaro, Jacopo, *Arcadia [1501] and Piscatorial Eclogues [1526]*, Ralph Nash, trans, Wayne State University Press, Detroit, 1966.

Seward, Desmond ed, *Naples: a Traveller's Companion*, Constable, London, 1984.

Shelley, Percy Bysshe, *The Letters*, Frederick L. Jones, ed, 2 vols, Oxford University Press, Oxford, 1964.

Shelley, Percy Bysshe, *Selected Poetry and Prose*, Alasdair D.F. Macrae, ed, Routledge, London, 1991.

Gaius Suetonius Tranquillus, *The Twelve Caesars* [c.115–130 A.D.], Robert Graves, trans, revised and expanded by Michael Grant, Penguin, Harmondsworth, 1980.

Virgil, *The Aeneid* [29–19 B.C.], Robert Fitzgerald, trans, Harvill, London, 1993. **Extract 1**.

Williams, R.D., *The Aeneid*, Allen and Unwin, London, 1987.

# *Extracts*

## (1) CUMAE

### Virgil, *The Aeneid*, 29–19 B.C.

*The Trojan (or 'Teucrian') Aeneas, ancestor of the Romans, lands in Italy for the first time near Cumae. Desiring to enter the underworld and speak with the dead – among whom are his father Anchises and the abandoned Dido – he consults the Sibyl.*

> Aeneas,
> In duty bound, went inland to the heights
> Where overshadowing Apollo dwells
> And nearby, in a place apart – a dark
> Enormous cave – the Sibyl feared by men. . . .
>
> The cliff's huge flank is honeycombed, cut out
> In a cavern perforated a hundred times,
> Having a hundred mouths, with rushing voices
> Carrying the responses of the Sibyl.
> Here, as the men approached the entrance way,
> The Sibyl cried out:
> 'Now is the time to ask

Your destinies!'
                    And then:
                                    'The god! Look there!
The god!'

            And as she spoke neither her face
Nor hue went untransformed, nor did her hair
Stay neatly bound: her breast heaved, her wild heart
Grew large with passion. Taller to their eyes
And sounding now no longer like a mortal
Since she had felt the god's power breathing near,
She cried:

                    'Slow, are you, in your vows and prayers?
Trojan Aeneas, are you slow? Be quick,
The great mouths of the god's house, thunderstruck,
Will never open till you pray.'

                    Her lips
Closed tight on this. A chill ran through the bones
Of the tough Teucrians, but their king poured out
Entreaties from his deepest heart.


## (2) NAPLES

### Giovanni Boccaccio,
### *The Elegy of Lady Fiammetta*, 1343–4

*Boccaccio's Fiammetta is one of the most psychologically con-*
*vincing women in late medieval literature. Unusually, she is*
*allowed to narrate her own unhappy adulterous love-story. In*
*this extract she has just seen her future lover, Panfilo, in the*
*church of San Lorenzo in Naples (Parthenope).*

Therefore, compassionate ladies, of all the noble, handsome, and
valiant young men who were available not only there but in my entire
beloved Parthenope, he was the one my heart chose with insane
judgment to be the first, last, and only lord of my life; he was the
one I loved and still love more than anyone else, the beginning and
cause of all my troubles and, as I hope, of my wretched death. . . .
Alas, miserable me, how wretched was that day to my virtue! But after
all, things badly done in the past can be more easily regretted than
corrected. As was said, I was caught anyway, and whether it was an
infernal fury or a malevolent fate that, envious of my innocent happiness, undermined it, on that day it could rejoice in the hope of certain
victory.

Therefore, surprised by this sudden passion, I sat among the ladies, nearly stunned and beside myself, and I let the sacred service, as well as my companions' various conversations, go by me, barely listening to them and much less understanding them. So entirely had this new and sudden love occupied my mind that either my thoughts or my eyes were constantly on the beloved young man, and deep inside me I hardly knew what an end I was demanding for myself from such a fervent love. How many times, wishing to see him closer to me, did I blame him for staying in back of the others and interpret as indifference what he was doing out of caution! The young men standing in front of him also annoyed me, because as I sometimes looked past them at the object of my interest, some of them thought that my gaze alighted on them and believed that it was they whom I loved. But while my mind was dwelling on these matters, the solemn ceremony had ended and my friends were already standing and about to leave when I became aware of this and recalled my soul to myself, which was wandering around the image of the young man I liked so much. Then I too stood up with the other ladies, and when I turned my eyes towards him, I seemed to perceive in his gestures what I was about to show him in mine, and in fact I indicated that it was painful for me to leave. Nevertheless, after a sigh or two and without knowing who he was, I left.

## (3) NAPLES

### Eduardo De Filippo, *Filumena Marturano*, 1946

*De Filippo's semi-dialect plays explore family conflicts and responsibilities, often through humour. Here the wealthy Domenico Soriano wants to find out which of three young men, the children of his long-term mistress and now wife Filumena Marturano, is his son.*

DOMENICO In my young days I was keen on singing. There was a group of us, seven or eight fellows. We'd have dinner out in the open, and end up with a singsong. Guitars, mandolins . . . Do any of you sing?

UMBERTO I don't.

RICCARDO I don't either.

MICHELE (*brightly*) I do.

DOMENICO (*delighted*) You do?

MICHELE I couldn't carry on working without singing. I'm always singing away in the shop.

DOMENICO (*hopefully*) Let's hear you sing.

MICHELE (*suddenly bashful*) Me? What do you want to hear?

DOMENICO Anything you like.

MICHELE I'm not sure . . . I'm shy . . .

DOMENICO But you just said you spend the whole day singing.

MICHELE That's different . . . all right. Do you know Core 'ngrato? That's a smashing song. (*Begins to sing, hopelessly out of tune and in a reedy colourless voice*) Core, Core 'ngrato – t'hai pigliato 'a vita mia – tutto e' passato – io non ce pienzo cchiu' . . .

RICCARDO (*breaks in*) I can sing like that. Do you call that a voice?

MICHELE (*slightly offended*) What do you mean?

UMBERTO Even I can do better than that.

DOMENICO Anyone can do better than that. (*To RICCARDO*) Let's hear you sing.

RICCARDO I hardly like to. I'm not as brazen as he is. Still, here goes. Core, core 'ngrato – t'hai pigliato 'a vita mia – (UMBERTO *joins in*) tutto e' passato – (MICHELE *joins in*) io non ce pienzo cchiu'.

(*The resulting discordant and inhuman noise is painful to the ear*)

DOMENICO (*interrupting them*) That's enough, thank you. (*They stop*) No need to go on. You're not quite yourselves today . . . (*Aside*) It's not possible . . . three Neapolitans who can't sing!

## (4) NAPLES

### George Gissing, *By the Ionian Sea*, 1900

*Much demolition and rebuilding took place in Naples in the 1880s and 1890s. George Gissing, en route for the wilds of Calabria in 1897, sets the tone for his meditations there on earlier lost worlds.*

Sirocco, of course, dusks everything to cheerless grey, but under any sky it is dispiriting to note the changes in Naples. *Lo sventramento* (the disembowelling) goes on, and regions are transformed. It is a good thing, I suppose, that the broad Corso Umberto I should cut a way through the old Pendino; but what a contrast between that native picturesqueness and the cosmopolitan vulgarity which has usurped its place! '*Napoli se ne va!*' I pass the Santa Lucia with downcast eyes, my memories of ten years ago striving against the dullness of today.

The harbour, whence one used to start for Capri, is filled up; the sea has been driven to a hopeles distance beyond a wilderness of dust-heaps. They are going to make a long, straight embankment from the Castel dell'Ovo to the Great Port, and before long the Santa Lucia will be an ordinary street, shut in among huge houses, with no view at all. Ah, the nights that one lingered here, watching the crimson glow upon Vesuvius, tracing the dark line of the Sorrento promontory, or waiting for moonlight to cast its magic upon floating Capri! The odours remain; the stalls of sea-fruit are as yet undisturbed, and the jars of the water-sellers; women still comb and bind each other's hair by the wayside, and meals are cooked and eaten *al fresco* as of old. But one can see these things elsewhere, and Santa Lucia was unique. It has become squalid. In the grey light of this sad billowy day, only its ancient foulness is manifest; there needs the golden sunlight to bring out a suggestion of its ancient charm.

## (5) NAPLES

### Norman Lewis, *Naples '44*, 1978

*Lewis worked in intelligence in desperately poor and disordered Naples in 1943–4, after its capture by the Allies in the wake of the Italian armistice of 8 September 1943. In this passage he dines with his indigent but resourceful civilian contact Vincente Lattarullo.*

No attempt was made to isolate the customers from the street. Ragged, hawk-eyed boys – the celebrated *scugnizzi* of Naples – wandered among the tables ready to dive on any crust that appeared to be overlooked, or to snatch up left-overs before they could be thrown to the cats. . . . An extraordinary cripple was dragged in, balancing face downwards on a trolley, only a few inches from the ground, arms and legs thrust out in spider fashion. Nobody took his eyes off his food for one second to glance down at him. This youth could not use his hands. One of the *scugnizzi* hunted down a piece of bread for him, turned his head sideways to stuff it between his teeth, and he was dragged out.

Suddenly five or six little girls between the ages of nine and 12 appeared in the doorway. They wore hideous straight black uniforms buttoned under their chins, and black boots and stockings, and their hair had been shorn short, prison-style. They were all weeping, and as they clung to each other and groped their way towards us, bumping into chairs and tables, I realized they were all blind. Tragedy and despair had been thrust upon us, and would not be shut out. I expected the indifferent diners to push back their plates, to get up and hold out their arms, but nobody moved. Forkfuls of food were thrust into open mouths, the rattle of conversation continued, nobody saw the tears.

Lattarullo explained that these little girls were from an orphanage on the Vomero, where he had heard – and he made a face – conditions were very bad. They had been brought down here, he found out, on a half-day's outing by an attendant who seemed unable or unwilling to stop them from being lured away by the smell of food.

The experience changed my outlook. Until now I had clung to the comforting belief that human beings eventually come to terms with pain and sorrow. Now I understood I was wrong, and like Paul I suffered a conversion – but to pessimism. These little girls, any one of whom could be my daughter, came into the restaurant weeping, and they were weeping when they were led away. I knew that, condemned to everlasting darkness, hunger and loss, they would weep on incessantly. They would never recover from their pain, and I would never recover from the memory of it.

## (6) PAESTUM

### Johann Wolfgang Goethe,
### *Italian Journey*, 1816–17

*The sixth and fifth century B.C. Doric temples of Paestum were among the more unfamiliar buildings encountered by Goethe during his time in Italy in 1786–8.*

Very early next morning, we drove by rough and often muddy roads towards some beautifully shaped mountains. We crossed brooks and flooded places where we looked into the blood-red savage eyes of buffaloes. They looked like hippopotamuses.

The country grew more and more flat and desolate, the houses rarer, the cultivation sparser. In the distance appeared some huge quadrilateral masses, and when we finally reached them, we were at first uncertain whether we were driving through rocks or ruins. Then we recognised what they were, the remains of temples, monuments to a once glorious city. . . . At first sight they excited nothing but stupefaction. I found myself in a world which was completely strange to me. In their evolution from austerity to charm, the centuries have simultaneously shaped and even created a different man. Our eyes and, through them, our whole sensibility have become so conditioned to a more slender style of architecture that these crowded masses of stumpy conical columns appear offensive and even terrifying. But I pulled myself together, remembered the history of art, thought of the age with which this architecture was in harmony, called up images in my mind of the austere style of sculpture – and in less than an hour I found myself reconciled to them and even thanking my guardian angel for having allowed me to see these well-preserved remains with my own eyes. Reproductions give a false impression; architectural designs make them look more elegant and drawings in perspective more ponderous than they really are. It is only by walking through them and round them that one can attune one's life to theirs and experience the emotional effect which the architect intended.

# (7) POMPEII

## Théophile Gautier, *Arria Marcella*, 1852

*The paradox of the eruption of Vesuvius which simultaneously destroyed the life of the inhabitants of Pompeii and preserved it in uncanny detail fascinated a number of 19th-century writers and painters. In Gautier's story a young French tourist, of melancholy and romantic disposition, falls in love with the mould of a woman found at the Villa Diomedes and is (all too briefly) transported to A.D. 79, the year of the destruction.*

A pair of earrings in the form of a balance, with pearls on each scale, gleamed in the light on her pale cheeks. A necklace of golden balls, to which were attached long pear-shaped beads, was draped across her breasts, which had been left casually half uncovered by the fold of a straw-coloured, black-bordered *peplum*. A fillet of black and gold shone here and there amid her ebony-black hair, and around her arm, like the asp around Cleopatra's, was entwined a golden snake, with precious stones for eyes, attempting to bite its tail.

Near the bed a small table with griffins' feet, encrusted with pearl, silver, and ivory, had been laid for two. It was loaded with different viands, served in dishes of gold and silver or of costly enamelled earthenware . . . Everything seemed to indicate that a guest was expected; there were piles of fresh flowers, and amphoras of wine cooling in urns full of snow.

Arria Marcella gestured to Octavien to recline beside her on the *biclinium* and partake of the meal. The young man, half-mad with amazement and desire, took a few mouthfuls at random from the dishes which were offered him by little Asiatic slaves with curled hair and short tunics. Arria did not eat, but she frequently sipped from an opal-tinted myrrhine vase filled with dark wine, purple as coagulated blood; as she drank, an imperceptible pinkness rose to her pale cheeks from that heart which had not beat for so many years; but her bare arm, which Octavien brushed against as he raised his goblet, was as cold as the skin of a snake or the marble of a tomb.

'Ah! When you paused at the museum to contemplate that piece of hardened mud . . ., ' said Arria Marcella as she turned to look, long and moist-eyed, at Octavien, 'and when your thought darted keenly towards me, my soul felt it in this world where I float, invisible to vulgar eyes. . . . A woman is only dead when she is loved no longer; your desire gave me life once more, the powerful evocation of your heart cancelled the distance which kept us apart.'

## (8) Vesuvius

### Charles Dickens, *Pictures From Italy*, 1846

*Dickens and his party (including the pseudonymous or invented 'Mr Pickle of Portici') are led up the volcano at night by a head-guide and his 30 men.*

From tingeing the top of the snow above us, with a band of light, and pouring it in a stream through the valley below, while we have been ascending in the dark, the moon soon lights the whole white mountain-side, and the broad sea down below, and tiny Naples in the distance, and every village in the country round. The whole prospect is in this lovely state, when we come upon the platform on the mountain-top – the region of Fire – an exhausted crater formed of great masses of gigantic cinders, like blocks of stone from some tremendous waterfall, burnt up; from every chink and crevice of which, hot, sulphurous smoke is pouring out: while, from another conical-shaped hill, the present crater, rising abruptly from this platform at the end, great sheets of fire are streaming forth: reddening the night with flame, blackening it with smoke, and spotting it with red-hot stones and cinders, that fly up into the air like feathers, and fall down like lead. What words can paint the gloom and grandeur of this scene!

The broken ground; the smoke; the sense of suffocation from the sulphur; the fear of falling down through the crevices in the yawning ground; the stopping, every now and then, for somebody who is missing in the dark (for the dense smoke now obscures the moon); the intolerable noise of the 30; and the hoarse roaring of the mountain; make it a scene of such confusion, at the same time, that we reel again. . . .

There is something in the fire and roar, that generates an irresistible desire to get nearer to it. We cannot rest long, without starting off, two of us, on our hands and knees, accompanied by the head-guide, to climb to the brim of the flaming crater, and try to look in. Meanwhile, the 30 yell, as with one voice, that it is a dangerous proceeding, and call to us to come back; frightening the rest of the party out of their wits.

What with their noise, and what with the trembling of the thin crust of the ground, that seems about to open underneath our feet and plunge us in the burning gulf below (which is the real danger, if there be any); and what with the flashing of the fire in our faces, and the shower of red-hot ashes that is raining down, and the choking smoke and sulphur; we may well feel giddy and irrational, like drunken men. But, we contrive to climb up to the brim, and look down, for a moment, into the Hell of boiling fire below. Then, we all three come rolling down; blackened, and singed, and scorched, and hot, and giddy: and each with his dress alight in half-a-dozen places.

## (9) VESUVIUS

### Pliny the Younger,
### letter to Publius Cornelius Tacitus, c.100 A.D.

*In 79 A.D. the author's uncle, Pliny the Elder, natural historian and naval commander, sailed from Misenum to Stabiae to investigate the eruption of Vesuvius and to attempt to rescue some of those endangered by it. This letter is a response to the historian Tacitus' request for details of his death.*

He embraced his terrified friend [Pomponianus], cheered and encouraged him, and thinking he could calm his fears by showing his own composure, gave orders that he was to be carried to the bathroom. After his bath he lay down and dined; he was quite cheerful, or at any rate he pretended he was, which was no less courageous.

Meanwhile on Mount Vesuvius broad sheets of fire and leaping flames blazed at several points, their bright glare emphasized by the darkness of the night. My uncle tried to allay the fears of his companions by repeatedly declaring that these were nothing but bonfires left by the peasants in their terror, or else empty houses on fire in the districts they had abandoned. Then he went to rest and certainly slept, for as he was a stout man his breathing was rather loud and heavy and could be heard by people coming and going outside his door. By this time the courtyard giving access to his room was full of ashes mixed with pumice-stones, so that its level had risen, and if he had stayed in the room any longer he would never have got out. He was wakened, came out, and joined Pomponianus and the rest of the household who had sat up all night. They debated whether to stay indoors or take their chance in the open, for the buildings were now shaking with violent shocks, and seemed to be swaying to and fro as if they were torn from their foundations. Outside on the other hand, there was the danger of falling pumice-stones, even though these were light and porous; however, after comparing the risks they chose the latter. In my uncle's case one reason outweighed the other, but for the others it was a choice of fears. As a protection against falling objects they put pillows on their heads tied down with cloths.

Elsewhere there was daylight by this time, but they were still in darkness, blacker and denser than any ordinary night, which they relieved by lighting torches and various kinds of lamp. My uncle decided to go down to the shore and investigate on the spot the possibility of any escape by sea, but he found the waves still wild and dangerous. A sheet was spread on the ground for him to lie down, and he repeatedly asked for cold water to drink. Then the flames and smell of sulphur which gave warning of the approaching fire drove the others to take flight and roused him to stand up. He stood leaning on two slaves and then suddenly collapsed, I imagine because the dense fumes choked his breathing by blocking his windpipe, which was constitutionally weak and narrow and often inflamed. When daylight returned on the 26th – two days after the last day he had seen – his body was found intact and uninjured, still fully clothed and looking more like sleep than death.

# Biographies and important works

BULWER-LYTTON, Edward (1803–73), English politician, novelist, and playwright (originally Edward Bulwer, later Lord Lytton), wrote *The Last Days of Pompeii*, 1834, mostly in Naples in 1832–3. Its sales were helped by a major eruption of Vesuvius in 1834 and by its combination of melodramatic plot (the villainous necromancer Arbaces attempts to 'frame' the innocent hero Glaucus for murder) with precise archaeological detail. W.M. Thackeray, in his novel *The Newcomes*, said that Bulwer-Lytton had 'illustrated the place by his text, as if the houses were so many pictures to which he had appended a story.' At times, as Edgar Johnson says in his introduction to *The Last Days*, the author is guilty of 'forgetting that he is a novelist and lecturing the reader like a scholarly cicerone to a literary Cook's Tour of ancient society'. Yet for more than a century the book rarely lacked readers. The appeal lay partly in the physical and emotional violence never far beneath the ordered classical surface, and culminating in 'a fierce eruption of subterranean fires bursting out and overwhelming the world with destructive fury'. (Johnson relates this to the violent failure of Edward and Rosina Bulwer's marriage.) The pride and the anxiety of empire also no doubt contributed to the British success of this tale of the sudden collapse of a prosperous town of imperial Rome.

DE FILIPPO, Eduardo (1900–84), was a popular Neapolitan actor, director, and playwright. With his sister Titina and brother Peppino he formed, in 1931, the Compagnia del Teatro Umoristico i de Filippo. He attracted the attention of Pirandello (◊Sicily), staging two of his stories in Neapolitan dialect versions and co-writing with him *L'abito nuovo* (*The New Suit*), 1937. In 1945 De Filippo, who was generally known simply as 'Eduardo', founded Il Teatro di Eduardo and began to write more morally and socially probing plays like *Filumena Marturano*, 1946, *Sabato, Domenica e Lunedì* (*Saturday, Sunday, Monday*), 1959, and *Il Sindaco del Rione Sanità* (*The Local Authority*), 1960. As Eduardo himself said, these plays are concerned above all with the conflict between the individual and society, and have their starting-point in a reaction against injustice or hypocrisy.

*Filumena Marturano* (which inspired Vittorio de Sica's 1964 film *Marriage Italian Style*) concerns the initial horror of the rich Domenico Soriano when he is trapped into marriage with Filumena, the mistress he has taken for granted for 25 years, and his eventual acceptance of the situation and of his responsibility – and growing affection for – all three of her sons regardless of which one is actually his. The play is generally somewhat more light-hearted than De Filippo's other post-war work, but continues to insist that people should be valued for themselves – should not, for instance, be treated as 'illegitimate'; De Filippo himself was the illegitimate son of the actor-playwright Eduardo Scarpetta (1853–1925).

DI GIACOMO, Salvatore (1860–1934), from Naples, wrote poems, plays and stories, mostly in dialect. His tales of jealousy, crime, prison, superstition, and daily life have led him to be considered a *verismo* writer, but are more sentimental than those of Verga (◊Sicily) or Luigi Capuana (1839–1915). The fluent and creative use of dialect is essential to the impact of his works; they have been little translated.

Closely involved throughout his life with his home city, Di Giacomo also wrote history, including a sympathetic study (1899) of prostitution in Naples between the 15th and 17th centuries.

GAUTIER, Théophile (1811–72), French writer in many genres, proponent of *l'art pour l'art*, travelled in Italy in 1850 and 1852. He was in Venice in 1850 with his lover Maria Mattei, who played some part in the writing of *Voyage en Italie* (*Journey in Italy*), 1851. In this collection of sketches, where Venice features largely, Gautier is concerned mainly with people and places, amorous encounters and daydreams about them. Sometimes the tone lifts into rapture; often it is more whimsical, more aware of – at the same time as it indulges in – the author's 'excessive love of local colour'.

From Venice Gautier's tour, partly described in the *Voyage*, continued to Ferrara, Rome, and Naples, from which he briefly visited Pompeii. The happenings there in *Arria Marcella*, 1852, are, according to the narrator, 'strange and hardly believable' but true. Elements of melodrama and excessive archaeology are somewhat off-set by the contrast between the romantic and abstracted Octavien and his two heartier companions; while he swells with emotion on being shown the place where Marcella's remains were found, his friends wonder whether the *osteria* just outside the site will serve only 'fossil steaks and eggs laid before the death of Pliny', and expound their systems of seduction under the influence of Falernian wine. The romantic idyll of Octavien and

Marcella is, besides, soon shattered by the furious entry of Marcella's stern Christian father, who reduces her once more to ash and bone. Octavien will never be able to love a modern woman. The story explores some of Gautier's favourite themes: sexuality and death, the unfulfillable ideal, the lure and the loss of the past.

GOETHE, Johann Wolfgang (von) (1749–1832), had for ten years held positions of increasing responsibility in the court and administration of the Duchy of Saxe-Weimar-Eisenach by the time he set off for Italy in September 1786. As a writer, he was still known mainly for the romantic *Leiden des jungen Werthers* (Sorrows of Young Werther), 1774, but had become steadily more interested in classical ideas and motifs. Seeing the classical sites was one reason for going to Italy; but he also yearned to experience the sun, fruits, and other sensual (including sexual) joys of the south. In 1782 or 1783 his character Mignon, in *Wilhelm Meisters Lehrjahre* (Wilhelm Meister's Apprenticeship, final version 1795–6) had asked longingly *Kennst du das Land, wo die Zitronen blühn,/Im dunkeln Laub die Goldorangen glühn?* ('Do you know the land where the lemon-trees bloom, the golden oranges glow among the dark leaves?'). The decision to fulfil such yearning in 1786 responded to Goethe's sense of weariness with official duties in Weimar, creative impasse, and general uncertainty of purpose.

Having crossed the Brenner, Goethe was soon feasting on figs and oranges and studying the Roman amphitheatre at Verona. Study, he continually assured his correspondents, was the main purpose of the journey; most of his absence, extended with the permission of the tolerant Duke until April 1788, was spent in Rome.

But antiquities were not his only interest. He worked hard at his painting and continued to make serious geological and botanical observations. And particularly in Naples, where he spent several months in 1787, he watched and wrote about street-life and social life: 'Naples is a paradise; everyone lives in a state of intoxicated self-forgetfulness, myself included. . . . Yesterday I thought to myself: Either you were mad before, or you are mad now'.

*Italienische Reise* (Italian Journey), 1816–17, was compiled on the basis of letters and a journal from 1786–8. It is as much an edited extract from Goethe's intellectual autobiography as a travel-book. He focuses frequently on his own aims and development, how Italy fits his personal programme. But he is by no means unresponsive to external stimuli; his reaction to the unfamiliar architecture of Paestum illustrates that adaptability which kept his art changing and developing through a 60-year career.

HAMILTON, Sir William (1730–1803), was British envoy in Naples 1764–1800. His *Campi Phlegraei: Observations on the Volcanoes of the Two Sicilies*, 1776, was the main published fruit of a lifetime's fascination both with Vesuvius and with the ancient sites and artefacts of the area. He was known to generations of Grand Tourists who came to see his unrivalled collection and, in his later years, his mistress and then wife Emma Hart, who gave the guests the mixed classical and erotic pleasure of seeing her arranged in various poses and costumes illustrative of ancient art. On their return to England in 1800 the Hamiltons were much derided as a result of Emma's liaison with Horatio Nelson, who had commanded the fleet which temporarily restored King Ferdinand to the throne of Naples in 1798–9. Hamilton's life in Naples is the basis of Susan Sontag's *The Volcano Lover: a Romance*, 1992, where the volcano is not only Vesuvius but the passion the ambassador discovers through Emma and Emma through Nelson.

LEWIS, Norman (born 1908), served, mostly in intelligence, in Sicily and southern Italy in 1943–4. *Naples '44*, 1978, based on notes taken at the time, describes Lewis's difficult and often frustrating work checking the records of locals seeking Allied employment and following up allegations of spying. In the process he provides data for an anthropology of Neapolitan life at the time, controlled less by the often naive or incompetent Allied authorities than by poverty, prostitution, black marketeering, police corruption, belief in the evil eye and the miraculous powers of the images of San Gennaro, vendettas and the Camorra. Lewis' book on the Mafia, *The Honoured Society*, appeared in 1964.

MALAPARTE, Curzio (1898–1957), was born in Prato. His father was German and his original name Kurt Erich Suckert. Malaparte worked as a journalist, playwright, poet and novelist, much of his work reflecting his chequered political history: he was early involved with Fascism, was imprisoned having offended Fascist leaders and released partly through the intervention of Mussolini's son-in-law Count Ciano, worked for the Americans in Naples in 1944, and later became a Communist, visiting Mao's China at the end of his life. His works include the novels *Kaputt*, 1944 – based in part on his experiences on the Russian front – and *La pelle* (*The Skin*), 1950, which deals with the moral and physical collapse of Naples in 1943–4, and a study of his fellow Tuscans, *Maledetti toscani* (*Those Cursed Tuscans*) 1956.

PETRONIUS ARBITER, Gaius, is very probably Nero's courtier and 'arbiter of elegance' (it is not clear whether the name prompted the appointment or vice versa) who, accused of conspiracy, bled himself to death at Cumae in 65 A.D. According to Tacitus' *Annales* (*The Annals*), c.116, Petronius died with some style, feasting and listening to frivolous songs and compiling a (lost) list of Nero's crimes and accomplices before drifting away at leisure in what appeared to be a postprandial doze. Such conduct, very different from that of the Roman Hero, fits well with the tone and contents of *Satyricon* (more correctly *Satyrica*, 'satyr stories'). In its main surviving portion Trimalchio, an ignorant millionaire of humble origins and ostentatious and fantastic tastes, gives a wild dinner-party, diversified by drunken singing and fisticuffs, failed acrobatics, the grand but ludicrous entry of dishes like pork disguised as a goose or a boar's head accompanied by hounds, the tale of a werewolf, and the host's maudlin account of his last will and testament. Among the guests are the narrator Encolpius and his boyfriend Giton. Only parts of books 14–16 remain from what must have been a huge and various picaresque, satirical, and erotic tale. The language is a fast-moving colloquial Latin, nearer to speech than all but a very few surviving works of the time. Federico Fellini filmed an adaptation of *Satyricon* in 1969.

PLINY THE YOUNGER – Gaius Plinius Caecilius Secundus (A.D. 61/2–113) – was a lawyer and senator advanced both by the tyrant Domitian (d. 96) and the reformer Trajan (ruled 98–117). He specialized in financial and property law, and ended his career as governor of Bithynia-Pontus (in Asia Minor) from about 110. His tenth, posthumously published book of letters is a version of his correspondence with Trajan from Bithynia, but the other nine books, issued between 100 and 109, are addressed to a variety of friends and acquaintances and concern public affairs, business and estate matters, literature, and life at Pliny's various country villas. The letters were revised – and probably written – with publication in mind. Rather more formal and public than much of Cicero's (◊Rome) correspondence, they are carefully structured and aim at a tone of consistent well-bred restraint.

Of the many writings of Pliny's uncle, the Elder Pliny (Gaius Plinius Secundus, 23–79), there survives *Naturalis historia* (*The Natural History*), 77, a 37-volume compendium of natural observations, art history, and much else.

ROGERS, Samuel (1763–1855), at one time a banker, established himself as a poet with *The Pleasures of Memory*, 1792. The first edition of his poem *Italy*, 1822–8, sold poorly, but the magnificent illustrated edition of 1830 secured its fame. (The artists included J.M.W. Turner and Samuel Prout.) The poem, in the measured style which many contemporaries continued to prefer to the new flights of the Romantics, concentrates on the expected classical sites and gives the expected responses. The *Italian Journal* (first published in 1956), another fruit of his European tours of 1814–15 and 1821–2, retains more immediacy.

SANNAZARO, Jacopo (c.1457–1530), Neapolitan poet in Italian and Latin, was honoured by the Aragonian kings of Naples and particularly close to Federico (ruled 1496–1501), whose exile he shared when he was ousted in 1501. After Federico's death in 1504 he returned home and lived quietly at Mergellina.

*Arcadia*, 1504, intersperses prose with verse in its account of an idealised but melancholy pastoral community. It is, as Ernest Hatch Wilkins (*A History of Italian Literature*) puts it, a mosaic of Virgilian, Ovidian and Theocritan 'gentle idyllicism'. This perhaps 'palls on the modern reader', but was immensely popular in the 16th century and it influenced the Spanish and Portuguese pastoral romances with which, in turn, it became an important source for Sir Philip Sidney's more robust 1580s *Arcadia*.

Sannazaro's principal Latin works are *Piscatoria* (*Piscatorial Eclogues*), 1526 (mostly written in the 1490s), a quasi-pastoral set among fishermen on the Bay of Naples, and *De partu virginis* (*On the Childbirth of the Virgin*), 1526, mingling Christian and pagan motifs.

SERAO, Matilde (1857–1927), born in Greece to a Greek mother and an exiled Neapolitan father, spent much of her life in Naples as a prolific and successful journalist and (sometimes less successful) newspaper editor and proprietor. *Il ventre di Napoli* (*The Belly of Naples*), 1884, contains some of her best campaign journalism. *Il paese di Cuccagna* (*The Land of Cockayne*), 1891, takes up some of the same themes, especially the effects of the Neapolitan lottery, in fictional form.

Between 1881 and 1887 Serao worked in Rome. *La conquista di Roma* (*The Conquest of Rome*), 1885, aimed amongst other things to conquer a Roman market for her work. The novel suggests that most politicians, however honestly and enthusiastically they begin, are prone to pettiness, love of compromise, indifference, 'stinted zeal'. When they have passion, it is directed at gaining power at all costs. In their pursuit of this aim, Angelica forces Sangiorgio to agree, minds capable of producing 'wonders of beauty and utility' in art or science 'often accomplish nothing' and 'all worthy initiative is frittered away in 25 public sittings and 14 discussions in committee. All words, words!' *The Conquest of Rome* does not, however, seriously address political issues: once Sangiorgio falls in love they fade into the background for the reader as much as for the deputy, in keeping with Serao's and many of her contemporaries' (and successors') cynicism about post-Unification Italian politics.

VIRGIL is the English name for the most celebrated and ambitious of Roman poets, Publius Vergilius Maro (70–19 B.C.), born at Andes near Mantua. His works are *Eclogae* (*The Eclogues*), 37 B.C. (pastoral poems), *Georgica* (*The Georgics*), 29 B.C. (on husbandry and rural life) and the epic *Aeneis* (*The Aeneid*), 29–19 B.C. According to tradition he studied for a time in Naples and lived in Campania for most of his life after 42 B.C.; he died at Brundisium (now Brindisi) soon after his return from a visit to Greece. Through his friend and patron Gaius Maecenas, Virgil became personally known to the Emperor Augustus. He was also associated with Horace (◊Rome); their poetry has been taken as defining a 'golden' standard against which later Latin verse used often to be measured and found wanting.

*The Aeneid* recounts the hero Aeneas' various adventures and vicissitudes – most famously his love for and divinely-prompted abandonment of Dido, Queen of Carthage – before and after his arrival in Italy, where his descendants are fated to build Rome and whence they will embark on their domination of the world. Aeneas' destiny, the gods' intervention for and against it, and his problems as a result of it, are among the main subjects of *The Aeneid*. It is an epic of national self-celebration, with the Romans and especially Augustus listed or implied as the dutiful and victorious heirs of *pius* Aeneas. (The status of Rome and *The Aeneid* is also enhanced by frequent allusion to or absorption of lines and scenes in Homer's *Iliad* and *Odyssey*.) But Virgil's complex poem is far removed from simple propaganda. The bloodshed which accompanies the hero's eventual success is not unambiguously glorified as it often is in Homer's heroic conflicts, and Dido's plight is sensitively explored.

Virgil's work has had immense influence on later artists. Scenes and landscapes from the poems were an acknowledged inspiration to Claude Le Lorrain. As a 'virtuous pagan' Virgil is Dante's guide through Hell and Purgatory in *The Divine Comedy*, and *The Aeneid* affected Milton's epic aims and style in *Paradise Lost*.

# ABRUZZO, CALABRIA AND THE SOUTH-EAST

'Calabria! – No sooner is the word uttered than a new world arises before the mind's eye, – torrents, fastnesses, all the prodigality of mountain scenery, – caves, brigands, and pointed hats, . . . costumes and character, – horrors and magnificence without end.'
Edward Lear,
Journals of a Landscape Painter in Southern Calabria

'In some books . . . southern Italy is a blessed and beautiful land in which the peasants go carolling joyfully to work, echoed prettily by a chorus of country girls in traditional costume, while nightingales trill in the neighbouring wood', observes Ignazio Silone) in the introduction to his novel *Fontamara*, 1933; in Fontamara and the real south the people 'dress as the poor do all over the world. There is no wood . . . The mountainside is parched and bare . . . The birds are few and timid, because of the pitiless way in which they are hunted, and there are certainly no nightingales . . . The peasants do not sing, either in chorus or alone. They do not sing, they swear'.

Many of the two-and-a-half million Italians who emigrated, mostly to the United States, between 1880 and 1914, came, not surprisingly, from the south. The harsh conditions endured by most of those who remained were little known – seen and reported in other lands by occasional eccentric or intrepid travellers, a shock for even a liberal north Italian like Carlo Levi) when he was forced to spend time in Basilicata in the mid-1930s. Yet much of the south, even mountainous Basilicata for a time, had prospered once as part of Magna Graecia. The lost city of Sybaris in Calabria – sunk beneath the diverted river Crati by its rival Croton (now **Crotone**) in 510 B.C. – gave its name to (excessive) luxury. Croton had been the home of the semi-legendary Greek mystic and mathematician Pythagoras (c. 580–500 B.C.) and his disciples, and the historian Herodotus is said to have died in about 425 B.C. at Thurii, founded to replace Sybaris. (Scanty remains of Thurii survive near Terranova di Sibari.) The ancient south was famous for corn and white oxen and remained so long enough – especially in naturally fertile Apulia (Puglia) – to be lengthily fought over by Byzantines, Arabs, and Normans. The Norman presence is visible in many castles and a group of striking Romanesque churches starting with the basilica of **San Nicola** at **Bari**, built to house the relics of St Nicholas (seized by sailors from the town from a shrine in Lycia in 1087). In the 13th century the emperor Frederick II often held court in Apulia. But a generation later the whole of the south was controlled from Naples and the decline into poverty and obscurity began. Some areas, particularly Apulia, have now recovered from this legacy, but the *problema del mezzogiorno*, the 'problem of the south', remains the subject of much division.

## ABRUZZO

Abruzzo (also known by the plural form Abruzzi) includes the high peaks of the Gran Sasso. Snow is widespread in winter, as in the neighbouring Molise region, and wolves, common into recent times, survive in the Parco Nazionale d'Abruzzo. To natural hardship was long added a quasi-feudal system which kept most of the fertile land in the hands of the powerful few, and which is one of the reasons why this region – the northernmost part of the former Kingdom of Naples – is often considered as part of the south. The villagers of Silone's◊ Fontamara (Extract 1) are even worse off than some of their ancestors. Not only are they deprived, tantalisingly, of rights to the good land of the reclaimed Lake Fucino, but they even lose control of their vital water supply at the behest of a Fascist mayor at least as unconcerned for the peasants' welfare as any earlier overlord. (Fontamara combines elements of Silone's home, **Pescina dei Marsi**, and the villages in the hills above it. His ashes are buried in Pescina, beneath local rock, by the bell-tower of San Berardo, all that survived of the church after the earthquake of 1915 which killed most of his family.)

For some, Abruzzo was a happier memory. Ovid◊ was born at **Sulmona**, the Roman Sulmo, in 43 B.C., on a well-watered plain surrounded by the mountains. In the *Amores*, c.3–2 B.C., he describes its corn, grapes, olives, and moistened earth by 'gliding streams'. Nevertheless in the absence of a lover this pleasant place might as well be barbarous Scythia or even the land of the 'woad-covered Britons'. And Ovid seems to have spent most of his life in Rome until his banishment in A.D. 8.

Gabriele D'Annunzio (◊Lombardy) also lived away from Abruzzo, leaving the then quiet seaside town of **Pescara** initially in order to continue his education and then for a life seeking fame, fulfilment and 'total art', far from the provincial scandals and jealousies which nevertheless provided material for such works as *Le novelle di Pescara*. His monument in the town, the **Casa di Gabriele D'Annunzio**, where he was born on 12 March 1863 (the son of a landowner with considerable estates in the area, several times mayor) contains manuscripts, family portraits, and other memorabilia.

## APULIA

Frederick II◊, German emperor and king of Sicily, built in the 1240s, in ashlar, a magnificent eight-towered, octagonal hunting-lodge at the remote **Castel del Monte**. Frederick probably died before the work was near completion – indeed it remained unfinished – but it has given less mighty visitors much joy. In September 1847 Edward Lear◊ felt it worth enduring five hours of slow riding, through 'dismal, shrubless' rocky country unrelieved by any 'distant prospect', to sketch the 'hunting-palace' and gaze, from its stony hill, north across 'one vast pale pink map, stretching to Monte Gargano', south to where the lands of Bari and Otranto fade into the horizon, and east to the blue Adriatic with, 'as in a chart', its succession of maritime towns from Barletta towards Brindisi (*Journals of a Landscape Painter in Southern Calabria and the Kingdom of Naples*, 1852). The journey back was lightened when Lear's guide 'indulged me with a legend of the old castle'. The tale relates that the emperor sent out a courtier to inspect the castle during its construction. The courtier, however, got no further than **Melfi**, 'where he became enamoured of a beautiful damsel, whose eyes caused him to forget Castel del Monte and his sovereign'. He lingered until a messenger from Naples arrived with orders for him to make his report at once. On his arrival, rather than admitting his negligence, the courtier brazenly told Frederick that so far the building was 'a total failure as to beauty and utility, and the architect an impostor'. Summoned angrily by the emperor, the architect preferred to kill himself and his whole family than 'to fall into the hands of a monarch notorious for his severity'. But hearing of this, the emperor travelled at once, 'with characteristic impetuosity', to Castel del Monte, taking with him the 'doubtless sufficiently ill at ease' courtier. Seeing the beauty of the building, polluted now by innocent blood and doomed to remain unfinished, Frederick, 'foaming with rage . . . dragged the offender by the hair . . . to the top of the highest tower, and with his own hands threw him down as a sacrifice to the memory of the architect and his family, so cruelly and wantonly destroyed'.

More accessible, and of particular interest for more classically-minded travellers, was **Taranto** – the Spartan colony of Taras, Roman Tarentum. The most distinguished of Greek Tarentines was the philosopher, general, and mathematician Archytas (c. 430–365 B.C.), friend of Plato (◊Sicily). (The city's Museo Nazionale has an important collection of ancient sculpture.) Horace (◊Rome) in his *Satires* and *Epistles* refers in passing to Tarentum as a comfortable, verdant, peaceful place (famous for its scallops). Later it developed a more exotic

reputation as the home of the poisonous tarantula and its danced
antidote the tarantella, commented on by the English traveller George
Sandys◊ in *The Relation of a Journey*, 1615 (Extract 4).

George Gissing◊, in his brief, thoughtful account of his lonely south
Italian journey *By the Ionian Sea*, 1901, winces at the new town with its
'great buildings of yellowish-white stone, as ugly as modern architecture can make them' and is not particularly enthusiastic about the old
'island part of the town' with its cathedral, castle, and maze of alleys:
'All is strange, but too close-packed to be very striking or beautiful'.
But at the sea-wall, looking over the Gulf of Taranto and its mountainous shore, Gissing found the delicate synthesis, the living intimation
of an idealised ancient past, which he sought in these rarely visited
lands: here the fishermen:

> 'are the primitives of Taranto; who shall say for how many
> centuries they have hauled their nets upon the rock? When Plato
> visited the schools of Taras, he saw the same brown-legged figures,
> in much the same garb, gathering their sea-harvest. When Hanni-
> bal, beset by the Romans . . . escaped from the inner sea, fisher-
> men of Tarentum went forth as ever, seeking their daily food. A
> thousand years passed, and the fury of the Saracens, when it had
> laid the city low, spared some humble Tarentine and the net by
> which he lived. Today the fisher-folk form a colony apart; they
> speak a dialect which retains many Greek words . . . I could not
> gaze at them long enough; their lithe limbs, their attitudes at work
> or in repose, their wild, black hair, perpetually reminded me of
> shapes pictured on a classic vase.'

The fishermen – although for some authors the contrast would work
to the detriment of vases, philosophers, and generals – enable Gissing
to make contact with the world of Plato and Hannibal, of his reading
and his dreams.

## BASILICATA AND CALABRIA

The bare, earthquake-riven, deforested province of Basilicata (the
ancient Lucania) became known to the world through a work by a
northern Italian political detainee, Carlo Levi's◊ *Cristo si è fermato a
Eboli* (*Christ Stopped at Eboli*), 1945. Gagliano in the novel closely
resembles the real **Aliano** where Levi was sent to live in 1935–6.
Surrounded by ravines and *calanchi* (erosions), the village was a prison
as much for its inhabitants as for those officially confined there; the
monotonous life of both groups is underlined by the insistent presence of this battered landscape: of treeless, grassless slopes of white
clay 'eroded into a pattern of holes and hillocks like a landscape of the
moon'. Living here amid poverty, wasting disease, and superstition,
Levi's peasants are resigned to fate, a force more real to them than the

Fascist state's ideological pronouncements and the very idea of a state (Extract 2). Those who can escape to America. Some return but usually curse the day they did. For the peasants of Basilicata Rome is only 'the capital of the gentry'; Naples, as 'the capital of poverty' has more claim on them; but New York would be their capital 'if these men without a country could have a capital at all. And it *is* their capital, in the only way it can be for them, that is as a myth'.

Levi left Aliano as a result of the amnesty granted to celebrate the Italian capture of Addis Ababa in 1936. After the Second World War, as he had promised, he often returned, worked for improvements, and himself sufficiently identified with the village, once the home of people 'without a country', to be buried there in 1975. (There is also a museum which houses objects connected with the author and agricultural life in the Basilicata of his time and a selection of his paintings.)

Levi came away from Aliano with a confirmed social agenda. Voluntary visitors to the south usually wandered in search of some more personal goal – to hear some echo of the ancient world like George Gissing◊ in *By the Ionian Sea*, 1901, for instance. (Gissing's disappointment at how rarely he succeeds in his aim helps to explain – though for Levi it would not excuse – his remarks about the 'coarse and bumpkinish' faces of Crotone (then called Cotrone), their 'vulgar ugliness'.) His main moment of epiphany comes when, lying feverish in bed, he is able to lose meagre, malarial, defeatist modern Calabria in a dream or vision, of hallucinatory sunlit clarity, of ancient Croton with 'great vases, rich with ornament and figures', sepulchral marbles, processions, 'the soldiers of Hannibal doing massacre', and such peculiarities of costume and architecture 'which could by no possibility have been gathered from books'.

The immediate source of Gissing's delirious vision had been his frustration at being prevented, through his illness, from reaching the one still standing column of the late sixth-century B.C. Temple of Hera at **Capo Colonna**, a few miles south of Crotone. Norman Douglas◊, tracing Gissing's footsteps for parts of his longer journey in *Old Calabria*, 1915, eventually reaches the column after several views of it from afar, and ends the book here, at torrid, silent noon in 'the meridian glow of all things', by declaring Calabria the objective correlative of his hedonistic beliefs. (Gissing knows that he seeks an unrealisable ideal while Douglas sees his ideal as eminently achievable.) Calabria's waters and bare rocks are 'actualities, the stuff whereon man is made'. The austere landscape:

'hints at brave and simple forms of expression; it brings us to the ground, where we belong; it medicines to the disease of introspection and stimulates a capacity which we are in danger of unlearning amid our morbid hyperborean gloom – the capacity for honest contempt: contempt of that scarecrow of a theory which would have us neglect what is earthly, tangible. What is life well lived but a blithe discarding of primordial husks, of those comfortable intangibilities that lurk about us, waiting for our weak moments?'

'From these brown stones that seam the tranquil Ionian, from this gracious solitude', the true sage will take into the roar of the city 'the rudiments of something clean and veracious and wholly terrestrial – some tonic philosophy that shall foster sunny mischiefs and farewell regret'.

In the far south of Calabria Douglas had earlier come to **Aspromonte**, which 'deserves its name' (*aspro* means 'rough', 'harsh') since 'it is an incredibly harsh agglomeration of hill and dale', the geology of which 'reveals a perfect chaos of rocks of every age, torn into gullies by earthquakes and other cataclysms of the past'. In this dramatic landscape Corrado Alvaro◊ was born, at **San Luca**, in 1895. His novel *Gente in Aspromonte (Revolt in Aspromonte)*, 1930, is concerned with the hard life of shepherds and peasants on the mountain (Extract 3), suffering the effects of extreme heat, cold, and deprivation. Yet at the same time Alvaro idealises and celebrates the people and their savage surroundings as instances of a purity not to be attained by their oppressors in the novel or by the author's Fascist opponents and critics. He remains romantic enough to share something of the spirit of Edward Lear's happy anticipation, at the beginning of *Journals of a Landscape Painter in Southern Calabria*, 1852, of the land which includes 'the lofty cloud-topped Aspromonte':

> 'Calabria! – No sooner is the word uttered than a new world arises before the mind's eye, – torrents, fastnesses, all the prodigality of mountain scenery, – caves, brigands, and pointed hats, . . . costumes and character, – horrors and magnificence without end.'

## OTHER LITERARY LANDMARKS

**Canne della Battaglia**: approximate site, south-west of Barletta, of the battle of Cannae, 216 B.C. Hannibal, although heavily outnumbered, inflicted a spectacular defeat on a Roman army, killing perhaps 30–40,000 men.

**Matera**: at the Centro Carlo Levi are paintings by Levi◊ from his time in Aliano.

**Metaponto**: ruins of the Greek and Roman city of Metapontum, where Pythagoras is said to have taught at the end of his life.

**Sila**: in central Calabria, the 'venerable granitic tableland' described in Norman Douglas'◊ *Old Calabria*.

**Venosa**: the ancient Venusia, Apulian birthplace of Horace (◊Rome), commemorated by a statue in Piazza Orazio. In the ruins of the abbey of La Trinità is the possible tomb of the Norman conqueror of southern Italy Robert Guiscard (d. 1085).

## BOOKLIST

Alvaro, Corrado, *Revolt in Aspromonte* [1930], Frances Frenaye, trans, New Directions, Norfolk, Connecticut, 1962. **Extract 3**.

Douglas, Norman, *Old Calabria* [1915], Jonathan Keates, intr, Picador, London, 1994.

Gissing, George, *By the Ionian Sea* [1901], Marlboro/Northwestern, Evanston, 1996.

Highet, Gilbert, *Poets in a Landscape*, Hamish Hamilton, London, 1957.

*Horace: Satires and Epistles. Persius: Satires*, Niall Rudd, trans, Penguin, Harmondsworth, 1979.

Lear, Edward, *Edward Lear in Southern Italy: Journals of a Landscape Painter in Southern Calabria and the Kingdom of Naples* [1852], Peter Quennell, intr, William Kimber, London, 1964.

Levi, Carlo, *Christ Stopped at Eboli* [1945], Frances Frenaye, trans, Penguin, Harmondsworth, 1982. **Extract 2**.

Origo, Iris, 'Ignazio Silone: a Study in Integrity', in *A Need to Testify*, John Murray, London, 1984.

Ovidius Naso, Publius, *The Erotic Poems*, Peter Green, trans, Penguin, Harmondsworth, 1982.

Ovidius Naso, Publius, *Metamorphoses*, A.D. Melville, trans, E.J. Kenney, ed, Oxford University Press, Oxford, 1987.

Sandys, George, *The Relation of a Journey Begun An. Dom. 1610* [1615], Theatrum Orbis Terrarum, Amsterdam, and Da Capo Press, New York, 1973. **Extract 4**.

Silone, Ignazio, *Fontamara* [1933], Eric Mosbacher, trans, Robert Gordon and Robin Fitzpatrick ed, Dent, London, 1994. **Extract 1**.

# *Extracts*

## (1) ABRUZZO

### Ignazio Silone, *Fontamara*, 1933

*Silone's novel about the exploitation of peasants by the rich and powerful was first published in the safety of Switzerland. The women of Fontamara (one of whom is the narrator at this point) have come to town to demand the restoration of their village stream, diverted by the ruthless Contractor, now also* podestà *or mayor. The lawyer Don Circostanza has a misplaced and carefully cultivated reputation as 'the Friend of the People'.*

The Contractor said nothing. He let the others do the talking, and smiled, with a cigar that had gone out in a corner of his mouth. It was Don Circostanza who found the solution.

'These women claim that half the stream is not enough to irrigate their land. They want more than half, at all events, that is how I interpret their wishes. So there is only one possible arrangement. The *podestà* must be left three-quarters of the water of the stream, and the three-quarters of the remainder must be left to the people of Fontamara. Thus both parties will have three-quarters, that is, each will have a little more than half. I appreciate,' he went on, 'that my proposal will inflict great hardship on the *podestà*, but I appeal to his heart as a philanthropist and public benefactor.'

The guests, having recovered from their fear, surrounded the Contractor and implored him to make this sacrifice on our behalf. After a great deal of persuasion he ended by giving in.

A sheet of paper was hurriedly produced. I saw the danger immediately.

'If there's anything to pay, you can count me out of it,' I hastened to say.

'There's nothing to pay,' the Contractor said at the top of his voice.

'Nothing to pay?' Zompa's wife whispered to me. 'If there's nothing to pay, it must be a swindle.'

'If you really want to pay, there's nothing to stop you,' I pointed out.

'Not if they threaten to put my eyes out,' she replied. 'But if there's nothing to pay it must certainly be a swindle.'

'Then it would be better if you did,' I said.

'Not if they put my eyes out,' she insisted.

The notary scribbled the terms of the agreement on a piece of paper, and after the Contractor and the communal secretary had signed it Don Circostanza added his signature as the representative of the people of Fontamara.

Then we set off for home. Actually not one of us had understood what the agreement consisted of.

'What luck there was nothing to pay,' Marietta kept repeating, 'What luck.'

## (2) ALIANO

### Carlo Levi, *Christ Stopped at Eboli*, 1945

*In the poor, barren region to which Levi was banished for his opposition to Fascism in 1935–6, he found problems too deep for easy solution but also a strength and humanity in the peasants which enabled him to retain some optimism for the future. In this extract the mayor has just treated all those villagers who have*

> not fled down the hill to work in the fields to an outpouring of his
> 'rapt and visceral eloquence' at the time of Italy's invasion of
> Abyssinia.

The gentry were all Party members, even the few like Dr Milillo who were dissenters. The Party stood for Power, as vested in the Government and the state, and they felt entitled to a share of it. For exactly the opposite reason none of the peasants were members; indeed, it was unlikely that they should belong to any political party whatever, should, by chance, another exist. They were not Fascists, just as they would never have been Conservatives or Socialists, or anything else. Such matters had nothing to do with them; they belonged to another world and they saw no sense in them. What had the peasants to do with Power, Government, and the State? The state, whatever form it might take, meant 'the fellows in Rome'. 'Everyone knows,' they said, 'that the fellows in Rome don't want us to live like human beings. There are hailstorms, landslides, droughts, malaria and . . . the state. These are inescapable evils; such there always have been and there always will be. They make us kill off our goats, they carry away our furniture, and now they're going to send us to the wars. Such is life!'

To the peasants, the state is more distant than heaven and far more of a scourge, because it is always against them. Its political tags and platforms and, indeed, the whole structure of it do not matter. The peasants do not understand them because they are couched in a different language from their own, and there is no reason why they should ever care to understand them. Their only defence against the state and the propaganda of the state is resignation, the same gloomy resignation, alleviated by no hope of paradise, that bows their shoulders under the scourges of nature.

For this reason, quite naturally, they have no conception of a political struggle; they think of it as a personal quarrel among the 'fellows in Rome'. They were not concerned with the views of the political prisoners who were in compulsory residence among them, or with the motives for their coming. They looked at them kindly and treated them like brothers because they too, for some inexplicable reason, were victims of fate.

## (3) ASPROMONTE

### Corrado Alvaro, *Revolt in Aspromonte*, 1930

*Alvaro's novel protests at the sufferings inflicted on the poor by the less poor, but finds poetry in the natural hardships and privations, as in the landscape, of his native southern Calabria.*

It is no easy life, that of the shepherds of Aspromonte, in the dead of winter when swollen streams rush down to the sea and the earth seems to float on the water. The shepherds stay in huts built of mud and sticks and sleep beside the animals. They go about in long capes with triangular hoods over their shoulders such as might have been worn by an ancient Greek god setting out upon a winter pilgrimage. The torrential streams make a deafening noise and in the clearings, amid the white snow, big black tubs, set over wood fires, steam with boiling milk curdled by a greenish ferment and a handful of wild herbs. The men standing around in their black capes and black wool suits are the only living beings among the dark surrounding mountains and the stiffly frozen trees. But even in the icy cold the nuts are ripening under the oak bark for the future delight of rooting pigs.

The men toss thick slices of bread into the tubs and draw them out with long carved wooden spoons, dripping and gleaming with a whiteness that only bread dipped in milk can acquire. Wood-carving is one of the shepherds' diversions. They cut flowering hearts into the ribs of their sweethearts' stays and sculpture figures out of olive branches to decorate their wives' distaffs. With red-hot spits they make holes in their reed flutes. They crouch at the entrance to their huts, looking across the shining white snow and waiting for the day when they can go down to the plain and hang up their capes and flasks on a tree of the lowlands. The new moon will break the cycle of rains and they will go down to the village, where there are houses with solid walls, heavy with the talk and sighs of women. The village is warm and its houses are huddled together like the sheep in a sheepfold. On fair days the oxen climb up the steep, rocky path like the animals in a Christmas play; white and well-built as they are, they seem larger than the trees, almost like huge, prehistoric beasts. . . .

Neither the sheep nor the oxen nor the black pigs belong to the shepherds. They are the property of the local gentry, who are waiting to send them to market to the whiskered traders who come from the coast.

## (4) Taranto

### George Sandys, *The Relation of a Journey*, 1615

*Calabria and southern Apulia were for centuries little known to outsiders; they were likely locations for such terrors and wonders as the tarantula and the tarantella.*

Hereabout [on the west coast of Calabria] are great store of tarantulas: a serpent peculiar to this country, and taking the name from the city of Tarentum. Some hold them to be of the kind of spiders, others of efts [newts]; but they are greater than the one, and less than the other, and (if that were a tarantula which I have seen) not greatly resembling either. For the head of this was small, the legs slender and knotty, the body light, the tail spiny, and the colour dun, intermixed with spots of a sullied white. They lurk in sinks, and privies, and abroad in the slimy filth between furrows; for which cause the country people do reap in boots. The sting is deadly, and the contrary operations thereof most miraculous. For some so stung are still oppressed with a leaden sleep; others are vexed with continued waking, some fling up and down, and others are extremely lazy. He sweats, a second vomits, a third runs mad. Some weep continually, and some laugh continually, and that is the most usual. Insomuch that it is an ordinary saying to a man that is extraordinarily merry, that he hath been stung by a tarantula. . . . The merry, the mad, and otherwise actively disposed, are cured by music; at least it is the cause, in that it incites them to dance indefatigably: for by labour and sweat the poison is expelled. And music also by a certain high excellency hath been found by experience to stir in the sad and drowsy so strange an alacrity, that they have wearied the spectators with continued dancing. In the meantime the pain hath assuaged, the infection being driven from the heart; and the mind released of her sufferance. If the music intermit, the malady renews, but again continued, and it vanisheth.

# Biographies and important works

ALVARO, Corrado (1895–1956), novelist and journalist, was born at San Luca, on Aspromonte. Although much of his adult life was spent away from Calabria (he was for a time a foreign correspondent of *La Stampa*), he was known chiefly for *Gente in Aspromonte* (*Revolt in Aspromonte*, 1930). This brief novel tells the story of the successive misfortunes which come upon the family of the shepherd Argirò as much as a result of the cruelty or indifference of the landowning Mezzatesta family as from natural hardships. In the mythic or wish-fulfilling end of the book Argirò's son Antonello takes the law into his own hands. This is why the English translation of the book is called *Revolt in Aspromonte*. But the *gente* – 'people' – of the title are important; many of the book's most effective scenes are evocations of the rough life of the peasants or the pampered pettiness of their exploiters: the bloated old Filippo Mezzatesta, for instance, 'breathing hard and leaning on the shoulders of two robust maidservants', the head of one of whom he uses as a support during 'the crucial stage of pulling on his trousers'. *Gente in Aspromonte* has little of the social depth or political cogency of the southern novels of Carlo Levi) or Ignazio Silone), but unlike them was actually published in Fascist Italy: it made as provocative a statement about conditions in Calabria as was possible without incurring censorship.

DOUGLAS, Norman (1868–1952), of Scottish and German family, entered the Foreign Office and was third secretary in St. Petersburg in 1894–6 until he left both Russia and the service in the wake of a sexual scandal (one of a number in which he was to be involved, first heterosexual and then homosexual). Douglas spent much of the rest of his life in Italy, mainly in Florence (where he lived for most of 1919–37), and Capri, his home for parts of 1903–12 and again in his last years. His travel-books include *Siren Land*, 1911 (on Capri and the Bay of Naples) and *Old Calabria*, 1915 (the result mainly of a brief tour of Calabria in the summer of 1909), idiosyncratic in structure and style, by turns erudite and ironic, plain-spoken and ornately wrought. *South Wind*, 1917, is a 'conversation-novel' set on an island with resemblances to Capri.

Douglas' hedonist philosophy is not only explicitly stated in his books but made evident in their delight in language, in people (as objects for both love and hate), topography, and knowledge – Douglas prided himself, with some justice, on his expertise in natural history and geology as well as the more usual classical topics.

FREDERICK II (1194–1250), of the house of Hohenstaufen, was king of Sicily from 1198, king of the Germans from 1215, and Holy Roman Emperor from 1220. Much of his reign was spent in contention with the papacy, attempts to consolidate his vast empire, and the suppression of rebellion. In the tradition of his grandfather Roger II of Sicily Frederick was tolerant towards and much interested in the scientific and philosophical culture of his Arab and Jewish subjects, but his reputation as an intellectual has, David Abulafia argues in his biography, often been exaggerated.

Five of the emperor's Provençal-inspired love-poems survive. (These are part of a larger body of work in this vein produced at his court by the 'Sicilian School', most spiritedly by Giacomo da Lentino (d. c.1245). In prose he wrote the more exceptional, keenly observed *De arte venandi cum avibus* (*The Art of Falconry*), c.1229, unusually early in its empirical emphasis.

Frederick, sometimes known as *Stupor Mundi*, 'the Wonder of the World', remained a familiar figure in legend, appearing for instance in several stories of the anonymous *Novellino* (*The Hundred Old Tales*), c.1280–1300, and in the traditional tale of Castel del Monte.

GISSING, George (1857–1903), is best known for *New Grub Street*, 1891, and other 'naturalistic' novels, but was also an assiduous reader of classical history and literature. His journey to Calabria was motivated chiefly by a desire to see what was left of the Greek and Roman civilization familiar from his reading. The sparseness of the remains, delays through illness at Crotone, and the general lack of interest in ancient sites among the Calabrians, contribute to the melancholy, wistful tone of much of *By the Ionian Sea*, 1901. While encounters with local fishermen, innkeepers, servants, the doctor at Crotone, are thoughtfully narrated, Gissing's main interests and manner here are fairly summed up by the book's closing words: 'and, as I looked my last on the Ionian Sea, I wished it were mine to wander endlessly amid the silence of the ancient world, today and all its sounds forgotten.'

LEAR, Edward (1812–88), landscape painter and nonsense poet, lived chiefly in southern Europe after 1837 and travelled also in the

Middle East and India. In 1870 he settled in San Remo. *Journals of a Landscape Painter in Southern Calabria*, published with lithographic plates in 1852, records Lear's tour of 1847 with characteristic attention to both the picturesque and the absurd.

LEVI, CARLO (1902–75), novelist and painter, was born and educated in Turin, where he qualified in medicine. As a result of anti-Fascist activities, Levi was sent in internal exile to the remote villages of Basilicata in 1935–6. He was confined first at Grassano and then at Aliano, which becomes the 'Gagliano' of *Cristo si è fermato a Eboli* (*Christ Stopped at Eboli*), 1945.

The novel – or quasi-fictional narrative – has been immensely popular in Italy and abroad since its first publication in 1945. (Francesco Rosi's film version appeared in 1979.) Its social and political analysis and protest are born of the author's passionate personal response to the people among whom he lived. Levi is fascinated by the peasants' powers of endurance, their kindness to him as a fellow sufferer, and their belief both in magic and in his ability to give them medical help. He describes individuals in considerable detail but makes them monumental, larger than life, a standing reproach to those who, century after century, have trodden such people down.

The only remedies available were indifference or, if possible, emigration. For those who remained, Christ – and with him humane relations between human beings, and 'hope, the link between cause and effect, reason and history' – stopped at Eboli, where the road and the railway turn from the coast towards desolate Basilicata.

*Cristo si è fermato a Eboli* was written in 1943–4 in Florence when, says Levi's introduction, 'savage death' roamed the streets. Writing the book was 'an act of defence that routed death.' After the war Levi was prominent in left-wing journalism and politics and continued to explore the suffering of the deprived in works including *Le parole sono pietre* (*Words Are Stones*), 1955, an account of Sicily.

OVID – Publius Ovidius Naso (43 B.C.-A.D. 17) – was born in Sulmo, now Sulmona. He studied rhetoric in Rome and briefly held minor public office there before dedicating the rest of his life to poetry. In A.D. 8 he was banished by Augustus to Tomis on the Black Sea, possibly in connection or involvement with the adultery of the emperor's grand-daughter, Julia, and died there.

Ovid's principal poems are *Amores* (sophisticated love poems first published in a lost version of c.20 B.C.; c.3–2 B.C.); *Heroides* (letters of unhappy heroines, c.1 B.C.-5 A.D.); *Ars Amatoria* (*The Art of Love*), c.1 B.C., semi-serious, detailed advice on seduction which is known to have been disapproved of by Augustus; *Metamorphoses*, c.A.D. 2–10, a long poem of mythological transformations (including the stories of Pyramus and Thisbe, Daedalus and Icarus, and Jason and Medea); and *Tristia* (*Sorrows*), A.D. 8–12, laments from exile. Of these the richest in language, texture, and influence, is the *Metamorphoses*. Its stories are culled from, and involve parody of and subtle allusion to, a very wide range of Greek and Roman authors. The poem is loosely defined as an epic but varies the model of Homer and Virgil to the point of unrecognisability, is concerned with the divine but principally in its effect on and mingling with the human, and excels both in its witty virtuosity and its exploration of states of extreme anguish. This poem of – metamorphic – variousness was open to allegory (as in the medieval *Ovide moralisé*) and provided plots, images, and even tones of voice for Renaissance literature and especially Marlowe and Shakespeare.

SANDYS, George (1578–1644), travelled in Italy, Turkey, Egypt, and Palestine and wrote *A Relation of a Journey Begun An. Dom. 1610*, 1615. This account was popular enough to to go through five further editions by 1673. Between 1621 and 1631 Sandys was in America as treasurer of the Virginia Company, member of the Council of Virginia, and plantation owner. His translation of the *Metamorphoses* of Ovid appeared in 1626.

SILONE, Ignazio (1900–78), was born at Pescina dei Marsi as Secondo Tranquilli. The name Silone was inspired by Quintus Pompaedius Silo, who led the Marsi to victory over the Romans in 90 B.C., helping to obtain civil rights for his people and other allies of Rome. Most of Silone's family died in an earthquake at Pescina in 1915. He was a founder member of the Italian Communist Party in 1921, and took an important part in clandestine operations after its banning by Mussolini in 1926, as well as editing party newspapers. He was forced to spend many years in exile. While he was in Switzerland in 1929–30 he broke with the Communists, partly in response to the Comintern's expulsion of Trotsky.

His best known works include *Fontamara*, 1933 (not published in Italy until 1949), *Pane e vino* (*Bread and Wine*, 1936; revised as *Vino e pane*, 1955), and his contribution to *The God That Failed: Six Studies in Communism*, edited by Richard Crossman, 1950.

*Fontamara* concerns the sufferings of the Abruzzese *cafoni*, the poor peasants whose name is 'a term of derision and contempt' but may become a term of honour 'when suffering ceases to be shameful in my country'. The newly appointed Fascist *podestà* (mayor) of the local administrative centre, an entrepreneur known as 'the Contractor', is one of the main agents of injustices like their being bullied and hoodwinked out of the water which has always irrigated their land (*fontamara* means 'bitter spring'). But Silone is at pains to show that Fascism only exacerbates the age-old problems of the abuse of power, whether by landowners, the clergy, or the lawyer and apparent 'Friend of the People' Don Circostanza, who gives the Fontamaresi fine words but works only to his own and the other exploiters' advantage.

*Fontamara* is narrated in turn by three villagers, a man and a woman and their son, whom Silone imagines as having escaped to join him in exile. Their language is simple and direct (although, as Silone points out, rendered in Italian rather than dialect), as befits the starkness of the story they have to tell. Silone's imperative was, as he put it in *The God That Failed*, 'to bear witness'.

# SICILY

'On one side stretched a bare and desolate landscape, the realm of the sulphur mines; on the other side, vineyards, olive groves, almond trees – untidy and beautiful.'
*Leonardo Sciascia,*
*Sicily as Metaphor*

For Phoenicians and Greeks Sicily was the 'America of antiquity', as Giuseppe Tomasi di Lampedusa says in *Il gattopardo* (*The Leopard*), 1958. The colonists were attracted to the island (already populated by the Siculi, Sicani, and Elymians) by its convenient position for trade and war – between Italy and Africa and between the eastern and western Mediterranean – and by its extraordinary fertility, the subject of myth and poetry since at least the time of Homer. Tradition identifies as Sicily, in *The Odyssey*, Book 9, the island of the Cyclopes who, although they are too savage to tend the land, are provided by nature with all the wheat, barley, and vines they need. And the corn-goddess Demeter and her daughter Persephone were much venerated in Sicily. Traditionally it was in the (once) violet-filled meadows by Lake Pergusa, near **Enna**, in the very centre or 'navel' of Sicily, that Persephone was seized and abducted by Hades, god of the Underworld, to be his queen. Demeter, as she wandered in search of her daughter, made the world barren, a state of affairs which prevailed until Hades allowed Persephone to return to the upper world annually for the months of harvest. Like the corn, she continued to spend most of the year beneath the surface of the earth, germinating; but in celebration of her seasonal re-appearance, the historian Diodorus Siculus says, 'we are told' that the flowers near Enna bloom all year and their sweet odour puts hunting dogs off the scent. (Most of the stone from the city's great fifth-century B.C. temple of Demeter was put to other uses in the Middle Ages, when Enna became known as Castrogiovanni, but the spirit of Demeter's cult still survives in such widespread local customs as the offering to the Madonna of the first ears of ripe wheat).

Other Greek myths (sometimes, as probably in the case of Demeter

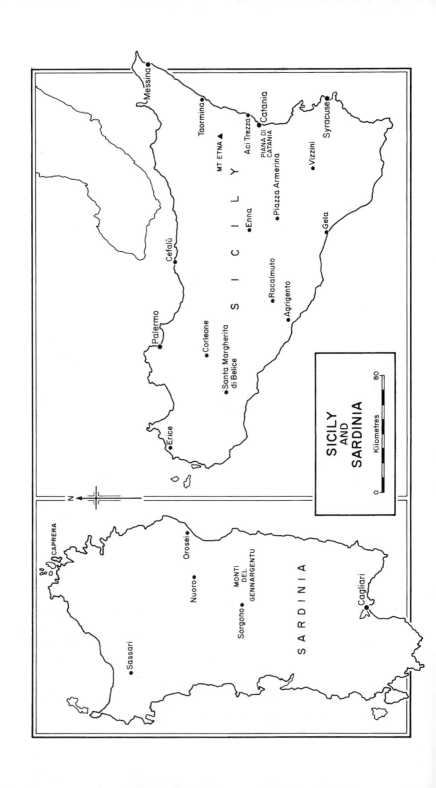

SICILY
AND
SARDINIA

Kilometres

0                    80

N

**SICILY**

Messina

Taormina

Aci Trezza
Catania
PIANA DI
CATANIA

MT ETNA ▲

Syracuse

Enna

Piazza Armerina

Vizzini

Cefalù

Gela

Racalmuto

Agrigento

Palermo

Corleone

Santa Margherita
di Belice

Erice

**SARDINIA**

CAPRERA

Orosei

Nuoro

MONTI
DEL
GENNARGENTU

Sorgono

Cagliari

Sassari

and Persephone, assimilated to indigenous traditions) are associated with Sicily: Odysseus must sail between the rock-dwelling six-headed monster Scylla and the whirlpool Charybdis in, legend says, the **Straits of Messina**. Scylla eats six of the ill-fated crew while they gaze terrified at the swirling vortex of Charybdis. The archetypal maker and craftsman Daedalus flew on his waxen wings from Crete to Sicily and wrought a golden honeycomb to honour Aphrodite at her temple (later replaced by a castle) in **Erice**. The nymph Arethusa fled from the god of the river Alpheus, in Arcadia, to the island of **Ortygia**, where she was changed into a spring, the **Fonte Aretusa**; he pursued her beneath the sea and finally flowed into the spring. More solid traces were left by the descendants of real Greek settlers, including, amongst much else, the remains of some of the largest and richest of all ancient temples at **Agrigento**.

The Sicilian city-states, caught in the path of warring Rome and Carthage, passed under Roman control in the third century B.C. Fertile Sicily was a valuable possession, 'the granary of the Republic, the nurse at whose breast the Roman people is fed', as the statesman Cato the Censor (234–149 B.C.) counselled all to remember. A tenth of the corn went to Rome (until the reign of Augustus, when alternative sources became available, and probably again later as the empire contracted). There were many other taxes, levies and restrictions. Governors, on their brief but lucrative tours of duty, lived magnificently; the wholesale extortion of Gaius Verres in 73–71 B.C. was only one of the more extreme examples of malpractice. Cicero (◊Rome), who exposed Verres' crimes after gathering prosecution evidence in Sicily in 70 B.C., discovered that he had even stolen the very ancient, very sacred bronze cult statue from the shrine of Demeter (or, to the Romans, Ceres) in Enna. As often in later centuries, local sentiment had been ignored. (In this case Roman religion itself was also affronted, as Cicero was not slow to point out.) The Sicilians believed, says Cicero, that their crops and fruit were failing (in fact the result of 'the many and various wrongs done them by Verres') because of the sacrilege against Ceres. It was as if 'the king of the shades' had returned to carry away the goddess herself, not her daughter.

The former Governor was able, apparently, to make off into exile with most of his ill-gotten gains before he could be convicted. Someone at least as rich as Verres must have built what was once Roman Sicily's most spectacular construction, the vast palace of Casale, south-west of **Piazza Armerina** in central Sicily. Here survive 3,500 sq.m. of richly detailed polychrome mosaics of the labours of Hercules, Ulysses (Odysseus) with the Cyclops Polyphemus, a chariot-race in the Circus Maximus in Rome and a mock race with children's carts drawn by birds, erotic scenes, hunting scenes, cupids, griffins, hippocamps, African wildlife being shipped for the arena. Possibly this was the palace of the co-emperor (286–305 A.D.) Maximian or his son

Maxentius, but more likely, Roger Wilson concludes in his study of the site, a man of senatorial rank from Rome with a passion for, and probably a business interest in, transporting exotic animals.

After the Romans came more invaders: Vandal, Byzantine, Arab, Norman. The Arabs introduced agricultural improvements and brought their architectural and scientific skills to the court of the Norman kings (see **Palermo**). Splendid mosaics adorned the walls of Roger II's monumental cathedral (founded 1131) below the rock of **Cefalù**. But the problems of Sicily, so often discussed and argued over by its modern inhabitants and writers, were about to increase. Deforestation was already beginning; later this would cause erosion and landslides (most dangerously at Agrigento in 1966). Less avoidably, the island continued to be shaken by earthquakes and volcanic eruptions: Etna devastated **Catania** in 1669 as did an earthquake in 1693; **Messina** (also victim of a terrible plague in 1743) was badly damaged in the earthquakes of 1783 and 1908 (when 84,000 people died). The economy also suffered from the absence of an enterprising mercantile class and the lack of good roads until well after 1800. The peasants were kept poor by the system of *latifundia* – large estates in the hands of single landowners – originally introduced by the Romans and not legislated against successfully until the 1950s. After the Norman period foreign domination – mainly Spanish – became more irksome. Taxes were high. Under Aragonese and Habsburg rule in the late 15th and 16th century the Inquisition became firmly established, enforcing orthodoxy in contrast to the policy of tolerance pursued in the Arab and Norman period, and helping to isolate Sicily from the Renaissance and the Reformation.

The Prince of Salina, in Giuseppe Tomasi di Lampedusa's *Il gatto-pardo* (*The Leopard*), 1958, diagnosed Sicily's ills and provoked a storm of controversy. Many Sicilians were angered, while others felt it to be only too true, as the Prince explains to a baffled Piedmontese official of the newly united Italy in 1862, that the Sicilians are worn out after 25 centuries as a colony and only want to sleep; 'our sensuality is a hankering for oblivion, our shooting and knifing a hankering for death; our languor, our exotic ices, a hankering for voluptuous immobility, that is for death again'. They have been formed so by 'events outside our control': by 'this landscape which knows no mean between sensuous sag and hellish drought; which is never petty, never ordinary, never relaxed' and the 'six times 30 days of sun sheer down on our heads' in a summer 'as long and glum as a Russian winter'; by foreign rulers – obeyed, detested, misunderstood – who could express themselves only through 'works of art we found enigmatic and taxes we found only too intelligible, and which they spent elsewhere'.

Such remarks were at first widely seen as exaggerated, ahistorical and defeatist – as in part they clearly are; they are intended as the utterance of a particular individual in a particular historical context rather than a simple declaration by the author. Leonardo Sciascia◊, soon to emerge as the leading Sicilian novelist and commentator, was among those who disapproved. But Sciascia later announced that he had misjudged Lampedusa; his experience in politics and in thinking and writing about the mafia brought him, too, closer to pessimism about the island's future. In one of the interviews published in France as *La Sicile comme métaphore* (*Sicily as Metaphor*), 1979, Sciascia states his belief 'that a world of liberty and justice can be realized, however imperfectly. But the whole of Sicilian history is a history of defeats – defeats of reason, defeats of reasonable men'. Scepticism is the appropriate response. The investigators of the murders in Sciascia's novels *Il giorno della civetta* (*The Day of the Owl*), 1961 and *A ciascuno il suo* (*To Each His Own*), 1966, lack the scepticism necessary to cope with a society in which there are wheels within wheels, the agents of law and order are not always what they appear, and sexual, family, political, and mafioso motivations and identities are inextricable. It is difficult for an outsider like Captain Bellodi, the policeman from Parma in *Il giorno della civetta*, to comprehend the depth of mafia roots, the complexity of the rivalries and deals between the different groups or *cosche* (Sicilian *cosca*, 'the thick cluster of artichoke leaves'), and the tendency of many Sicilians to admire the men of blood in spite of themselves.

An organised mafia seems to have originated in the late 19th century. (But any statement on the subject tends still to be hotly disputed; there have always been those who have denied the existence of the organisation.) Before this, mafia was a positive term associated with qualities of masculine assertiveness. In the 1960s, 'many *mafiosi* still appeared to enjoy some popular support. In a cruel world, they could pose as realists' (Denis Mack Smith). 'When I denounce the Mafia I suffer at the same time', said Sciascia; 'the residues of *sentire mafioso*, in me as in all Sicilians, are still there. Thus in struggling against the Mafia, I struggle with myself and it hurts'.

Many Sicilian writers – Verga◊, Pirandello◊, Vittorini◊, for instance – have spent long periods in Rome and further north. But for all the problems and complications, the poverty and violence and at times hopelessness, they have felt impelled to return to Sicily either literally or, often taking up the problems and exploring the complications, in their fiction. Others, including Sciascia, remained longer at home, which for him was firstly in **Racalmuto**, north of Agrigento, poised between two Sicilies: 'on one side stretched a bare and desolate landscape, the realm of the sulphur mines; on the other side, vineyards, olive groves, almond trees – untidy and beautiful'. Here he was born, returned in later years each summer to write, and in the 1950s tried to teach hungry children about the Renaissance and the Risorgimento. They were quicker at arithmetic, since they ran errands for the better-off, and geography (almost all of them went on to follow the traditional solution to Sicilian problems, emigration).

## SYRACUSE

Syracuse was founded by colonists from Corinth in 733 B.C. Its natural attractions included the magnificent sweep of the **Great Harbour** and the sheltering rocky island of **Ortygia**. One of its periods of greatest prosperity was initiated by the defeat of the Carthaginians at Himera in 480 B.C. – long before Rome was a power to be reckoned with – by Gelon, Tyrant of Syracuse, and Theron of Akragas (**Agrigento**). The same year, Gelon replaced an earlier sanctuary on Ortygia with the Temple of Athena, which has survived in good condition thanks to its later incorporation in the **Cathedral**. Other rulers embellished the city with further rich temples, a theatre, and successive fortifications commanding the long ridge to the west of Syracuse at the Euryalus citadel (**Castello Eurialo**). Gelon's successors also provided patronage or subject matter for the foremost Greek writers of the time.

Gelon's brother, Hieron I (ruled 478–467 B.C.) was summed up by the historian Diodorus Siculus) as violent, miserly and ignoble, but he cut a rather different figure among some of his contemporaries. His repeated victories in horse and chariot-racing at the Olympic and Pythian games in Greece – vital for his prestige in the mother-country – were celebrated, together with his military prowess, in the odes of Pindar (518–c.446 B.C.). Hieron also seems to have invited the tragic playwright Aeschylus (525–456 B.C.) to visit his court. When the Tyrant re-founded Katane (**Catania**) as Aetna, Aeschylus produced a play (now lost) for the occasion, *The Women of Aetna*, and he may also have been involved in productions – in an earlier, simpler form of the Syracuse theatre – of his Prometheus plays. He died in 456 B.C. at **Gela**, on the south coast, from which Hieron's family originated. An improbable but unforgettable tradition holds that an eagle, mistaking the playwright's bald head for a stone, fatally dropped a tortoise on it.

Tyrants were for much of the fifth century discarded in favour of a 'democratic' regime. Under this Syracuse scored perhaps its most signal military success when, in 413, it resoundingly defeated a large and well-equipped Athenian force which, two years previously, had invaded with 134 triremes. Thucydides, the Athenian historian, describes the progressive destruction of his compatriots' army, fleet (trapped in the Great Harbour) and morale. In all Hellenic history, he concludes, this was 'to the victors the most brilliant of successes, to the vanquished the most calamitous of defeats; for they were utterly and entirely defeated; their sufferings were on an enormous scale . . . and, out of many, only few returned' (*The Peloponnesian War*, c.430–400 B.C.). As many as 7000 prisoners were consigned to cramped stone quarries, now the Latomie del Paradiso garden, east of the Greek theatre. Their ration was, according to Thucydides, a pint of corn and half a pint of water a day, and many died of disease, summer heat or autumn cold before the survivors were finally released or sold as slaves after about ten weeks. But according to one story perhaps designed to assert an ideal of panhellenic fellow-feeling rather at odds with this treatment, those who could recite verses from the plays of Euripides were released.

Tyranny returned with Dionysius I (ruled 405–367 B.C.), a successful warlord who ruled most of Sicily. He also wrote poems and plays which were much derided in antiquity (justly, to judge by the few surviving fragments). Plato apparently came to Syracuse during his reign, but left in disgust at the amount of unphilosophical gorging at the proverbial 'Syracusan table'. Dionysius contributed to Plato's image of the archetypal unjust ruler in *Politeia* (*The Republic*), c.375 B.C. (Brian Caven, in his life of the ruler, argues that he has been judged rather too harshly on Plato's word: he found in Syracuse all the vices his philosophy told him to expect.) The story of his later visits to the court of Dionysius II (367–44) is told in the seventh letter of the work known as Plato's *Epistles*. This may not be by Plato himself but is widely regarded as true to the facts at least as he would have interpreted them. (It is perhaps the work of a disciple.) It was at the urgent request of Dion, a powerful kinsman of the Tyrant, who had studied with Plato in Athens, that he agreed to attempt to turn the young monarch into a philosopher-king, the only figure who, in Platonic philosophy, could hope to impose just rule. He had made little headway in this design when Dionysius banished Dion. Plato wanted to follow his friend at once, but the tyrant wanted him to stay and 'the requests of tyrants are coupled, as we know, with compulsory powers'. He was moved to accommodation near the royal residence. According to Plutarch's version of events ('The Life of Dion', in *Bioi paralleloi* (*Parallel Lives*, c.105–20) Dionysius was seized with such tyrannical affection for the older man that he required that 'in return of his kindness' he should 'love him only, and attend to him above all other men'. 'This extravagant affection was a great trouble to Plato, for it was accompanied with petulant and jealous humours, like the fond passion of those who are deeply in love'. Dionysius wanted passionately to study Plato's philosophy, 'and yet he was ashamed of it with those who spoke against it and professed to think it would ruin him'. There were many such speakers: some no doubt were worried that never again would there be at court, as Plutarch claims there once had been, a 90-day orgy of 'drinking, singing, dancing, and buffoonery'; others feared that Dion intended to distract Dionysius with philosophy and then seize his domains.

Eventually Plato obtained permission to return to Athens. But somehow – motivated by wounded *amour-propre*, the Epistle suggests – the tyrant persuaded him to come back several years later. He even listened to Plato – once – and told him that he was already very knowledgeable about philosophy. When Dionysius deprived Dion of agreed income from property, Plato 'perceived clearly what kind of love Dionysius had for philosophy'. A quarrel soon blew up between the tyrant and the sage who, apparently, had the effrontery to contradict him in public. On a pretext, Plato was sent now to live outside the safety of the acropolis of Syracuse. Here fractious mercenaries threatened his life; in 360 B.C. his friend Archytas of Taras (Taranto) despatched a trireme to rescue him.

Plato regretted the civil war which broke out soon afterwards on Dion's angry return to the island to try whether swords would influence Dionysius more than words, but remained convinced that Dion's aims were fundamentally his own, that he would, had he not been murdered by former allies after briefly taking power in Syracuse, have aspired to the status of philosopher-king. After Dion's death (353 B.C.) civil war continued. Order was restored only by the Corinthian Timoleon, who arrived from the mother-city on Syracuse's appeal in 345 and later led the citizens to a new victory over the ever-menacing Carthaginians. Meanwhile Dionysius II travelled in the opposite direction to live (hostile sources rather gleefully assure us) in sordid poverty in Corinth.

There is archaeological evidence of much re-building in eastern Sicily in Timoleon's time. A longer period of peace – made possible by a prescient decision to court Roman rather than Carthaginian friendship – and public construction occurred during the reign of Hieron II (265–215 B.C.), who was responsible for many of the extant ancient remains. He much expanded the **Greek Theatre** of Aeschylus' day (it was adapted further for gladiatorial combat by the Romans, while plays transferred to the smaller Roman theatre, before the opening of the large Roman amphitheatre in the third century A.D.). Nearby, some time after 241, he built his Nymphaeum and long sacrificial **Altar of Hieron II** (once 40 feet high). He was saluted in verse by Theocritus◊, and took an interest in the work of the great mathematician Archimedes◊, to whom he was related. Plutarch ('The Life of Marcellus', in *Parallel Lives*) tells the traditional story of how Hieron, astonished by Archimedes' claim that he could move any given weight with any given force and its proof – the lifting of a heavy ship by means of a system of pulleys – commissioned him to build engines of defence and attack. Hieron never had cause to use them, but when, after his death, Syracuse did fall foul of the now apparently invincible Romans, the machinery and its maker came into their own. The Romans attacked by land and sea but were beaten back by repeated almost Spielbergian displays of Archimedes' technical skill (Extract 7). In the end, says Plutarch, the Romans took the city by storming an ill-defended tower while the Syracusans were 'given over to wine and sport' during a festival of Artemis. The general Marcellus 'is said to have wept much' as he looked down from a high place on 'the beautiful and spacious city below' which was about to be pillaged;

he would not contemplate razing it or enslaving its free-born citizens, but neither he nor any of his captains dared try to deprive the legionaries of their plunder. But Marcellus mourned above all the death of Archimedes. Plutarch gives several versions of how this is said to have occurred. The most popular recounts how he was so intent on working out a mathematical problem that he did not so much as notice that the Romans had entered the city. While he was transported with contemplation, a soldier came upon him and ordered him to go with him to Marcellus. His answer – that he must work out the problem first – so enraged the Roman that he ran him through. Archimedes' absorption was apparently usual: he was so divinely possessed by his love of his work that he would forget to eat and would bathe only when forcibly carried to the bath. There he would 'trace geometrical figures in the ashes of the fire, and diagrams in the oil on his body'. Plutarch's Archimedes is no doubt largely legendary, an archetype of the wondrous and eccentric man of science; but he was clearly a great mathematician and engineer, one more instance of the richness of Greek Syracusan culture.

## ETNA AND CATANIA

In myth the tremendous bulk of **Mount Etna** weighs upon a tormented creature vanquished by the gods – the hundred-headed monster Typhon or the giant Enceladus. The volcano's fires and rumblings are the victim's restless or angry movements or, according to a different tradition, the work of the smith and fire-god Vulcan. Virgil's Aeneas (◊Naples and Campania), who reports the Enceladus theory, describes the fury of eruption as the loud-roaring mountain expels black smoke, boiling lava and balls of flame which 'lick the stars', and the rocks which are its very entrails.

Aeneas' Trojans take refuge in a forest, unable, through the muffling mists, to see the cause of the commotion. Since the next day they have to flee the Cyclops Polyphemus with all possible speed, they have no chance to investigate further. Among those who did ascend Etna in ancient times the best known is the philosopher Empedocles◊. Legend has it that he hurled himself to his death in the crater; having apparently disappeared on the numinous heights of Etna, he would be taken for a god. But the ruse failed because the volcano threw up one of his bronze sandals. Empedocles was much on the mind of Patrick Brydone◊ (*A Tour Through Sicily and Malta*, 1773, Extract 4) when he journeyed up from the village of Nicolosi to the **Torre del Filosofo** which tradition had made his. The view from here was fit for a philosopher, indeed 'the mind enjoys a degree of serenity here, that even few philosophers, I believe, could ever boast'. But 'in the very midst of these meditations, my philosophy was at once overset, and in a moment I found myself relapsed into a poor miserable mortal'.

Brydone's leg had folded under him on the ice 'and your poor philosopher was obliged to hop on one leg, with two men supporting him,
for several miles over the snow; and our wags here allege, that he left
the greatest part of his philosophy behind him, for the use of Empedocles' heirs and successors'.

William Ewart Gladstone (1809–98), the future British Prime Minister, was not deterred so easily from the 'higher uses' of the wonderful sight of Etna's rolling and flying lava (*The Gladstone Diaries 1833–
9*). 'Standing in such a presence of the aweful functions and powers of
Nature, the material form of Providence, a man finds that he is in
respect of his physical being, a plaything in her hands, a feather upon
the wind'. Therefore he should desire to live more in the spirit, 'that
part of himself which is more subtle than the flame' and which can be
made purer than it by God. Furthermore, 'these terrible orifices of the
subterranean fire' portend the Last Judgement: they are meant:

> 'to give a palpable assurance to our faith in the declarations of
> scripture concerning the final conflagration of the heavens and
> the earth that now are. We look upon beds of lava which we know
> to be the graves of cities, and upon the ever fresh and fertile
> caverns of the mountains: we see the match and the combustibles,
> and nothing is hidden from us but the Hand, and the Time, which
> are to bring them together.'

Volcanic activity has left indelible traces on the countryside and towns
around Etna. The eruption of 1669 had, says Brydone, 'laid waste the
whole country betwixt' Etna and Catania, 'scaled the walls of that city,
and poured its flaming torrent' into the sea, reducing 30,000 people to
beggary, forming hills where once were valleys, and filling up 'a large
deep lake'. Maps, properties, livelihoods were mercilessly rearranged
by the lava. In one of Giovanni Verga's short stories a man already in
financial difficulties loses everything as the black mountain looms over
his vineyard, 'smoking, collapsing here and there, with a rattling of
stones as if a mountain of broken pots were slipping down'. Trees flare
up, then one by one the images of the saints which have been desperately set up in the path of the lava, then the vineyard. There is no
point in saving the casks and implements, the owner points out to his
man; 'I shall have nothing left now, there'll be nothing to put in the
casks'. (*I galantuomini* ('The Gentry'), in *Novelle rusticane* (*Little Novels
of Sicily*), 1883.)

Verga's birthplace can be visited in Catania at 8 Via Sant' Anna,
where exhibits include manuscripts of some of his novels and tales.
Here too, in 1922, he died. But there was also an ancestral home, the
Palazzo Verga at **Vizzini**, a hill-town to the south-west of Catania, and
here or in the surrounding countryside he and his family often spent
the summers. The setting for a number of his works is the **Piana di
Catania**, the low-lying plain west and south of the city, in the 1880s a

place of dire poverty, extreme summer heat, and pestilential marsh-land (Extract 6). Etna glowers ominously in the background, as it does in one of Verga's other most famous settings, **Aci Trezza**, then a small fishing village, whose Malavoglia family lose their boat and their house but not their self-respect in *I Malavoglia* (*The House By the Medlar Tree*), 1881. The hostility of the volcanic land and the sea are com-bined in the story, first found in Homer's *Odyssey*, that the rocks off Aci Trezza – the Isole Ciclopi – were hurled there by the angry Cyclops Polyphemus at the escaping Odysseus.

## AGRIGENTO

Agrigento was once Akragas, which was founded, probably in 581 B.C., by colonists from nearby Gela and from Rhodes and other islands. Its first known Tyrant was Phalaris (ruled 571–56), who became proverbial for cruelty; allegedly he roasted people alive in a bronze bull, starting – with grim justice – with its maker. After Pha-laris' time Akragas was more happily famous for its philosopher Empedocles◊ and for its wealth and luxury, the product of fertile lands and the successes against the Carthaginians of the more civilised tyrant Theron (488–72). Diodorus Siculus◊ records examples of the wealth of Akragas at this time: an Olympic victor conducted home into the city by three hundred chariots, each drawn by two white horses; the general use by the citizens of 'exceedingly delicate clothing and gold ornaments' and even oil-flasks and strigils of silver or gold; a noble wedding celebrated, at a signal from the acropolis (occupied now by modern Agrigento) in a blaze of brushwood fires from every temple, courtyard, and shop so that, as a procession of torch-bearers followed the bride through the streets, 'the city was filled with light'. What is left of the glory of this sizeable city – taking in the area both of much of the modern town and of the present **Valle dei Templi** to the south – are the remains of some of the grandest temples in the Greek world, a constant reminder to later dwellers of their dwindled fortunes or of the transience of all earthly power and wealth. Salvatore Quasi-modo◊ contemplates the sad windy ancient place in his poem 'Strada di Agrigentum' ('Street in Agrigentum'), 1936 (Extract 3). His 'doleful telamons' and 'giants thrust down from the sky' are inspired mainly by the huge *telamon* (one of the male figures, once 25 feet high which, together with concealed iron beams, supported the architrave) now prone among the tumbled, earthquake-stricken and plundered ruins of the enormous **Temple of Olympian Zeus**. (A copy of the giant has now replaced the original, which is to be seen in the Museo Regionale Archeologico, as is a model reconstruction of the temple.)

In 406 B.C., when Zeus' temple was still unfinished, Akragas was sacked by the Carthaginians. It never fully recovered. Its doom was brought on, ancient moralists liked to feel, by its love of luxury.

Diodorus claims that when the city was under siege a decree was passed that guards at their posts must have no more than 'one mattress, one cover, one sheepskin, and two pillows'. ('Two' pillows is the sort of detail an unfriendly source would be particularly pleased to supply.) 'When such was their most rigorous kind of bedding, one can get an idea of the luxury which prevailed in their living generally'. After re-settlement and further vicissitudes Akragas survived as the Roman Agrigentum, which in turn became the Arab Kerkent, whence the later Girgenti until the adoption of the modern name in 1927 as part of Mussolini's campaign to reassert *Romanitas*.

Girgenti was a pale shadow of Akragas. Luigi Pirandello, in his novel *I vecchi e i giovani* (*The Old and the Young*), 1908, remembers it as a place of narrow, steep, and dirty lanes, bad smells, women on doorsteps 'watching the same people' and 'listening to the same quarrels'. This was, of course, ideal material for a writer of fiction and plays. But a more profound influence, or at least aptness, may be attributed to the name and position of his birthplace, his family's house of **Il Caos**. Its name (in dialect *Càvusu*) seems to be connected with the ancient Greek *Chaos* – 'nothingness', the void before creation; one can, if so minded, take either that meaning or the later sense of 'confusion' as appropriate to the Pirandello who regards the world as an arbitrary place, life as necessarily sustained by illusions beyond which there exists nothing but the void; the idea of mutual human understanding is a delusion 'based on the hollow abstraction of words' (1925 preface to *Sei personaggi in cerca d'autore* (*Six Characters in Search of an Author*), 1921).

Il Caos, close to Villaseta, stands at the edge of a profoundly fissured 'arid plateau of blue loamy soil whose crumbling cliffs fall sheer to the African sea' ('*Un cavallo sulla luna*' ('A Horse in the Moon'), 1907). Also of symbolic potential was its location between highly contrasting places, old Agrigento (looking down on one side at ruined Akragas) and **Porto Empedocle**, the growing industrial harbour where (in life as in *I vecchi*) sulphur was heaped in great yellow piles on the beach amid the noise of trains and shouting and the grinding of carts arriving from dawn to dusk from the railway station or the mines. Pirandello worked at the port in the summer of 1886 for his father, manager of a sulphur deposit.

Pirandello was relieved to withdraw from 'the savage war of profit' to university in Palermo and a literary future beyond Sicily. But in his fiction he often revisited cramped Girgenti and its toiling port, the constricting codes of chastity, honour, and revenge, the hot sulphur mines, burning plains and chalky rocks of his homeland. He remains aware of the void, of how easily, in the distorting heat or in the silhouetting light of the 'enormous, vapoury copper disc' of the moon in *Un cavallo sulla luna* (Extract 1), one can be 'assailed by the suspicion that everything' is unreal: the thought further explored, outside the Sicilian context, in many of the plays. But even Pirandello's ironic but mostly unwavering belief in the nothingness at the heart of things is slightly qualified by the love of origins, the inescapable nature of identity: he instructed that his body should be burnt and his ashes thrown to the winds but added that if this was not possible his urn should be 'walled into some rough stone in the country near Girgenti, where I was born'. Ten years after his death this suggestion was carried out and the ashes interred, a few hundred yards from Il Caos, which became a national monument soon afterwards, beneath a rock by a tall pine. (In a late fragment of an autobiographical novel he described his birth as a dropping down 'one night in June . . . like a firefly beneath a huge pine tree standing completely alone in an olivegrove'.)

## PALERMO

In 1186 a Muslim scholar, poet and administrator from Granada, Ibn Jubair, came to Palermo on the way back from his pilgrimage to Mecca and found 'an ancient and elegant city, magnificent and gracious, and seductive to look upon'; there are 'plains filled with gardens, with broad roads and avenues', a river and springs, buildings all of cut limestone. 'The King, to whom it is his world, has embellished it to perfection and taken it as the capital of his Frankish Kingdom – may God destroy it'. More than a century after Norman or 'Frankish' rule had replaced Arab in Sicily, Ibn Jubair still found Palermo congenial – dangerously so, he felt, since, appearances notwithstanding, it was a Christian capital.

Arabs (Saracens) had settled in large numbers from the ninth century onwards, bringing with them their language, religion and legal systems, poetry and scientific knowledge, efficient irrigation systems, melons and citrus fruits, aubergines, sugarcane and pistachio nuts. The Arab capital Palermo (called al-Madinah) rapidly became a prosperous, multi-racial commercial centre, one of the largest cities in Europe. When the Norman de Hauteville family took control of the island (Palermo fell in 1071) they adapted much from the Arabs and continued their policy of broad racial and religious toleration. The most astute and magnificent of the Hautevilles, Roger II (Count and then, between 1130 and 1154, King of Sicily) was particularly cosmopolitan in his interests – and adept at so advancing Arab, Greek, Italian, French and English courtiers, churchmen, soldiers and administrators as not to become dependent on any one group. Physically the most convincing tribute to Roger's eclecticism is the **Palatine Chapel** in the Palazzo dei Normanni, 'a seemingly effortless fusion of all that is most brilliant in the Latin, Byzantine and Islamic traditions into a single, harmonious masterpiece' (John Julius Norwich), with its western form and decorations, Greek Christ Pantocrator, and resplendent

Islamic 'stalactite' ceiling. It might appear to be a monument only to Roger's syncretising secular power but, as Norwich remarks, Christ is enthroned prominently over the royal dais, backed with marble where the dais is backed with gold'; all the throbbing colour, 'the interplay of verd-antique, ox-blood and cipollino, every inch of it burnished by the million glinting tesserae of the walls, create an atmosphere not of ostentation but of mystery, not of royal pride but of man's humility before his maker'.

Different traditions are also harmoniously combined in the former church of **San Giovanni degli Eremiti** (1132–48) with its five red domes; in the remains of the **Zisa** palace (from Arabic *aziz*, 'magnificent') of Roger's successors William I and William II, once surrounded, in oriental manner, with orchards, gardens, and pools and still hailed, in an Arabic stucco inscription, as 'the earthly paradise'; and in the more Byzantine **Martorana**, properly Santa Maria dell' Ammiraglio (consecrated in 1143), which struck Ibn Jubair on Christmas Day 1186 as:

> 'beyond dispute the most wonderful edifice in the world. The inner walls are all embellished with gold. There are slabs of coloured marble, the like of which we had never seen, inlaid throughout with gold mosaic and surrounded with branches formed from green mosaic. In its upper parts are well-placed windows of gilded glass, which steal all looks by the brilliance of their rays, and bewitch the soul. God protect us from their allurement!'

Probably the Muslim traveller had feelings at least as mixed about the mosaic in the nave of the Martorana in which King Roger, described in Greek script as 'Rogerios Rex', is crowned by Christ himself in a gesture which, it has often been noted, identifies him as an absolute, divinely appointed ruler in the Byzantine tradition. This attitude asserts, in a manner highly unusual in the feudal 12th century, independence from Pope and emperor, and states and helps to consolidate his success in ruling his disparate subjects. It was reinforced by the use of eastern imperial ceremonies including the prostration of his subjects when they came before him. In this context it seems unsurprising that the royal servant, the scholar al-Idrisi̧, should introduce his *Nuzhat al-mushtāq fī 'khtirāk al-āfāq* (*A Recreation for the Person Who Longs to Traverse the Horizons*), 1154, with claims that Roger's 'acts of generosity are like the waves of the ocean and as beneficent as the rains which make fecund the land'; al-Idrisi's lungs would weary, his breath be insufficient, if he had to enumerate the wonders for which his monarch has been responsible. But it does appear to be true, as his loyal servant would have it, that Roger was highly knowledgeable about mathematics, literature, and the sciences. Over a period of 15 years travellers were called before the king and questioned – perhaps by Roger himself, probably by al-Idrisi or lesser officials. When several travellers agreed on what they had seen, their reports were taken as proven, and on the basis of this research a great silver planisphere was constructed to show the different regions of the earth. The planisphere perished in a riot not long afterwards, but al-Idrisi's authoritative book of geography, part of the same project, survived as a monument to the varied interests of the reign and the advantages of empirical method.

In many ways Roger II provided an example for his grandson the Emperor Frederick II, king of Sicily 1198–1250. He too delighted in science and poetry and Arab ways (like Roger, he spoke Arabic and kept a harem). He himself wrote Provençal-influenced love poetry and drew to him a group of poets, known subsequently as the 'Sicilian school', who were credited with introducing vernacular love poetry to Italy. Roger and Frederick are buried near each other in porphyry sarcophagi in the south side of the nave of Palermo **Cathedral**. But the vibrant days of Norman-Sicilian culture were already over. Frederick was away from Sicily for much of his reign, fighting the Pope, enemies in Italy north and south, rivals and rebels in Germany, or holding court at the castles in Apulia where, in his later years, he seems to have been most happy. Sicily, the bedrock of the Normans' power in southern Italy, was an increasingly marginal part of a larger empire; hundreds of years of subordination to French and Spanish interests were about to begin.

Palermo remained an attractive city of golden stone with views of Monte Pellegrino and the sea and the Norman cathedral of **Monreale** on its heights, a city of palms and of orange blossom whose 'Islamic perfume' evokes 'houris and fleshly joys beyond the grave' (Giuseppe Tomasi di Lampedusa, *Il gattopardo* (*The Leopard*), 1958). But in Lampedusa's novel, set mainly in the 1860s, this was also the city whose many convents and monasteries gave it 'its grimness and its character, its sedateness and also the sense of death which not even the vibrant Sicilian light could ever manage to disperse'. During and after Lampedusa's lifetime Palermo became less sedate as the traffic and the violence increased. Amidst the noise there are quieter pockets like the garden of San Giovanni degli Eremiti. There are a few well restored buildings like the Zisa. But many of the old buildings of Palermo are, notoriously, in a state of collapse, the consequence of Allied bombing in 1943, earthquake, or neglect. These include the family homes of the Princes of Lampedusa, the 'lost paradise' remembered by the last of the line in *I luoghi della mia prima infanzia* (*Places of My Infancy*), 1961, and used also in various combinations in *Il gattopardo*. Outside the town near the La Favorita park at San Lorenzo are the ruins of the Villa Lampedusa, main source of the Villa Salina in the novel. (Salina is the name of one of the Aeolian Islands, north of Sicily, origin of the fictional Prince's title as the remote southern island of Lampedusa was of the author's.) The larger **Palazzo Lampedusa**, in Via Lampedusa, was left as a sad shell after the bombing; in the mid-1980s David Gilmour, working on the prince's biography, slipped in having noticed a loose plank in the padlocked gates and found amid the rubble 'scattered pages of Lampedusa's favourite authors', documents, photographs, even intimate letters from his mother. Here as a child, *I luoghi* recalls, he had the freedom of three courtyards, four terraces, a garden, huge staircases, halls, corridors, stables, servants' rooms and offices, 'a real kingdom for a boy alone, a kingdom either empty or sparsely populated by figures unanimously well-disposed', a world of 'surprises ever renewed and ever fresh'.

Lampedusa also remembered the great ballroom of the palazzo 'with its enamelled floor and its ceiling on which delicious gold and yellow twirls framed mythological scenes where with rude energy and amid swirling robes crowded all the deities of Olympus'. This lost room was partly recreated (Extract 5) in the ball in *Il gattopardo* where the Prince wanders, broods on death and the decline of his order, and, in a few contrasting moments of forgetting, waltzes magnificently with the beautiful Angelica. In the film version of this scene Luchino Visconti uses the surviving opulent Salone degli Specchi of **Palazzo Valguarneri-Gangi**.

## Santa Margherita Di Belice

The palace where Giuseppe Tomasi, Prince of Lampedusa spent summers until he was 20 is, like his former haunts in Palermo, in a sorry state. Already sold out of the family, it was largely destroyed in the earthquake of 1968, 11 years after his death; only one wall remains. But what was once here is recorded in loving detail in *I luoghi della mia prima infanzia* (*Places of My Infancy*), 1961, and equally lovingly transformed and enlarged in the Donnafugata of *Il gattopardo* (*The Leopard*), 1958. (The name Donnafugata is taken from a castle in southern Sicily.)

The second chapter of *The Leopard* opens memorably with the Salina family's long hot journey south from Palermo to Donnafugata by carriage in August 1860, with level trots, uphill trudges and downhill shuffles 'merging . . . into the constant jingle of harness bells, imperceptible now to the dazed senses except as sound equivalent of the blazing landscape'. When they finally arrive they are greeted by the town dignitaries and band and hear a *Te Deum* in the cathedral next door to the palace (another casualty of the earthquake), are welcomed by their own retainers, and only then can subside into bed, the bath, or the shady gardens.

The palace at Santa Margherita, built in 1680 and partially restored in 1810, was owned by Lampedusa's maternal ancestors. It remained 'a kind of 18th century Pompeii, all miraculously preserved intact'. As a child Lampedusa would 'wander through the vast ornate house as in an enchanted wood', through rooms with 'walls covered in rough crumpled white silk', or portraits of his forebears, or tapestries, past the great bed used by the visiting King Ferdinand (an 'Empire *lit-bateau*'), or in the gardens' long alleys meeting in a central fountain. There was a pink dining-room with 'four big console tables covered with pink marble' and on the main table a silver centre-piece 'surmounted by Neptune who threatened guests with his trident, while beside him an Amphitrite eyed them with a hint of malice'. There was even a Louis XVI theatre of white and gold and light blue velvet, capable of holding three hundred people. Strolling players performed there for two or three weeks each summer, improvising sets with some of the house's second-rank armchairs, tables, and wardrobes; Lampedusa's mother once lent the leading lady 'a low-cut robe of Nile green covered in silver spangles' for *La Dame aux camélias*. The acting was not good, but full of gusto and fire.

The First World war brought such 'poor and picturesque wandering companies' to an end, and soon afterwards Santa Margherita became only a memory for Lampedusa. *Places of My Infancy* breaks off with the wish that 'these lines which no one will read [may] be a homage to its unblemished memory'. A more expansive homage is paid by Donnafugata in *The Leopard*, with its 'inextricable complex of guest rooms, state rooms, kitchens, chapels, theatres, picture galleries, odorous saddling rooms, stables, stuffy conservatories, passages, stairs, terraces and porticos'. Many of the details of the rooms actually come from the family home in Palermo, or are imaginary, but this simply adds to the richness of the visionary transformation of the real palace, particularly now that it is almost completely lost to us.

## OTHER LITERARY LANDMARKS

**Catania**: the birthplace of the composer Vincenzo Bellini (1801–35), in Piazza San Francesco, houses the **Museo Belliniano**.

**Cefalù**: setting of Vincenzo Consolo's novel, of the 1920s, *Nottetempo, casa per casa (Night-Time, House by House)*, 1992.

**Corleone**: Mafia stronghold which provides one of the settings for Mario Puzo's *The Godfather*, 1969, and a name for the family of the godfather himself, Don Corleone.

**Palermo**: many of the French victims of the popular uprising of 1282 known as the Sicilian Vespers (because tradition says that it broke out at the time of evening prayer) were buried in the now dilapidated **Piazza Croce dei Vespri**.

**Taormina**: the **Teatro Greco**, a Greek theatre transformed in the first century A.D. for gladiatorial use, impressed travellers including Goethe with its spectacular views.

**Taormina**: '**Fontana Vecchia**' was the house, then on the edge of the town, where D.H. Lawrence (◊Sardinia) and his wife Frieda lived in 1920–22.

# BOOKLIST

Bassnett-McGuire, Susan, *File on Pirandello*, Methuen, London, 1989.

Brydone, Patrick, *A Tour Through Sicily and Malta in a Series of Letters to William Beckford, Esq.*, London, 1773. (There is unfortunately no modern edition.) **Extract 4**.

Caven, Brian, *Dionysius I: War-Lord of Sicily*, Yale University Press, New Haven and London, 1990.

Cicero, Marcus Tullius, *The Verrine Orations* [70 B.C.], L.H.G. Greenwood, trans, Heinemann, London, and Harvard University Press, Cambridge, Mass., 1967.

Diodorus Siculus, *Diodorus of Sicily* [*Bibliotheke-Historike*, c.60–30 B.C.], C.H. Oldfather, trans, vol. 5, Heinemann, London, and Harvard University Press, Cambridge, Mass., 1962.

*Empedocles: the Extant Fragments*, M.R. Wright, ed, Bristol Classical Press, Gerald Duckworth, London, and Hackett Publishing, Indianapolis, 1995.

Finley, M.I., Denis Mack Smith and Christopher Duggan, *A History of Sicily*, Chatto and Windus, London, 1986.

Gilmour, David, *The Last Leopard: a Life of Giuseppe di Lampedusa*, Quartet Books, London, 1988.

Giudice, Gaspare, *Pirandello: a Biography*, Alastair Hamilton, trans [and considerably abridged], Oxford University Press, London, 1975.

Gladstone, William Ewart, *The Gladstone Diaries*, vol. 2 (1833–9), M.R.D. Foot, ed. Clarendon Press, Oxford, 1968.

Guido, Margaret, *Sicily: an Archaeological Guide*, Faber, London, 1967.

Kinkead-Weekes, Mark, *D.H. Lawrence: Triumph to Exile, 1912–1922*, Cambridge University Press, 1996. (Vol 2 of *The Cambridge Biography: D.H. Lawrence, 1885–1930*.)

Lampedusa, Giuseppe Tomasi di, *The Leopard* [1958], with a Memory and Two Stories, Archibald Colquhoun, trans, Collins Harvill, London, 1986. **Extract 5**.

Norwich, John Julius, *The Normans in Sicily: the Normans in the South 1016–1130 and The Kingdom in the Sun 1130–1194*, Penguin, London, 1992.

Plato, *Timaeus. Critias. Cleitophon. Menexenus. Epistles*, R.G. Bury, ed and trans, Heinemann, London, and Harvard University Press, Cambridge, Mass., 1956.

Plutarch, *Plutarch's Lives*, Bernadotte Perrin, trans, vol. 5, Heinemann, London, and Harvard University Press, Cambridge, Mass., 1917, 1961.

Pirandello, Luigi, *The Late Mattia Pascal* [1904], Nicoletta Simborowski, trans, Dedalus, London, and Hippocrene Books, New York, 1987.

Pirandello, Luigi, *Tales of Madness: a Selection from Luigi Pirandello's Short Stories for a Year* [1922–37], Giovanni R. Bussino, trans, Dante University of America Press, Brookline, MA, 1984. **Extract 2**.

Pirandello, Luigi, *Six Characters in Search of an Author* [1921], Felicity Firth, trans, in *Collected Plays*, vol. 2, Robert Rietty, ed, John Calder, London, and Riverrun Press, New York, 1988.

Plutarch, *Plutarch's Lives*, Bernadotte Perrin, trans, vol. 5, Heinemann, London, and Harvard University Press, Cambridge, Mass., 1961. **Extract 7**.

*Booklist continued*

Quasimodo, Salvatore, *Complete Poems*, Jack Bevan, trans, Anvil Press Poetry, London, 1983. **Extract 3**.

Sciascia, Leonardo, *To Each His Own* [1966], Adrienne Foulke trans, Carcanet Press, Manchester, 1989. **Extract 1**.

Sciascia, Leonardo, *Sicily as Metaphor: Conversations Presented by Marcelle Padovani* [1979], James Marcus, trans, Marlboro Press, Marlboro, Vermont, 1994.

Thucydides, *The Peloponnesian War*, Rex Warner, trans, Penguin, Harmondsworth, 1954.

Verga, Giovanni, *The House By the Medlar Tree* [1881], Raymond Rosenthal, trans, University of California Press, Berkeley, Los Angeles, and London, 1983.

Verga, Giovanni, *Little Novels of Sicily* [1883], D.H. Lawrence, trans, Penguin, Harmondsworth, 1973. **Extract 6**.

Vittorini, Elio, *Conversation in Sicily* [1941], Wilfrid David, trans, Quartet, London, 1988.

Wilson, R.J.A., *Piazza Armerina*, University of Texas Press, Austin, 1983.

# Extracts

## (1) SICILY

### Leonardo Sciascia, *To Each His Own*, 1966

*The idealistic Professor Laurana is attempting to solve a murder-case. Don Benito, whom he meets in the course of his investigations, outlines the wider problems. Raganà is 'one of the respectable, unpunished, untouchable criminals' who order or commit violent crimes in Sicily.*

'I want to tell you something you surely know about already, but the story has a moral. . . . A big industry decides to build a dam above a populated area. Ten or more deputies, acting on the opinion of technical experts, ask that the dam not be built because of the threat it poses to the area below. The government permits the dam to be built. Later, when it has been built, and is already in operation, there is some warning of danger. Nothing is done. Nothing until the disaster, which some people had foreseen, actually happens. The result: 2000 people dead. . . . 2000 – as many people as all the Raganàs who flourish around here liquidate in ten years. And I could tell you a number of other fables but you know them perfectly well.'

'The analogy doesn't hold. . . . You take no account of the fear, the terror –'

'You think the people around Longarone weren't afraid when they looked up at that dam?'

'But that isn't the same. I agree, yes, it was a very serious thing.'

'That will go unpunished exactly as do our choice and more characteristic crimes.'

'But, after all, if this Raganà, and all the Raganàs whom we know and don't know – if it is possible finally to get at them in spite of the protection they enjoy, it seems to me that it will be a big, a significant step forward.'

'You really think so? Given the situation we're in?'

'What situation?'

'A half-million emigrants, which is to say, almost the entire able-bodied population; an agriculture that is completely abandoned; sulphur mines that are closed; salt mines that are about to close; a petroleum industry that is a joke; regional authorities each more addlepated than the next; a national government that lets us stew in our own juice. . . . We are drowning, my friend, drowning. . . . This corsair that has been Sicily, with the splendid leopard rampant on its prow . . . with its crew of headline-seeking *mafiosi* and the politicians secretly in cahoots with them, with its *engagé* writers, its screwed-up logicians, its madmen, its high-noon and nocturnal demons, its oranges and its sulphur and its booted corpses – the ship is sinking, my friend, sinking. And you and I – I mad maybe, and you perhaps *engagé* – with the water already to our knees, we sit worrying about Raganà, whether he's jumped into the Deputy's lifeboat or stayed aboard with those who are about to die.'

'I don't agree,' Laurana said.

'All in all, neither do I,' Don Benito said.

## (2) AGRIGENTO

### Luigi Pirandello, 'A Horse in the Moon', 1907

*Pirandello's short story of nightmarish mental and physical anguish is set in the countryside near Agrigento, still parched, in September, 'from the furious rays of the long summer sun', gloomy and bristling with blackened stubble. The characters have come upon a dying horse.*

He remained there, alone, sitting on the rock, completely at the mercy of those increasing tremors; and, as he sat there, huddling like a great owl upon a perch, he suddenly caught a glimpse of what seemed to him to be . . . why yes, of course, now he could see it, howsoever horrible it was, howsoever much it looked like a vision of another world. The moon. A large moon, rising slowly from that yellow sea of stubble. And silhouetted in black against that enormous, vapory copper disc, the skeletal head of that horse, still waiting with its neck outstretched; it would perhaps always wait like that, so darkly etched upon that copper disc, while the ravens, circling overhead, could be heard cawing high up in the sky.

When the disappointed and indignant Ida returned, after making her way back through the plain, all the while shouting 'Nino! Nino! the moon had already risen; the horse had again collapsed to the ground as if dead; and Nino . . . where was Nino? Oh, there he was; he, too, was lying on the ground.

Had he fallen asleep there?

She ran over to him. She found him with the death rattle in his throat. His face, too, was on the ground, and it was almost black. His eyes were swollen and tightly shut. He was flushed.

'Oh, God!'

She looked around as if in a trance. She opened her hands where she held a few dried beans which she had brought from the village in order to feed the horse. She looked at the moon, then at the horse, then at this man lying here on the ground, he, too, looking like a corpse. She felt faint, suddenly assailed by the suspicion that everything she saw was unreal. Terrified, she fled back towards the villa, calling for her father in a loud voice, calling for her father to come and take her away – oh, God! – away from that man who had that death rattle . . . who knows why! . . . away from that horse, away from that crazy moon up above, away from those ravens cawing up in the sky . . . away, away, away . . .

## (3) AGRIGENTO

### Salvatore Quasimodo, '*Street in Agrigentum*', 1936

*Agrigento, with its many visible reminders of a glorious past, is especially suited to Quasimodo's poetry of loss. 'Doleful telamons' refers to a gigantic male figure among the ruins of the Temple of Olympian Zeus and the name of the 'saracen olive trees' is a reminder that the town was once, from 857, Arab. A marranzano is a Sicilian form of 'Jew's harp'.*

The wind is still there that I remember
kindling the manes of horses coursing
oblique along the plains; a wind
that stains and gnaws the sandstone and the heart
of the doleful telamons lying
felled on the grass.
Ancient soul grey with bitterness
you return with the wind, sniff

the delicate moss that clothes
the giants thrust down from the sky.
How lonely you are in the space that remains to you;
and greater your grief, if you hear again the sound
as it moves far off and opens out to the sea
where morning Hesperus now creeps.
The marranzano twangs
sad in the carter's throat as he climbs
slow the moon-sharpened hill
In the murmur of saracen olive trees.

## (4) ETNA

### Patrick Brydone,
### A Tour Through Sicily and Malta, 1773

*Brydone's book, the first detailed account of its subject in Eng-
lish, was popular with travellers and readers until the mid-19th
century. He responds to Etna as an instance of the Sublime – the
pleasingly terrifying – as well as a fascinating scientific phenom-
enon and well known mythological site. (Vulcan is the blacksmith of the gods; he trapped his wife Venus and her lover Mars
in a net.)*

This mountain reunites every beauty and every horror; and in short,
all the most opposite and dissimilar objects in nature. Here you
behold a gulf, that formerly threw out torrents of fire and smoke,
now covered with the most luxurious vegetation; and from an object
of terror, become one of delight. Here you gather the most delicious
fruit, rising from what was but lately a black and barren rock. Here the
ground is covered with every flower; and we wander over the beauties,
and contemplate this wilderness of sweets, without considering that
hell, with all its terrors, is immediately under our feet; and that but a
few yards separate us from lakes and liquid fire and brimstone. . . .

After incredible labour and fatigue, but at the same time mixed with
a great deal of pleasure, we arrived before dawn at the ruins of an
ancient structure, called *Il Torre del Filosofo*, supposed to have been
built by the philosopher Empedocles, who took up his habitation here
the better to study the nature of Mount Aetna. By others, it is supposed to be the ruins of a temple of Vulcan, whose shop, all the world
knows (where he used to make excellent thunderbolts and celestial
armour, as well as nets to catch his wife when she went astray) was ever
kept in Mount Aetna. Here we rested ourselves for some time, and
made a fresh application to our liquor bottle, which, I am persuaded,
both Vulcan and Empedocles, had they been here, would have greatly
approved of after such a march.

## (5) PALERMO

### Giuseppe Tomasi di Lampedusa,
### The Leopard, 1958

*This scene of the novel takes place in 1862, when social life has
again begun to flourish after the fighting which preceded Sicily's
entry into a united Italy. A culture based on money is increasingly replacing one based on deference, and it is a sign of the
times that Don Fabrizio Corbera, Prince of Salina, has agreed,
with some misgivings, to a marriage between his nephew and the
daughter of the unrefined but newly rich and powerful Don
Calogero Sedàra.*

The ballroom was all golden; smoothed on cornices, stippled on door-
frames, damascened pale, almost silvery, over darker gold on door
panels and on the shutters which covered and annulled the windows,
conferring on the room the look of some superb jewel-case shut off
from an unworthy world . . . From the ceiling the gods, reclining on
gilded couches, gazed down smiling and inexorable as a summer sky.
They thought themselves eternal; but a bomb manufactured in Pitts-
burgh, Penn., was to prove the contrary in 1943.

'Fine, Prince, fine! They don't do things like this nowadays, with
gold leaf at its present price!' Sedàra was standing beside him; his
quick eyes were moving over the room, insensible to its charm, intent
on its monetary value.

Quite suddenly Don Fabrizio felt a loathing for him; to the rise of
this man and a hundred others like him, to their obscure intrigues and
their tenacious greed and avarice, was due the sense of death looming
darkly over these palaces; it was due to him and his colleagues, to their
rancour and sense of inferiority, their incapacity for putting out
blooms, that the black clothes of the men dancing reminded Don
Fabrizio of crows veering to and fro above lost valleys in search of
putrid prey. He felt like giving a sharp reply and telling him to get out
of his way. But he couldn't; the man was a guest, he was the father of
that dear girl Angelica; and maybe, too, he was just as unhappy as
others.

'Fine, Don Calogero, fine. But our young couple's the finest of all.'
Tancredi and Angelica were passing in front of them at that moment,
his gloved right hand on her waist, their outspread arms interlaced,
their eyes gazing into each other's. The black of his tail-coat, the pink
of her interweaving dress, looked like some unusual jewel. They were
the most moving sight there, two young people in love dancing
together, blind to each other's defects, deaf to the warnings of fate,
deluding themselves that the whole course of their lives would be as
smooth as the ballroom floor, unknowing actors set to play the parts
of Juliet and Romeo by a director who had concealed the fact that

tomb and poison were already in the script. Neither was good, each self-interested, turgid with secret aims; yet there was something sweet and touching about them both; those murky but ingenuous ambitions of theirs were obliterated by the words of jesting tenderness he was murmuring in her ear, by the scent of her hair, by the mutual clasp of those bodies destined to die.

## (6) PIANA DI CATANIA

### Giovanni Verga,
### 'Malaria', in *Little Novels of Sicily*, 1883

*The low-lying Plain of Catania was, until efficient land recla-*
*mation began here after Verga's time, rife with malaria and*
*other diseases known by the same name – 'evil air'. (The 'lake of*
*Lentini' is now reclaimed land.) The translation is by D.H.*
*Lawrence.*

And you feel you could touch it with your hand – as if it smoked up from the fat earth, there, everywhere, round about the mountains that shut it in, from Agnone to Mount Etna capped with snow – stagnating in the plain like the sultry heat of July. There the red-hot sun rises and sets, and the livid moon, and the *Puddara* [the Pleiades] which seems to float through a sea of exhalations, and the birds and the white marguerites of spring, and the burnt-up summer; and there the wild-ducks in long black files fly through the autumn clouds, and the river [Simeto] gleams as if it were of metal, between the wide, lonely banks, that are broken here and there, scattered with pebbles; and in the background the lake of Lentini, like a mere, with its flat shores, and not a boat, not a tree on its sides, smooth and motionless. By the lake-bed the oxen pasture at will, forlorn, muddied up to the breast, hairy. When the sheep-bell resounds in the great silence, the wag-tails fly away, noiselessly, and the shepherd himself, yellow with fever, and white as well with dust, lifts his swollen lids for a moment, raising his head in the shadow of the dry reeds.

And truly the malaria gets into you with the bread you eat, or if you open your mouth to speak as you walk, suffocating in the dust and sun of the roads, and you feel your knees give way beneath you, or you sink discouraged on the saddle as your mule ambles along, with its head down. In vain the villages of Lentini and Francofonte and Paternò try to clamber up like strayed sheep on to the first hills that rise from the plain, and surround themselves with orange groves, and vineyards, and evergreen gardens and orchards; the malaria seizes the inhabitants in the depopulated streets, and nails them in front of the doors of their houses whose plaster is all falling with the sun, and there they tremble with fever under their brown cloaks, with all the bed-blankets over their shoulders.

## (7) SYRACUSE

### Plutarch,
### 'The Life of Marcellus', in *Parallel Lives,*
### c.105–120

*Archimedes' spectacular devices probably derive partly from sources anxious to explain why Syracuse fell to the Romans only after a siege of two years. Plutarch, moreover, seeks the essence of the figures discussed as much as the exact historical truth about them: in this case, the machines pay tribute to the reputation of Archimedes as one of the greatest mathematicians.*

When, therefore, the Romans assaulted them by sea and land, the Syracusans were stricken dumb with terror; they thought that nothing could withstand so furious an onset by such forces. But Archimedes began to ply his engines, and shot against the land forces of the assailants all sorts of missiles and immense masses of stones, which came down with incredible din and speed; nothing whatever could ward off their weight, but they knocked down in heaps those who stood in their way, and threw their ranks into confusion. At the same time huge beams were suddenly projected over the ships from the walls, which sank some of them with great weights plunging down from on high; others were seized at the prow by iron claws, or beaks like the beaks of cranes, drawn straight up into the air, and then plunged stern foremost into the depths, or were turned round and round by means of enginery within the city, with great destruction of the fighting men on board, who perished in the wrecks. Frequently, too, a ship would be lifted out of the water into mid-air, whirled hither and thither as it hung there, a dreadful spectacle, until its crew had been thrown out and hurled in all directions, when it would fall empty upon the walls, or slip away from the clutch that had held it. . . .

However, Marcellus made his escape, and jesting with his own artificers and engineers, 'Let us stop,' said he, 'fighting against this geometrical Briareus, who uses our ships like cups to ladle water from the sea . . . and with the many missiles which he shoots against us all at once, outdoes the hundred-handed monsters of mythology.' For in reality all the rest of the Syracusans were but a body for the designs of Archimedes, and his the one soul moving and managing everything.

# Biographies and important works

ARCHIMEDES (c.287–212 B.C.), the great Syracusan Greek mathematician, probably studied at Alexandria. The most popular story about him was recorded by the architect Vitruvius in the first century A.D.: called upon by Hieron II to find out whether the gold in a votive crown had in fact been partly replaced by silver, Archimedes came upon the method for measuring the difference when, in the bath, he noticed the displacement of water by his body. He then rushed about, naked, crying *heureka!* (or, less accurately, *eureka!*), 'I have found [it]!' How literally this tale can be taken is, like the real scope of Archimedes' military machines (Extract 7), uncertain. His surviving works include treatises on the verbal expression of large numbers, the surface and volume of the cylinder and square and – the first known book on the subject – mechanics, including a section on the principle of the lever.

DIODORUS SICULUS (d.21 B.C.?) is the Latin name (*Siculus*, 'Sicilian') of the historian, born at Agyrion (now Agira), who wrote his *Bibliotheke Historike* (*Historical Library*) between about 60 and 30 B.C. Originally this was in 40 books, of which 14 have survived together with fragments of the others. Diodorus aims to give a complete history of Greece and Rome, with an emphasis in the first books in particular on their mythical beginnings. A detailed account of his native Sicily is included.

EMPEDOCLES (c. 493–c. 435 B.C.), of Akragas (Agrigento) engaged in politics (he upheld democracy having refused the crown of Akragas), the theory and practice of healing, and philosophy. The core of his beliefs, as far as it can be ascertained from the fragments of his hymns and his poem on nature, is that the four eternal elements of fire, air, water, and earth are repeatedly brought together by the force of Love and divided by the force of Strife.

The legend that Empedocles ended his life by hurling himself into the crater of Etna to prove himself a god results partly from a line in which he claims to have reached – metaphorically but perhaps also physically – a state of divine purification. It also follows, perhaps, from his view that 'life on earth is an exile from an earlier and more ideal state' (M.R. Wright). In Matthew Arnold's 'dramatic poem' *Empedocles on Etna*, 1852, he becomes essentially a troubled 19th century thinker who 'sees things as they are . . . in their stern simplicity', lacks 'the religious consolation of other men', and hurls himself into the crater in order to be reunited with the universe before depression and loneliness can rob him of the joys and truths he can still glimpse.

IDRISI, Abu Abdullah Mohammed al- (c. 1100–65), was born at Ceuta in Morocco and educated at Cordoba. He had settled in Palermo by 1138. He drew on his own travels in Iberia, France, England and Asia Minor as well as on the verbal accounts of other travellers in the composition of *Nuzhat al-mushtāq fi 'khtirāk al-āfāq* (*A Recreation for the Person Who Longs to Traverse the*

*Horizons*), 1154, conceived as an accompaniment to the planisphere commissioned by Roger II and to some 70 maps. The *Recreation* was often known as *The Book of Roger*. It divides the earth – 'round like a sphere', with the waters 'adhering to and kept upon it by means of a natural and unvarying equilibrium' – into its seven climes and is concerned particularly with the accurate statement of distances and locations, often left uncertain in earlier works of this sort. Sicily, not surprisingly, is most fully described. It is a well ruled, fertile and well irrigated island, whose cisterns, water-mills, rivers, and springs and fountains al-Idrisi often mentions.

PIRANDELLO, Luigi (1867–1936), was born at Il Caos near Agrigento, studied in Palermo and Bonn, and lived most of the rest of his life in Rome. The mental collapse there of his wife Antonietta in 1903 (she was eventually committed to hospital in 1919) was one source of his interest in problems of identity: she imagined him a liar and adulterer, constructing an identity for him quite foreign to the one he knew; 'to see life being transposed in the mind of my poor companion enabled me later to convey the psychology of the alienated'. The ironic pessimism of Pirandello's work contrasts more puzzlingly with his membership of the Fascist party from 1924. (His enthusiasm for Mussolini cooled within a few years.) By this time Pirandello was established as a playwright. Much of his writing before 1915, and some of it later, took the form of short stories, many of them rearranged as *Novelle per un anno* (*Short Stories For a Year*), 1922–37. His novels include *Il fu Mattia Pascal* (*The Late Mattia Pascal*), 1904, and *I vecchi e i giovani* (*The Old and the*

*Young*), 1908, set in Sicily in the social unrest of the 1890s. Among his many plays are *Sei personaggi in cerca d'autore* (*Six Characters in Search of an Author*), 1921, *Enrico IV* (*Henry IV*), 1922, and *Questa sera si recita a soggetto* (*Tonight We Improvise*), 1930. Between 1925 and 1928 he wrote, managed and directed for the Arts Theatre company, based in Rome and touring widely in Europe and America. In 1934 Pirandello was awarded the Nobel Prize for Literature.

The *novelle* vary considerably in setting, tone, and length. Many, however, are concerned with jealousy, delusion, and the gap between people's socially constructed and internal images, a theme intensified by the author's background in formal Sicilian society. Not far from an apparently solid, conventional world are dream-states of passion and grief and, particularly in some of the Sicilian stories, deceptive shadows and illusions, the madness-inducing moon and heat-crazing sun. (These aspects are prominent in *Kaos*, the Taviani brothers' film based on some of the stories.) *Il fu Mattia Pascal* further explores the construction and partial dissolution of identity in the tale of a man who, mistakenly believed to have killed himself, decides that Fate has released him from all entanglements, 'made me a spectator of the intrigues amid which other people still struggled'. His new identity, or lack of one, leads, however, to practical difficulties and to the giddying sense that 'I was still alive as far as death was concerned, and dead as far as life was concerned', that he is no more real than his shadow, has a head but can 'only use it for considering and accepting the fact that it was the head of a shadow and not the shadow of a head'. He becomes Mattia Pascal again, but his identity – as, for instance, he inspects his 'own' tombstone – remains problematic. (Pirandello himself comments, in a late notebook entry, 'There is someone who is living my life. And I know nothing about him'.)

Reality is also much debated, played with and problematised in the plays. In *Enrico IV* a man appears to have lived for 20 years under the illusion that he is the Emperor Henry IV as the result of a head injury sustained during a masquerade. In fact he is not mad so much as trying to avoid the terrible knowledge of the sane that time destroys all, that flux is everywhere. While art, like madness, appears fixed, life changes continually; the Characters who burst in on a rehearsal to search for an author in *Sei personaggi* should, Pirandello stipulates, be as distinct as possible from the Actors and Director they confront – they 'must not . . . seem to be phantasms; they must appear as figures of created reality, immutable constructs of the imagination' and therefore 'more real and more consistent . . . than the natural and volatile Actors'. The Characters are even more completely prisoners of their situation of jealousy, betrayal, and recrimination, than real people would be; concessions, comprehension, forgiveness are impossible between characters who are intended, Pirandello explains in his preface of 1925, 'to appear at the exact stage of development each had reached in the author's imagination at the moment when he decided to be rid of them'. The very degree of their presence, their aliveness in the play, rather than only whether they play leading or supporting roles, is unalterably determined: the dominant Father and Stepdaughter drag behind them 'the practically dead weight of the others: the demurring Son, the submissive, suffering Mother, and

. . . the two children who consist of little more than their appearance and have to be led by the hand'. The Actors have great difficulty in understanding that these are not roles to be played in a particular way; the play ends with them in great confusion as to what is and is not real. There is no Author in the cast: no-one to finish the Characters' stories neatly, to provide answers, and so no avoiding the challenging questions about the nature of theatre and of reality raised by the encounter between Characters and Actors. To complicate matters further, the Characters are themselves played by actors. This is 'a play about the nature of the play constructed on a Chinese box principle, where the answering of one question merely opens the lid to another' (Susan Bassnett-McGuire).

PLATO, in Greek Platōn (427–347 B.C.), with Aristotle the greatest and most influential of Greek philosophers, set out in *Politeia* (*The Republic*), c. 375 B.C., his belief that the ideal state would be ruled by a class of 'guardians', men whose rigorous philosophic education enabled them to perceive justice and the good. At the opposite extreme is the tyrannical man, a type perhaps modelled partly on Dionysius I of Syracuse.

The 13 *Epistles*, regarded as Plato's from ancient times but probably by one or more of his followers, are mostly concerned with his relations with Dion and Dionysius II of Syracuse. The aim appears to be to explain and justify Plato's involvement in Syracusan affairs. The portrayal of the rulers (the tyrannical father and the son who failed to become a philosopher-king) is inevitably one-sided; Dionysius II 'had sinned against the Light, and (what was worse) had made Plato look foolish. He had to be portrayed as a person wholly contemptible' (Brian Caven).

PLUTARCH, in Greek Ploutarkhos (c. 46–120 A.D.), visited Rome but lived mostly in his native Greece. His *Bioi paralleloi (Parallel Lives)*, c. 105–120, the fruit of wide reading, clear principles, and experience of both the Greek and the Roman world, are paired biographies of Greeks and Romans, mostly politicians and generals, from the legendary time of Theseus to the imperial Rome of the first century A.D. His primary aim is moral evaluation and comparison of these famous figures. In the process he gathers a wealth of anecdotes, which he sought out on the grounds that 'a slight thing like a phrase or a jest often makes a greater revelation of a character than battles where thousands fall . . . or the sieges of cities'.

The *Lives*, translated into French and thence into English by Sir Thomas North in 1579, are the main sources of Shakespeare's *Julius Caesar*, *Antony and Cleopatra*, and *Coriolanus*.

QUASIMODO, Salvatore (1901–68), was born in Modica in southeastern Sicily and studied in Palermo and Rome. He gave up his engineering degree as a result of financial hardship but eventually qualified as a surveyor and between 1926 and 1938 was employed by the army engineering corps. At the same time, with the assistance and encouragement of his brother-in-law Elio Vittorini¢ in Florence, he began to publish poems. In 1941 he became Professor of Italian Literature at the Milan Conservatory. He was awarded the Nobel Prize for Literature in 1959.

Quasimodo's early style in, for instance, his first two volumes *Acque e terra (Waters and Land)*, 1930, and *Oboe sommerso (Sunken Oboe)*, 1932, is allusive, analogical, 'hermetic'. Here especially Sicily recurs as a lost, now unobtainable paradise. The focus of the later verse collections is more social and the style arguably less original. Quasimodo also published many translations, most sensitively of *Lirici greci (Greek Lyric Poets)*, 1940.

SCIASCIA, Leonardo (1921–89), worked from 1941 at the grain depot, and from 1949 as an elementary-school teacher, in his native Racalmuto, then from 1956 in educational administration in Caltanisetta, retiring in 1970. He was elected as an independent Communist city councillor in Palermo (1975–7) and as a Radical member of the European parliament in 1979.

Poverty, deprivation and violence in Racalmuto were a major source of Sciascia's crusading zeal against social injustice, political corruption, and the Mafia. (Racalmuto figures as Regalpetra in several books including *Le parrocchie di Regalpetra* (translated as *Salt in the Wound*), 1956.) As well as short stories and novels he wrote essays and articles, many on Sicily but many, too, on national issues. One of his more controversial interventions was *L'Affaire Moro (The Moro Affair)*, 1978, condemning the Christian Democrats and Communists who had refused to bargain with the kidnappers of the consequently murdered politician Aldo Moro. Corrupt authorities, he argued, were in no position to claim that contact with terrorists was corrupting. Since in fiction and non-fiction alike Sciascia denounced injustice, he was happy to call himself a 'pamphleteer' as much as a novelist.

*Il giorno della civetta (The Day of the Owl)*, 1961, concerns the investigation of a Mafia murder similar to that of a Communist trades unionist, Miraglia, at Sciacca in southern Sicily in 1947. The carabiniere captain Bellodi, from distant Parma, regards 'the authority vested in him as a surgeon regards the knife: an instrument to be used with care, precision and certainty'; he is 'a man convinced that law rests on the idea of justice and that any action taken by the law should be governed by justice'. But most of the Sicilians he deals with cannot imagine such an attitude, so alien to their experience of those in authority. In the most extreme instance, the Mafia leader Don Mariano can picture 'the world of sentiment, legality and normal human relations' only as 'a blind man pictures in his mind, dark and formless, the world outside'. Bellodi is reasonable and intelligent and solves mysteries with an acumen which amazes his subordinates, but cannot beat a system in which crime is protected by higher powers in Rome as well as Sicily.

In *A ciascuno il suo* (*To Each His Own*), 1966, Professor Laurana, the reserved, innocent teacher who correctly works out the murderer's identity and suffers the consequences, has even less possibility of success than Bellodi. Unlike amateur detectives in more conventional examples of the genre, Laurana has no chance of outwitting the powers ranged against him (or rather surrounding him in a whole culture of violence and concealment). Similarly the reader, whom convention usually places in the satisfying position of supporter or alter ego for his or her fellow sleuth, is not allowed to rest easy at the end: investigators perish or fail, while the larger problems remain unsolved. Italo Calvino (◊Liguria) wrote to Sciascia, on reading the manuscript of *A ciascuno* for the Einaudi publishing house, of the

delight of reading a *giallo* – 'yellow', a detective story, from the traditional colour of the cover – with the added pleasure of seeing it deconstruct itself.

Deconstructing detective novels is only one of Sciascia's favourite activities. Other fiction includes the historical novel *Il consiglio d'Egitto* (*The Council of Egypt*), 1963, where the conventions of the genre are again interestingly undermined, and *Candido, ovvero un sogno fatto in Sicilia* (*Candido, or a Dream Dreamed in Sicily*), 1977, a variation on Voltaire's *Candide*. Most of Sciascia's work is set, explicitly or not, in Sicily, but its substance, as he says of *Il giorno*, is 'that of a fable about power anywhere in the world, about power that, in the impenetrable form of a concatenation that we can roughly term *mafioso*, works steadily greater degradation'.

THEOCRITUS (third century B.C.), generally regarded as the first pastoral poet, was probably born in Syracuse. Later he lived on the Aegean island of Kos and in Egypt, but readers have felt that at least some of his landscapes are Sicilian. Theocritus was an important influence on the *Eclogues* of Virgil (◊Naples and Campania) and on most later pastoral poetry.

TOMASI DI LAMPEDUSA, Giuseppe (1896–1957), was born in Palermo. He succeeded his father as Duke of Palma and then Prince of Lampedusa. His only novel *Il gattopardo* (*The Leopard*), 1958, written at the end of his life and set mainly in 1860–2, is the fruit both of his awareness of his position as the last heir of a once mighty aristocratic house and of many years of intensive reading in European literature and history. Unusually for an Italian of his time, Lampedusa was at least as interested in English literature as in French. He admired English understatement and humour, which are perhaps a source, in *Il gattopardo*, of the irony of Don Fabrizio Corbera, Prince of Salina. Another strong influence was Stendhal (◊Lombardy), particularly for the combination of personal and political narrative.

Lampedusa's breadth of reading in five languages helps to explain both the carefully crafted language of his novel and why it is not simply a Sicilian aristocrat's nostalgic and biased account of a world of lost privilege. The view of Sicily as incapable of reform or energetic activity expressed by the Prince to a naive visiting Piedmontese bureaucrat created a furore on the book's first publication, but its politics are usually more subtle than that passage suggests. Don Fabrizio rejects the passing of the old order but knows its deficiencies and goes some distance to adapt himself to the new ways. (He is, besides, an astronomer, like Lampedusa's great-grandfather on whom he is partly based, and longs for the cool certainties of the stars, far removed from the human imperfections and mortality which he cannot otherwise forget.)

The flexibility of viewpoint in *Il gattopardo* in fact results from the close focus on its central character. Frequently the narrative takes the form of his own lyrical interior monologue. His awareness of death, both a personal characteristic and a response to the decay of his position and class, ebbs and flows. The Prince's initial contempt for the new rich Calogero Sedàra is softened by further contact, by reflection, by the appeal of Sedàra's self-confident and beautiful daughter Angelica. He cannot gainsay the practical sense of his beloved nephew Tancredi in taking up the tricolour of a united Italy

in 1860 and in marrying Angelica's wealth. (Such acceptance is again, however, qualified by the habitual scepticism.)

The proud lion or leopard (from his family crest) Don Fabrizio, already a rarity among the Bourbon nobility, loses his claws under the new dispensation. Lampedusa writes an elegy for him and for the palaces of his own younger days, now sold, dilapidated, or destroyed. (The desire to recall and record them in detail had an immediate origin in the author's rereading of Stendhal's autobiographical *La Vie de Henry Brulard* (*The Life of Henry Brulard*), 1835.) *Il gattopardo* is an elegy also for lost experience and opportunity (as in the unfulfilled life of the Prince's daughter Concetta, who loved Tancredi) which at the same time imaginatively reconstructs them. Luchino Visconti's film *The Leopard*, 1963, continued the process.

**VERGA, Giovanni** (1840–1922), was born into a prosperous landed family in Catania. In 1865 he moved to Florence, and in 1872 to Milan, while continuing to spend summers in Sicily. It was in 1874 that he began to publish stories and novels of the *verismo* school, a movement influenced by the French realist and naturalist novel. Verga wrote mainly about Sicilian villagers, mostly poor or precariously better-off, in simple and accessible language and attempting to tell their stories as much as possible from their own points of view without an omniscient authorial presence. They live in a world of repeated misfortune, disease, and death, social and sexual taboos which cannot be broken with impunity, and fierce passions and obsessions.

Verga's most important works are *I Malavoglia* (*The House By the Medlar-Tree*), 1881, *Novelle rusticane* (*Little Novels of Sicily*), 1883, and Mastro-don Gesualdo, 1889. He adapted his short story of jealousy and revenge Cavalleria rusticana – 'rustic chivalry' – as a play (1883) in which Eleonora Duse's performance as the heroine was much fêted. More famously, the play became an opera with music by Pietro Mascagni in 1890. Disputes over payments due to Verga in connection with the opera were among the factors that embittered his later years. In 1894 he returned to live in Catania. In 1920 he was appointed Senator.

I Malavoglia was intended to be the first of a five-novel cycle representing 'the struggle for life' of people ranging, as Verga puts it in a letter of 1878, 'from the rag-picker to the minister, to the artist'. The title of the cycle was to be I vinti, 'the vanquished'. The Malavoglia, poor fishermen of Aci Trezza, lose at sea their boat, their most able crew member, and their cargo, and as a result lose their house to their creditors. Traditional wisdom and heroic resignation, it becomes evident, remain the best available weapon against persistent misfortune in a poor and restricted social setting. Mastro-don Gesualdo was intended to be the second novel of the incomplete I vinti. Here a bricklayer, Don Gesualdo Motta, becomes rich enough to marry 'above his station', but remains, socially and psychologically, an outsider.

VITTORINI, Elio (1908–66), born in Syracuse, the son of a railwayman, left home in 1924 and found employment in the far north of Italy as, amongst other things, a construction worker in Gorizia. His period as a manual labourer contributed to his enduring commitment to social reform; after service as a partisan at the end of the Second World War he remained a Communist party member until

1951. After 1929 Vittorini spent most of his life in Florence and Milan, first as a proof-reader and book-reviewer. From the early 1930s to his death he was an immensely influential figure, becoming an editor for the publishers Einaudi, Mondadori, and Bompiani, translating and introducing American literature (especially Hemingway and Faulkner), and advancing younger authors like Italo Calvino (◊Liguria). As an editor, Vittorini's most controversial decision was to reject the manuscript of Lampedusa's Il gattopardo (The Leopard), 1958, a novel foreign in almost every respect to the literature of social commitment and formal experiment which he espoused. In 1959, with Calvino, Vittorini launched Il Menabò (1959–67), one of the leading radical literary reviews of its day.

Vittorini's first important novel is Il garofano rosso (The Red Carnation), serialised in 1933–4 when it was subject to censorship for its evident allusions to the violence and superficial attractiveness of Fascism. The book appeared in volume form only in 1948. Conversazione in Sicilia (Conversation in Sicily), 1941 (serialised 1938), avoided the same fate by referring more obliquely to, and further universalising, contemporary events. Fascism and the Spanish Civil War were much on Vittorini's mind as he wrote, but his character Silvestro, who returns to Sicily for the first time in fifteen years, starts as a sufficiently generalised victim of the times, 'haunted by abstract furies', by 'some sort of furies concerning the doomed human race'. Through a series of encounters, some realistic, some more surreal, with other travellers, his mother, the ghost of his brother killed in battle, and various oppressed Sicilians, Silvestro acquires new fellowship with those who suffer dictatorship, poverty, and illness; 'One persecutes and another is persecuted; not all the human race is human, but only the race of the persecuted . . . A man who is sick or starving is more than a man'. Largely composed of dialogue, almost incantatory in its repetitions, full of question marks, *Conversazione* wants to force attention onto the unresolved problems of the poor and oppressed. Like other 'neo-realist' novelists including Pavese (◊Piedmont), Vittorini rejects the formal and stylistic elegance of much late 19th and early 20th century Italian writing, but, more than most, his prose aspires to the condition of poetry. 'A word', he says with a characteristic mixture of the obvious and the profound, 'may give a new meaning to a fact which is not new'.

# SARDINIA

'An island of rigid conventions, the rigid conventions of barbarians, and at the same time, the fierce violence of the instinctive passions.'
D.H. Lawrence, preface to The Mother by Grazia Deledda

'Still Sardinia is one of the wildest, remotest parts of Europe, with a strange people and a mysterious past of its own. There is still an old mystery in the air, over the forest slopes of Mount Gennargentu, as there is over some old Druid places, the mystery of an unevolved people.'

D.H. Lawrence's idea of Sardinia, expressed here in his 1922 preface to Grazia Deledda's novel *La madre* (*The Mother*), 1920, is strongly influenced by his restless desire to find somewhere the pure, instinctual, uncorrupted place; the search will take him on to Mexico, the South Seas, Australia. But his stress on the primeval or mysterious aspects of the island would not have surprised Deledda, a native of the stony hill of **Nuoro**, at the time of her birth in 1871 still a very remote town ('nothing but a perch for the crows' according to her fellow Nuorese Salvatore Satta) (Extract 1) in *Il giorno del giudizio* (*The Day of Judgment*), 1979.)

Certainly the Deledda family house (now the birthplace museum in Via Deledda) had a more solid emphasis than 'old Druid places' tend to – life centred, as described in the autobiographical *Cosima*, 1937, on the kitchen with its solid furniture and utensils and *focolare* or central fire above which pecorino cheeses were cured – but there was a view of Mount Ortobene from the house, wild country all around Nuoro, and a local life of ancient festivals and costumes, extempore poems and songs, bandits' deeds and vendettas, and shepherds' tales and superstitions. Sards were and continued to be intensely aware of an individual, non-Italian identity to be kept alive in costume, language (varying greatly from region to region, often as close to Latin as Italian) and story. Prehistoric remains, especially the *nuraghi* – hollow structures made with huge blocks of stone – and so-called 'giants' tombs, are a more frequent and imposing presence in the country than any traces left by successive Carthaginian, Roman, Arab, Pisan, Genoese, Spanish, or Austrian rulers over the centuries before Sardinia was apportioned to Piedmont in 1720. Such changes of ownership, culminating in unification with the new kingdom of Italy in 1861, rarely alleviated the island's deep poverty, experience of which formed Italy's great Communist thinker and activist Antonio Gramsci), born at **Ales** north-west of Cagliari in 1891. (The family lived mainly, however, at **Ghilarza**, some miles further north.)

Sardinia is, continues Lawrence's preface, 'an island of rigid conventions, the rigid conventions of barbarians, and at the same time, the fierce violence of the instinctive passions. A savage tradition of chastity, with a savage lust of the flesh. A barbaric overlordship of the gentry, with a fierce indomitableness of the servile classes'. There is 'a determined savage individualism often breaking with the law, or driven into brigandage; but human, of the great human mystery'. In Deledda, the 'instinctive passions' are often defeated, after much struggle, by the 'rigid conventions'. The conventions themselves, indeed, have an emotional, instinctive hold on dwellers in traditional communities. In *La madre*, for instance, Agnese, a rich, respected single woman, intends to denounce her lover, the priest Paolo, before the congregation, but cannot, when the time comes, bear so to shame herself. A 'primitive and monotonous' ancestral hymn calls to her in the voice of her past and her whole race, including 'the men and women who had built and furnished her house, and ploughed her fields and woven the linen for her swaddling clothes'.

Lawrence's direct experience of Sardinia was an expedition from Sicily, with his wife Frieda, in January 1921. The resulting *Sea and Sardinia*, written soon afterwards, came out at the end of the year. Landing in Cagliari, they travelled into the interior by slow country train as far as Sorgono then on, by the very recently introduced motor-bus service, to Nuoro and eventually to the east coast. There were frustrations in plenty: cold and filthy inn-rooms, unavailability of tolerable food, a communal latrine (not, for a cold and hungry Lawrence at least, a good example of uninhibited naturalness), and occasional hostility. The natives encouraged poor service by pitying the inn staff at Sorgono as simply *ignoranti* – 'what they need is not pity but prods'. As he is aware, disappointment sometimes follows expectations as high as his. But frequently he does find what he seeks. He savours the people and their black, white, or flaring red costumes. The men's long 'stocking-caps', worn all the time but in various permutations – down the back, rising over the brow 'martial and handsome', over the nose with points like fox-ears above – become in Lawrence's account 'superb crests', signs of the islanders' 'splendid, animal-bright stupidity' and perilously surviving escape from homogeneity. The landscape complements the people, substituting for Italy's 'toppling crags of romance' (Extract 2) a sense of space among the 'unremarkable ridges of moor-like hills' in the south (Celtic hills, were not the heath and scrub 'too big and brigand-like' for Celtic lands), grey stony expanses, the 'savage, dark-bushed, sky-exposed' shore near **Orosei**. Earlier in the journey, in the central interior, the mountains of **Gennargentu** are like the peasants, 'more human and knowable' than Etna, 'with a deep breast and massive limbs, a powerful mountain-body'.

Much else catches Lawrence's attention: in **Cagliari**, for example, a steep street 'like a cork-screw stairway', the cathedral which once must have been a fine fortress but now has come 'through the mincing machine of the ages, and oozed out baroque and sausagey', one market glowing with eggs ('a Sierra Nevada of eggs, glowing warm white') and another with massed fruit, with 'piles of sugar-dusty white figs and sombre-looking black figs, and bright burnt figs'. Later incidents on the bus include an altercation when a man with two black pigs in sacks is outraged that he must pay for each of them 'as if it were a Christian'. ('How much do you charge for the fleas you carry?' asks a sarcastic youth.)

Elio Vittorini (◊**Sicily**), in *Viaggio in Sardegna* (*Journey to Sardinia*), 1936, recorded many and various sights, including some of the things and places the Lawrences did not see, from the 'nothingness of daily labour' in the coal-mines, where the use of toil is a bit of bread and the use of a bit of bread is the strength for new toil, to **Sassari**, the second city of Sardinia, the baroque facade of whose cathedral looks at first like 'a gigantic worm-eaten piece of furniture' before it is seen to be towering dove-coloured stone swarming with, positively infested with, leaves and heads of angels.

North of Sardinia on the mountainous island of **Caprera** is the white house of Giuseppe Garibaldi◊. This was, for disciples like C.A. Vecchi, 'the humble abode of the greatest man of the age'. In 1855 Garibaldi bought half Caprera with the aid of a legacy from his brother Felice; later an English-based fund raised the money to buy the other half for him. During 1856 a small group of friends helped him to build the Casa Bianca and its outhouses. He also built dry-stone walls and established a vineyard. (On one occasion Vecchi, after a hard morning writing letters for his leader, was summoned for some 'relaxation' which turned out to consist of a hard afternoon's pruning and planting.) Here, after his part in the momentous events of the early 1860s, Garibaldi returned to till the soil, a figure still viewed with suspicion by the rulers of the new kingdom he had done so much to bring about but revered as a hero by thousands in Europe and the Americas. The island was conveniently placed for journeys to both Nice and Genoa, the cities where Garibaldi had the closest ties, and where he continued to address workers' and other groups. There were more dramatic absences, as when he slipped away in a small boat before dawn, and before he could embarrass or be intercepted by the Italian authorities, to fight against the Prussians in France in 1870–1. Most of his remaining years, however, were spent on Caprera, writing memoirs and (avowedly for the money) novels, dealing with correspondence, tending his land, sheep and cattle, and presiding over meals and family music parties. (Vecchi heard him sing an aria from Bellini's *I Puritani* and join the company in a loud rendering of the revolutionary *Marseillaise*.)

Some unknown admirers of the great man inevitably penetrated this rural retreat, but access was only possible by boat – there was at this stage no causeway between Caprera and its more fertile and cultivated neighbour **La Maddalena**. (Garibaldi was, however, a tolerant man. At the Hotel d'Angleterre in Naples in 1860 he submitted meekly, according to one observer, when English ladies asked 'for a kiss-a-piece, and that each might cut off a lock of his hair'. General Türr, one of his right-hand men, 'looked somewhat out of patience, standing over Garibaldi with a comb, and raking down his head after each operation'.)

Garibaldi died in his house, preserved as the present **Museo Garibaldi**, on 2 June 1882. The hero of the Risorgimento, as he became to even more people once he was safely dead, was buried (as befitted a hero – he had asked to be cremated) in a granite tomb in the garden.

## Other Literary Landmarks

**Cagliari**: ruins of the **House of Tigellius**, the supposed home of a Sard poet known only from unflattering remarks by Horace (◊Rome) and Cicero (◊Rome). The dead Tigellius, says Horace in his First Book of *Satires*, is mourned by flute-girls, quacks, beggars, buffoons; he was one of those singers who would never perform when asked to (even Julius Caesar couldn't make him) but who, when the fancy took him, 'would keep chanting 'Io Bacche'' through the feast from hors-d'oeuvre to fruit.

**Nuoro**: the **Museo Etnografico** (Via Antonio Mereu) contains a very extensive collection of costumes of the sort often described in Sard and visitors' literature, including those worn at the end of August at the Festa del Redentore.

**Nuoro**: in the church of **Santa Maria della Solitudine** is the tomb of Grazia Deledda◊.

## BOOKLIST

Deledda, Grazia, *Cosima* [1937], Martha King, trans, Quartet, London, 1988.

Deledda, Grazia, *Elias Portolu* [1903], Martha King, trans, Quartet, London, 1992.

Deledda, Grazia, *La Madre: the Mother* [1920], M.G. Steegman, trans, foreword by D.H. Lawrence [1922], introduction by Eric Lane, Dedalus, London, and Hippocrene, New York, 1987.

Joll, James, *Antonio Gramsci*, Penguin, Harmondsworth, 1977.

Kinkead-Weekes, Mark, *D.H. Lawrence: Triumph to Exile, 1912–1922*, Cambridge University Press, 1996. (Vol 2 of The Cambridge Biography: D.H. Lawrence, 1885–1930.)

Lawrence, D.H., *D.H. Lawrence and Italy: Twilight in Italy, Sea and Sardinia, Etruscan Places*, introduction by Anthony Burgess, Viking Penguin, New York, 1972; Penguin, London, 1985. **Extract 2**.

Ridley, Jasper, *Garibaldi*, Constable, London, 1974.

Satta, Salvatore, *The Day of Judgment* [1979], Patrick Creagh, trans, Collins Harvill, London, 1987. **Extract 1**.

Wood, Sharon, *Italian Women's Writing 1860–1994*, Athlone, London, 1995.

# Extracts

## (1) NUORO

### Salvatore Satta, *The Day of Judgment*, 1979

*These are the last, retrospective and reflective pages of Satta's unfinished evocation of life in the small provincial capital in the late 19th and early 20th centuries.*

After many months I once more take up this tale, which perhaps I should never have begun. I am swiftly growing old, and feel that I am preparing myself for a sad end, because I have chosen not to accept the first condition for a good death, which is oblivion. Maybe it was not Don Sebastiano, Donna Vincenza, Gonaria, Pedduzza, Giggia, Baliodda, Dirripezza and all the others, who begged me to set them free from their lives: it is I who have called them up to rid me of mine, without calculating the risk to which I was exposing myself, in making myself eternal. And then today, outside the windows of this remote room where I have taken refuge, it is snowing: a light snow that settles on the streets, and the trees, as time settles upon us. In a little while everything will look the same. In the cemetery of Nuoro one will not be able to tell the old from the new, and 'they' will have some fleeting peace beneath the cloak of whiteness. I too was once a little boy, and I am beset by the memory of when I watched the swirl of the snowflakes with my nose pressed against the windowpane. We were all there then, in the room enlivened by the fire, and we were happy, because we did not know ourselves. To know ourselves we have to live our own lives to the bitter end, until the moment we fall into the grave. And even then we need someone to gather us up, to revive us, to speak about us both to ourselves and to others, as in a last judgment. It is what I have done myself these last few years, which I wish I had not done: yet I will continue to do it, because by now it is not a question of the destinies of others, but of my own.

## (2) Sardinia

### D.H. Lawrence, Sea and Sardinia, 1921

*Lawrence visited Sardinia from Sicily for a week in January 1921. This excerpt is from his characteristically eager, insistent, observant, opinionated account of the train-journey in the interior from Mandas to Sorgono. (Wilhelm Meister is the eponymous hero of Goethe's novel of 1795–6.)*

But soon we begin to climb the hills. And soon the cultivation begins to be intermittent. Extraordinary how the healthy, moor-like hills come near the sea; extraordinary how scrubby and uninhabited the great spaces of Sardinia are. It is wild, with heath and arbutus scrub and a sort of myrtle, breast-high. Sometimes one sees a few head of cattle. And then again come the greyish-arable patches, where the corn is grown. It is like Cornwall, like the Land's End region. Here and there, in the distance, are peasants working on the lonely landscape. Sometimes it is one man alone in the distance, showing so vividly in his black-and-white costume, small and far-off like a solitary magpie, and curiously distinct. All the strange magic of Sardinia is in this sight. Among the low, moor-like hills, away in a hollow of the wide landscape one solitary figure, small but vivid black-and-white, working alone, as if eternally. There are patches and hollows of grey arable land, good for corn. Sardinia was once a great granary. . . .

This is very different from Italian landscape. Italy is almost always dramatic, and perhaps inevitably romantic. There is drama in the plains of Lombardy and romance in the Venetian lagoons, and sheer scenic excitement in nearly all the hilly parts of the peninsula. Perhaps it is the natural floridity of limestone formations. But Italian landscape is really 18th-century landscape: . . . aqueducts, and ruins upon sugar-loaf mountains, and craggy ravines and Wilhelm Meister water-falls: all up and down.

Sardinia is another thing. Much wider, much more ordinary, not up-and-down at all, but running away into the distance. Unremarkable ridges of moor-like hills running away, perhaps to a bunch of dramatic peaks on the south-west. This gives a sense of space, which is so lacking in Italy. Lovely space about one, and travelling distances – nothing finished, nothing final. It is like liberty itself, after the peaky confinement of Sicily. Room – give me room – give me room for my spirit: and you can have all the toppling crags of romance.

# Biographies and important works

DELEDDA, Grazia (1871–1936), was born at Nuoro into a middle-class family which regarded it as highly unsuitable for a young woman to write for money. Nevertheless she succeeded in publishing her first short story in a Rome magazine in 1886. Initially she wrote romantic love stories, but in the 1890s moved further towards a realist or *verismo* emphasis. In 1899 she moved to Cagliari and married a civil servant. From 1900 they lived in Rome. Deledda rarely revisited Sardinia, but continued to set almost all her fiction there. She was awarded the Nobel Prize for Literature in 1926, occasioning some controversy because Mussolini may have backed her candidacy against more morally and politically challenging authors including Matilde Serao (◊Naples and Campania).

Among Deledda's most characteristic novels are *Elias Portolu*, 1903, where the eponymous character loves his brother's fiancée but, unable to take decisive action, becomes a priest, and *La madre*

(*The Mother*), 1920, where, as D.H. Lawrence◊ says in his foreword to an English translation of 1922, 'the old, wild instinct of a mother's ambition for her son defeats the other wild instinct of sexual mating'. The novels and tales repeatedly examine the tension between individual desires and age-old Sardinian social and familial hegemonies. Lawrence judges that Deledda does not probe her characters' passions and motives very deeply but 'what she does do is to create the passionate complex of a primitive populace'.

The struggle of the individual against the social order in Deledda can also be read 'as the literary correlative of the relations between an island which is only in theory part of a post-Unification reality, torn between the old world and the new, and the newly-formed nation state, the Kingdom of Italy' (Sharon Wood).

GARIBALDI, Giuseppe (1807–82), was born at Nice, recently incorporated into France under Napoleon, of a Genoese family. As a seaman in 1833 he came under the influence of Mazzini's (◊Liguria) republican ideas, took part in an abortive attempt at revolution in Piedmont, and fled abroad to avoid a death sentence. From 1836 to 1848 he was in South America, where he learnt his skills as a guerrilla and naval commander, fighting for the Rio Grande do Sul separatists in Brazil and for Uruguay against Argentina. In 1848 he returned to Italy and was prominent in the defence of Mazzini's Roman Republic. After its defeat Garibaldi returned to seafaring, becoming captain of a merchantman and travelling widely in Europe, Asia, and the United States. In 1859 he led a volunteer force in support of the Piedmontese army in northern Italy, having abandoned his early republicanism in favour of support for King Vittorio Emanuele II. (In later years, however, he developed sympathies with socialism.) Garibaldi's greatest achievement was the conquest of Naples and Sicily in 1860 at the head of his 'Thousand'. After a period as Dictator, he dismayed many of his followers by handing all captured territory over to Vittorio Emanuele, an action which greatly facilitated the establishment of a united Italy. Garibaldi wished to move on to attack Rome, but this did not accord with the more cautious and subtle policy of the Prime Minister of Piedmont, Cavour, or his allies. Captured at Aspromonte, he made his peace once more with the king and Piedmont. Nevertheless he left Caprera to take part in two more attempts to take Rome, in 1862 and 1867, and to fight against the Prussians for republican France in 1870–1. Garibaldi clearly possessed great personal charisma. He was particularly popular in England, which he visited several times.

Garibaldi's most readable and important piece of writing, *Le memorie* (*Memoirs*), concerned primarily with his military campaigns, appeared first in an English translation in 1859 and then in other longer versions and translations. He also wrote poems and novels which overtly advance the causes he believed in. *Clelia, ovvero Il governo del monaco* (*Roma nel secolo XIX*) (*Clelia, or the Rule of the Monk* (*Rome in the 19th Century*), 1870, is, as its title suggests, fervently anti-clerical; the villainous Cardinal Procopio not only persecutes liberals and revolutionaries but has a penchant for dishonouring beautiful maidens. (Procopio is inspired by the papal secretary of state Cardinal Antonelli, after whom one of Garibaldi's donkeys on Caprera was caustically named.)

GRAMSCI, Antonio (1891–1937), was born at Ales and grew up, chiefly in Ghilarza, in poverty caused partly by the imprisonment of his father, a minor bureaucrat, on charges of embezzlement. In 1911 he won a scholarship to the University of Turin and soon became a Socialist and a prolific journalist. He was involved in the strikes and factory occupations of 1920. From 1921 he was a member of the central committee of the new Italian Communist Party, travelling twice to Moscow. He was elected to the Chamber of Deputies in 1924. Arrested under Fascism in 1926, Gramsci was held in various prisons and finally clinics until his death from a brain haemorrhage in 1937. *Lettere dal carcere* (*Letters from Prison*), published in 1947, and particularly *Quaderni del carcere* (*Prison Notebooks*), published in 1948–51, have had an enormous influence on European Marxism and Italian intellectual life more generally. One of Gramsci's most important concepts is 'hegemony' – 'the way in which a minority can impose its leadership and its values on a majority' (Joll). The hegemony of working class intellectuals is a necessary first step towards the establishment of rule by the working class. This idea, which is at odds with Lenin's conception of the (party-imposed) 'dictatorship of the proletariat', has been particularly useful for Marxist politicians forced to function in liberal parliamentary regimes. Gramsci's ideas are often pursued, in the notebooks, through reflections on history and literature, which explain the current context of political action and are important vehicles of the moral and intellectual reform which, Gramsci believes, must, accompany social.

LAWRENCE, D[avid] H[erbert] (1885–1930), lived and travelled in northern Italy for much of 1912–14 and mainly in the south in 1919–22; between 1925 and 1929 he lived on the Riviera di Ponente and near Florence. He rented the house at Taormina in Sicily from 1920, and visited Sardinia in 1921. His books about Italy, like all his work, have sermons to preach, axes to grind, a non-'mechanistic' ideal civilisation to glimpse and yearn for. In the process not just the vividly striking externals of a place emerge – although those too fascinate Lawrence, often as evidence of its spiritual qualities – but what seems to him, albeit temporarily, their essence.

*Twilight in Italy*, 1916, is a series of sketches mainly of Lake Garda. What makes *Sea and Sardinia*, 1921, so different from this first Italian book is, as Mark Kinkead-Weekes says, the 'characters': the irascible 'I' and the queen-bee or 'q-b' (Frieda Lawrence), 'not easily moved, but formidable when offended'. The comic irascibility allows what is beautiful and serious to come through undiminished,

'while what is annoying and uncomfortable gets dramatized into vivacity, or made material for comedy, or held at tolerable distance by self-awareness. A persona so deliberately prickly can help to turn Lawrence's abiding self-consciousness into lively drama, where his perceptions and descriptions of the oddness of others get visibly sharpened by awareness of the oddity he seems to be'. *Etruscan Places*, published posthumously in 1932, retains some of the travel-journal structure of *Sea and Sardinia*, but is more meditative, lyrical, and focused. The Etruscans, dead and mysterious, can bear the weight of Lawrence's sexual and ethical idealism more easily, more sustainedly, than living people and peoples.

Lawrence also wrote some of his more famous novels, short stories, and poems in Italy. *Cypresses*, 1920, again explores the opposition between Etruscan (manifested in sinuous Tuscan cypresses) and Roman, life and what denies it as 'mechanical America' still denies Montezuma; in 'Snake', 1921, set in the heat of Taormina in summer, the voice of 'accursed human education' tells the speaker to try to kill the snake; similar tensions characterize *Bat* and *Man and Bat*, 1921, set in Florence.

SATTA, Salvatore (1902–75), from Nuoro, lived in mainland Italy ('the Continent') for much of his life. An authority on legal procedure, he held university posts in Genoa and Rome and contributed extensively to the early volumes of the comprehensive *Enciclopedia del Diritto* (*Encyclopedia of Law*), 1958–95. His unfinished novel *Il giorno del giudizio* (*The Day of Judgment*) was published four years after his death.

At the end of his life Satta felt a pressing need to record the Nuoro of his youth and to reflect on the mystery of living beings now dead. Although his book tells a family story it does so most often in sketches, interspersed with authorial musings and digressions on mortality and identity, telling of life which is over and yet continues as – effectively because – he writes, until, conversely, his own life seems to exist only in the writing.

# ACKNOWLEDGEMENTS

The author and the publisher are very grateful to the many literary agents, publishers, translators, authors and other individuals who have given their permission for the use of the extracts listed below or who have helped to trace copyright holders. Every effort has been made to identify and contact copyright owners or their representatives. The publisher would welcome any further information.

**VENICE**: (2) Carlo Goldoni, *Four Comedies*, Frederick Davies, trans, Penguin, London, 1968. Copyright © Frederick Davies 1968. (*All rights whatsoever in this play are strictly reserved and application for performance etc., must be made before rehearsal to Casarotto Ramsey Ltd., National House, 60–66 Wardour Street, London W1V 4ND. No performance may be given unless a licence has been obtained.*) (4) Thomas Mann, *Death in Venice*, H.T. Lowe-Porter, trans, Penguin, London, 1955. © Martin Secker and Warburg, London, 1928. (5) Filippo Tommaso Marinetti, *Selected Writings*, R.W. Flint, ed, R.W. Flint and Arthur A. Coppotelli, trans, Secker and Warburg, London, 1972. Reprinted by permission of Farrar, Strauss and Giroux Inc. © 1972 Farrar, Strauss & Giroux, Inc. **VENETO**: (1) *For Love of Laura: Poetry of Petrarch*, Marion Shore, trans, University of Arkansas, Fayetteville, 1987. (2) Guiseppe Ungaretti, *Selected Poems*, Patrick Creagh, trans, Penguin, Harmondsworth, 1971. (3) Italo Svevo, *Confession of Zeno*, Beryl de Zoete, trans, Copyright 1930 and renewed 1958 by Alfred A. Knopf Inc. Reprinted by permission of the publisher. (4) Dacia Maraini, *Isolina*, Sian Williams, trans, Peter Owen, London and Chester Springs, PA, 1993. **LOMBARDY**: (1) Stendhal, *The Charterhouse of Parma*, C.K. Scott Moncrieff, trans, David Campbell, London 1992. (2) Antonio Fogazzaro, *The Little World of the Past*, W.J. Strachan, trans, Oxford University Press, London 1962. By Permission of Oxford University Press. (4) Alessandro Manzoni, *The Betrothed*, Bruce Penman, trans, Penguin, Harmondsworth 1983. (5) Giorgio Vasari, *Lives of the Artists*, George Bull, trans, Penguin, Harmondsworth 1987. **PIEDMONT**: (1) Umberto Eco, *How to travel with a Salmon and Other Essays*, William Weaver, trans, Secker and Warburg, London 1994. (2) Natalia Ginzburg, *Voices in the Evening*, Carcanet, Manchester 1990. © Hogarth Press. (3) Primo Levi, *The Periodic Table*, Raymond Rosenthal, trans, Sphere Books, London 1986. © Shocken Books Inc. 1984. (4) Cesare Pavese, *The Moon and the Bonfires*, Louise Sinclair, trans, Sceptre, Sevenoaks 1988. © Peter Owen, London 1952. **LIGURIA**: (2) Guiseppe Ungaretti, *Selected Poems*, see VENETO 2. (3) Eugenio Montale, *Poesie/Poems*, George Kay, trans, Edinburgh University Press, Edinburgh 1964. (4) Italo Calvino, *The Road to San Giovanni*, Tim Parks, trans, Jonathan Cape, London 1993. **EMILIA-ROMAGNA**: (1) Giosuè Carducci, *Selected Verse*, David H. Higgins, ed and trans, Aris and Phillips, Warminster 1994. (2) Ludovico Ariosto, *Orlando Furioso*, Barbara Reynolds, trans, Penguin, Harmondsworth 1975. (3) Giorgio Bassani, *The Garden of the Finzi-Continis*, Isabel Quigly, trans, Quartet, London 1974. © Faber 1965. (5) Dante, *The Divine Comedy: Hell*, Mark Musa, trans, Penguin, Harmondsworth 1984. © Indiana University Press. **FLORENCE**: (1) Boccaccio, *The Decameron*, Guido Waldman, trans, Jonathan Usher, ed, Oxford University Press, Oxford and New York, 1993. By permission of Oxford University Press. (4) E.M. Forster, *A Room with a View*, Penguin, Harmondsworth 1976. Published 1923 by Alfred A. Knopf Inc. Reproduced by permission of the Provost and scholars of King's College,

Cambridge and The Society of Authors as the Literary Representative of the E.M. Forster Estate. (5) Lorenzo de' Medici, *Selected Poems and Prose*, Jon Thiem, ed and trans, Pennsylvania State University Press, 1991. Copyright © Pennsylvania University Press. Reproduced by permission of the publisher. (6) Vasco Pratolini, *Family Chronicle*, Martha King, trans, Quartet, London 1991. (7) Niccolo Macchiavelli, *The Literary Works of Macchiavelli; Mandragola, Clizia, a Dialogue on Language, Belfagor, With Selections from the Private Correspondence*, J.R. Hale, ed and trans, Greenwood Press, Westport, CT 1979. © Oxford University Press 1961. By permission of Oxford University Press. **TUSCANY:** (1) Heinrich Heine, *Selected Prose*, Ritchie Robertson, trans, Penguin, London 1993. (2) Dante, *The Divine Comedy: Hell*, see EMILIA-ROMAGNA 5. (3) E.M. Forster, *Where Angels Fear to Tread*, Penguin, Harmondsworth 1974. Copyright 1920 by Alfred A. Knopf Inc and renewed 1948 by Edward Morgan Forster. Reprinted by permission of the publisher. Reproduced by permission of the Provost and Scolars of King's College, Cambridge and The Society of Authors as the Literary Representative of the E.M. Forster Estate. (5) Iris Origo, *War in the Val d'Orcia*, John Murray, London 1984. **UMBRIA:** (1) *Francis and Clare; the Complete Works*. Regis J. Armstrong and Ignatius C. Brady, trans, SPCK, London 1982. © Missionary Society of St Paul the Apostle in the State of New York. (2) *A Leopardi Reader*. Ottavio M. Casale ed and trans, University of Illinois Press, Urbana, Chicago and London 1981. (3) Baldesar Castiglione, *The Book of the Courtier*, George Bull, trans, Penguin, Harmondsworth 1967. (4) John Mortimer, *Summer's Lease*, Penguin, London, 1988. Reprinted by permission of The Peters Fraser and Dunlop Group Limited on behalf of © John Mortimer. **ROME:** (1) Sibilla Aleramo, *A Woman*, Rosalind Delmar, trans, Virago 1979. Copyright © Giangiacomo Feltrinelli Editore, Milano 1973. (2) Reprinted from ARTEMISIA by Anna Banti, translated by Shirley D'Ardia Caracciolo, by permission of the University of Nebraska Press. Copyright © 1988 by the University of Nebraska Press. (3) Carlo Emilio Gadda, *That Awful Mess on Via Merulana*, William Weaver, trans, Quartet, London 1985. © George Braziller Inc. (5) Juvenal, *The Satires*, Niall Rudd, trans, Clarendon Press, Oxford 1991. By permission of Oxford University Press. (6) Livy, *The Early History of Rome*, Aubrey de Selincourt, trans, Limited Editions Club, 1970. © Penguin

1960. (7) Michelangelo Buonarotti, *The Sonnets of Michelangelo*, Elizabeth Jennings, trans, Carcanet Press, Manchester 1987. © The Folio Society 1961. (8) Alberto Moravia, *The Woman of Rome*, Lydia Holland, trans, Granada, London 1984. © Martin Secker and Warburg. **LAZIO:** (1) Giorgio Bassani, *The Garden of the Finzi-Continis*, see EMILIA-ROMAGNA 3. (3) Pier Pasolini, *The Ragazzi*, Emile Capouya, Paladin, Grafton Books, London 1989. © Grove/Atlantic Inc. 1968. **NAPLES AND CAMPANIA:** (1) Virgil, *The Aeneid*, Robert Fitzgerald, trans, Harvill, London 1984. First published in the United States by Random House, Inc. First published in Great Britain in 1984 by The Harvill Press. Translation copyright © 1981, 1982, 1983 by Robert Fitzgerald. Reproduced by permission of The Harvill Press. (2) Boccaccio, *The Elegy of Lady Fiammetta*, Mariangela Causa-Steindler and Thams Mauch, trans, University of Chicago Press, London and Chicago 1990. (3) Eduardo de Filippo, *Four Plays: the Local authority, Grand Magic, Filumena Marturano*, Carlo Arditto, trans, Methuen Drama, London 1992. (5) Norman Lewis, *Naples '44*, Collins, London 1978. (6) J.W. Goethe, *Italian Journey*, W.H. Auden and Elizabeth Mayer, trans, Penguin 1970. © Collins 1962. (9) *The Letters of the Younger Pliny*, Betty Radice, trans, Penguin Books, Harmondsworth 1963. **ABRUZZO-CALABRIA AND SOUTH-EAST:** (1) Ignazio Silone, *Fontamara*, Eric Mosbacher, trans, J.M. Dent, London 1994. (2) Carlo Levi, *Christ Stopped at Eboli*, Frances Frenaye Lanza, trans, Penguin, Harmondsworth 1982. Translation copyright © Penguin 1963/Farrar, Strauss 1947 and copyright renewed © 1974 by Farrar, Straus & Giroux. (3) Corrado Alvaro, *Revolt in Aspromonte*, Frances Frenaye, trans, New Directions, Norfolk, CT, 1962. Copyright © 1962 by New Directions Publishing Corp. Reprinted by permission of New Directions Publishing Corp. **SICILY:** (1) Leonardo Sciascia, *To Each His Own*, Adrienne Foulke, trans, Carcanet press, Manchester 1989. © Copyright Sciasca Estate. The book is published in Italy by Adelphi Edizioni, Milano. (2) *Tales of Madness: a Selection from Luigi Pirandello's Short Stories for a Year*, Giovanni Bussino, trans, Dante University of America Press, Brookline, MA, 1984. (3) *Street in Agrigentun* is taken from COMPLETE POEMS OF SALVATORE QUASIMODO, translated by Jack Bevan, published by Anvil Press Poetry in 1983. (5) Giovanni Tomasi di Lampedusa, *The Leopard*, Archibald Colquhorn, trans, William Collins,

# Index of Places

Abruzzo, 62–3, 246–7, 251–2
Adige, river, 31, 34
Agrigento, 261, 262, 269–71, 278–80
Alba, 70
Alban Hills (Colli Albani), 210
Ales, 293
Alessandria, 70, 71–2
Aliano, 248–9, 252–3
Amalfi, 228
Amiata, Monte, 155
Anacapri, 227
Anchiano, 149
Ancona, 164
Anzio, 211
Apulia, 246, 247–8, 250, 254–5
Arezzo, 148
Arona, 54
Arpino, 212
Arquà Petrarca, 29, 39–40
Asolo, 29–31, 38
Aspromonte, 250, 253–4
Assisi, 161–2, 165–6
Asti, 70
Avernus (Averno), Lake, 218

Bagni di Lucca, 148
Baia (Baiae), 226–7
Bari, 246
Basilicata, 245, 248–9, 250, 252–3
Baveno, 49
Bergamo, 46, 54
Bologna, 89–91, 98, 100
Bolzano (Bozen), 31
Bomarzo, 212
Borromean Islands, 46, 50
Bosisio Parini, 65
Brindisi, 219
Burano, 13
Busseto, 98

Cagliari, 294, 295

Calabria, 245, 249–50, 253–4
Caldonazzo, Lago di, 31
Campagna (Roman), 209–10
Campania, 217–44
Campi Flegrei, 226
Canne della Battaglia, 250
Caos, Il, 270, 271
Capo Colonna, 249
Caprera, 294–5
Caprese Michelangelo, 148
Capri, 227–8
Careggi, 113
Carrara, 141
Carso, 37, 45
Casale, 70
Caserta, 221
Castel del Monte, 247
Castello Euriale, 264
Catania, 262, 264, 268, 275
Catania, Piana di, 268–9, 282–3
Caudine Forks, 228
Cefalù, 262, 275
Certaldo, 148
Cerveteri, 211, 213–14
Cinque Terre, 80
Clitunno, Fonti del, 160
Colloredo di Montalbano, 38
Como, Lake, 51–2, 56–7
Corleone, 275
Cremona, 46, 54
Crotone, 245, 249
Cumae (Cuma), 217, 218, 227, 230–1

Duino, 38

Eboli, 257
Elba, 148–9
Emilia-Romagna, 89–109
Enna, 259
Etna, 262, 267–9, 280
Euganean Hills, 29

Ferrara, 89, 92–6, 98, 100–02
Fiume (Rijeka), 52, 63
Florence, 110–40
Frascati, 210, 214–15
Friuli, 26, 216

Garda, Lake, 52
Gardone Riviera, 52
Gela, 264
Gennargentu, 294
Genoa, 81–2, 83–4, 294
Ghilarza, 293
Gombo, Il, 142
Gorizia, 38
Gradara, 92
Gran Sasso, 246
Grianta, 56
Grotte di Catullo, 52
Gubbio, 159

Herculaneum (Ercolano), 225

Ischia, 228
Isola Bella, 50

La Verna (or Laverna), 149
Langhe, 69
Lazio, 209–16
Lecco, 51, 54
Lerici, 79
Lido di Venezia, 12, 16–17
Liguria, 79–88
Livorno (Leghorn), 142
Lodi, 46, 49
Loreto, 160
Lucca, 146–7, 149, 150–1
Lugano, Lake, 51, 57–8

Maggiore, Lake, 50–1
Mantua, 53–4, 58–9
Marche, 160–1, 163–5, 166–72
Marengo, 72
Marmore, Cascate delle, 160
Matera, 250
Melfi, 247
Mergellina, 218
Messina, 262
Messina, Straits of, 261
Metaponto, 250
Milan, 46, 47–50, 59–61
Mira, 38
Miseno, 227, 228
Modena, 89, 95

Molise, 246
Monferrato, 69
Monreale, 273
Montecristo, 149
Montegufoni, 149
Montenero, 142
Montepulciano, 149
Monterosso al Mare, 80, 85

Naples, 218–24, 228, 231–5
Norcia, 164
Nuoro, 292, 293, 295, 296–7

Oria, 51
Orosei, 294
Ortygia, 261, 264
Orvieto, 160
Ostia Antica, 211
Ostia, Lido di, 211, 215

Padua (Padova), 31–3
Paestum (Pesto), 218, 235–6
Palermo, 271–4, 275, 281–2
Palestrina, 212
Parma, 91
Pavia, 46
Pergusa, Lake, 259
Perugia, 160
Pesaro, 164
Pescara, 246–7
Pescina dei Marsi, 246
Piacenza, 89
Piazza Armerina, 261–2
Piedmont, 67–78
Pienza, 149
Pieve di Cadore, 38
Pisa, 144–5, 149, 151–2
Pompeii, 225–6, 236–7, 240–1
Portici, 221
Porto Empedocle, 270
Portofino, 82
Posilippo, 219
Pozzuoli, 226
Pratica di Mare, 212
Procida, 228
Puglia *see* Apulia

Racalmuto, 263, 287
Rapallo, 82
Ravenna, 89, 96–8, 102–4
Recanati, 160–1, 166–7
Reggio Emilia, 89, 98
Rimini, 91–2, 104–5

Romano d'Ezzelino, 38
Rome, 173–208, 211
Roncole Verdi, 98
Rubicone, river, 92

Sabbioneta, 54
San Gimignano, 147–8, 153
San Giovanni Battista, 80, 85–6
San Luca, 250
San Marino, 92
San Mauro Pascoli, 92
San Michele, Monte, 37, 40
San Remo, 80–1, 85–6
San Terenzo, 79
Sant' Andrea in Percussina, 119, 130–1
Santa Margherita di Belice, 274–5
Santa Maria delle Grazie, 54
Santo Stefano Belbo, 69, 74–5
Sardinia, 292–301
Sassari, 294
Sicily, 259–91
Siena, 142–4, 149, 154
Sila, 250
Sirmione, 52
Solfatara, 226
Sorgono, 293
Sorrento, 218, 234
Spoleto, 159, 164
Stresa, 54
Sulmona, 246
Sybaris, 245
Syracuse (Siracusa), 264–7, 283

Taormina, 275
Taranto, 247–8, 254–5
Tarquinia, 211
Terni, 160

Terranova di Sibari, 245
Thurii, 245
Tivoli, 210
Todi, 160, 164
Torcello, 13–14
Torre del Lago Puccini, 149
Trasimene, Lake, 160
Trevi, 160
Trieste, 36–8, 40–1
Turin, 67–9, 70
Tuscany, 110, 141–58
Tusculum, 212, 214

Udine, 38
Umbria, 159–60, 161–2, 164–6, 169–72
Urbino, 163–4, 167–9

Val d'Orcia, 141–2, 155, 157
Valdicastello Carducci, 149
Vallombrosa, 149
Valsolda, 51
Veneto, 29–45
Venice, 1–28
Venosa, 250
Verona, 33–5, 41–2
Vesuvius (Vesuvio), 224–6, 237–9
Viareggio, 142
Vicenza, 35–6
Villa Adriana, 210
Villa della Ginestra, 226
Villa Rotonda (Almerico), 29, 36
Villa San Michele, 227
Vinci, 149
Vittoriale degli Italiani, Il, 52
Vizzini, 268
Volterra, 141, 148
Vulci, 212

# Index of People

Aeschylus, 264
Albany, Countess of, 117
Alberti, Leon Battista, 92
Aleramo, Sibilla, 179, 192–3, 201
Alexander VI, Pope (Rodrigo Borgia), 93, 119
Alfieri, Vittorio, 70, 117
Alfonso the Magnanimous, King of Naples, 220
Alvaro, Corrado, 250, 253–4, 255
Ambrose, St, 46
Andersen, Hans Christian, 178, 190
Angelico, Fra, 114, 119
Antony, Mark (Marcus Antonius), 184, 203
Aquinas, St Thomas, 135
Arbes, Cesare, 24
Archimedes, 266–7, 283, 284
Archytas of Taranto, 247, 266
Aretino, Pietro, 4, 22
Ariosto, Ludovico, 92, 93–4, 94, 100–02, 105–6, 109, 212
Arnim, Elizabeth von, 82
Arnold, Matthew, 284
Arnold, Thomas, 52
Auden, W.H., 228
Augustus, 91, 182, 184–5, 244, 287

Ballantyne, R.M., 190
Banti, Anna, 193–4, 201–2
Barberini, Pope Urban VIII, 178
Bassani, Giorgio, 95–6, 98, 102, 196, 211, 213–14
Beckford, William, 31, 34, 53, 58–9, 61, 209, 221
Beerbohm, Max, 82
Belisarius, 96
Bellini, Vincenzo, 275, 295
Bembo, Pietro, 29–31, 32, 42, 94, 221
Benedict, St, 164, 212
Bernini, Gianlorenzo, 177, 178, 188

Blessington, Marguerite Power, Countess of, 222
Boccanegra, Simon, 81
Boccaccio, Giovanni, 110, 111–12, 112, 122, 123–4, 131–2, 148, 149, 216, 219–20, 227, 231–2
Boethius, Anicius Manlius Severinus, 96, 106
Boiardo, Count Matteo Maria, 98, 107
Bologna, Giovanni (Giambologna), 114, 120
Bonaparte, Napoleon *see* Napoleon Bonaparte
Bonaventure, St, 161, 169
Borgia, Cesare, 137
Borgia, Lucrezia, 42, 93, 94
Borromeo, St Carlo, 48, 54
Borromeo, Federigo, 48, 49
Botticelli, Sandro, 118
Bronson, Katharine de Kay, 11–12, 31
Browning, Elizabeth Barrett, 114, 120–1, 121, 132–3
Browning, Robert, 4, 11, 31, 114, 120–1, 124–5, 133–4, 141, 175–6, 178, 209–10
Bruni, Leonardo, 116–17
Bruno, Giordano, 189, 190
Brydone, Patrick, 267–8, 268, 280
Bulwer-Lytton, Edward, 176, 225, 239
Burckhardt, Jacob, 92, 93
Byron, George Gordon, Lord, 1, 7, 8, 9, 10–11, 12, 14, 16, 22, 25, 51, 94, 95, 97–8, 102–4, 117, 145, 157, 160, 181, 185, 189

Caesar, Gaius Julius, 62, 92, 173–5, 184, 295
Calvino, Italo, 68, 80–1, 85–7, 288, 290
Canova, Antonio, 14
Canuti, Isolina, 34–5
Cappello, Bianca, 151

Carducci, Giosuè, 62, 91, 98, 100, 107, 149, 160, 186
Carpaccio, Vittore, 4
Carracci family, 91
Carretto, Ilaria del, 146–7
Casanova, Giacomo, 4, 8–9, 23
Castiglione, Count Baldassare, 42, 53, 54, 163, 163–4, 167–8, 169–70
Catherine of Siena, St, 143, 156
Catiline (Lucius Sergius Catilina), 183, 184
Cato the Censor, 261
Catullus, Gaius Valerius, 52, 61–2
Cavalcanti, Guido, 134
Cavour, Count Camillo, 57–8, 67–8
Cellini, Benvenuto, 121, 186, 188–9, 202
Cenci, Beatrice, 189, 207
Charles V, emperor, 46
Charles VIII of France, 48
Chaucer, Geoffrey, 131, 216
Cherubini, Luigi, 117
Chiari, Pietro, 24
Cicero, Marcus Tullius, 173, 183, 184, 202–3, 212, 214, 215, 217, 261
Cione, Nardo di, 111, 112
Clairmont, Claire, 25, 122, 207
Clare, St, 162
Claude Le Lorrain, 244
Clement VII, Pope, 188
Clodia, 62
Clodius Pulcher, Publius, 62
Clough, Arthur Hugh, 121
Coleridge, Samuel Taylor, 113
Colonna, Vittoria, 206
Condivi, Ascanio, 119
Consolo, Vincenzo, 275
Cornaro, Caterina, 29–31
Coryat, Thomas, 3, 4–5, 10, 23, 33
Croce, Benedetto, 228

D'Annunzio, Gabriele, 52, 62–3, 246–7
Dante Alighieri, 33, 38, 42, 43, 89, 92, 97, 104–5, 110–12, 117, 134–5, 144–5, 151–2, 206, 219, 244
Deledda, Grazia, 292, 293, 295, 298
Demeter, 259–61, 261
Depretis, Agostino, 223
De Filippo, Eduardo, 224, 232–3, 239–40
De Sanctis, Francesco, 228
De Sica, Vittorio, 106, 240
Dickens, Charles, 48, 53, 53–4, 81–2,

83–4, 87, 95, 209, 218, 222, 226, 237–8
Di Giacomo, Salvatore, 224, 240
Diodorus Siculus, 259, 264, 269, 270, 284
Dion, 265–6
Dionysius I of Syracuse, 265
Dionysius II of Syracuse, 265–6, 286–7
Donizetti, Gaetano, 54, 153
Doria, Andrea, 81
Dostoevsky, Fyodor, 121
Douglas, Norman, 218, 228, 249–50, 250, 256
Dumas, Alexandre *père*, 149
Duse, Eleonora, 38, 62, 290

Eco, Umberto, 70, 71–2, 75–6
Einaudi, Giulio, 68
Eliot, George, 119, 125–6, 135–6
Eliot, T.S., 135
Emerson, Ralph Waldo, 121
Empedocles, 267, 269, 280, 284
Enzo, King of Sardinia, 91, 100
Este, Cardinal Ippolito d', 210
Este, Duke Alfonso I d', 93
Este, Duke Alfonso II d', 95, 108
Este, Duke Ercole I d', 92–3
Este, Isabella d', 53, 93
Euripides, 265
Evelyn, John, 2, 9, 89, 91, 177–8, 188, 210, 214–15, 216, 221
Ezzelino III of Treviso, 38

Falier, Marin, 7
Fellini, Federico, 179, 180–1, 242
Fenoglio, Beppe, 70
Ferdinando IV of Naples, 222
Ficino, Marsilio, 112, 113, 118, 136
Fo, Dario, 50, 51, 63
Fogazzaro, Antonio, 51, 57–8, 63–4
Forster, E.M., 47, 116, 117, 126–7, 136–7, 147–8, 153
Foscari, Iacopo, 14
Francesca da Rimini, 29, 104–5, 157
Francis, St, 116, 149, 159–60, 161–2, 165–6, 170
Franco, Veronica, 3–4, 23
Folgore da San Gimignano, 148, 156
Foscolo, Ugo, 117, 137
Frederick II, emperor, 247, 256, 273

Gadda, Carlo Emilio, 180, 194–5, 203–4
Galilei, Galileo, 117

Galuppi, Baldassare, 4
Garibaldi, Giuseppe, 26, 67, 294–5, 298–9
Gatto, Alfonso, 139
Gautier, Théophile, 1, 5–6, 10, 31–2, 32–3, 94, 121, 190, 225, 236–7, 240–1
Gell, Sir William, 225
Gelon of Syracuse, 264
Gentileschi, Artemisia, 193–4, 202
Gherardesca, Count Ugolino della, 144–5, 151–2
Ghiberti, Lorenzo, 117
Ghirlandaio, Domenico, 112, 113, 121
Gibbon, Edward, 46, 50, 96, 173, 182–3, 204
Ginzburg, Leone, 68, 76
Ginzburg, Natalia, 64, 68, 69, 72–3, 76
Giotto di Bondone, 33, 111, 114, 127, 219
Giovanna I of Naples, 220
Giovanna II of Naples, 220
Giraldi Cinzio, Giambattista, 94, 107
Gissing, George, 223, 233–4, 248, 249, 256
Gladstone, William Ewart, 268
Goethe, Johann Wolfgang (von), 33, 36, 94, 95, 161, 162, 190, 218, 224, 235–6, 241, 275
Gogol, Nikolai, 190
Goldoni, Carlo, 11, 14, 17–18, 23–4
Gozzi, Carlo, 11, 24
Gozzoli, Benozzo, 113
Gonzaga family, 53, 58–9
Gramsci, Antonio, 190, 293, 299–300
Graves, Robert, 96, 205
Gregorius, Master, 175
Guarini, Battista, 108
Guarino of Verona, 93
Guicciardini, Francesco, 110
Guiccioli, Teresa, 22, 97–8
Guiscard, Robert, 250

Hadrian, 210, 226
Hamilton, Emma, 241–2
Hamilton, Sir William, 226, 241–2
Hannibal, 160, 248, 249, 250
Hare, Augustus, 223
Hawthorne, Nathaniel, 114–15, 178, 181–2, 185–6, 204
Heine, Heinrich, 47, 147, 148, 150–1, 156–7
Hemingway, Ernest, 54
Herodotus, 245

Hieron I of Syracuse, 264
Hieron II of Syracuse, 266
Homer, 244, 259, 260, 269
Horace (Quintus Horatius Flaccus), 185, 205, 212, 244, 247, 250, 295
Hunt, Leigh, 145, 157
Huxley, Aldous, 144, 148, 157

Ibn Jubair, 271, 272
Ibsen, Henrik, 228
Idrisi, Abu Abdullah Mohammed al-, 272–3, 284–5

James, Henry, 1, 5, 6, 8, 10, 11–12, 18–19, 24–5, 122, 143, 144, 154, 177, 179, 182, 186, 187–8, 191, 195–6
Johnson, Samuel, 204
Jonson, Ben, 4, 7
Joyce, James, 36–7, 42
Julius II, Pope, 177, 187
Justinian, 96
Juvenal (Decimus Junius Juvenalis), 185, 196–7, 204–5

Keats, John, 132, 189–90, 222
Kesselring, Albert, 180

Lamartine, Alphonse de, 228
Lampedusa see Tomasi di Lampedusa, Giuseppe
Landor, Walter Savage, 121
Lawrence, D.H., 148, 211, 212, 228, 275, 292, 293–4, 297–8, 298, 300
Lear, Edward, 80, 247, 250, 256–7
Leighton, Frederick, 135
Lentino, Giacomo da, 256
Leonardo da Vinci, 47–8, 53, 54, 60–1, 149
Leopardi, Giacomo, 145, 161, 166–7, 170–1, 219, 225–6
Leopardi, Monaldo, 160–1
Levi, Carlo, 245, 248–9, 250, 252–3, 257
Levi, Primo, 68, 69, 73–4, 76–7
Lewis, Norman, 224, 234–5, 242
Lippi, Fra Filippo, 114, 124–5, 164
Livy (Titus Livius), 160, 175, 181, 182–3, 197–8, 205, 210, 228
Loy, Rosetta, 69, 77
Lucretia, 175, 197–8
Lucullus, Lucius Licinius, 228

Macaulay, Thomas Babington, Lord, 205

Machiavelli, Niccolò, 110, 117, 119, 127, 135, 137–8
Mackenzie, Sir Compton, 228
Maecenas, Gaius, 185, 205, 244
Magris, Claudio, 38
Malamud, Bernard, 13
Malaparte, Curzio, 224, 242
Malatesta family, 91–2, 104
Malatesta, Sigismondo, 92
Manin, Daniele, 7
Manin, Ludovico, 7
Mann, Thomas, 1, 9, 19–20, 25, 82
Mantegna, Andrea, 53
Manutius, Aldus, 2
Manzoni, Alessandro, 48, 49, 51, 54, 59–60, 64–5
Maraini, Dacia, 34–5, 41–2, 43
Marcellus, Marcus Claudius, 266–7, 283
Marin, Carlo, 26
Marinetti, Filippo Tommaso, 5, 20, 25–6
Marius, Gaius, 228
Marlowe, Christopher, 138, 258
Mascagni, Pietro, 24, 290
Mazzini, Giuseppe, 67, 81, 82, 87–8, 149, 299
Medici, Alessandro de', 120
Medici, Anna Maria de', 114
Medici, Cosimo de', 112, 136
Medici, Cosimo I de', 119–20
Medici, Ferdinando I de', 114, 120
Medici, Francesco I de', 121
Medici, Giuliano de', 118
Medici, Lorenzino de', 120
Medici, Lorenzo de' ('The Magnificent'), 44, 113, 118, 127–9, 138, 139
Medici, Lorenzo de', Duke of Urbino, 114
Medici, Lorenzo di Pierfrancesco di, 118
Medici, Piero de' ('The Gouty'), 112–13
Michelangelo Buonarotti, 110, 114, 117, 119, 141, 148, 176, 177, 186–7, 188, 198–9, 205–6
Michelino, Domenico di, 111
Michelozzo (di Bartolommeo), 112
Middleton, Thomas, 121
Milton, John, 28, 109, 117, 149, 226, 244
Montale, Eugenio, 79–80, 85, 88
Montefeltro, Federico da, 163
Monteverdi, Claudio, 109

Morante, Elsa, 180, 206
Moravia, Alberto, 179–80, 199–200, 206–7
Moro, Aldo, 287
Mortimer, John, 142–3, 164, 168–9, 171
Mozart, Wolfgang Amadeus, 36
Munthe, Axel, 227
Musset, Alfred de, 14, 120
Mussolini, Benito, 26, 52, 63, 270

Napoleon Bonaparte, 8, 46, 49, 148–9, 161
Nelson, Horatio, 241–2
Nietzsche, Friedrich, 70
Nievo, Ippolito, 7, 26, 38

Odysseus, 218, 261
Origo, Iris, 114–15, 142, 155, 157
Ouida (Louise de la Ramée), 148
Ovid (Publius Ovidius Naso), 246, 257–8

Palazzeschi, Aldo, 116, 138
Palestrina, Pierluigi da, 212
Palladio, Andrea, 29, 35–6
Palmer, Samuel, 87
Papini, Giovanni, 141, 157
Parini, Giuseppe, 49, 65
Pascoli, Giovanni, 92, 108
Pasolini, Pier Paolo, 132, 181, 211, 215, 216
Paul, St, 183
Paul II, Pope, 187
Pavese, Cesare, 68, 68–9, 74–5, 77–8
Pellico, Silvio, 9, 26–7, 50
Persephone, 259–61
Peter, St, 183, 190
Petrarch (Francesco Petrarca), 29, 39–40, 42, 43–4, 89, 110, 132, 148, 176, 181, 219
Petronius Arbiter, Gaius, 218, 242
Phalaris, 269
Piccolomini, Enea Silvio (Pope Pius II), 143–4, 149, 157–8
Pico della Mirandola, Giovanni, 113, 121, 138–9
Piero della Francesca, 92, 157, 163, 168–9
Pindar, 264
Pinturicchio (Bernardino di Betti), 144
Piozzi, Hester Lynch, 32, 54, 67, 78, 164
Pirandello, Luigi, 240, 263, 270–1, 278–9, 285–6

Pisanello, Antonio, 53, 92
Plato, 248, 265–6, 286–7
Plautus, Titus Maccius, 24, 93
Pliny the Elder, 238–9, 243
Pliny the Younger, 225, 238–9, 242–3
Plutarch, 184, 190–1, 210, 228, 265, 266–7, 283, 287
Poliziano, Angelo, 113, 118, 121, 139, 149
Pompilius, Numa, 182–3
Porta, Carlo, 50, 65
Porta, Luigi da, 33–4
Pound, Ezra, 13, 26, 82, 92, 135, 145, 158
Pratolini, Vasco, 116, 129–30, 139–40
Prokofiev, Sergei, 24
Propertius, Sextus, 161, 171–2
Proust, Marcel, 6, 27
Puccini, Giacomo, 24, 149
Pulci, Luigi, 22, 121
Puzo, Mario, 275
Pythagoras, 245, 250

Quasimodo, Salvatore, 269, 279–80, 287

Raimondo of Capua, 143
Rame, Franca, 63
Raphael (Raffaello Santi), 163, 176
Régnier, Henri de, 14
Reni, Guido, 91
Rienzo, Cola di, 43, 176
Rilke, Rainer Maria, 38
Robbia, Luca della, 114
Robert of Anjou, King of Naples, 219–20
Roger II de Hauteville, 271, 272–3
Rogers, Samuel, 222, 243
Rolfe, Frederick ('Baron Corvo'), 13, 27
Romano, Giulio, 53–4, 58
Rosi, Francesco, 257
Rossetti, Biagio, 93
Rossini, Gioacchino, 164, 222
Ruskin, Effie (Euphemia), 14, 27
Ruskin, John, 1–2, 5, 13–14, 14, 21, 27–8, 34, 91, 146–7
Ruzzante, Il (Angelo Beolco), 32, 44

Sand, Georges (Aurore Dupin, baronne Dudevant), 14
Sandys, George, 248, 254–5, 258
Sallust (Gaius Sallustius Crispus), 183
Sannazaro, Jacopo, 220–1, 243
Santi, Giovanni, 163

Sarpi, Fra Paolo, 2–3, 28
Satta, Salvatore, 292, 296–7, 300–1
Savonarola, Fra Girolamo, 119, 125, 135, 136, 139
Scala, Cangrande della, 34, 111
Scamozzi, Vincenzo, 35, 54
Scarpetta, Eduardo, 240
Sciascia, Leonardo, 89, 263, 277–8, 287–8
Serao, Matilde, 178–9, 223, 243–4, 298
Severn, Joseph, 189
Sforza, Ludovico 'Il Moro', 47, 48, 61
Shakespeare, William, 2, 4, 6, 24, 33–4, 44, 46, 107, 132, 138, 173–5, 181, 184, 191, 210, 211, 258, 287
Shelley, Mary Wollstonecraft, 25, 79, 142, 207
Shelley, Percy Bysshe, 12, 16–17, 25, 79, 142, 145, 148, 186, 189, 190, 191, 200–1, 207–8, 222, 226, 226–7
Sidney, Sir Philip, 44, 243
Sienkiewicz, Henryk, 190
Silone, Ignazio, 245, 246, 251–2, 258
Sitwell, Sir Osbert, 80, 149
Smollett, Tobias, 78, 144
Sophocles, 35
Sontag, Susan, 242
Spenser, Edmund, 106, 109
Staël, Anne-Louise-Germaine de, 191
Stampa, Gaspara, 4, 28
Stendhal (Henri Beyle), 47, 49–50, 51–2, 65–6, 91, 117, 121, 190, 289
Story, William Wetmore, 178, 190
Stradivari, Antonio, 46
Suetonius, Gaius Tranquillus, 184, 227
Svevo, Italo, 37, 40–1, 42, 44–5
Symonds, John Addington, 89, 96–7, 108, 190

Tacitus, Publius Cornelius, 238, 242
Tasso, Torquato, 89, 94–5, 108–9
Taviani, Paolo and Vittorio, 285
Theocritus, 266, 288
Theodora, 96
Theodoric, 96
Theron of Akragas, 264, 269
Thomas of Celano, 162, 172
Thomas, William, 2
Thucydides, 264
Thurn und Taxis, Princess Marie von, 38
Tiberius, 227
Tigellius, 295

Tintoretto, Jacopo, 14, 27
Titian (Tiziano Vecellio), 14, 22, 38, 53
Todi, Iacopone da, 160, 164, 170
Tomasi di Lampedusa, Giuseppe, 259,
    262–3, 273–5, 281–2, 288–9
Trajan, 164, 243
Trelawny, Edward John, 142, 190
Trissino, Giangiorgio, 35
Trollope, Frances (Fanny), 121, 122
Trollope, Thomas Adolphus, 122
Turner, Joseph Mallord William, 1–2,
    243
Twain, Mark, 190

Ubaldini, Ruggieri degli, 144–5, 151–2
Ugolino di Monte San Michele, 159
Ungaretti, Giuseppe, 37–8, 40, 45, 80,
    84–5
Unsworth, Barry, 160

Vasari, Giorgio, 47, 60–1, 66, 110, 117,
    124, 148, 186–7, 198, 205–6
Vecchi, C.A., 294, 295
Verdi, Giuseppe, 14, 64, 81, 98

Verga, Giovanni, 263, 268–9, 282–3,
    289–90
Veronese, Paolo, 8
Verres, Gaius, 261
Verrocchio, Andrea del, 118
Vespucci, Simonetta Cattaneo, 118
Vico, Giambattista, 228
Virgil (Publius Vergilius Maro), 54, 185,
    217–18, 218–19, 228, 230–1, 244, 267
Visconti, Luchino, 274, 289
Vitruvius, 35
Vittorini, Elio, 263, 287, 290–1, 294
Vittorio Emanuele II, King, 299
Vogelweide, Walther von der, 31

Wagner, Richard, 14, 176, 190
Webster, John, 228
William I of Sicily, 272
William II of Sicily, 272
Wotton, Sir Henry, 2, 177
Woolf, Virginia, 143

Yeats, William Butler, 82
Yourcenar, Marguerite, 210

47 Milan
50 Lakes - 52

16/18 Non chalance